Walt Whitman

Walt Whitman

by

FREDERIK SCHYBERG

————❖————

TRANSLATED FROM THE DANISH BY

Evie Allison Allen

WITH AN INTRODUCTION BY

Gay Wilson Allen

————❖————

New York

Columbia University Press

1951

Translator's Preface

THIS AMERICAN VERSION of Dr. Frederik Schyberg's valuable study of Walt Whitman has been twice revised, first by my husband, who helped both in checking the accuracy and in improving the style. Then the manuscript went to Dr. Schyberg himself, who read it again for accuracy, and at the same time made whatever changes in the text he thought necessary or desirable. He originally wrote the book nearly two decades ago, when he was just beginning his career as a literary critic. The book that he published in 1933 is still essentially a sound interpretation, but reading my translation in manuscript gave him an opportunity—which many an author would covet—to substitute "second thoughts" for first ones and to correct a few minor errors, inevitable in the first edition of a complicated study such as this.

Dr. Schyberg found his final chapter, "Walt Whitman in World Literature," more out of date than the others. Therefore he has made extensive changes and additions in that chapter. He has largely rewritten and expanded the German and Scandinavian sections, and these will probably be a revelation to Whitman students in the United States.

Consequently this translation is not an exact rendering of the book published in Copenhagen, but it is in some respects an improved version, like a second edition—certainly not through my efforts, but because of the author's acumen. My only claim is that I have tried to respect his words, whether written in the early 1930's or in the late 40's as emendations and additions to my manuscript.

I am deeply grateful not only to Dr. Schyberg for his patient and kindly scrutiny of my typescript but also to his friend Mr. Jørgen Andersen, English language consultant for the Danish Broadcasting Company, whose suggestions have helped me over many a pitfall and have improved my translation in numerous places. As to my own part in the work, I have verified quotations and checked facts so far as it has been within my power to do so. Every quotation from *Leaves of Grass* has been verified in the original editions—in each case the one the author was at the moment examining or discussing. Since these editions are not available to many readers, however, the section numbers refer to the "authorized" version, such as Holloway's "Inclusive" edition.

At the expense of sometimes cluttering the page with brackets, but with the hope of making the book useful to as many readers as possible, I have translated all foreign titles and quotations. The translated titles appear in brackets (not italicized unless a translation has been published in English). The foreign quotations are translated in the text, but have been retained in the original form in the footnotes. This arrangement may annoy multilingual readers, but should be appreciated by those not so fortunate or gifted.

E. A. A.

ORADELL, N.J.
August 30, 1950

Contents

Introduction   3

America in *1850*   14

Walt Whitman at Thirty-six   30

Leaves of Grass, *1855–89*   77

Whitman in World Literature   248

Notes   329

Bibliography   360

Index   367

An Introduction to Frederik Schyberg and His *Walt Whitman*

By Gay Wilson Allen

I N THE SUMMER OF 1935, while doing research for a
Whitman paper in Library of Congress, I came across an attractive book entitled *Walt Whitman*, by Frederik Schyberg,
published in Copenhagen, 1933. Though it had been in print for
two years, during which time I had been engaged in Whitman
studies, I had never heard of the book, and I could find no reviews of it in scholarly journals—though some years later I
learned that Dr. Jens Nyholm had published a short notice in
Books Abroad. Apparently none of the scholars in American
literature could read Danish—and neither could I. But my curiosity was aroused by the chapter headings, especially the one
obviously on the editions of *Leaves of Grass* (with its subheads
on "Første Udgave," "Anden Udgave," and so forth), and the
final lengthy chapter on "Whitman i Verdenslitteraturen."

Promptly I ordered a copy of the book, a Danish grammar,
and a *Dansk-Engelsk Ordbok*. When these arrived, my wife (who
was equally interested) and I plunged into Danish. Fortunately
for us, this language has probably the simplest grammar in the
world, and the vocabulary is nearer to English than modern
German is. Danish idioms, like those of almost every language,
can cause trouble, but we were soon able to read enough of the
book to arouse our curiosity to an even higher pitch. My wife
became so absorbed in finding out just what Schyberg knew

about Whitman that she dropped everything else to learn Danish
—and quickly outdistanced me.

Before long we were convinced that the Danish author had
penetrated farther into Whitman's psychology than anyone else
and that he had succeeded in doing so mainly by tracing the
poet's development and unconscious self-revelation through all
the editions of *Leaves of Grass*. He had discovered no new external biographical facts (probably impossible for a scholar
working in a foreign library), but being a remarkably acute
literary critic, he had uncovered enough subjective evidence to
upset many of the theories and interpretations of the leading
biographers and critics writing in English. Moreover, his astounding knowledge of comparative literature had enabled him
to see Whitman in relation to schools, movements, and similar
literary or psychological types in a manner that illuminated
both Whitman and his contributions to world literature. Nothing
like this had been done, or scarcely attempted, before—though
W. S. Kennedy had made an awkward beginning in *The Fight of
a Book for the World* (1926). To the present day I have not
found any other book on Walt Whitman that has given me so
many "leads" for further investigation or has so stimulated me
to continue my own studies of Whitman.

After my wife and I had become acquainted with the true value
of Frederik Schyberg's interpretation of Whitman, we got in
touch with the author through his Danish publisher, Gyldendal,
and we have kept up a correspondence with him ever since, except
for the duration of the German occupation of Denmark. We
learned that he had received the degree of doctor of philosophy
at the University of Copenhagen in 1933, having successfully
"defended" his book on Walt Whitman as his thesis. His first
book, *Moderne Amerikansk Litteratur, 1900–1930*, was published in 1930. Despite the fact that a reviewer in *The American
Mercury* called it better than any similar work in English, it is
still almost unknown in this country. Had it been published in
English, French, or German it would almost certainly have attracted wide attention.

Meanwhile, Dr. Schyberg was making a name for himself in
Denmark as a dramatic critic on leading Copenhagen news-

papers. The son of two well-known actors and having been closely associated with the theater all his life, even while a university student, he was remarkably well qualified to interpret and judge theatrical performances. Consequently, most of his books since 1933 have been concerned with dramatic or theatrical criticism (he carefully distinguishes between the two). They have included *Dansk Teaterkritik, indtil 1914* (a history), 1937; *Ti Aars Teater, 1929–1939* (a collection of reviews), 1939; and an edition in 1943 of the diary and letters of Michael Rosing, a Danish actor who toured Europe in 1788. Rosing's observations, written on the eve of the French Revolution, have unusual social as well as theatrical value, and it is to be hoped that this book, with its masterly historical introduction by the editor and the text of Rosing's diary, kept secret for many years, may yet be translated into English.

During the German occupation Dr. Schyberg worked secretly with other patriotic writers on an "underground" newspaper. Twice he gave a radio address on Walt Whitman, because the "poet of democracy" provided subtle propaganda against Nazism, but the third attempt was prevented by the German censor. Later Dr. Schyberg was arrested and placed in a concentration camp. There he amused himself by translating E. T. A. Hoffmann's *Klein Zaches*, the story of the little homunculus who became prime minister and through magic help deceived everyone concerning his real nature. The German guards thought that because their prisoner read Hoffmann he must be becoming sympathetic toward Germany, but Dr. Schyberg saw in the tale a perfect allegory for Hitler and Goebbels. Dr. Schyberg was permitted to publish his translation, *Lille Zacharias, Kaldet Zinnober* [Little Zacharias, called Zinnober] in 1944. His introduction to the book is a brilliant contribution to Hoffmann criticism. Since then Dr. Schyberg has published *Digteren, Elskeren og den Afsindige* [The Poet, the Lover, and the Lunatic], 1947, a collection of literary essays and reviews, and *Theatre in War*, 1949, a collection of theatrical criticism. At present he is writing and lecturing on the psychology, theory, and history of acting. He has given courses of lectures on this subject in several universities in Sweden, Denmark, and Norway.

His three lectures at the University of Lund have been published at Lund under the title *Skådespelarkonst* [The Art of the Theater], 1949.

Although Dr. Schyberg has not written about Whitman since the publication of his two books in 1933 (he supplemented his critical biography by a little book of translations from *Leaves of Grass*), his success as a critic bears testimony to the kind of mind and literary judgment that he brought to the task of interpreting America's great poet. Furthermore, he has influenced the reception of Whitman in Scandinavia since the publication of his *Walt Whitman*, for there has been a decided quickening of interest in Whitman in Sweden and Norway, as well as Denmark, since 1933, and most of the critics and translators of Whitman in these countries mention Frederick Schyberg or reveal by their attitudes and comments their obvious debt to him. Indebtedness is freely acknowledged by K. A. Svensson in the introduction to his excellent *Strån av Gräs*, Stockholm, 1935, and recently by Per Arneberg in his brilliant translation of *Sangen om Meg Selv*, Oslo, 1947. This recent growth of Scandinavian interest in Whitman, so largely the result of Dr. Schyberg's efforts, has now completed the circle by returning to Denmark—indicated by the fact that the Schyberg book of translations, entitled *Walt Whitman Digte*, was handsomely reprinted in 1949 by Gyldendal.

Two of Dr. Schyberg's interpretations have particularly appealed to poets and critics in Scandinavia, perhaps especially in Sweden: recognition that Whitman's mysticism, like Swedenborg's—who also saw "hot visions of Paradise"—was rooted in unappeased sex urges and realization that the unity and harmony of which Whitman dreamed for his nation, and devoted most of his life to achieving in and through his poems, he did not have in his own life. Nor did America herself have this dreamed-of unity, or American literature in general, for Whitman proclaimed it just before the Civil War. In fact, in Whitman, Mark Twain, Emily Dickinson, Henry Adams, and on down to Dos Passos, there is a duality of mind and an undertone of irony and pessimism that often accounts for both the strength and the weakness of American literature. Thus, Whitman's problems were to a large extent his nation's problems, and *Leaves of Grass* is more truly symbolical than even the poet himself could ever have understood.

Recently in reviewing Sven Møller Kristensen's *Amerikansk Litteratur, 1920–1940* (1947), Dr. Schyberg referred again to the duality in Whitman, the paradox that continues to puzzle the intellectual in America, especially the author, who is proud of his country's freedom and yet is ironically conscious that the "Democracy" envisioned by Jefferson, Lincoln, and Walt Whitman is still not a reality. Two paragraphs deserve to be quoted to show Dr. Schyberg's point of view.

From its earliest days American literature, despite its conspicuous surface optimism, has had a concealed but deep, uneasy undertone of doubt and distrust. It was first of all a social literature, and early concerned itself with the question of freedom in the States, the great "experiment in Democracy," as Upton Sinclair once called it. This literature proclaimed Democracy—until it began to doubt and criticize it. Doubt of Democracy has been the strongest undercurrent in modern American poetry since the turn of the century, when the numerous American naturalistic depicters of social conditions came to the fore. But this literary period was actually inaugurated by and had its roots in Walt Whitman's little prose work of 1871, *Democratic Vistas*—a book one cannot read today without being impressed by it. *It is the manifesto of what we call modern American literature.* It pays homage to the expected, dreamed-of Democracy, draws up the plan for an intellectual awakening (and the awakening has since then truly taken place), but at the same time it betrays a nagging doubt about political freedom. This can only be because the growing materialistic conditions of the social life were slowly gaining control and might transform the dreamed-of democratic State into a dreadful failure, "the most tremendous failure of time," a State that would corrupt its citizens until their lives became that of the "fabled damned."

The duality in Whitman's writings is the duality of modern American poetry. Johannes V. Jensen has called him, not without reason, "the gateway to America," or at least a gateway to *modern* America. What the great social authors of the first decade of the twentieth century showed us was indeed such pictures of the life of the damned and a preview of the "American Tragedy." Just as Whitman in his refulgent prose defied at the same time that he glorified his rich, mighty nation, so have the poets after him glorified it, in sheer defiance and devotion—with an expansive diction tinged with dark undertones, which is deeply indebted to the language created by Whitman.

In my remarks on Frederik Schyberg's *Walt Whitman* in my *Walt Whitman Handbook* (remarks that opened the way for the publication of this translation by my wife), I referred to his first two chapters as "superficial" and of "little value for the American student." When the publication of this translation was being discussed with the Columbia University Press, I at first suggested that these two chapters be combined, and possibly condensed. I held these opinions because the long chapters on *Leaves of Grass* and "Whitman in World Literature" had contained the great revelations for me. But on re-reading the book I realized that Dr. Schyberg's "triad"—the country, the man, and the book—should be kept inviolate. The discussion of the country may tell American readers little about their history that is not commonplace with them, and the account of Whitman scholarship is sketchy, though it serves the useful purpose of orienting Dr. Schyberg's contribution. But Chapter I helps to introduce this Danish study of Whitman by showing us what Europeans thought of America at the time Fredrika Bremer visited our shores in the decade of the first *Leaves of Grass*. It helps to explain why Walt Whitman had to await discovery by Europeans —why, in fact, they still understand him more readily than do his own countrymen, as Dr. Schyberg's book itself demonstrates. These introductory chapters are necessary reminders that this is a book by a European, a very acute European, one who lives in a small country and is therefore in close contact with other languages and literatures. His cultural and geographical position has enabled Dr. Schyberg to see Walt Whitman more clearly in the great world stream than is possible for Americans themselves to see him, since they live on a continent so spacious that they view the literary currents of the world from a hazy distance.

This book is not the final word on Whitman or his art. As the author says, "When we have unanimously agreed about a poet he is on the point of dying." But it should bring a fresh impulse and perhaps new life to Whitman scholarship in this country, as well as a more intelligent understanding of the reputation of America's best-known poet in other lands.

After the above paragraphs were in type, word was received that Dr. Schyberg had died suddenly on August 11, 1950. The University of Copenhagen had just created a chair in theatrical history especially for him. At the time of his death he was acknowledged as the greatest contemporary literary critic in Denmark, and probably the greatest since Georg Brandes. Although he was little known in America, this country has also lost a brilliant critic of her literature. Had he lived, I believe he would have become of increasing importance to us.

Walt Whitman

Introduction

———◆•••◆———

"**MY** BOOK is a candidate for the future," wrote Whitman
in his seventieth year, when he had finished the final edition of *Leaves of Grass*. How right he was the succeeding years
have revealed, especially since the turn of the century, for Walt
Whitman, after having been the most controversial and con-
demned American author, has become *the* American author and
has gradually acquired a following in world literature. *Leaves of
Grass* set the pattern for the younger generation of American
writers, and one of the main purposes of this biography is to
show that it was equally important to intellectual groups in
Europe, particularly in England, Germany, and France. Today
Walt Whitman is not so much an individual, interesting for his
peculiarities and his many American traits, and of course his
remarkable poetic talent; rather he is a *trend in world literature*,
like Zola, Dostoyevsky, or Nietzsche, and is therefore of especial
interest to the literary historians, who are more concerned with
the connecting links of literary history than with individuals.

In the relationships of recent literature Walt Whitman occupies a very prominent place, and the number of studies of him
or works in which he is mentioned increases year by year. He will
always be a disputed subject, but that is not the point. Like him
or not, we cannot ignore him. He is one of the most fundamental
impulses in recent world literature. "Poetic talent" is scarcely
an adequate designation for Whitman. In his finest moments he
has poetic genius. "What is genius?" Georg Brandes once asked.
"Genius is the power in a human being which generates an
epoch." He was undoubtedly thinking of himself when he said
this, but he mentioned Rousseau as an example. In a like sense

and with the same human limitations as Rousseau, Whitman can
as surely be pronounced a genius.

In 1906 Bliss Perry, the gifted successor of Longfellow and
Lowell at Harvard, compared Rousseau and Whitman in his
outstanding book, the first long critical study of Whitman's
poetry and its importance. In spite of the fact that Whitman
was "discovered" in the literature of the seventies and eighties
of the preceding century, recognition of his place in literary
history has long been delayed. With the exception of John Addington Symonds's excellent little book *Walt Whitman, a Study*,
1893, all the early interpretations were to a large extent influenced by or written by his disciples and admirers. They were
propaganda and panegyric, not criticism. Naturally, this was
especially true of the earliest little books: W. D. O'Connor's
The Good Gray Poet, 1866, and John Burroughs's *Notes on
Walt Whitman as Poet and Person*, 1867; but in reality it was
true also of Dr. Bucke's well-known *Walt Whitman*, 1883, of the
German Johannes Schlaf's *Walt Whitman*, 1904, and in England of Henry Bryan Binns's *The Life of Walt Whitman*, 1905.
The latter, because of the author's intimate knowledge of the
subject, his explicitness and his skillful charting of trends and
currents, is still one of the most important sources of information about Whitman. It actually incorporates most of the material used by his predecessors. But all these writers were among
Whitman's closest adherents, we might almost say his congregation, and their enthusiasm often made them hysterical and in-
fatuated. Bliss Perry wittily christened them "the hot little
prophets" in 1906 in his book, the conclusion of which otherwise
was a sincere recognition of Whitman's literally unique position
in American literature: "No American poet now seems more
sure to be read, by the fit persons, after one hundred or five hundred years."

After Bliss Perry, Whitman scholarship gained momentum.
Dr. Bucke had already published, in 1897–98, the two collections of letters: to Peter Doyle, *Calamus*, and to the poet's
mother, *The Wound-Dresser*. Between 1906 and 1914 the loyal
but naïve "Prophet" Horace Traubel published the three-
volume *With Walt Whitman in Camden*, which, with inexorable

minuteness, reported every casual and trivial observation by
Whitman in his old age. In 1906 also appeared Edward Carpenter's *Days with Walt Whitman*, one of the most important source
books, because Carpenter, even in his profound admiration for
Whitman, never lost his critical judgment. On the basis of these
publications and of Bliss Perry's critical study, Whitman research could actually begin. The first long account of the American poet-prophet was the French literary historian Léon Bazalgette's *Walt Whitman, l'homme et son œuvre*, 1909, a work
which at the time deserved great consideration because it had
tremendous influence on Whitman's reputation in France; but it
was to a large extent based on the reports of admirers of Whitman and blindly accepted a number of the myths and legends
which Whitman himself, in his later years, helped to shape and
to circulate and which Bliss Perry had already tried to dis-
credit. Somewhat like Bazalgette's French work was the English
Walt Whitman, a Critical Study, 1914, by Basil de Selincourt,
but otherwise a fine penetrating analysis of the poet and his
poetry.

As the study of Whitman progressed, it became apparent,
however, that the results did not provide a clearer and more
elaborate picture of Whitman the man, but that the outlines
were blurred in the process. He had concealed himself behind
the myths. Research pushed through these myths—especially
after the publication of what was left to be published: Thomas
Harned's edition of the *Letters of Anne Gilchrist and Walt
Whitman*, 1918; Cleveland Rodgers and John Black's *The
Gathering of the Forces*, 1920 (Whitman's journalistic work
from the Brooklyn *Daily Eagle*, 1847–48) ; and in 1921 Holloway's valuable and extensive *The Uncollected Poetry and
Prose of Walt Whitman*. But it was increasingly obvious that
these contributions merely swept away the myths without pro-
ducing any facts to take their places. It was negative research,
not positive. Walt Whitman's private life was concealed in
darkness; with unique and admirable consistency he had destroyed everything which could throw light on the puzzling and
—for the poetry—decisive periods of his life around 1848, 1859,
and 1865. For the last twenty years of his life, after his illness

and paralysis in 1873, he was a passive sharer in existence, and his book was his own and better "I." It was to be his dynamic "I" then and in the future. With his mystic romanticism he intended that in it should live the real Walt Whitman and that everything which might detract from the book or from the author's posthumous reputation must be removed.

Unless we clearly realize Whitman's absolutely religious belief in *Leaves of Grass* we cannot understand him. With this understanding, much about him that seemed ludicrous and trivial before becomes explicable and forgivable. He invented myths about himself to conceal the periods of his life in which nothing particular had happened to him (and not much did happen to Whitman; it was in his inner life that the greatest and finest things always took place and were transformed into poetry) or in which he had been overcome by innate weakness of character. Was it not a very human concealment of what he thought concerned him and him only? What concern was it of his readers? Especially when he had fought his way through and was done with his past life? Thus, his naïvely vain preoccupation with his own mausoleum during his last years—which suggests immediately an amusing comparison with his contemporary Mary Baker Eddy, the talented founder of Christian Science—becomes only a consistent and sustained effort to establish the *official* portrait of Walt Whitman the eminent American poet. And then there is the astounding and ingenuous self-advertising in anonymous reviews and character sketches written by himself, which Symonds and Perry had already noted and which Holloway has made one of his chief tasks to discover—and has found a surprisingly large number of examples in the contemporary American newspapers. Subterfuges of this sort, so regrettable to Europeans, throw a somewhat humorous light on the insatiable vanity which made them possible, but they also reveal the sublime faith in himself that enabled Whitman to produce the great book *Leaves of Grass*. This method, for better or for worse, is fundamentally as American as is the book itself.

Whitman *is the* American poet. It is not going too far to say that through him America first achieved a position in world literature. Intellectually, both Cooper and Poe were deeply

rooted in the European inheritance. Walt Whitman broke with
European academic tradition in both style and content, and
he was fully aware of it. That was part of his program. He
celebrated modern reality, modern America and her democracy.
In a manner quite different from that of Cooper, but similar to
that of Rousseau a hundred years earlier, he introduced "the
divine average" into literature. Whitman's complaint against
both earlier and contemporary literature is that it was written
for a minority, an elite few. No writer, he said in his 1855
Preface and again in *Democratic Vistas*, 1871, had spoken
straight to the people or had created a single work especially
for them. In "Song of the Exposition," 1871, he declared his
poetic intention "to teach the average man the glory of his daily
walk and trade." Today we can see that *Leaves of Grass* is
not a book for the masses, for perhaps more than any other
great book it appeals to a literary elite, and it is a fact that
it never attracted the ordinary American reader, whom it was
always Whitman's ideal to reach. On the contrary, it was first
"discovered" in Europe and spread its influence among the
literary people there before, in the present century, it began
to win acceptance among the young and very limited American
vanguard. We know now that Whitman was no more a "divine
average" than Lincoln, whom he resembled and whom from
the beginning he hailed as a kindred spirit. We know that in
spite of his psychological peculiarities he was one of the finest
of the American writers of the last half of the nineteenth century, along with Poe, Melville, Thoreau, Hawthorne, who were
the astonishing outgrowth of a culture which was at once callow
and senile, with early signs of degeneration. This does not affect
his book or the fact that he first introduced into literature his
America, with all her swaggering dreams of a young and strong
democracy, or the fact that with "Song of Myself" he actually
added the great American personality to the many personalities
in world literature. The rest of the world can now see the ob-
jectionable side of this indigenously American personality, especially in the light of historical developments since then, but
naturally this does not detract from Whitman's importance. As
the Danish poet Johannes V. Jensen said in 1919 with mature

understanding: "Whitman is a Prince of words and a gateway to America."

At one time Whitman's followers wanted to make him more than a poet; they wanted to make him a philosopher and a prophet. Both roles were impossible. There is nothing systematic in Whitman's philosophy, which is essentially the Spinozan-romantic philosophy instilled in him by his reading of Carlyle, Emerson, and the American Transcendentalists, and a very superficial Hegelianism, which he got, not directly from Hegel, but from popular journalistic reports. He made his philosophy important by the expression which he frequently gave it, and this wins forgiveness for his contradictions and inconsistencies. Whitman was a lyricist, not a logician; he was a mystic, not a philosopher.

We cannot accept Whitman as a religious prophet, because his "preaching" in *Leaves of Grass* is at once too defiant and too feeble. But in religious history he is an interesting example of a mystic. He resembles the first Quaker, George Fox, in his "new religion" with its "inner light"; there is a similarity to Jacob Böhme and also to Swedenborg, whose daily life offers many interesting parallels to Whitman's. Just as in his poetry Whitman included much of the contemporary American philosophy, Transcendentalism, he also included part of its religion, because there are many traces of both American Quakerism and Unitarianism in *Leaves of Grass*. In addition there is an oriental note in his poetry, which made Tagore exclaim, while visiting the United States, that no American poet had such an extraordinary grasp of the essential oriental tone of mysticism as Whitman. This, along with his own assertions that in the future poets would supersede priests in democratic society, has made his disciples hail him hysterically as a modern Christ. Nothing could be more exaggerated or fallacious. Whitman is a religious prophet in the same way and to the same extent as were Carlyle and Nietzsche; in fact, Whitman's democracy of "great individuals" has at times a paradoxical resemblance to Nietzsche's "superman" theories. The "congregation" which in the last years of his life and those immediately following collected about Whitman and which has gradually become quite literally

world-wide he created for himself through his pre-eminent poetic
power. In *Some Friends of Walt Whitman,* 1924, Carpenter
says: "Thousands of people date from their first reading of his
poems a new era in their lives." *Leaves of Grass* does not offer
its readers a new experience; like all great lyric poetry it offers
them a new emotion. Everyone who has read Whitman at a receptive moment can testify to that. This emotion is a natural
accompaniment of "the cosmic consciousness" which Dr. Bucke
reports Whitman as having had to such a marked degree, and
it is one of the characteristics which made Whitman's mind akin
to the feminine, receptive, and comprehensive consciousness of
oriental mysticism. In his memoirs Tagore tells how, when
he saw two friends walking along the street with their arms
around each other, he suddenly felt something which reached
beyond the present, and "the vital rhythm of the world itself
vibrated in those two and in all humanity, every day, everywhere." That is the very emotion Whitman produces. How
strong an impression he makes with this "perceptiveness" in his
poetry we can see by the effect a first reading of his book made
on such people as Symonds and Stevenson, to choose only two
representative examples. Symonds says: "Leaves of Grass,
which I first read at the age of twenty-five, influenced me more
perhaps than any other book has done except the Bible; more
than Plato, more than Goethe." Stevenson characterizes it as
"a book which tumbled the world upside down for me."

We can say that in this extremely personal sense Whitman
created an epoch. But he did the same thing in literary history.
His huge shadow forms the background for the *Revolution der
Lyrik,* which Arno Holz inaugurated in Germany in 1899, and
may be detected behind the Vers-librists of France in the nineties.
Free verse, or prose verse, is found in literature before Whitman, but it was he who most effectively and with the most far-
reaching results introduced it into the literature of our time as
modern verse. During the period of the First World War and
afterwards free verse lyricists—at times too free—could and always did point to Whitman as their great ancestor and master.
On still another count Whitman created an epoch—in his treatment of sex. That had been a part of other programs before his—

for example, Rousseau and Blake—but he was the first to praise
the erotic act in poetry with complete frankness. As we know,
this part of his program especially gained followers in modern
American literature. And in modern European literature D. H.
Lawrence, a direct pupil of Whitman, is particularly interesting because of similar psychological traits. It is a gospel of
defiance, originating, not in an emotion of sexual superiority,
but of sexual inferiority. In this sexual poetry some people see
Whitman's real importance as a pioneer. For example, Frank
Harris in his famous autobiography, *My Life and Loves*, 1926,
proclaimed that Whitman was "the first of the great men who
wrote frankly about the erotic, and for the next five hundred
years that will be his particular and greatest distinction."

Whitman also revolted from the conventions in literature,
and for that reason alone it is obvious that he would arouse
extraordinary and unusually prolonged controversy and opposition, especially in his own country. At the same time it is
astounding to see how difficult it has been for European critics
to place him in world literature. In 1888 the German Adolf
Stern wrote: "Only a period that is filled with a languishing
yearning for novelty could see more in those triumphant rhap-
sodies than one of those phenomena which regards the true
poetic vocation as the complete destruction of all form." [1]
Edmund Gosse thought in 1896 that Whitman must be doomed
"to sit forever apart from the company of poets." In 1906 the
Norwegian Just Bing spoke of him as "the strange American
poet, or no-poet, Walt Whitman." Otto Hauser, in *Weltgeschichte der Literatur*, 1910, called him in a condescending
way "the good natured, thundering giant child." According to
Professor Moore Smith, in the *Contemporary Review*, Georg
Brandes never paid any attention to Whitman and mentioned
him only once, while on a trip to England in 1913: "I do not
see much in Walt Whitman or Oscar Wilde. I consider them as
one." [2] Leon Kellner, in *Geschichte der nordamericanischen
Literatur*, 1913, said: "The esthetes stand helpless before Whitman." And as late as 1928 Régis Michaud, in his *Panaroma de
la littératur américaine contemporaine*, wrote: "Nothing in
the literature of his country prepares for or explains him. No

one announces him, and no one follows him." What could be more tempting than at last to evaluate Walt Whitman's position in the development of world literature?

The years after the First World War produced a number of publications valuable in Whitman research: Clifton J. Furness collected and edited Whitman's rough drafts in *Walt Whitman's Workshop*, Harvard University Press, 1928, and in 1931 Dr. Clara Barrus published *Whitman and Burroughs Comrades*, an important collection from John Burroughs's papers. Emory Holloway's distinguished *Whitman, an Interpretation in Narrative* appeared in 1926, and in France, Jean Catel, a pupil of Baldensperger's, made a special study of Whitman's childhood and youth, *Walt Whitman, la naissance du poète*, 1929, with a very special and personal survey of Whitman's style and his eroticism. But so far a contemporary European study of Whitman has not been written, however obvious the lack of such a book seems to be.

In the present work I have tried to write a Danish book on Whitman, because I regard it as one of the chief responsibilities of the younger Scandinavian historians of literature to furnish monographs on the great central figures in world literature comparable to Brandes's *Shakespeare, Voltaire*, and *Goethe;* Vedel's *Corneille, Racine*, and *Molière;* Poul Levin's *Victor Hugo;* and Rimestad's *Baudelaire*. Such distinguished company must not intimidate us; there is work to be done which is of cultural importance. I have chosen Walt Whitman because of personal interest in the subject, but I feel sure that in the history of literary relations and developments he is equally significant.

The history of Walt Whitman in world literature is the history of his book. The literary world recognizes that he wrote only one book, although William Dean Howells once expressed a personal preference for Whitman's prose. That comment can only be regarded as a curiosity and an example of the faulty judgments to which Whitman was constantly exposed in his own country even in the following generation. Most of his *Prose Works* have long since vanished from the surface of literature, and even before they sank to the bottom they had little influence.

Like the other journalistic writings, they must only be considered as material for the reconstruction of the growth of *Leaves of Grass*. Symonds once compared the poetry to "the rings in a majestic oak or pine." Whitman even told J. W. Wallace, one of his English admirers, "I have felt to make my book a succession of growths like the rings of trees." Now that all the biographical material available has proved, for the most part, to be of a negative sort,[3] we may try to read Whitman's private life from his book as it now exists. That would appear to be simple and easy with the help of the "annual rings." But here we find one of the main points in Whitman's very effective disposal of himself and his work. The destruction of all sources of knowledge concerning his private personality which Whitman undertook corresponds to the *exclusion of every trace of chronological sequence in the integration of his book*. The poems were published between 1855 and 1889, but many of the introductory verses are from the later years, and his farewell poem, "So Long," was written in 1860. The book is a living unit, but in its present form its history is *not* shown by annual rings of growth.

I see it as my task to weave the intricate web, to present the gradual development of *Leaves of Grass* through the eight editions from 1855 to 1889, when the final edition appeared, and to reconstruct Whitman's life with its recurrent crises, struggles, conquests, and defeats, which can be read plainly, though naturally not in detail, in the several versions of *Leaves of Grass*. This weaving constitutes the main chapter of my work, the growth of a book and of a poet, with an account of Whitman's poetic style and its peculiarities based on "Song of Myself" in the 1855 edition. Two introductory chapters describe America in 1850 and Whitman before he wrote his book at thirty-six years of age. The three chapters form a triad: the country, the man, and the book. The final chapter discusses Whitman's place in world literature.

And now we come to the fact that I have written a critical book, often far from flattering, about the author on whom I, some years ago, would have preferred to write a panegyric such as he deserves here in Denmark, where as a poet he is

primarily a candidate for the future. I must comfort myself
with the same defense which Bliss Perry made when he for the
first time touched some of the myths and they crumbled away
between his fingers. The superman myth about Whitman has
been completely exploded, and instead we have a human being, at once simple and self-contradictory, sometimes genial,
sometimes all too human—but vital. And it is my hope that in
the study of *Leaves of Grass* I have made clear not only the
importance of this wonderful book in world literature but also
its poetic and human value. My work has led me round about
in literature and in the history of literature—into the relation
between various phenomena between poets and their themes,
between reciprocal themes, between critics or writers who use
the same themes—and my findings have often surprised and
stimulated me. If some of this surprise and stimulus conveys
itself to the reader, I shall not have failed entirely in my purpose—and this must be my consolation for not having written
a better book. In conclusion I want to express my admiration
for Georg Brandes, the *Altmeister* of Scandinavian literary
criticism, who in his *Main Currents of European Literature*,
1871–90, was able, with such unique, synthesizing ability, to
survey and to command such a large portion of world literature,
and to pay homage to my teacher Professor Vald. Vedel, a master of the art we all hoped to learn from him: to be able to strike
a single chord in literature and make the whole orchestra of
world literature ring.

America in *1850*

——◆•••▶——

After a struggle for light and freedom, which to a large extent mistook its goal and never clearly knew what it wanted,
half of Europe seemed to have sunk back under a despotism
which knew better what it wanted and had gained for a time
the right of power; in that gloomy season my soul turned in
deep faith and love toward that distant land whose people
have raised the banner of human freedom, have declared their
right and ability to govern themselves and on this right have
established a group of states—the beginning of the world's
greatest form of government.

What I sought there was a new man and his way of life,
a new humanity, and a glimpse of its future in the new world.
Fredrika Bremer, *Homes of the New World*, Letter No. 29.[1]

IN SEPTEMBER, 1849, the world-renowned Swedish writer
Fredrika Bremer went to America. At that time she was
about fifty years old and had already written *Sketches of Daily
Life, The President's Daughters, Nina*, and *Neighbors*. The
religious and political movements of the time, especially the sudden rise of Women's Rights during the forties, had aroused her
interest; and she went to America, which at that time appeared
to Europeans to be the land of unlimited opportunity, where
originated so many new movements concerning both women and
peace. She had intended to use her trip through the States to
gather material for a new long novel—but she soon relinquished
that plan. Fact and reality in this strange world completely
engrossed her. The novel disappeared, she wrote; reality remained. "And I felt that my best work would be merely a faithful transcription of the truth." [2] Her most successful work
was the travel book *Homes of the New World*, which was pub-

lished in three volumes in Stockholm in 1853–54 and is still one of the best sources of our knowledge of the social, religious, political and literary conditions in America at that time. The book is made up of letters written by Fredrika to her sister Agatha, the first dated September 23, 1849, and the last September 12, 1851, supplemented by some important letters to Danish friends, Dowager Queen Caroline Amalie, H. C. Ørsted, the eminent physicist who discovered electro-magnetism, Martensen, bishop and professor, and to the Swedish pastor I. P. Böklin. After her return the letters were revised, corrected, amplified to give them the unmistakable literary form of a travel book rather than that of casual letters accidentally collected. For the reader of today there is undeniably something very appealing and stimulating in this kind of travel book; for Scandinavians are still interested in the Scandinavian point of view, which has scarcely changed during the course of the years. We see America of 1850 as if with our own eyes. It is primarily the date 1850 which makes this the invaluable source book it is even to English and American readers.

Fredrika Bremer arrived in the United States at just the right time, or rather at a critical time. It was in 1850 that the great cauldron really began to boil; during the twenties and thirties the fire had been built; the first bubbles had appeared in the forties, but now it steamed in earnest. A new world was in the crucible. Women's Rights, peace, prohibition—all emerged in the 1840's, along with socialism and communism (or what at that time was called socialism and communism) and the establishment of many "experimental communities" led by idealistic enthusiasts and reformers. The controversy over slavery, which occupied the attention of the public to an increasing and alarming degree, reached the first crisis with the fateful 1850 Compromise Debate in Washington, which Fredrika Bremer attended and of which she has given a series of unforgettable glimpses. This debate gave the decisive stamp to the irreconcilable and implacable friction between North and South and between the two great political parties, Democrats and Whigs; it affected the attitude of the whole country by its foreshadowing of the storm that dissolved the Union, the most tragic event

of all. The War with Mexico, 1846–48, the discovery of gold
in California in 1849, and the great migration to the West in
1850 played their roles along with "gold fever" and the other
fevers of anticipation. Finally there was even a tense, expectant
attitude in the literary America of that year. Throughout the
forties there had been a stronger and stronger demand by
Transcendentalism for an original American literature, as in
the works of Emerson (*Essays*, 1841, 1848), Margaret Fuller
(*Papers on Literature and Art*, 1845), and Lowell (*A Fable
for Critics*, 1848). In the year 1850 people expected some result. What would happen and how? It fell to Fredrika Bremer's
lot to reproduce faithfully and circumstantially in her book
all this mood of hysteria, optimism, expectation, and anticipation, because, in contrast to the earlier European travelers in
America, she entered the States at the decisive and critical moment.

The attention of Europe had long been directed toward
America, the country of the Declaration of Independence, the
land of Fulton and the novels of Cooper. The romantic poets
had enthusiastically extolled the new land of freedom—Chateaubriand, Coleridge (who with Southey considered founding an
experimental community in Pennsylvania), Eichendorff (*Ahnung und Gegenwart* [Past and Present], 1815), and George
Sand, who under the influence of Chateaubriand wrote *Mauprat*,
1837, and saw her ideas about women's emancipation and socialism realized on the other side of the Atlantic. In Denmark
we know the romantic poet's social dreams of America from
Hauch's novel *Robert Fulton*, 1853. In *Wilhelm Meister's
Travels*, 1821–29, the aged Goethe had hailed America as the
new cradle of culture, and in 1829, in his *Zahme Xenien*, he
had expressed his view in the famous lines:

> America, thou art better
> than our old continent;
> thou hast no crumbling castles
> and no basalt.
> Thy soul is not cut off
> from the vital present
> by useless memories and vain strife.[3]

To Goethe, America symbolized the emancipation of the working man, an idea which can also be found in the second part of *Faust* and can be explained by Goethe's transition from "culture-worshiper" to practical idealist. The vision of the New World was responsible for Robert Owen's emigration in 1824 and his founding of the New Harmony Colony in Indiana and for the many other colonies, phalanxes, and co-operatives patterned after Fourier; French socialism followed English socialism in America. These visions of social betterment and a new future for the human race constituted one side of the European conception of America. But naturally there were opposing points of view. For America was also the world of Negro slavery, the Monroe Doctrine, and the new political imperialism; and the belligerent attitude toward England, particularly after the War of 1812, helped to stamp the American-European relationship as inimical and contentious. English authors regarded it as a duty to take issue with the New World. America was a controversial subject in Europe at the beginning of the nineteenth century in much the same way as it was at the beginning of the twentieth century. Was it the world of the future or was it a crude, barbaric place, a threat to European culture? That question was propounded then as now. The enemies of America got unexpected support (also then as now) from one of America's own writers, James Fenimore Cooper, who had achieved literary fame in 1826 with *The Last of the Mohicans* and had come to Europe for a seven-year stay. With *Notions of the Americans Picked Up by a Travelling Bachelor*, 1828, and *Gleanings in Europe*, 1830, he added fuel to the flame. These attacks won Cooper the hatred of his compatriots, but his attitude can only be regarded as coming from the same paradoxical nationalism which today has made most of the important American writers belabor their country. Cooper attacked his homeland for its rampant materialism, its position on slavery, and its press, whose stupidity, ignorance, and corruption he never tired of pointing out.

European travel books on America began in the thirties; authors and authoresses wanted to see with their own eyes the conditions in the New World and to tell their contemporaries about them. The first was *Domestic Manners of the Americans*, 1832, by the Englishwoman Frances Trollope, mother of Anthony Trollope, a book which created a sensation at the time and evoked great resentment in America by its ridiculously distorted representation of American conditions. In 1837 came Harriet Martineau's famous *Society in America*, in three volumes, and in 1839 Marryat's *Diary in America*, likewise in three volumes, very dependent on Cooper, whom he chivalrously defended against Harriet Martineau. In New England Miss Martineau had plumped down in a circle of Cooper's enemies and had accepted their opinions pretty much as dictated. In 1842 occurred Dickens's visit, which resulted in his feeble, dull *American Notes* and *Martin Chuzzlewit* (1843–44), with their grotesque, exaggerated, irresistibly comic but violent and unjust American caricatures. Among other American subjects Dickens emphasized slavery, tyranny of the press, political corruption, religious hypocrisy, the lack of personal freedom in the "land of the free," and especially the American's naïve conceit and total ignorance of European conditions. As Marryat had already noted, Americans simply could not bear to hear criticism. Literature, like the press, should praise America. The writer who failed to do so, like Cooper, brought on himself personal and intellectual persecution of every imaginable description.

Contrasted with these representations, all of which show the influence of the peculiar English attitude toward America, there were others, particularly the French and the Germans, who showed the development of the New World with greater sympathy and accuracy. Such a writer was the German K. A. Postl (Charles Sealsfield), who in his fictionized *Life in the New World*, 1835, gave an alluring description of America in the style of Chateaubriand or Cooper. Most important of all was the French nobleman Alexis De Tocqueville, whose *De la démocratie en Amérique* (Vols. I–IV, 1835), was a masterful account of the democratic form of government and played a great role in European liberalism of the 1840's. Even Sealsfield considered it "the most fundamental and penetrating work from a French pen since Montesquieu." In the United States

De Tocqueville saw the great pattern for future governments, although he was not blind to the dangers of democracy, "which often permits those on a lower level to strive for equality, not by elevating themselves, but by dragging all down and thus restricting all in order to bring about apparent equality." [4] And he also observed the increasing and perilous conflict between North and South. Another friend of America was the German historian Friedrich von Raumer, who in 1845 published his two-volume *Die Vereinigten Staates von Nordamerika* [The United States of North America], which in many ways is comparable to De Tocqueville's work, and gave illuminating statistical details about the conditions of church, politics, and the press. Another voice raised against the chorus of European disapproval was that of James Fenimore Cooper. Nothing is more characteristic of Cooper than his persistent wish to divide praise and blame equally between America and Europe, thus arousing discontent on both sides. In *Excursions in Switzerland*, 1836, he had countered some English attacks on America by saying it was a regular English habit "to blackguard those who stood in the way of national interests," and in the same book he said, as American authors of today say, when Europeans snub America: Only one thing is comparable with an American's ignorance of conditions in Europe and that is a European's complete ignorance of actual conditions in America, both good and bad.

It is in this connection and with these predecessors in mind that we must consider Fredrika Bremer's great picture of America in 1850 if we are to judge it correctly. The label of incompleteness and inadequacy applied by the earlier travel books to the new society was part of the equally temporary and unfinished condition of the America they described. In none of them is there any mention of American intellectual life. It was simply nonexistent. Though Harriet Martineau mentioned Washington Irving, Bryant, and Cooper (the last as "a much regretted failure"),[5] for her there seems to have been only female writers of the rank of the Fannie Hurst of the period, Catharine Sedgwick, whose somewhat weird figure occasionally appears also in the pages of Fredrika Bremer as an example of the popular authoress. And Marryat, in corroboration of De Tocqueville, who had said much the same thing, records of Americans "that with the exception of newspapers, they are not a reading nation." [6] For Harriet Martineau, herself an ardent opponent of slavery, American intellectual life was most nearly represented by the Abolitionists and the two prominent leaders of the anti-slavery party: William Lloyd Garrison, who in 1831 had founded the newspaper *The Liberator*, and Dr. W. E. Channing, whose *Slavery*, 1835, was unquestionably one of the great moral achievements of America in the thirties. But it was in the period between Harriet Martineau and Fredrika Bremer that the real intellectual life of America began to take form, and it is this beginning of which we can get such an interesting interpretation in her book.

American Unitarianism arose in 1787 as a protest against the rigorously dogmatic Puritanism and new Calvinism in the States. Aside from the purely doctrinal reforms (denial of the Trinity, original sin, damnation, and so forth), after its revival in 1819 it had, under Channing's leadership, successfully fought for greater tolerance and more freedom of thought in the religious life of the States. In the middle thirties the Unitarians had become the American Transcendentalists, under the direct influence of German romantic philosophy. The word Transcendentalism came from Kant's *Critique of Pure Reason*, but the young New Englanders who joined the new movement were neither systematic nor dogmatic, and for them the new philosophy was "more a spirit and an attitude of mind than a consciously reasoned out theory of the world." [7] The general public considered the attitude of the school merely as "transcending from common sense," and in *American Notes* Dickens quotes a common American *bon mot*, "Whatever was unintelligible would be certainly *transcendental!*" The movement was founded in 1836 by Ripley, who was originally a Unitarian minister, and it got its manifesto in Emerson's *Nature*, 1836, and *American Scholar*, 1837. Ecclesiastical ceremony and authority are rejected; God is everywhere and reveals himself in each individual, particularly in communion with nature. These are some of the general principles of Transcendentalism. Tol-

erance and optimism are its fixed concepts; the designation
for God is "The Over-Soul"—true German romanticism. Unitarianism, which in 1819 had seemed radical, was conservative
in comparison. As we know, Emerson soon resigned from his
position as a Unitarian minister; even the simplified Unitarian
service was too ceremonial for him. However, Transcendentalism did not necessarily mean a break with Unitarianism. Until
his death in 1842 the noble Dr. Channing was a moderator
between the two groups, and many other Transcendentalists
remained Unitarian ministers, such as Ripley until 1840, when
he resigned to put Fourier's socialistic theories into practice
in the experimental community at Brook Farm (1841–46).
Today the "program" of the new school seems foggy, amor-
phous, and the definition of "the new mind" as the power to
conceive a higher meaning of existence than that which can be
defined by the five senses appears indeterminate and vague; but
it is impossible to overestimate their effects on American intellectual life of that period. Transcendentalism meant a religious, political, and literary revival, and the widely diverse
individuals who met within its framework under the common
designation of Transcendentalists, each in his own field did pioneer work for the future American literature. The anti-slavery,
abolitionist group, which was finally organized into a political
party in 1840, got its most zealous supporters and champions
from the ranks of the Transcendentalists. Thoreau, H. W.
Channing (nephew of Dr. Channing), and Theodore Parker
were among those who boldly, in defiance of the law, received
fugitive slaves into their homes. To a great extent the social
reform movement came from the same group, as in the Brook
Farm of Ripley and Hawthorne and even in Alcott's vegetarian colony, "The Community of Fruitlands." The American
Women's Rights movement got its chief advocate in the talented
Margaret Fuller, the author of *Woman in the Nineteenth Century*, 1846. Margaret Fuller was also one of the editors of the
famous Transcendental magazine, *The Dial*, founded in 1840,
which, through its contributions from all the most promising
young writers of the period, probably did more than anything else to smooth the way for future American literature.

The intellectual spadework of the forties, performed in the midst of the terrific social tension, was just reaching its final stages when, in 1850, Fredrika Bremer arrived in America and began her observation of the new intellectual life.[8]

On the voyage Fredrika Bremer got a taste of the literature of the country she was to visit. She read with interest Longfellow's *Evangeline*, which had appeared in the preceding spring; and soon after her arrival in New York her host, Mr. Downing, gave her copies of the three writers he considered most characteristic of the period: Bryant, Lowell, and Emerson. The Swedish writer was instantly captivated by Emerson, "a philosopher rather than a poet, yet poetic in his prose philosophical essays . . . a new and peculiar character, the most unusual of the three." [9] She compared him with her countryman the poet Thorild, and was greatly impressed by his break with Unitarianism. "I have never as yet gone a step to see a literary lion; but I would go a considerable way to see Emerson, this pioneer in the moral forests of the New World." [10] She was not long in discovering that intellectual life in the New World was primarily associated with New England, especially with Massachusetts, from which issued not only literature but also socialism and abolitionism. She went there on her first trip, and in addition to meeting Emerson became acquainted with practically all the important people in American politics, science, the church, and art. In philosophy there was the "Christian Socialist" Henry James, father of the two brothers of later fame, William and Henry; the historian George Bancroft; the preacher and abolitionist Theodore Parker; the scholarly blacksmith Elihu Burrit, just returned from the first Peace Congress, in Paris; also, there was the great educational organizer Horace Mann, and the two fiery agitators and abolitionists William Lloyd Garrison and Wendell Phillips. Among the Transcendentalists she met H. W. Channing, Bronson Alcott, the mild dreamer and vegetarian, "whose Pythagorean wisdom will hardly make people wiser nowadays," [11] and Thoreau, who had returned from his solitude at Walden, but had not yet written about it. She met Longfellow, the Quaker poet Whittier, whose Puritan ascetism attracted her ("Both soul and spirit have overstrained the nervous chords and wasted the body"),[12] and Lowell—but he disappointed her. "Singularly enough I did not discern in him that deeply earnest spirit which charmed me in so many of his poems." [13] She saw the work of the only important American sculptor, Hiram Powers, whose *Eve* had already been admired by the Danish sculptor Thorwaldsen. In Boston she heard the famous sailor-preacher Father Taylor, whose astonishingly simple, rough eloquence Dickens had also described. She met the two great actresses of the time, Fanny Kemble and Charlotte Cushman, both of a pronounced masculine character. Charlotte Cushman was from an old Puritan family, with which she had broken to go into the theater. Fredrika Bremer saw her as Meg Merrilies and Lady Macbeth. Although Fanny Kemble was English, she had lived in the States since 1832, and her Shakespearean recitals were the sensation of the season. Fredrika Bremer wrote that occasionally she undeniably lacked feminine grace, but as a compensation was "brimful of life."

We must not overestimate this new "free thought," however, because of the tolerance, fermentation, and reform in these Boston circles. After all, this was the land of the Puritans, and complete freedom was essentially a literary matter; even Emerson remained *bourgeois*, and social "good form" was always an important measuring stick for the Boston literary set. Therefore, it is very interesting to hear from Fredrika Bremer about an affair that shows clearly the limits of free thought. It is the story of Margaret Fuller, whose career caused distress in the group. She had always been the *enfant terrible* of the Transcendentalists, and Lowell, who tried by his writing to arouse a new intellectual life, but always remained aloof when it appeared, had treated her roughly in *A Fable for Critics*. Nevertheless, she was generally recognized as one of the keenest intellects of the period, and Fredrika was disappointed not to meet her. She was on a trip to Italy, and "a report has now reached this country that she has connected herself with a young man . . . and a Fourieristic or Socialistic marriage, without the external ceremony, is spoken of; certain it is that the marriage remained secret for a year and that she has a child. . . . They who love neither herself nor her turn of mind believe the worst." [14] The proud, inflexible Margaret Fuller, who had formed a friendship with George Sand in Paris, was one of the period's most stimulating personalities. Consequently the greatest sensation of the year was the report in July, 1850, that on her way home from Europe Margaret Fuller Ossoli, with her husband, Marquis Ossoli, and their child, had been lost in a wreck off the American coast.

The year 1850 had other sensations and other events of importance and interest. Hawthorne's *Scarlet Letter* was published. Fredrika met Hawthorne much later, and he scarcely spoke to the Swedish guest, but still she regarded him as one of the most significant authors of the literary future. Jenny Lind also made her American tour in 1850, but the two famous fellow countrywomen did not meet, though in letters and through the newspapers Fredrika Bremer followed the singer's career with interest and pride. Finally, 1850 was the year of two deaths most fateful for American politics, Taylor's and Calhoun's. President Zachary Taylor, hero of the War with Mexico, died when the Congressional action on the slavery question was in progress. Although a Southerner by birth, he sided with the North. Calhoun, the most important Southern statesman, died at the same critical time for his party. The two great parties, the Whigs and the Democrats, were at an explosive impasse on the slavery question. In 1840 the Abolitionist party had split, in 1848 the antislavery members of the Whig and Democratic parties had united to form the Free Soil party, and in 1850 at last the main question before Congress was whether the District of Columbia and the new territories of California, Utah, and New Mexico should be slave or free. The balance of power between the North and the South stemmed from 1820, when the number of slave states equaled the number of free states. Since then the formation of each new state had raised the question to which party it should belong. Previously Missouri had been the dividing line between North and South, but the abolitionists made stronger and stronger protests against the disgrace of introducing slavery into any more states. In 1850 the final and decisive blow was expected; instead, the notorious and hopeless "Compromise" was brought about by the two most powerful statesmen on each side, Henry Clay for the South and Daniel Webster for the North. Fredrika described them both [15] and eagerly followed the proceedings each day.[16]

The Compromise provided that each new state must decide for itself whether it was to be free or slave, but the South had the right to demand the return of fugitive slaves from the free states if they sought refuge there. This last provision, which was enforced, led, among other things, to the famous Boston Slave Delivery when some fugitive slaves were held in custody. This act contributed so much to heighten the tension between the North and the South that it became *the* constant source of irritation that finally led to the outbreak of the Civil War. Webster was hated in the North for his "ardent enthusiasm over freedom for the Hungarians while he indifferently saw three million Americans in slavery." [17] As an interesting example of the way in which the times were ripe for a book, which was "in the air" even before it was written, it may be mentioned that Fredrika Bremer felt a glowing desire to compose a story, a long novel, about a "fugitive negro couple as it seems to me it ought to be written." [18] She began to collect material, but felt "that it should belong to some one else. I hope and wait for the American mother." It was two years later that Harriet Beecher Stowe's *Uncle Tom's Cabin* produced the effect in Europe and America for which Fredrika Bremer had hoped. Her active interest in the slave question colored her whole tour, and her aversion toward and disgust with the "institution" was sharpened by a trip through the South.

The Swedish authoress did not get caught in the snare which Marryat had previously noted in reference to Harriet Martineau as a threat to the traveler in America, that is, falling into the hands of a determined clique who posed as typical and leading figures and attempted to "surround the traveler with an atmosphere of their own." [19] Fredrika Bremer did not stay with her friends in the North, but traveled through both the West and the South, and even as far as Cuba, and she made her observations first hand. In some cases she suffered for the sins of her predecessors, for example, when a ship's captain refused on patriotic grounds to sail for South Carolina with her as a passenger. After their experience with Dickens, Americans had acquired a distrust of European travelers, but in most places she was treated frankly and hospitably even by Southern planters, who were not unaware that her sympathies were with the North. Regarding a conversation which she had had with one of the planters on contemporary American literature, she made the important and characteristic observation: "It is remarkable how very little, or not at all, the authors of the Northern States, even the best of them, are known in the South. They are afraid of admitting their liberal opinions into the slave states." [20]

From Fredrika Bremer we get an overwhelming impression of the innumerable religious sects in the America of that period. Being vitally interested in religion, she visited as many of the sects as possible and took part in divine services of all kinds. Always she reported them faithfully and objectively. Some states had a preponderance of one religious creed: Maryland was Catholic; Virginia, Episcopalian; Pennsylvania, Quaker. In South Carolina she met descendants of the emigrant Huguenots, whom she called "the French Puritans" to distinguish them from the English Puritans in Massachusetts. In addition she attended meetings of Unitarian, Mormon, Baptist, and Moravian congregations, and gives an excellent account of Swedenborgianism, which, after the publication of Wilkinson's book on Swedenborg in the forties, suddenly caught on, especially influencing Emerson. She visited the Dunkers in the Valley of Virginia and the mystical Shaker community at Canterbury, whose ascetic life and dancing at divine service had seemed so irresistibly funny to Dickens. To Fredrika the industrious daily life of men and women to whom all sexual intercourse was forbidden was "the most rational . . . of all the convent orders. I should be very glad for similar foundations in every country." [21]

Most amusing of all is her characterization of what we are tempted to call "the eternal America," which is ever present in this account of 1850, the constantly reiterated grievances and

arguments: money as the chief interest of Americans, the un-
pardonable imitations of Greek and Gothic architectural styles,
the autograph craze, of which Fredrika jokingly complains—
and above all the dominant role women play in the intellectual
life. At first with interest, but soon with distaste, the Swedish
writer mentions some twenty women writers and says, "In general I have little faith in woman's ability as a creative artist." [22]
In social life, however, she predicts a great future for women,
even if shortly after her arrival she made an observation concerning the ordinary type of American women which might
have been written today: "The ladies dress with taste, have
small hands and feet, reminiscent of the French. Something
however is wanting in their faces, but what I don't rightly
know—I fancy it is expression." [23] That is today's description
of the Hollywood-type sketched a hundred years in advance.[24]

In spite of all the criticisms, all the internal tensions, the
conflicts, contradictions, and discussions, in 1850 the United
States was still a *young* America and primarily a latent force.
What Goethe and De Tocqueville had seen in America could
in 1850 still be regarded as a résumé of what Europe expected
of the great New World. The surge toward California set the
tone of fervent anticipation and emphasized still further that
at that time the people of the Eastern States considered the
expected settlement and development of the Mississippi Valley
as the great future of America. It was in mid-America that a
new people, a new race would develop "through the union of
all peoples" into a stronger, better humanity. Thus Fredrika
Bremer described the contemporary mood of hope and belief
that America was the model state that De Tocqueville had
thought it would be.

On one other point De Tocqueville had ventured a prophecy.
European authors had not been very optimistic about an American literature. In *De l'amour* Stendhal talked of "the complete
lack of artists and writers" there, and Lenau, whose visit to
America in 1832–33 had been such a bitter disappointment,[25]
thought it would require the voice of a Niagara to awaken
an American intellectual life. But De Tocqueville firmly believed in a future American intellectual life.[26] He noted the

difficulties of writing in a new democratic state, the necessity
for detachment from European form and style, and the industrial stamp that readily colors democratic literature (the
people will seek the utilitarian rather than the esthetic) ; but
while the literature of the old world is always conscious of the
past, the New World has really an "instinctive distaste for what
is old," and therefore the great task of its writers is to describe
the new wonders of nature, to gather accounts of man, of the
universal working man of our day—and the future. To com-
prise all mankind in one image ("recognizing humanity as a
single unity"),[27] therein, according to De Tocqueville, resides
"a very prolific source of poetry." Furthermore, the ability to
see *man in relation to the universe* is a rich source of poetry:
"Man is born, traverses time, and disappears forever in the
bosom of God." [28] For whatever the new democratic poetry
loses in subject matter through the loss of the old legends and
historic figures, it will gain in the portrayal of man, both as
"generic humanity" and as individual. De Tocqueville says:
"All these resources are lacking, but *man* remains, and that is
enough. Human destiny, *man himself, removed from his setting
in time and country, and placed face to face with nature and
God, with his passions, his doubts, his rare prosperity and incomprehensible misery, will become for these people the principal and almost the only source of poetry."* [29]

Fredrika Bremer went to America when the spadework for
the intellectual life of the country was being finished. She was
conscious that she went not to something already in existence
but to something yet to be, as she said in the final letter to
Martensen, a humanity and an intellectual life of the future.
That was the keynote of American literature in the forties.
Emerson and Lowell invoked "the future poet." [30] In the
twenties and thirties Cooper and Channing had insisted that
there must be an original and independent American intellectual life, and in *A Fable for Critics* Lowell had voiced the dependence of American literature on England.

You steal Englishmen's books and think Englishmen's thought,
With their salt on her tail your wild eagle is caught.

.   .   .

Forget Europe wholly, your veins throb with blood,
To which the dull current in hers is but mud.

But in January, 1850, when Fredrika Bremer in conversation
with Emerson praised him for "the genuine American" quality
in some of his poetry, he thanked her for her appreciation, but
replied in a very noteworthy and significant statement: The
states have no poet yet who has grown naturally from the new
form of government or the new nature. "The poet of America is
not yet come. When he comes he will sing quite differently." [31]

It is interesting to review the significant American books that
appeared after Lowell's declaration of independence: in 1848
Lowell's *A Fable for Critics*, in 1849 Longfellow's *Evangeline*,
in 1850 Hawthorne's *Scarlet Letter*, in 1851 Whittier's *Songs
of Labor* and Melville's *Moby Dick*, in 1854 Thoreau's *Walden*,
in 1855 Longfellow's *Hiawatha*—and Walt Whitman's *Leaves
of Grass*. When we have this wonderful, original, strong, eloquent, democratic book in our hands it is impossible not to think
of Emerson's "future poet," of De Tocqueville's poet who was
to depict man and the universe, of Fredrika Bremer's "new
man"—or of the voice of Niagara which Lenau [32] thought
would be necessary for an American poet. In the original version of "Starting from Paumanok" (then called "Proto-Leaf")
Whitman speaks of himself on the very first page as a "resounding Niagara."

We find the complete poetic and historic expression of the
new man and his new world in the 1855 *Leaves of Grass*, along
with an expanding poetic vision of "the future in the New
World." That this vision was an illusion, a *Fata Morgana*, does
not matter. The history of literature is always the history of
the great dreamers and their greatest dreams throughout the
centuries. But when Whitman appeared in 1855 he was a natural, an inevitable product of a powerful intellectual process in
the people, a product of the tendencies, the struggles, the
crises of America in 1850.

Walt Whitman at Thirty-six

There was a child went forth every day,
And the first object he looked upon and received
    with wonder or pity or love or dread, that
    object he became,
And that object became part of him for the day or
    a certain part of the day . . . . or for many
    years or stretching cycles of years.

The early lilacs became part of this child,
And grass, and white and red morning glories, and
    white and red clover, and the song of the
    phœbe-bird,
        •   •   •

And all the changes of city and country wherever
    he went.
        •   •   •

These became part of that child who went forth
    every day, and who now goes and will always
    go forth every day, . . .
      There Was a Child Went Forth (1855)

WHITMAN was born in 1819, the same year as Lowell
and Melville, on "fish-shaped" Long Island, almost on
the borderline separating the Dutch and the English colonies.
Originally the Dutch formed the majority of the inhabitants on
the west side of the Island, opposite the city which had been
founded across the river in 1623 and called New Amsterdam,
and arbitrarily christened New York by the English soldiers in
1663. About 1800 English and Dutch were in almost equal
numbers on the Island, and Whitman had both English and

Dutch blood in his veins. His mother was the daughter of Major
Cornelius Van Velsor; his father was of an old English family
that had emigrated to America before 1640. Both families considered themselves "American," and in the war against England
fought in the Continental armies. One great-uncle was killed in
the Battle of Long Island, at Brooklyn, on August 22, 1776,
an early battle of the War of Independence. The mother of this
great-uncle and of Jesse Whitman, Walt's paternal grandmother, was famous in the annals of Long Island for her doughty
manners; she smoked, drank, rode, and swore—and was notorious for the masculine vigor with which she chastened her
slaves. Jesse's wife, on the other hand, was a typical Eastern
American woman of the time, a former schoolmistress, and, like
Jesse himself, with a leaning toward the Quaker faith. Jesse was
a personal friend and admirer of Elias Hicks, the great enigmatic figure of American Quakerism, and that friendship was
inherited by his son and grandson. The Whitman–Van Velsor
union took place in 1816, and Walt Whitman was the second
child of the marriage. On his mother's side there was also a
Quaker inheritance. His grandmother, Naomi Williams, previous to her marriage to Major Van Velsor, had belonged to the
Island's Quaker community.

The existence of Quakers on Long Island goes far back in
the history of New York State,[1] and the English founder of the
sect, George Fox, on his visit to America in 1672, preached there
under the oak trees of Flushing. In the beginning the sect
suffered violent persecution, "Almost as much as the Jews in
Europe in the Middle Ages," Whitman wrote in *November
Boughs;* but the vigorous reaction against the infamous persecution in New England benefited the Long Island congregation
so that it flourished and at the end of the eighteenth century
produced its great leader, Elias Hicks. Briefly, the teaching of
the Quakers is this: In each person there is an "inner light,"
which it is his duty to heed—to develop the inner Christ, Elias
Hicks called it. All church ceremonies such as christenings and
communion are forbidden; there is complete freedom of conscience, and—what strongly impressed Fredrika Bremer and
greatly influenced Whitman's ideal of democracy—equality be-

tween men and women. The Quakers dressed alike, were easily recognized by their broad-brimmed hats, addressed every one as "thou" and "friend," and removed their hats to no one, neither to those in authority nor in church. They were forbidden to take an oath or to bear arms; their weapon was passive resistance. They had no ministers; in their meetings one of the congregation stood up and spoke if he had a mind to—if no one spoke there was a so-called "silent meeting." We are familiar with the importance of the sect in America, especially in the Quaker City of Philadelphia (City of Brotherly Love), founded by William Penn in 1682, and in all Pennsylvania. Although by 1850 their greatness was declining, many Quakers participated in the movements of the period, particularly in Women's Rights and Peace. Many leading men of the States have been of Quaker descent. Fredrika Bremer visited Philadelphia in 1850 and gave an enthusiastic account of the Quaker community there: "The women please me particularly, from that quiet refinement of demeanor, both inward and outward . . ." [2] She was critical of them for discarding the Holy Writ, which to them was only a "history of religion," but she found their idea of equality noble, "a rich seed which must germinate through a wider sphere." [3] But the sect was disintegrating; inner conflict and external conditions had weakened its position, especially the schism between the orthodox Quakers and the "Hicksites" which took place while Walt was a child.

From Whitman's own hand we have a valuable account of the Quakers and a eulogistic and vivid description of Elias Hicks,[4] whom he heard as a child in 1829 when Hicks was 81 —about the time he broke with the Orthodox Quakers and a few months before he died. By that time the Whitman family had moved to Brooklyn, where the father was a carpenter, and it was in a hotel on the Heights overlooking New York "and its North and East Rivers fill'd with ships" that Elias Hicks spoke that evening. The child's impression of the old Quaker's eloquence was overwhelming. "A pleading, tender, nearly agonizing conviction, and magnetic stream of natural eloquence" is the way he described Hick's sermon, and he said that if he had to name anything in his later life which reminded him of that it would be Father Taylor, in Boston, and his "passionate unstudied oratory." Whitman summarized the essence of Hicks's teaching as follows:

Elias taught throughout, as George Fox began it, or rather re-iterated and verified it, the Platonic doctrine that the ideals of character, of justice, of religious action . . . are to be conform'd to no outside doctrine of creeds, Bibles, legislative enactments, conventionalities, or even decorums, but are to follow the inward Deity-planted law of the emotional soul. . . . E. believ'd little in a church as organiz'd—even his own—with houses, ministers, or with salaries, creeds, Sundays, saints, Bibles, holy festivals, &c. But he believ'd always in the universal church, in the soul of man, invisibly rapt, ever-waiting, ever responding to universal truths.[5]

Whitman says of the break with the orthodox Quaker congregation that it occurred in September, 1827, at a great meeting in Philadelphia, where Hicks spoke and said, among other things:

The blood of Christ—the blood of Christ—why, my friends, the actual blood of Christ in itself was no more effectual than the blood of bulls and goats—not a bit more—not a bit.

Almost instantly there was pandemonium. That was "the definite utterance" which divided the Quaker congregation.

There can be no question of the significant influence which the ideas of Quaker faith and the personality of Elias Hicks had on Whitman. In the two phrases he quotes about "the emotional soul" and "the universal truths" and the expression about Christ's blood, which was for that time paradoxically bold, we recall three frequently varied ideas of Whitman's own poetry. In the account of Hicks's growing up on Long Island as a "thorough gunner and fisherman," "a singer fond of vain songs . . . a dancer, too at the country balls," there are characteristics which recall his own youth. There is a real similarity between Whitman and the young carpenter Hicks, whom frequent roaming about in the open air "preserved from falling into hurtful associations"! Older people told Whitman later that behind his religion Elias Hicks had basically "a large element of personal ambition." Nothing could be more typical than Whitman's defense. "Very likely. Such indeed seems the means, all through progress and civilization, by which strong men and strong convictions achieve anything definite." Better than most people Whitman knew ambition and personal vanity as the motive power behind his own poetic and religious teaching. But at the same time he stressed Hicks's ability to attract people by radiation of "powerful human magnetism"; he knew that people said that he too had this faculty. On the whole Whitman fully recognized his intimate connection with and spiritual kinship to the Quakers, and in later years he emphasized it in his dress and diction. In his last book of prose, *Good-Bye My Fancy,* he repeated many times: "I am partly of Quaker stock," "For I am at least half of Quaker stock," and once he considered joining the Quaker congregation.[6] The influence of Quakerism on his poetry is mixed with the Emersonian influence and with that of romantic philosophy and oriental mysticism. He even compared Hicks with Goethe, Emerson, and Omar Khayyám, always giving prominence to the "magnetic personality" of Elias Hicks. "The feeling and intention never forgotten yet" is the way he begins the Hicks article in *November Boughs,* written in his seventieth year.

Today Long Island, or Paumanok, as Whitman in his fondness for the Indian name called it in his poetry, is affected in the hundred miles from Brooklyn to Montauk Point by the monstrous development of the great city of New York. But in Whitman's childhood it was a stretch of wild and uncultivated nature, and that nature more than any other is almost exclusively in the background of all his descriptions of nature in *Leaves of Grass* —the north shore where he was born, the flat prairielike plains in the center of the Island, and finally the romantic South Bay, "the habitat of every sort of fish and aquatic fowl of North America." In *Specimen Days,* 1882, his first book of prose, Whitman gave a detailed account of the significance which nature on his native island had for him.

. . . the successive growth-stages of my infancy, childhood, youth and manhood were all pass'd on Long Island, which I sometimes feel as if I had incorporated . . .[7] many a good day or half-day did I have, wandering through those solitary cross-roads, inhaling the peculiar and wild aroma. Here, and all along the island

and its shores, I spent intervals many years, all seasons, sometimes riding, sometimes boating, but generally afoot, (I was always then a good walker,) absorbing fields, shores, marine incidents, characters, the bay-men, farmers, pilots—always had a plentiful acquaintance with the latter, and with fishermen . . .[8]

The strongest impression of nature came from the sea, sailing among the many lighthouses to the north, seal-catching and wild birds to the south—the sea which was Whitman's first inspiration to write poetry,[9] the sea with which his first romantic experience was linked; the wreck of the ships "Bristol" and "Mexico" in 1836 and 1837, which he witnessed and refers to in "Song of Myself" and "The Sleepers"—the sea whose wave beats are visible in his verse, in the typography, changing and undulating, like tidal marks in the sand on the beach. It is scarcely necessary to point out how important ships and marine incidents are in his poetry. They can all be traced back to his first youthful experiences on the coast of Long Island, where the ship "Elizabeth" went down in 1850 with Margaret Fuller on board.

In Whitman's childhood Long Island had about 60,000 inhabitants, and the city of Brooklyn, to which the family moved in his fifth year, had between ten and sixteen thousand. In Whitman's seventh year Lafayette visited New York again and rode through the streets of Brooklyn. In the poet's official biography we learn that on the ride through Brooklyn, Lafayette passed a group of children, took little Walt onto his saddle and kissed him. It is a childish memory which grew clearer and clearer with each of the three repetitions.[10] Whitman has attached a definite importance to making it authoritative. Probably there was nothing more than that as a child he saw Lafayette ride through Brooklyn. This is Myth No. 1 and a characteristic example of Whitman's later conscious romanticizing of his life.

Like the mother city, New York, Brooklyn was developing rapidly. Between Whitman's tenth and sixtieth years the population increased from 16,000 to 400,000. This was the child's first and decisive impression of a modern city: Brooklyn, with its churches, its theaters (where the boy early witnessed an unforgettably terrifying performance of "Timour the Tartar"), its old fortifications from Revolutionary days, its In-

dians from their reservation on the Eastern part of the Island,
who came gliding soundlessly into the city and vanished again
silently (the red squaw in "The Sleepers"), its picturesque fire
engines, which still today with clang and clamor roar through
the pages of *Leaves of Grass*—and above all Brooklyn with its
ferries, "Old Ferry" and "New Ferry," whose trips from shore
to shore between Manhattan and Long Island always moved
Whitman's thoughts to poetic rhythm. In 1862 he wrote a series
of articles, "Brooklyniana," about the old Brooklyn, and his
childish impressions remained of important significance in his
whole writing. A peculiarly childlike characteristic of his poetry
is the ability to reproduce fresh, simple impressions, often as
primitively as a child interprets people and events; and the
actual experiences of his childhood have gone into his poetry
as part of his "I." In the 1855 poem "There Was a Child Went
Forth" he himself indicates to what extent this is true.

There was a child went forth every day,
And the first object he looked upon and received with wonder or
    pity or love or dread, that object he became,
And that object became part of him for the day or a certain part
    of the day . . . . or for many years or stretching cycles of
    years.

Lilacs, the grass, apple trees, school children, Negro children,
the streets, the ferries, the people on the streets, the ships, the
clouds.

His own parents . . he that had propelled the fatherstuff at night,
    and fathered him . . and she that conceived him in her womb
    and birthed him . . . . they gave this child more of them-
    selves than that,
They gave him afterward every day . . . . they and of them be-
    came a part of him.

The mother at home quietly placing the dishes on the suppertable,
The mother with mild words . . . . clean her cap and gown . . . .
    a wholesome odor falling off her person and clothes as she
    walks by:
The father, strong, selfsufficient, manly, mean, angered, unjust,
The blow, the quick loud word, the tight bargain, the crafty lure,

The family usages, the language, the company, the furniture . . . .
    the yearning and swelling heart,
Affection that will not be gainsayed . . . . etc.

One interesting thing about this poem intended for the future is that this is the only place in which we get a glimpse of the friction in his childhood home which has indirectly but clearly left a mark on his poetry. Contrary to what he himself—and therefore most biographers—asserted, it is obvious that his home life could not have been happy, and his parents' marriage was far from harmonious. Walter Whitman was "strong, self-sufficient, manly, mean, angered, unjust," a tyrant with the wayward inclinations of a dreamer. He ran through with the old family place at West Hills, and his building ventures in Brooklyn were not always successful. In ten years the family moved from Front Street, near the Ferry, to Cranberry Street, to Johnson Street, Tillary Street, Henry Street, according to whether the building ventures sold or not. A family constantly on the move, constantly upset, was naturally painful for the mother, whose ideal was domesticity and comfort. Louisa Whitman was completely untaught—she could scarcely read or write —but she had a lively imagination and a natural gift for story-telling. She had nine children, of whom eight lived. Jesse was the oldest, a replica of his father and never congenial to his mother or to Walt; Walt was next; then, in 1821 and 1823, came two girls, Mary and Hannah; finally, in 1827, 1829, and 1833, the three boys, Andrew Jackson Whitman, George Washington Whitman, and Thomas Jefferson Whitman, whose ostentatious names were intended as so many declarations of their father's loyalty to the Democratic party. In 1835 the youngest boy was born, the half-imbecile cripple Edward. Aside from the latter, Walt felt closest to his sister Hannah and brother Jeff, who was later his companion on the trip to New Orleans. Edward, whose condition was Whitman's constant care until his death, was perhaps in his later years a reminder that his family was not the model of primitive health which he would have liked it to be. Eduard Bertz, in his pathological study of Whitman [11] (1905), stressed this as the explanation of his

psychological peculiarities and of his later illness. On the basis
of observations by Dr. D. G. Brinton and C. P. O'Connor,[12]
Bertz states that paralysis was a hereditary trait in Whitman's
family and thinks that a strong degenerative character could
be traced in the family. Jesse died an inmate of Queens Hospital,
and Whitman himself was white-haired at an early age.

To Whitman the family meant primarily his mother. Even
if he had not recorded it again and again, we could guess this
from his poetry, in which the mother always has a place which
hovers between monomania and mythology. If we wanted to
construct a "mother-religion" from the works of any modern
poet, it would be Whitman's. He is the perfect example of
Bachofen's "mother's son." [13] The mother completely dominates
his concept of the female; woman as mother is for him the most
neglected theme in world literature,[14] and the primeval forces
in his poetry are always, quite naturally, the mother figure:
the Great Mother America, the Great Mother Sea, the Great
Mother Earth. Nothing is said of the father except in a few
poems in which the negative principle is presented. One of his
most famous *Drum-Taps* poems is "Come Up from the Fields,
Father," but it is exclusively concerned with the mother's grief
over her son's death. And the fact that Whitman, in spite of his
dependence on his mother, left home at an early age can only
be explained by his unpleasant relationship with his father.

The boy had to get out and earn his living. At the age of
eleven he was in the office of a Brooklyn lawyer, Edward Clarke,
who took an interest in him and gave him books to read—*The
Thousand and One Nights* and novels by Scott and Cooper.
In 1831 he was working for S. E. Clements, publisher of *The
Long Island Patriot*. He learned the fundamentals of typeset-
ting under the old printer Hartshorne, of whom he has given
such a sympathetic picture in "Brooklyniana." [15] The old man
made a profound impression on the boy with his stories of Washington and Jefferson, and inspired in him a love for printing
that lasted throughout the years and left its own whimsical
stamp on many editions of *Leaves of Grass*, which Whitman
liked to set himself. Later we know he was with the *Long Island*

Star and that, young as he was, he had short journalistic pieces printed in that and other papers.

But already we find the first lacuna in our knowledge of his life. Whitman's deliberate expurgation of all traces of everything except his "official" life goes back as far as his childhood roaming between 1832 and 1836. We learn that shortly after the cholera epidemic in 1832 the family left Brooklyn and returned to the country ("my dear mother very ill for a long time, but recover'd"),[16] but he stayed behind in Brooklyn. Why? Where? Here, as for the later periods of his life, we can "read" it in his work—a procedure which is as stimulating for psychology as it is discouraging for biography. Only one thing is positive: he finally took the ferry from Brooklyn to New York and in one way or another established himself there.

New York, which Fredrika Bremer found less a city than "a huge hotel, a caravansary for the whole world," [17] had in the 1830's more than 200,000 inhabitants. The city had recently been ravaged by two great catastrophies, cholera and the great fire, but the latter only served to make the city still more romantic for young Whitman, who in 1835, the year of the fire, seems to have had his daily occupation there. That the city made a deep impression on his mind we can see in his poems; we know from *Leaves of Grass* the "Manhattan day-dreams" of the harbor and ships which his contemporary Melville described so vividly in the introductory chapter of *Moby-Dick*. Above all, in New York the boy came under the influence of the theater, the other great spiritual factor next to Quakerism in his youth. The city had two theaters of importance. After 1825 Italian opera, which always appealed to Whitman as the zenith of theatrical art, was performed at the old Park Theater, but there was also good comedy. Forest made his debut there; the English actors Macready and Kean made guest appearances, and Fanny Kemble played there regularly. She made a profound impression on the boy: "Nothing finer did ever stage exhibit—the veterans of all nations said so, and my boyish heart and head felt it in every minute cell. . . . It was my good luck to see her nearly every night she play'd at the old Park—certainly in all her principal characters." [18] From the other, more popular theater, the Old Bowery, with its 3,000 seats, the dominant impression seems to have been the acting of the elder Booth. At least, Whitman referred to him again and again, and in *November Boughs* devoted a whole section to him. He praised him as Richard III, King Lear, and Sir Giles Overreach. Concerning his personality Whitman made a comment that we cannot fail to note: "He illustrated Plato's rule that to the forming an artist of the very highest rank a dash of insanity or what the world calls insanity is indispensable." [19] The Bowery was in its prime during the thirties. Afterwards Whitman speaks of the Park and names some of its famous patrons—the presidents Adams, Jackson, Van Buren, the writers Cooper, Bryant, Irving, Fitz-Greene Halleck—and complains that after 1840 the old theater went into a decline. However, the main point is that the theater was a fundamental experience for Whitman. Henry Bryan Binns compares the effect Booth had on the boy with that made by Elias Hicks, and explains the strong attraction the theater had for Whitman as being for him "a new world of expression." "For the first time, he understood how far gestures, and a presence more powerful than words, can express the heights and depths of emotion." [20] In any event, the theater influenced the *oratorical* side of Whitman's art. But the biographical problem is, *how* did he get there? How did he manage to see Booth and Fanny Kemble in all their chief roles? Jean Catel, who in *Walt Whitman, la naissance du poète* [Walt Whitman, the Birth of the Poet] [21] made the most careful study imaginable of Whitman's awakening, without always getting results in proportion to his efforts, offers the hypothesis that Whitman, having failed at journalism, became a chocolate vender, a program seller, or a prompter (!) in the Park or Bowery, an opinion Holloway seems to support,[22] but we *know* nothing. We can guess at a few harried, transitional, homeless years from certain features of the novel *Franklin Evans*, 1842, and the horrors of cheap boarding and rooming houses can be followed through the prose writings which in "Brooklyniana" he says belong to his first stay in New York. We know that in 1836 the seventeen-year-old boy was for a while with his family on Long Island, taking in August a position as schoolmaster in the country town of Babylon on the southern shore of Long Island.

If Whitman's development was typically "American," no part of it was more so than this appointment as schoolmaster. Many followed that path. Melville was also a schoolmaster at that time, but we must not take the title too seriously. In those days a schoolmaster might be anyone who came wandering into the community and applied to the parents; the pay was next to nothing, and the young man got board and room. John Erskine has pictured it in his satirical novel on America's awakening, *Uncle Sam in the Eyes of His Family*, 1930, in which school teaching is presented as one of the typical employments for Americans of that period. Erskine reveals also the embarrassment of the poorly paid teacher at having to take turns eating with the parents of the children he taught. Whitman afterwards wanted to give the impression that he had ability as a teacher. There is nothing which bears it out; it is part of the Whitman mythology. In the two years he taught he changed schools no less than seven times, and in the account of an early pupil with whom Dr. John Johnston talked on a visit to Long Island in 1890 [23] we learn that the parents regarded him as a sort of harmless vagabond, usually to be found outside of school hours lying on his back somewhere in the sun with a book in his hand. Dr. Johnston showed an old farmer with whom he talked the picture of Whitman in the 1855 edition. The farmer did not recognize the face, but he knew the sloppiness of the clothes, the unbuttoned shirt, and the tilt of the hat. Whitman himself never gave any account of these years. In *Specimen Days* he says only that he had many of the best experiences of human nature during this period. He certainly remembered primarily the hunting and fishing trips with contemporary country youths, which he afterwards described so colorfully and romantically, for example, in "Song of Joys."

It was journalism which attracted him most of all, and that was typically American too; in the land of newspapers, as Marryat called America, the road to the intellectual life led through journalism. The writers were all journalists, even

Bryant and Poe. In 1838 Whitman went to his native town of Huntington, and there, at nineteen, he founded his own paper, *The Long Islander* (weekly), which he wrote, printed, and delivered himself by horse and buggy: "I never had happier jaunts." [24] After one year the paper naturally failed, and the youthful editor went back to his desk—this time, however, only as a compromise. He lived with the editor, James S. Brenton, in Jamaica, for whose reputable paper, *The Long Island Democrat*, he wrote outside school hours. Some of these contributions, especially a series with the significant title "From the Desk of a Schoolmaster," Holloway has included in *The Uncollected Poetry and Prose of Walt Whitman*. But they are of little interest. From the daughter-in-law of Editor Brenton, Mrs. Orvetta Hall Brenton, Holloway got an account of Whitman during his stay with the Brenton's, as family tradition preserved the memory.

Mrs. Brenton wrote, among other things:

My mother-in-law, Mrs. Brenton, was a practical, busy New England woman, and very obviously, from her remarks about Whitman, cared very little for him and held him in scant respect. He was at that time a dreamy, impracticable youth, who did very little work and who was always "under foot" and in the way. Except that he was always in evidence physically, he lived his life very much to himself. One thing that impressed Mrs. Brenton unfavorably was his disregard of the two children of the household—two small boys—who seemed very much to annoy him when they were with him in the house.

Mrs. Brenton always emphasized, when speaking of Whitman, that he was inordinately indolent and lazy and had a very pronounced disinclination to work! During some of the time he was in the household, the apple trees in the garden were in bloom. When Whitman would come from the printing office and finish the mid-day dinner, he would go out into the garden, lie on his back under the apple tree, and forget everything about going back to work as he gazed up at the blossoms and the sky. Frequently, at such times, Mr. Brenton would wait for him at the office for an hour or two and then send the "printer's devil" up to the house to see what had become of him. He would invariably be found still lying on his back on the grass looking into the tree entirely oblivious of the fact that he was expected to be at work. When spoken to, he would get up reluctantly and go slowly back to the shop. At the end of such a day, Mr. Brenton would come home and say, "Walt has been of very little help to me to-day. I wonder what I can do to make him realize that he must work for a living?" and Mrs. Brenton would remark, "I don't see why he doesn't catch his death of cold lying there on the ground under that apple tree!"

Whitman was such an annoyance in the household that Mrs. Brenton was overjoyed when he finally decided to leave the office of the *Democrat*. Mr. Brenton, however, was sorry to have him go, for, even in those early days, he showed marked ability as a writer and was of great value to the "literary" end of the newspaper work. How long he was in Jamaica, or what salary he received, I do not know. Of course, in those days, a considerable part of the salary consisted in "board and lodgings."

. . .

Another detail comes to mind in regard to his behavior in the house. He cared nothing at all about clothes or his personal appearance, and was actually untidy about his person. He would annoy Mrs. Brenton exceedingly by "sitting around" in his shirt sleeves, and seemed much abused when she insisted on his putting on his coat to come to the family table. . . .

I am sorry I cannot tell you more. My impression has always been of a dreamy, quiet, morose young man, evidently *not at all in tune with his surroundings* and feeling, somehow, that fate had dealt hard blows to him. I never heard him spoken of as being in any way bright or cheerful. I cannot see how he could have been an interesting or successful teacher because of *his apparent dislike of children* at the time we knew him. I never heard a word against his habits.[25]

In my opinion this is one of the most important biographical documents that has been procured. It fills a blank in our knowledge of a very important and, for young people in general, a very significant year of life; and it seems to me that it reveals with stupendous clarity his whole personality, a personality very different from the "official" representation of the young Whitman. It strikes a decisive blow at the myths about his ability as a teacher, which were repeated as late as 1922 in Hans Reisiger's otherwise excellent introduction to the big two-volume

German translation (Fischer Verlag, Berlin). And instead of
a picture of the presumptuous, audacious, enthusiastic young
American we would expect from the poems in *Leaves of Grass*—
the singer of modern life—we see a somewhat sad, apathetic
youth, not too keen on doing any work, actually the picture of
a young man who was not at all mature then. Whitman matured
late. We get an impression of anticipation and contemplation,
of a young man lying on his back in the grass and staring at
the sky. "How I do love a loafer!" he begins one of his articles
in "From the Desk of a Schoolmaster"; the exclamation is
noteworthy not only because of Whitman's personal fondness
for a completely free and unfettered life, but also because in
this whole sentiment there is something which became the foundation for his later poetry, such as the opening of "Song of Myself" fifteen years later:

I loafe and invite my soul,
I lean and loafe at my ease . . . . observing a spear of summer
    grass.

In 1841 there was again an opening for Whitman in New
York. He had to begin as a typesetter on *The New World*, but
at the same time he began to write. Even while on Long Island
he had been occupied with the idea of writing "a wonderful and
ponderous book." In one of the articles in "From the Desk of a
Schoolmaster" and in an awkward little poem, "Fame's Vanity," [26] he argued the question with himself. "Yes: I *would*
write a book! And who shall say that it might not be a very
pretty book? Who knows but that I might do something very
respectable?" [27] The tone is pathetic in its caution, and it seems
not at all clear to him what kind of book it would be. It appeared
most likely that it would be didactic or moral. In the beginning
it was only news articles, poems, and stories in the most diversi-
fied New York papers, and finally, in 1842, there was the long
novel, *Franklin Evans*, on the terrible consequences of drunkenness. It is to Holloway's credit to have brought to light all this
material which Whitman himself chose to forget or mentioned
only with reluctance. These youthful writings are interesting,
not because of their literary quality—which is negligible—*but*

*because they are our only sources for an estimate of Whitman's
mentality in those years.* We know only from his stories, poems,
and newspapers articles what his spiritual attitude, his sentiments, and his emotions were during the long New York period
between 1841–48. In 1908 the always optimistic Bazalgette
tried to establish how happy and exhilarating these New York
years were for Whitman ("a superb human animal, eager to
test his magnificent health . . . he seemed to take possession
of a Paradise, to take an account of a heritage to which he had
fallen heir"),[28] but this does not agree with the impressions
that we get from his work from his twentieth to his thirtieth
year, and even later, in which, on the contrary, we see the picture of unrealized expectations.

The world reverberated noisily around the young poet. The
ferries sailed from shore to shore. The omnibuses, for whose
drivers and conductors he always felt such a romantic interest,
rumbled. On the streets newsboys shouted. At the theater Kean,
Fanny Kemble, and Charlotte Cushman played, and the famous
Havanna musicians under Maretzek were at Castle Garden. In
1842 Dickens came to New York and was acclaimed by the
crowds. Whitman was a member of Tammany Hall, the gathering place of the Democrats, afterwards the center of so much
corruption and so many scandals. There he took part in the
discussions of the slavery question. He became acquainted with
Bryant and wrote some poetry for his *Evening Post;* he met
Poe, who was not yet famous ("The Raven" was first published
in 1845), and wrote for his *Broadway Journal* also.[29] In 1845
the war with Mexico broke out. In 1846 Whitman had progressed to the editorship of the democratic Brooklyn *Daily
Eagle,* a position which he held for two years before his diverg-
ing political views (he was closer to the Free Soilers), or more
likely his laziness and his incapacity for direct, practical work,
led to his dismissal. But *what* had happened in his mind? What
were his writings like?

His first literary success in New York was the story "Death
in the Schoolroom," published in 1848 in the *Democratic Review,*
a periodical in which all the best literary authors of the day had
appeared: Bryant, Longfellow, Whittier, and Hawthorne. It is

a macabre story about a poor boy who is flogged to death by a wicked teacher. When it succeeded, Whitman wrote a whole series in the same vein: "Wild Frank's Return," "The Boy Lover," "One Wicked Impulse," and stories in which wicked men are reformed by little children, "The Child and the Profligate," and "Little Jane." In all these there is a note of macabre *Weltschmerz*, which we find also in his poems: "Our Future Lot" (*i. e.*, death), "Fame's Vanity," "The Death of the Nature Lover"—or whatever these awkward, trivial jingles were called! In all the stories there is a pale young man who carries within him the germs of an insidious illness or is too "unearthly fair for health," and in all he philosophizes somberly on death, which comes to all of us. The only one in which there is really any literary value is "Bervance, or Father and Son," [30] a story of a father who through an instinctive hatred of his son had him shut up in an asylum. It is told with a sort of impassioned melancholy reminiscent of Poe, and at the same time there seems to be something personal in it. In this story Whitman aired his "father complex." Characteristically, the opening concerns a theatrical performance which the son was forbidden to attend, but to which he went anyway. It is easy to see in this a picture of the elder Whitman's Quaker dissatisfaction with Walt's artistic propensities, a dissatisfaction the whole family always shared, which must have hurt Whitman terribly. In the delineation of the obstinate, harsh father-figure it is impossible not to see a portrait of Walter Whitman. Very interesting is his comment on the personal similarity between father and son ("a decided personal resemblance"), something which Whitman reverted to only once in his later work, in "As I Ebb'd with the Ocean of Life," 1860; when the poet broods over his shipwreck and failure, he suddenly feels a kinship with his father. We can put it this way: Whitman saw in his mother all the good and positive side of himself, while his father represented the negative principle, all the germs of defeat and failure. It is interesting, too, that in this story Whitman was concerned with the question of insanity, which undoubtedly played a part in his problems. We find confirmation in his remark about Booth. Was he at one time fearful of going crazy himself? While Lombroso and Max

Nordau overshot the mark in the nineties when they used Whitman as an example of an insane poet,[31] Bliss Perry correctly said in 1906: "There was some evidences, probably unsuspected by himself, of a neurotic tendency." [32]

There is nothing good to be said for the novel *Franklin Evans*, published by the *New World* in 1842. Henry Bryan Binns comments: "It is difficult to treat *Franklin Evans* seriously," [33] and in his later years Whitman was ashamed of its callow propaganda and awkward style, but he once pretended to J. G. Schumacher that in reality he had written it as prohibition propaganda—in a reading room of Tammany Hall, stimulating his fancy by gin cocktails.[34] That is a typical story. *Franklin Evans*, which was issued in a large edition and could not be suppressed or explained away, was—with this comment—suddenly fitted into the official picture of the swaggering, daredevil, non-existent young Walt Whitman! It is myth No. 3. The hero of the novel is a young Long Islander who is ruined in New York. (Does this imply a confession from Whitman of the bitter years around 1836?) He gets married, reforms, loses his wife, goes to Virginia, reverts to drunkenness, marries a Creole, is unfaithful to her with another woman, loses them both—and then takes the pledge of total abstinence. *Franklin Evans* sold 20,000 copies. Whitman got seventy-five dollars for it.

In several short stories of the following years there is a clear picture of the young writer's doubt, uncertainty, and sadness. The naïve and crude style of these early works developed into a poetic mood of an entirely different kind. "The Tomb Blossoms" [35] is about an old woman who, uncertain which of two graves was her husband's, put flowers on both and wished to be buried between them. "A Legend of Life and Love" is about two brothers who were separated in childhood and only met again as old men. Finally two stories, "The Angel of Tears" [36] and "Eris, a Spirit Record," [37] are both in theme and style as far as possible from the usual idea we have of Whitman. Alza, the angel of tears (that could be from Poe, Hugo, Wergeland, or Hans Andersen), hovered in space, waiting for the repentance of a criminal who had murdered his brother. When he does repent, Alza goes instantly and offers pity and comfort.

Oh, it is not well to look coldly and mercilessly on the bad done by our fellows . . . Who might say there was no premature seducing aside from the walks of honesty—and no seed of evil planted by others in his soul during his early years? . . . Who might dare cast the first stone?

"Eris" is the story of the Angel Dai, who was stricken blind for falling in love with a young girl whose deathbed he was set to watch. Dai roams, lonely, blind, and full of longing. "Wandering in the confines of earth, or restlessly amid the streets of the beautiful land, goes Dai, earnestly calling on one he loves."

"Wherefore is there no response?"

Much of Whitman's journalistic work during these years has been collected, some by Holloway and some by Rodgers and Black in the imposing *Gathering of the Forces*, which contains the greater part of his articles from the *Daily Eagle*. Stylistically the articles and editorials are not very valuable, but they do clearly define his spheres of interest. There are poetic descriptions of the ferries, skating rinks, and nocturnal fires. There are bombastic editorials about America's greatness, portraits of national heroes such as Taylor and Jackson, impassioned attacks on the death penalty and slavery. Articles on the theater are numerous. One of the best is called "Why Do the Theatres Languish? And How Shall the American Stage Be Resuscitated?" in which, in full agreement with the disposition of the decade, he asserts that all the ills are the fault of the cultural dependence on Europe, especially England. Like Emerson and Lowell he declares that a break is the only way to progress. "*It is full time.*—English managers, English actors, and English plays . . . must be allowed to die among us, as usurpers of our stage." [38] It is extremely interesting that Whitman's book reviews of the period have been preserved, and from them we can form a clear concept of his reading and his literary horizon. Holloway remarks: "I believe it safe to say that Whitman reviewed more books, and knew more about books, than any contemporary editor in Brooklyn, if not in New York, exclusive of the editors of the literary periodicals." [39]

Whitman first mentioned Fredrika Bremer's name in April,

1846, and in August he reviewed the Harper Edition of her works. "If we ever have children, the first book after the New Testament . . . that shall be their household companion—a book whose spirit shall be infused in them as sun-warmth is infused in the earth in spring—shall be Miss Bremer's novels." [40] Of Carlyle's *Heroes and Hero-Worship* he said, on October 17, 1846: "Under his rapt, weird . . . style the writer of this work has placed—we may almost say *hidden*—many noble thoughts." [41] Margaret Fuller's *Papers on Literature and Art* was always one of Whitman's favorite books and as late as in *Good-Bye My Fancy* he quoted her opinions of American literature. On November 9, 1846, he said: "We think the female mind has peculiarly the capacity, and ought to have the privilege, to enter into the discussion of high questions of morals, taste &c. We therefore welcome Miss Fuller's papers, right heartily." [42] He praises Raumer's book on America, because in a *kindly* way it calls the attention of Americans to the fact that not everything in the United States is perfect. Whitman called Melville's South Sea romance *Omoo* "most readable sort of reading," and Channing's essay on "Self-Culture," which was also important to him, "an unsurpassed piece." [43]

Finally there is Emerson, whom he mentions for the first time in his life on December 15, 1847, when he speaks of his "inimitable lectures." [44] This date is important for our knowledge of Whitman's acquaintance with Emerson, because once in later years he tried to say he had not read him before he wrote *Leaves of Grass*.

One of Whitman's places of resort in that period was Fowler and Wells's Bookshop and Phrenological Institute on Broadway, which later was one of the shops that offered his book for sale. Whitman was actively interested in phrenology and once had his own cranium examined. He often jokingly referred to the characterization which Mr. Fowler had given him and seemed almost to have been influenced by it. Henry Bryan Binns reports it this way:

. . . capable of deep friendship and sympathy, with tendencies to stubbornness and self-esteem, and a strong feeling for the sublime . . . Whitman's danger lay in the direction of indolence and sensuality, "and a certain reckless swing of animal will" . . . the quality of caution largely developed.[45]

We cannot deny that it is really a good estimate of Whitman's character, for most biographers admit, and in his old age Whitman himself told Carpenter frankly that "caution was his predominant trait." With admiration and regret Whitman scholars have to agree.

The world reverberated around the young poet. Whitman was twenty-nine, but the whole period between 1841 and 1848, as regards his personal life, is shrouded in silence and mystery. The truth is that it was a difficult period for him, but quite uneventful. We hear of no woman or other friends. If there had been, it would have been revealed in his writing, or they would have been among those who wanted to talk about him after he became famous, or to criticize him, regardless of consequences. To the best of his ability the young writer struggled with an unsympathetic world, quite alone, and certainly filled with longing. "Wherefore is there no response?" In that sentence we can almost hear the refrain of the whole period. When we realize the part unrequited love was to play in his writings, it is not fantastic to look for the origin of this consuming feeling of loneliness in these very years between his twentieth and thirtieth birthdays. Those who declare their love for all the world are often the most lonely. "Wherefore is there no response?" In his thoughts revolved themes of "the seed of evil planted by others," or he struggled with the gloomy problem of insanity. Lonely in a boarding house room, or doubly lonely in the crowds on the streets or ferries, he wrote his naïve story of the lovers who never found each other. Dai roamed the world, lonely and blind, with the beloved name on his lips. "Wherefore is there no response?" In one of the last articles for *The Long Island Democrat*, in which for the first time he speculated on the book he wanted to write, he had also said:

At the same time that I would do all this, I would carefully avoid saying any thing of woman; because it behoves a modest personage like myself not to speak upon a class of beings of whose nature, habits, notions, and ways he has not been able to gather any knowledge, either by experience or observation.[46]

Everything indicates that this naïve and poignant declaration of his twenty-first year was equally true in his twenty-eighth year. Fantastic and unbelievable as it may seem,[47] the zealous scholars Holloway and Catel have not succeeded in finding any trace of a love affair in these "happy years." Catel bases his theory of Whitman's auto-eroticism on that fact. But perhaps that is confusing cause with effect. Whitman matured slowly, but he was also, as we know from the part of his erotic poetry which concerned him personally, surprisingly shy and erotically passive, a characteristic that is often united with the capacity for friendly intercourse and the ability to attract many people —and many different kinds of people—which Whitman had to such a marked degree. In his twenty-eighth year Whitman was still dreaming (and loafing) under the apple tree, half-passive, half-expectant. He let life go by, while his writings reflected, like a mirror, the bustle and traffic of the streets, ferries, and omnibuses, the pageant and the parade. He imbibed it, absorbed it—a great passive acceptance and assimilation. The title which the two Brooklyn journalists have given their collection of Whitman's editorials for 1846–48 is, perhaps, the most accurate designation of this whole period of Whitman's life: *The Gathering of the Forces.*

But the abnormal, the surprising, the exceptional in the whole history of the young writer made the early biographers concentrate eagerly and intensively on the brief period of Whitman's life which followed, called the New Orleans period. Whitman had been discharged from the Brooklyn *Daily Eagle* and was in New York, unemployed. One evening he was at the old Broadway Theater (as he himself tells it in *Specimen Days*) [48]—and there, during one of the intermissions, he was suddenly offered a position on *The Crescent*, a newly established paper in New Orleans.

One of the owners, who was north buying material, met me walking in the lobby, and though that was our first acquaintance, after

fifteen minutes' talk (and a drink) we made a formal bargain, and
he paid me two hundred dollars down to bind the contract and bear
my expenses to New Orleans. I started two days afterwards; had a
good leisurely time, as the paper wasn't to be out in three weeks.
I enjoy'd my journey and Louisiana life much. Returning to Brooklyn a year or two afterward I started the "Freeman" . . .

Elsewhere in *Specimen Days* he reports the trip and says that
his fifteen-year-old brother, Jeff, was with him.[49] This is all
we knew at first of Whitman's stay in the motley city of the
South, a stay that furnished the basis for countless conjectures,
and in particular supplied the place where biographers located
the erotic experience which it was impossible to find anywhere
else in his life. Henry Bryan Binns called his chapter on the
visit to New Orleans "Romance"; Johannes Schlaf translated
that into German "Roman," meaning "novel," and other biographers followed suit. In any case, "Times South," where the
young writer for the first time met life and let himself go, was
the "romantic" point in Whitman's life; here was a sanctuary
for "the prophets," and the myth about this part of Whitman's
life outgrew any of the others. Whitman himself was naïvely
responsible for that. To begin with, he intentionally kept the
period blank; the romantic tinge which rested on all the Southern trip and experiences in the strange, colorful city suited him.
In a decisive moment, in one of the biographical storms which
he had foreseen would arise after a time, it assumed for him
the function of the ground wire of a lightning rod. John Addington Symonds (1840–93), the English esthetician, author
of *Studies of Greek Poets* and *Renaissance in Italy*, still valuable
today, was working on a book on Whitman during his last years,
for he was one of Whitman's ardent champions in England. To
him it seemed that a line connecting the Greek lyricists and the
Renaissance poets was continued in Whitman's *Calamus* poetry,
which he regarded as the heart of *Leaves of Grass*. Moved by a
natural desire to get at once full, clear information as to how
the erotic in *Calamus* was to be understood, in 1890 he wrote
Whitman a letter in which he asked about that dangerous and
inflammatory question. Whitman's reaction is understandable,
though not unimpeachable. Once and for all he wanted to dis-

pose of the charges of abnormality which more than anything seemed to be the obstacle to his future as the poet-prophet and "lyricist of America," and which, since *Calamus* first appeared, in 1860, had made him the target of so many attacks and so much scandal. On August 19, 1890, he wrote Symonds curtly and angrily (we have the exact words in Carpenter's *Days with Walt Whitman*) : [50]

My life, young manhood, mid-age, times South &c., have been jolly bodily, and doubtless open to criticism. Though unmarried I have had six children—two are dead—one living Southern grandchild, fine boy, writes to me occasionally—circumstances (connected with their fortune and benefit) have separated me from intimate relations.

This letter was Whitman's last word about an affair he never mentioned himself, not even to his closest friends. The astonishment, great astonishment, which this letter aroused in Symonds was revealed in his book,[51] published in 1893, the year after Whitman's death and in the last year of Symond's life. Carpenter was equally surprised, and in his writing about Whitman frequently referred to it. Most of Whitman's intimate friends welcomed that categorical conclusion of a discussion which would always be unpleasant. Those of the biographers, like Bazalgette in France, who had no doubt of Whitman's unassailable hetero-sexuality, have used that letter and the poem "Once I Pass'd" as proof and a basis for their representations of Whitman's erotic mentality.

Nevertheless, some writers have had their doubts about the truth of the peculiar information in the letter, and Dr. Clara Barrus's valuable *Whitman and Burroughs Comrades*, 1931, fully confirms that not only Burroughs but also the whole inner circle of Whitman's friends were convinced that the letter did not tell the truth,[52] that it was a deliberate falsification by Whitman. Even Burroughs declared: "I really doubt Walt's ever having had a child of his own." Stedman: "If Walt wrote it, it was for effect merely." Moncure Conway, one of Whitman's earliest admirers, observed quite frankly that Whitman had yielded to "a senile temptation to pose as a papa!" Dr. Barrus herself calls the letter "an intentional fabrication—for rea-

sons!" Here we face one of the most glaring, but at the same
time, one of the most typical examples of myth-formation to
which Whitman himself made his life subject, which naturally
had to be most positively expressed where it touched the
"dangerous" subject. There is something very pathetic in his
attempt to maintain to the last the fiction of his children in
the South. Henry Bryan Binns reports that one day he told
Traubel he had a visit from his grandson. Traubel regretted
that he had not been present. "God forbid," said Whitman,
and in the succeeding days destroyed letters and papers.[53] At
the same time we can undeniably agree with Bliss Perry that to
a certain extent he failed "in the finer obligations of friendship"
by never telling his most intimate friends how things really
stood. It appears from Traubel's notes [54] that Whitman was
several times on the point of confiding in him, but at the last
moment could never get it out: "Some other time, some other
time!" Clara Barrus quotes a significant remark of Burroughs
on the subject: "Whatever secrets there were in his life, he kept
to himself. That was Walt." [55] We cannot help thinking of
the phrenological characterization of him in which "cautious-
ness" was mentioned as a leading trait.

Another document supported the New Orleans myth—the
1860 poem.

Once I passed through a populous city, imprinting my brain, for
    future use, with its shows, architecture, customs, and tra-
    ditions;
Yet now, of all that city, I remember only a woman I casually met
    there, who detained me for love of me,
Day by day and night by night we were together,—
    all else has long been forgotten by me,
I remember I say only that woman who passionately clung to me,
Again we wander—we love—we separate again,
Again she holds me by the hand—I must not go!
I see her close beside me, with silent lips, sad and tremulous.

It is one of Whitman's most famous and most beautiful poems
in the *Children of Adam* section, and has always been connected
with his memories of the South.[56] However, Holloway found a
draft in a private collection in New York [57] and printed it

"because of its uncommon biographical significance." The poem
in its original form reads as follows:

Once I passed through a populous city, imprinting on my brain,
    for future use, its shows, architecture, customs and traditions,
But now of all that city I remember only the man who wandered
    with me there, for love of me,
Day by day, and night by night, we were together.
All else has long been forgotten by me—I remember, I say, only
    one rude and ignorant man who, when I departed, long and
    long held me by the hand, with silent lip, sad and tremulous.

In reality it is a *Calamus* poem, which in publication was
transferred to the *Children of Adam* section. Holloway uses it
as an example showing how we must always be aware that in
Leaves of Grass the author deliberately tries "to mystify the
reader."

The rich and prominent lady of the South whose parents and
family forced Whitman to return home—as the myth gradually
came to have it—has certainly never existed. Jean Catel, on
the basis of Holloway's discoveries, points out in his long philosophical chapter discussing Whitman in the South that the
whole famous stay in New Orleans which has filled such a disproportionate space in Whitman biography, and about which
the poet himself wanted to give the impression that it had
lasted a year or two, actually was of only three months duration,
from February 25 to May 27, 1848, that the reason for Whitman's leaving *The Crescent* was no more romantic than the
cause for his separation from the other papers he had worked
for: he was not fitted for systematic work (and in his poetry
never made a secret of it). "As for locating a love affair in New
Orleans, whose unhappy end caused the sudden departure of
Whitman, there is no authority for it." [58] Nevertheless, the
Southern sojourn naturally had a great significance for Whitman, in its many varied and strange impressions, in the whole
experience of the trip across the Allegheny Mountains and by
boat down the Mississippi. For the first time Whitman became
acquainted with his country. It is not at all improbable that in
the colorful, frivolous Southern city he had one or two love
affairs of either a romantic or profane kind, possibly with one

of the half-breed women who, repudiated by "society," were
literally forced to live as prostitutes in the great port city, and
whose beauty Whitman often mentioned with admiration in his
prose writing and conversation.[59] A new note of maturity, we
are tempted to say *sexual* maturity, can be traced in the journalistic writing in New Orleans which Holloway has collected,
in which a series of portraits of noteworthy southern street
figures reveals Whitman's surprisingly keen and minute powers
of observation, later turned to good account in *Leaves of Grass*.
The trip was very significant for Whitman's political attitude;
he always tried to keep clear of parties. Holloway says that
while in the South, Whitman developed his opinion about the
Negroes: "His residence in the South having taught him that
slavery was not an unmixed evil for the negro at his present
state of development, his attitude was not one of mere sentimental humanitarianism like that of the Abolitionists." [60] For
Whitman the Civil War was not so much over the Negroes as
the preservation of the Union.

Inevitably the Southern aspects of nature made a deep impression on him. Fredrika Bremer describes various zoological
and botanical observations which she made in the South,[61]
mentioning among others "the mocking bird," the nightingale
of the South, "called the hundred-tongued by the Indians,"
and the live oak: "most magnificent and most numerous of all
the trees is the live oak, an evergreen, an immense tree from
whose branches hang mossy growths in thick masses (often four
or five yards in length). These gray-green masses on the huge
branches are exceedingly picturesque, and where the trees grow
in any regularity they form splendid, natural Gothic churches,
with beautiful arcades and vaulted colonnades." We know that
the mocking bird ("the American mimic," as Whitman calls it
in "O Magnet South") and the live oak were included in Whitman's great descriptions of nature as "poetic requisites," the
live oak in particular as one of the most important.[62] It is interesting to have it corroborated by the report of the Swedish
writer. We naturally associate the strange, colorful, at times
almost barbaric, mixture of languages in *Leaves of Grass* with
the stay in New Orleans; in any case, the poet's fragmentary

French and his transitory knowledge of Italian and Spanish plainly grew out of it. How rich was the poetic inspiration he himself felt in this trip is apparent in "O Magnet South," from the 1860 edition:

O MAGNET-SOUTH! O glistening, perfumed South! My South!
O quick mettle, rich blood, impulse and love! Good and evil! O all
    dear to me!

Whitman went home by way of the Mississippi to Chicago, over the Great Lakes to Niagara and through "lower Canada, finally returning through central New York and down the Hudson; traveling altogether probably 8000 miles this trip, to and fro." [63] It was Whitman's only long trip before he wrote his famous poems. How it loomed in his memory and what it meant as inspiration is best realized by the fact that from this one really brief trip stems the whole myth of Whitman as a sort of inveterate wanderer, a mixture of Wotan and vagabond in his poetry. In reality Whitman was of a sedentary nature, a creature of habit, a home-keeping person, who in the next forty-two years left his daily circle and ordinary routine only when necessary. That all these myths grew up about him can only be taken as proof of the inspiration, the force, and the imagination of his poetry—the poetry which was about to come into existence.

Whitman was thirty when he began to wake up. There is no doubt that on the trip to New Orleans he got the first impulse toward *Leaves of Grass*. Inspiration began to stir; something indefinite and imminent began to take form. "Imprinting my brain for future use," as he says in "Once I Pass'd." Two of his articles in *The Crescent* were on the nude in art, and a third described a police investigation of some arrested prostitutes,[64] in which the tone of sympathy and compassion is an obvious foreshadowing of his future poems. At the same time he began to fill notebooks with prose outlines and loosely formed sentences in which we plainly find the first raw material not only of the ideas in *Leaves of Grass* but also of the new form, which came into existence between 1849 and 1855, between Whitman's thirtieth and thirty-sixth years.

For a short time after his return home Whitman was editor of the Free-Soil paper *The Freeman*, but his dislike of professional party politics soon put an end to that. This aversion to American politics and office seekers in Congress he shared with Emerson, who that same year said to Fredrika Bremer: "The crookedness and corruption of party spirit prevents the honest person from joining any party." [65] There is no question but that the U.S. Congress, of which Dickens, in *American Notes,* had given such an indignant and scandalized picture,[66] revealed its worst phases in the legislative enactments on slavery between 1844–50. Moreover, it is extremely interesting that it was the desperate 1850 Compromise that shocked Fredrika Bremer and incited Whitman to write poetry for the first time—at least to write in the peculiar style which we now regard as Whitmanesque. In 1850 he wrote a whole series of political poems. One, called "Dough-Face Song," was printed in Bryant's *Evening Post* on May 2:

> Beyond all such we know a term
>   Charming to ears and eyes,
> With it we'll stab young Freedom,
>   And do it in disguise;
> Speak soft, ye wily dough-faces—
>   That term is *"compromise."*

This poem expresses his indignation at the Compromise, but it is written in the traditional old form. It is not included in *Leaves of Grass,* but Whitman thought well enough of it not to destroy it, and later included it in his *Prose Works,* where it is now to be found undated in *Pieces in Early Youth.* That same year he wrote the first *Leaves of Grass* poem, "Resurgemus," which was printed in *The Daily Tribune,* June 21, 1850, and afterwards included in *Leaves of Grass* as "Europe, the 72d and 73d Years of These States." Under the impact of political events in Europe and his own country's political failure, the poet expresses his hope and faith in spite of everything. Liberty let others despair of you. . . . I never despair of you.

Is the house shut? Is the master away?
Nevertheless be ready . . . . be not weary of watching,
He will soon return . . . . his messengers come anon.

Here, in 1850, we see clearly for the first time Whitman's own personal form of expression, in glaring contrast to the verse he had written previously. The poetry, moreover, is quite typical in its content. It describes defeat, but the mood is optimistic and full of faith. It thus lays a foundation for all Whitman's lyricism. Just as his love poems grew out of the conflict between what he dreamed and what he actually attained, so his political lyric emerged out of the discrepancy between the America he saw and the America he wished for. That is the background of Whitman's whole paradoxical political position throughout all the editions of *Leaves of Grass*, as well as his prose writings in the seventies and eighties. Evincing a surprising insight into the corruption and degeneration of his country, he proclaims at the same time America as the young, new world. Optimism of defiance—that is the formula of Whitman's lyricism.

But it is part of the spiritual experience we must assume he had somewhere between 1848 and 1855, the years of economic difficulty. Journalism was almost closed to him. Once he became a carpenter, like his father, and helped to build houses; for the first time in twenty years he moved in with the family, scarcely to the satisfaction of the father or brothers, who quite naturally considered him an incurable dreamer and loafer. They could not know the kind of book which was slowly taking form in his consciousness, or what importance posterity would ascribe to it.

When authorship is of the peculiarly lyrical-mystical kind such as Whitman's, it is quite natural that it should go back to a spiritual experience, psychologically or perhaps pathologically conditioned, as in Jacob Böhme's account of his "enlightenment," or Swedenborg's "illumination," or in the more recent examples of "mystical experiences" of Amiel or Malwida von Meysenburg, which William James cites in Chapter XVI of his *Varieties of Religious Experience*, mentioning Whitman as especially typical. In Danish literature we can point to *Gabrielis Breve*,[67] describing a similar cosmic experience with all its characteristics. It is the writer or thinker whose Ego expands so that he suddenly discovers his *cosmic conscious-*

ness, as Dr. Bucke called it in his book in 1901.[68] In the mysticism of the Orient or of the church such experiences are frequent; why should we refuse to accept them in modern people? We find Whitman's own description in Section 5 of "Song of Myself":

Loafe with me on the grass . . . . loose the stop from your throat,
Not words, not music or rhyme I want . . . . not custom or lecture, not even the best,
Only the lull I like, the hum of your valved voice.

I mind how we lay in June, such a transparent summer morning;
You settled your head athwart my hips and gently turned over upon me,
And parted the shirt from my bosom-bone, and plunged your tongue to my barestript heart,
And reached till you felt my beard, and reached till you held my feet.

Swiftly arose and spread around me the peace and joy and knowledge that pass all the art and argument of the earth;
And I know that the hand of God is the elderhand of my own,
And I know that the spirit of God is the eldest brother of my own,
And that all the men ever born are also my brothers . . . . and the women my sisters and lovers,
And that a kelson of the creation is love . . .

This experience, this acknowledgment, which is so vital in the whole tenor of *Leaves of Grass,* is Whitman's "mystical experience." It corresponds exactly to the poet-philosopher Sibbern's sudden and inspired acknowledgment on the shore of a lake in Seeland "that thus the supreme vital force moves throughout the world in the unceasing surge of time" and his acknowledgment of "the divinity in me whose inner life was at one with my life without distinction or opposition. . . . It was the supreme bountifulness which revealed itself to me in the most sacred, the most profound, the most beautiful felicity." [69] Or Dr. Bucke's "simple consciousness of the cosmos," "not a conviction that he shall have eternal life, but the consciousness that he has it already," as he himself describes his own experience in Chapter One of *The Cosmic Consciousness*. We see in Whitman's case just how important that astoundingly spiritual and all-encompassing emotional experience can be for a lyricist. It is interesting that we have from a great modern lyricist, a kindred spirit of Whitman's, a similar account of a mystical experience which is so obviously the impulse for his whole poetic work. In a famous poem Franz Werfel describes his sudden cosmic emotional experience on one afternoon in a wood as he lay on his back under a tree and suddenly felt at one with the wind, the grass, and the leaves "while the great Rigoletto quartet of creation" [70] intoned around him.

For Whitman this inner stimulation to write poetry was supplemented by a series of external events in the crucial years preceding 1855. There was the Crystal Palace Fair in New York in 1853, to which Whitman was such a naïve and enthusiastic visitor; [71] there were his friendships with the poorer people of New York, especially with the Broadway bus drivers —"the drivers—a strange natural, quick-eyed and wondrous race . . . how many exhilarating night-times I have had . . . riding the whole length of Broadway, listening to some yarn . . . Yes, I knew all the drivers then . . . Not only for comradeship, and sometimes affection—great studies I found them also. (I suppose the critics will laugh heartily, but the influence of those Broadway omnibus jaunts and drivers and declamations and escapades undoubtedly enter'd into the gestation of 'Leaves of Grass.' ") [72] Besides, there was the influence of the American oratory of the period, Whitman's musical experiences, and last, but not least, his reading.

Whitman had heard both William Lloyd Garrison and Wendell Phillips; he heard Emerson lecture in 1850, and received a deep impression from Henry Ward Beecher, Harriet Beecher Stowe's brother, who was a fashionable preacher at Plymouth Church in Brooklyn and unquestionably one of the most compelling personalities of the period. Fredrika Bremer describes the young minister and abolitionist, whose fiery oratory impressed her, though she was repelled by his self-conceit. "Even in his sermons this *I* was too prominent." [73] That Whitman admired Beecher is evident from an article he wrote for the Brooklyn *Daily Advertiser,* which Holloway has reprinted,[74] and it is not impossible that the Beecher "I" put its stamp on the tone of "Song of Myself." Beecher was one of the first who visited Whitman after the publication of *Leaves of Grass.* At any rate it is important to stress Whitman's interest in oratory; he himself walked along the Long Island shore declaiming verse, usually Shakespeare, and his emphatic opinion of the superiority of the spoken word over the written determined the whole tone and style of *Leaves of Grass.*

In music we know that Whitman's two great experiences between 1850 and 1855 were—not Jenny Lind's appearances, which he regarded somewhat coolly [75]—but the great Italian tenor Bettini's appearance in Castle Garden in 1851 and Marietta Alboni's concert in 1853.[76] Later in life he referred time and again to both of these occasions as the peak of theatrical art that he had seen and heard. It is plain that the famous "musical passages" in *Leaves of Grass* such as in "Song of Myself," "Thought," "That Music Always around Me," 1860, and especially the whole of "Proud Music of the Storm," 1869, go back to the impression these two artists made on his mind at a critical time—just as the recitative of the Italian opera has entered into his whole style. In *Good-Bye My Fancy* he has told how eagerly he studied the librettos of the operas he heard. It is very important that in a review Whitman wrote of Bettini's concert [77] we are on one happy occasion able to point directly to the significance of the impression, not merely for inspiration but also for the development of his style.

In this article he says in part:

Have not you, in like manner, while listening to the well-played music of some band like Maretzek's, felt an overwhelming desire for measureless sound—a sublime orchestra of a myriad orchestras—a colossal volume of harmony, in which the thunder might roll in its proper place; and above it, the vast pure Tenor—identity of the Creative Power itself—rising through the universe, until the boundless and unspeakable capacities of that mystery, the human soul, should be filled to the uttermost, and the problem of human cravingness be satisfied and destroyed?

And the description of Bettini's performance concluded thus:

Listen. Pure and vast, that voice now rises, as on clouds, to the heaven where it claims audience. Now, firm and unbroken, it spreads like an ocean around us. Ah, welcome that I know not the mere language of the earthly words in which the melody is embodied; as all words are mean before the language of true music.

In the notebooks in which Holloway has found that Whitman at that time was writing the tentative sketches for *Leaves of Grass*, his first groping attempts to put the new ideas and visions into poetry, there is a passage which is obviously the initial poetic result of this musical experience and a positive step toward a personal style.

I want that tenor, large and fresh as the creation, the orbed parting of whose mouth shall lift over my head the sluices of all the delight yet discovered for our race.—I want the soprano that lithely overleaps the stars, and convulses me like the love-grips of her in whose arms I lay last night.—I want an infinite chorus and orchestrium, wide as the orbit of Uranus, true as the hours of the day, and filling my capacities to receive, as thoroughly as the sea fills its scooped out sands.—I want the chanted Hymn whose tremendous sentiment shall uncage in my breast a thousand wide-winged strengths and unknown ardors and terrible ecstasies—putting me through the flights of all the passions—dilating me beyond time and air— startling me with the overture of some unnamable horror—calmly sailing me all day on a bright river with lazy slapping waves— stabbing my heart with myriads of forked distractions more furious than hail or lightning—lulling me drowsily with honeyed morphine—tightening the fakes of death about my throat, and awakening me again to know by that comparison, the most positive wonder in the world, and that's what we call life.[78]

Here we have not only a wonderfully inspired description of a musical experience—of a sexual kind similar to the cosmic— but we have also a series of expressions and phrases in which we can plainly recognize for the first time the Whitman that is to be. The language already has much of the rhythm which was being born. In *Leaves of Grass*, 1855, in "Song of Myself,"

Section 26, these two sketches, these two prose drafts, have become the following familiar and remarkable passage.

I think I will do nothing for a long time but listen,
And accrue what I hear into myself . . . . and let sounds contribute toward me.

I hear the bravuras of birds . . . . the bustle of growing wheat
. . . . gossip of flames . . . . clack of sticks cooking my meals.

I hear the sound of the human voice . . . . a sound I love,
I hear all sounds as they are tuned to their uses. . .

. . .

I hear the violincello or man's heart complaint,
And hear the keyed cornet or else the echo of sunset.

I hear the chorus . . . . it is a grand-opera . . . . this indeed is music!

A tenor large and fresh as the creation fills me,
The orbic flex of his mouth is pouring and filling me full.

I hear the trained soprano . . . . she convulses me like the climax of my love-grip;
The orchestra whirls me wider than Uranus flies,
It wrenches unnamable ardors from my breast,
It throbs me to gulps of the fartherest down horror,
It sails me . . . . I dab with bare feet . . . . they are licked by the indolent waves,
I am exposed . . . . cut by bitter and poisoned hail,
Steeped amid honeyed morphine . . . . my windpipe squeezed in the fakes of death,
Let up again to feel the puzzle of puzzles,
And that we call Being.

Thus, on three occasions we can closely follow the evolution of Whitman's style during these years—in the very time between Bettini's concert in 1851 and the publication of his book in 1855. We can follow his development by the language. At the same time we have his own description of his musical experiences,

undoubtedly quite as fundamental and determinative for him
as the cosmic-mystical one with which it has so much in common, particularly in the sexual character which is unquestionably a conspicuous element in the passage last quoted. In a later
poem, "That Music Always around Me" 1860, he has again,
though more vaguely and feebly, pictured the importance of
music as an inspiration.

His reading was naturally an essential and fundamental
factor. As spontaneous and independent a poetic expression
as *Leaves of Grass* was, it is still clearly reminiscent of certain
definite figures and types in world literature, and it is part of
my aim to show to what extent Whitman was aware of that.

From his own account we know fairly well what he read. Besides the books we know about from his reviews in *The Daily
Eagle*, there was a long list which he read on his own initiative.
In his old age he told Traubel how he visited the secondhand
book dealers in Brooklyn and carefully "searched them through
and through." [79] Here he found the edition of Epictetus's moral
handbook which he kept throughout his life, and here also he
provided himself with the editions of the classics or modern
writers which particularly appealed to him and affirmed something in himself. He took Homer and Shakespeare on swimming
trips to Coney Island and declaimed them aloud "to the surf
and sea-gulls by the hour." [80] Later there was Dante—and
Ossian, whom he found somewhat obsolete and European, but
with which he was nevertheless so strongly impressed that thirty
years later in *Specimen Days*, in a description of "a real Ossianic night," [81] he quoted Ossianic verse as the best expression
of his emotions in old age. But he did not want his own book
to be influenced by Ossian's style. In a notebook of the early
fifties we find the following characteristic admonitory exclamation: "Don't fall into the Ossianic *by any chance*." [82] Among
the lyricists, Burns made a vivid impression. In *November
Boughs* Whitman wrote a whole critical essay on the Scottish
poet, whom he called "almost the tenderest, manliest, and (even
if contradictory) dearest flesh-and-blood figure in all the streams
and clusters of by-gone poets." As with Elias Hicks, he stressed
the "personal magnetism": "Probably no man that ever lived

—a friend has made the statement—was so fondly loved, both by men and women, as Robert Burns." [83] He frequently read Bryant, who in "Hymn of the City," "The Prairies," and "The Crowded Street" had sung of America's plains and the throngs on the streets, though he had never been able to free himself from the stiff, stilted eighteenth-century verse form. Still he was the only one of the older poets who could come close to Whitman's ideal of "the American lyricist": "I am not sure, but his name ought to lead the list of American bards." [84] Then there is Tennyson, whom Whitman loved right up to old age with an almost paradoxical devotion. "Ulysses" was one of his regular declamation pieces. We can scarcely conceive of a greater contrast than Whitman and Tennyson. If there is a European or feudal poet he is Tennyson. But in an article in *November Boughs,* called "A Word about Tennyson," Whitman explained his devotion by a *bon mot* from Burroughs: "His [Tennyson's] glove is a glove of silk, but the hand is a hand of iron."

Of the novelists of the period, besides Scott and Cooper, Whitman was especially attracted by Dumas and Eugene Sue. Sue's long democratic propaganda novels played an important role in that period and were, for example, among Margaret Fuller's favorite reading. More important is Whitman's strongly emphasized liking for George Sand. (Again following Margaret Fuller's taste! [85]) *Consuelo* was always one of his favorite books and, according to Kennedy, was the direct inspiration for "Song of the Open Road"; [86] likewise Whitman's whole attitude on the emancipation and his constant stressing of woman's importance in the state are scarcely uninfluenced by his enthusiastic reading of the French writer. Even Whitman's connection with Rousseau, who celebrated as no other author did, the poesy of the vagabond life, is less the result of reading him than of the emphatically expressed Rousseauism on every page of George Sand's *Consuelo.*

Next comes a very essential point. Whitman's relation to the thinkers and philosophers, chiefly to Rousseau and to Hegel, whose influence on *Leaves of Grass,* especially the later editions, is so obvious, but almost never direct. Whitman was never a systematic reader of scientific works. In *Good-Bye My Fancy*, his last prose work, he confesses that "I . . . cannot study and never did." [87] His knowledge of the philosophical theories of the day he got through literature or the newspapers. Binns says: "His knowledge of modern thought came to him chiefly through the more popular channels of periodical literature, and through conversations with thoughtful men. *Probably the largest and most important part of his reading, then and always, was the daily press.*" [88] That is the journalist and American Walt Whitman in a nutshell. But still we cannot sufficiently emphasize the extent to which he occupied himself with the scientific accounts and results, or how important and essential he found them for his poetry. In Denmark about that time H. C. Ørsted, the physicist and natural philosopher, commanded poets to desert the old armory of poetry and to consider it one of the duties of the modern poet to put in his poetry all the imagery of the modern world, the modern discoveries and inventions, modern science and modern mechanics, as an emancipation from the romantic metaphysicians. Ørsted regarded the old-age Goethe as the ideal poet of natural science,[89] and Hans Andersen's enthusiastic effusions on railroads, steamships, and the telegraph cable in the Atlantic ("the great sea-snake," as he called it in one of his stories), was a direct result of Ørsted's teaching; but in world literature Whitman's is undoubtedly the most spontaneous contemporary expression of this view. He is the first poet whose whole lyrical expression is fundamentally colored by modern life. "In the beauty of the poems are the tuft and final applause of science," he proclaimed first in his 1855 Preface, and later in "Indications," 1860, which is completely in the spirit of Ørsted. "Passage to India" and "Song of the Exposition" are his two most typical songs of the new conquests of the mind.

As to Whitman's attitude toward the science of his century, Binns has said briefly and succinctly what there is to say: The theory of evolution was the century's most conspicuous idea in any field; Goethe, Hegel, and Comte had led up to it; Darwin, Wallace and Spencer had expressed it decisively. Relationship and development were solved. "Every form of life has its secret, and is worthy of study, for that secret is a part of the World's Secret, the Eternal Purpose which affects every soul. We are each a part of that progressive purpose which we call the universe." [90] Whitman preached that philosophy in his poetry; it was his religion. The optimism which startles us who are familiar with his life was in the age. "The era of Mazzini, Browning, Ruskin, Emerson, was an era of affirmations, not an era of doubt. And Whitman caught the spirit of his age: eagerly he accepted and assimilated it." [91] That could not be more precisely or fully phrased.

But there are yet to be discussed the two most important authors who at that time completed the ripening process and gave final impetus to *Leaves of Grass*, the two authors who in those years meant most to Whitman: Carlyle and Emerson.[92] Whatever effect Transcendentalism can be said to have had on the development of Whitman's ideas, it is agreed that this influence can always be traced back to these two. (Lowell asserted in one essay that Carlyle was the real founder of Transcendentalism.) Thus, Emerson and Carlyle are the important links between Whitman and Goethe—and between Whitman and the whole school of European romantic philosophy.

It was the early writings of Carlyle that made a special impression on Whitman. The bitterness and pessimism of the older Carlyle often goaded him to contradict the spiteful and impassioned sorties against democracy. Once he even went so far as a direct reply to Carlyle's article "Shooting Niagara," 1867, in which the Scottish writer foresaw the drowning of all Western culture in the Niagara of American democracy. Primarily it is the influence of *Sartor Resartus* which can be detected in Whitman's philosophy. By a publisher's caprice this book originally appeared in America in 1835, the same year of De Tocqueville's *Démocratie* and Channing's *Slavery*, and it was no less important in the States than were they. Naturally Whitman was least influenced by all the romantic conceits and affectations. The style of *Sartor Resartus* is a choice specimen of Jean Paul's manner and of "romantic irony" fully orchestrated by a German apprentice. The entire milieu of Professor Teufelsdröckh and Hofrat Heuschrecke and the cities of Weissnichtwo,

Hinterschlag, and Entepfühl, had a message for more fastidious literary souls than Whitman, but much greater strength lay in the pantheistic cosmic creed behind all the ironic tomfoolery, especially in Carlyle's impassioned rhetoric, which in many ways influenced Whitman's ideal of what a direct poetic style should be.

In the picture of the strange Professor der Allerley-Wissenschaft Teufelsdröckh, Carlyle had assumed characteristics which must very definitely have appealed to Whitman. Teufelsdröckh lived above the city and looked down on its inhabitants and homes. "That living flood, pouring through these streets, of all qualities and ages, knowest thou whence it is coming, whither it is going? *Aus der Ewigkeit, zu der Ewigkeit hin.*" [93] At the inn he suddenly jumped up and proposed a toast to "*Die Sache der Armen in Gottes und Teufels Namen* (The cause of the Poor, in Heaven's name and ——'s)." Occasionally he was filled with "soft wailings of infinite pity; he could clasp the whole Universe into his bosom and keep it warm," [94] and the publication of his "The Philosophy of Clothes" emphasized his boldness of language. "He speaks out with a strange plainness; calls many things by their mere dictionary names"; [95] and later there is an account of his rambling life through the world and evidently among all sorts of people. Now he is a scientist in Europe, then Hadschi in the neighborhood of Mecca. From Goethe's *Faust* comes the notably pantheistic theme of the earth spirit which permeates the whole book:

'Tis thus at the roaring Loom of Time I ply
And weave for God the Garment thou see'st Him by.[96]

But also there is the violent modern spirit in *Wilhelm Meister:* here where we now are, here is our America, as Lothario puts it —or as Carlyle's variation goes in the chapter, "The Everlasting Yea: 'Do the Duty which lies nearest thee.' . . . Yes, here, in this poor, miserable, hampered, despicable Actual, wherein thou even now standest, here or nowhere is thy Ideal." That is Goethe's and Carlyle's greatest lesson for Whitman. And Carlyle sketches the new poet who must arise as one "who, Prometheus-like, can shape new Symbols" [97] for emancipation from the rags and tatters of the old symbols which are now on the point of strangling us. This whole idea of leaving antiquity behind, old society, old church, old literature, is one of Whitman's most important themes. In his own way Goethe had hit on it in his salute to America unhampered by "useless memories"; Carlyle and later Emerson (also H. C. Ørsted) had taken up the theme. Emerson spoke of Europe as "an old faded garment of dead persons." [98] Whitman gave the old idea its most baroque expression in "Song of the Exposition":

Come Muse migrate from Greece and Ionia,
Cross out please those immensely overpaid accounts,

.   .   .

Placard "Removed" and "To Let" on the rocks of your snowy
    Parnassus,

.   .   .

For know a better, fresher, busier sphere, a wide, untried domain
    awaits, demands you.

Carlyle's picture of George Fox, the first Quaker, and his homage to the busy unwearied life of the farmer must have been after Whitman's own heart. A direct influence on Whitman's style can be traced in the following passage. After praising the great procession ("not I do it but fathers and distant forefathers determine it and carry it out through me!") Carlyle says: "Detached, separated! I say there is no such separation: nothing hitherto was ever stranded, cast aside; but all, were it only a withered leaf, works together with all; is borne forward on the bottomless, shoreless flood of Action and lives through perpetual metamorphoses. The withered leaf is not dead and lost, there are Forces in it and around it, though working in inverse order; else how could it *rot?* Despise not the rag from which man makes Paper, or the litter from which the Earth makes Corn. Rightly viewed no meanest object is insignificant; all objects are as windows, through which the philosophic eye looks into Infinitude itself." [99] That is almost like a prose draft of sections of "Song of Myself." On the whole, this book of Carlyle's prose comes nearer to Whitman's than anything else in contemporary literature at the time that his special *prose-verse* was in the process of metamorphosis.[100] Carlyle's optimism in *Sartor Resartus* influenced Whitman's whole religious mysticism. "Then sawest thou that this fair Universe, were it in the meanest province thereof, is in very deed the star-domed City of God; that through every star, through every *grass-blade,* and most through every Living Soul the glory of a present God still beams!" [101]

It is impossible not to notice the pulpit style in these quotations from Carlyle; and that very quality is an important link with Whitman. Like Emerson, Carlyle was originally to have been a minister, but scruples similar to Emerson's stopped him. Both were ministers in their own way and thus in a certain sense anticipated Whitman's idea of the poet as the minister of the new era. The sermonizing entered into their form (Emerson's essays were first given as "Lectures," then published in book form).[102] Much of their writing is often addressed directly to the reader in a manner which showed Whitman the way to his "prophetic" and direct style.

Whitman had heard Emerson speak. In *Good-Bye My Fancy* he mentions Emerson among those whom he had heard in the years when he had attended the New York Tabernacle on Broadway and the Athenaeum Society. It was to Emerson he first sent his book, and in the letter to Emerson at the end of the second edition he openly acknowledged his debt. To Kennedy in 1887 (as to Burroughs in 1867) he tried to deny that Emerson had influenced him before 1855.[103] This must be regarded as an attempt at myth-formation which later had to be abandoned, and which he did publicly give up. In an article on Whitman in *The Atlantic Monthly,* February, 1902, Trowbridge quotes a letter and an important talk with him. Whitman frankly mentioned that among the books he had carried with him out on Long Island there was a volume of Emerson which made an ineffaceable impression on him: "I was simmering, simmering, simmering; Emerson brought me to a boil." [104] We cannot doubt that in this absurdly simple metaphor Whitman has given an accurate characterization of his condition in 1854.

Considering Whitman's mental state at that time, it is obvious what Emerson must have meant to him. He was the con-

firmation of what seethed in Whitman's own consciousness; he
was the stimulus to follow the path along which Whitman felt
himself drawn. With his gift of expression,[105] Emerson had
clearly formulated what was still hazy and formless in the young
poet's world of ideas. Furthermore, by his constant invocation
of the future American poet, he had, so to speak, conjured forth
this poet in Whitman! Emerson's "The Poet" (1844) can be
taken as almost a direct prophecy of Whitman.[106] And his exclamation "I look in vain for the Poet whom I describe" must
have appeared to Whitman when he read it as an invitation he
could scarcely fail to answer. Whitman's attitude in the first
edition of *Leaves of Grass* left no doubt as to whom he considered himself to be. He sent the book to Emerson, and in
Emerson's famous letter he got confirmation that he really
was what he believed himself to be—America's poet.

Many details from Emerson's writings we find repeated more
emphatically or more baroquely in Whitman. Emersonian ideas
and pithy comments were used as *leit motifs*, and whole poems
were written on them. For example, "Miracle" (1856), is
merely a development of Emerson's remark in "Nature": "The
invariable mark of wisdom is to see the miraculous in the common" and "to the wise, therefore, a fact is true poetry and the
most beautiful of fables. The wonders are brought to our own
door." From "The American Scholar," one of Emerson's most
characteristic addresses, the manifesto of Transcendentalism,
there are two passages which plainly became the *leit-motif* of
Whitman's work: "the one thing in the world, of value, is the
active soul" and ". . . I embrace the common, I explore and
sit at the feet of the familiar, the low. Give me insight into today, and you may have the antique and future worlds. What
would we really know the meaning of? The meal in the firkin;
the milk in the pan; the ballad in the street; the news of the
boat; the glance of the eye; the form and gait of the body;—
show me the ultimate reason of these matters . . . let me see
every trifle bristling with the polarity that ranges it instantly
on an eternal law; and the shop, the plough, and the ledger, referred to the like cause by which light undulates and poets
sing." Even the diction (note the reiteration) shows the con-

nection. In fact, parallels to Emerson's *Essays* are innumerable. Outcries like this from "The Poet," "A rhyme in one of our sonnets should not be less pleasing than the iterated nodes of a sea-shell," or "The pairing of the birds is an idyll, not tedious as our idylls are," Whitman used in one of his most beautiful poems, "The Dalliance of the Eagles"; the love-making of the eagles, was for him really a beautiful and wonderful "idyll." In "The Over-Soul" there is a passage which is absolutely Whitmanesque in form: "Great is the soul, and plain. It is no flatterer, it is no follower; it never appeals from itself. It believes in itself." This is the nucleus of that whole individual concept of the soul in Whitman's poetry, to which we will return later. In "Circles": "I am God in nature; I am a weed by the wall." In "Friendship": "Who hears me, who understands me, becomes mine—a possession for all time." From "Self-Reliance": "No law can be sacred to me but that of my nature," etc., etc. One can understand what all this meant in encouragement and stimulation to the young poet in whom such thought had hitherto been seething and fermenting. In his notebooks we find a series of original sentences of similar nature which were later worked out in *Leaves of Grass*.[107]

> I am the poet of sin,
> For I do not believe in sin
>
> . . .
>
> And of whatsoever I have I bestow upon you.
> And first I bestow of my love.
>
> . . .
>
> All truths lie waiting in all things.

And a long series of similar lines.

Emerson's purely religious influence is not the least phase. More definitely than Carlyle, Emerson developed a completely pantheistic creed that united Unitarian pantheism with German Romantic pantheism and produced the "new religion" for Whitman to preach to America in his cosmic democratic poetry. Emerson is, moreover, Whitman's chief and only link with the earlier mystics of world literature: Plato, Plotinus, and Jacob Böhme, who are so frequently quoted and mentioned in

Emerson's writing—and also, and most important of all, Swedenborg, whose ideas and visions engaged much of Emerson's
thought, and whose teachings on symbols played a large part in
Leaves of Grass.

Emerson's poetry probably had little influence on Whitman.
Although Emerson, like Goethe, experimented with "free verse,"
it is his *prose* rhythm we recognize in Whitman's style. One of
his poems, however, could not have helped being an inspiration
to Whitman, who later expressed similar ideas in his prefaces
and in *Democratic Vistas.* The poem is "Merlin" (1847), in
which Emerson once more introduces the new poet who is to
come and break away from the contemporary enervating twang-
ings.

> No jingling serenader's art,
> Nor tinkle of piano strings,[108]
> Can make the wild blood start
> In its mystic springs.
> The kingly bard
> Must smite the chords rudely and hard,
>
> .   .   .
>
> With the pulse of manly hearts;
> With the voice of orators;
> With the din of city arts;
> With the cannonade of wars;
> With the marches of the brave;
>
> .   .   .
>
> Great is the art,
> Great be the manners, of the bard.
> He shall not his brain encumber
> With the coil of rhythm and number;
>
> .   .   .
>
> But mount to paradise
> By the stairway of surprise.

Among the many "prophecies" about Whitman in Emerson's
work this is not the least remarkable. In a special way it was
Whitman's fate to mount "the stairway of surprise" in world
literature, and Emerson himself was far from being able to
follow his pupil or completely approve his "surprises." But it

is very tempting to regard all Whitman's new prose-verse, which awakened such a sensation and so much ridicule, as a direct and noteworthy literary result of the Emersonian invitation and permission. Emerson brought the simmering pot to boil.

Without any external events worth mentioning having happened to him, Whitman's years of "preparation and growth" came to an end. These years, strangely expectant and receptive, as we have seen, can be regarded as a mighty generating of the poetic power which was to follow. Also we know that in human dissatisfaction lies a source of great artistic power. What was he like? How did he look? The picture from this period, the 1854 daguerrotype, "the Christ portrait," as it is frequently called from a comment of Anne Gilchrist's, tells us in part. It reveals among other things that the myth about Whitman as "the strong man," a sort of Atlas in the poetic ranks, has no basis. Some of the "Whitmaniacs" were never reconciled to that picture, which justifies Burroughs in one of his later published characterizations: "He was not an athlete, or a rough, but a great tender mother-man." [109] The picture shows us a dreamer and a mystic in whose face traits of both sensuality and effeminacy are united with something at once very artless and very "surprised." Binns mentions Whitman's "wonder at the world" [110] and says that during these years it was constantly increasing. That is fundamental. There was in Whitman's attitude always something surprisingly receptive and frank, and this is significant for his kind of writing. As late as 1877 Carpenter noted the peculiar expression of his face: "I remember how I was most struck, in his face, by the high arch of the eyebrows, giving a touch of child-like wonder and contemplation to his expression." [111] But all of a sudden that passivity would give way to something active, Carpenter continues, and his receptivity would be replaced by an aggressive mien. Whitman himself felt in 1855 that his long awaited moment had at last arrived. In *A Backward Glance o'er Travel'd Roads* he says that in his thirty-third year he was filled with a "feeling or ambition to articulate and faithfully express . . . my own physical, emotional, moral, intellectual, and aesthetic Personality, in the midst of, and tallying, the momentous spirit and facts of its immediate days, and of current America—and to exploit that Personality, identified with place and date, in a far more candid and comprehensive sense than any hitherto poem or book." In "Song of Myself," Section 25, he expressed it more baroquely, giving a wonderfully clear image of his momentary condition.

Speech is the twin of my vision . . . . it is unequal to measure itself.

It provokes me forever,
It says sarcastically, Walt, you understand enough . . . why don't you let it out then?

The moment had come to express what he had in his heart. The inner vision, "my vision" (by which he clearly means the cosmic vision) is no longer enough. It must be presented to the world. "Speech is the twin of my vision." And some lines further on he compares his long hesitation to the flower-buds which lie "waiting in the gloom, protected by the frost." There is no doubt that in that imagery Whitman thought of himself in his own long gestation during his twenties and thirties, waiting in the dark protected by the frost.

Anyway, to the consternation of his family, for whom these years had been worse than ever (the father always ill, Jesse away from home, and Hannah still unmarried), in the spring Whitman laid down the carpenter's tools which had earned for him a reasonable income that he had turned over to his mother untouched. He locked himself in his room or went on all-day trips while he put his book into final form. At last he marched into a little printing shop on Cranberry Street belonging to some friends and with his own hands set up *Leaves of Grass,* a quarto with green cover and the title in gold on the binding. Inside there was a picture of the poet in negligent, slouching pose, with open shirt, and hat cocked on one side. "The Rowdy portrait" in contrast to "The Christ portrait." Early in July, just after his father's death, he advertised the book for sale in the New York *Tribune.* America then in the 79th year of the States had her poet.

I, now thirty-six years old,—begin!
("Starting from Paumanok")

Leaves of Grass, *1855-89*

THE GROWTH OF A BOOK AND A POET

Thou shalt have the whole land for thy park and manor, the sea for thy bath and navigation, without tax and without envy; the woods and the rivers thou shalt own, and thou shalt possess that wherein others are only tenants and boarders. Thou true land-lord! sea-lord! air-lord! Wherever snow falls or water flows or birds fly, wherever day and night meet in twilight, wherever the blue heaven is hung by clouds or sown with stars, wherever are forms with transparent boundaries, wherever are outlets into celestial space, wherever is danger, and awe, and love,—there is Beauty, plenteous as rain, shed for thee, and though thou shouldst walk the world over, thou shalt not be able to find a condition inopportune or ignoble.

R. W. Emerson, *The Poet.*

THE BOOK of ninety-five pages which in the summer of 1855 was put on sale by an obscure author at the Phrenological Institute of Fowler and Wells on Broadway we now recognize as a masterpiece of American literature, as the first actually original contribution of the New World, whose significance for later writers it is difficult to overestimate. But we also know that on its first appearance in the United States the book was a complete failure. None of the many people who had invoked the new poet recognized in Whitman the realization of their dream. Emerson was the exception, for immediately after reading the book he wrote the famous letter to Whitman greeting him "at the beginning of a great career" (a letter which Emerson quickly regretted and wished that he had never

written). We know that *Leaves of Grass* had a long struggle
ahead, that in the next edition it aroused almost fanatical vitu-
peration in America, and that it first had to win fame and recognition in Europe through Whitman's loyal champions Rossetti,
Freiligrath, Rudolf Schmidt, Anne Gilchrist, Swinburne, Buchanan, and others, before America gradually began to accept
it for what it was.

This is consistent with the conventional prejudice which
always opposes the "new." The New England professors and
Boston moralists had impressively demanded a "new" poet,
as in the words of young Lowell:

> He who would be the tongue of this wide land
>
> .   .   .
>
> One who hath dwelt with Nature well attended,
> Who hath learnt wisdom from her mystic books,
>
> .   .   .
>
> Who as the clear northwestern wind is free,
>
> .   .   .
>
> Who to the Right can feel himself the truer
>
> .   .   .
>
> Who sees a brother in the evil-doer,
> And finds in Love the heart's-blood of his song;— . . .[1]

This is a characterization that fits Whitman as accurately as
Emerson's various prophecies about the future poet. But Lowell,
even more than Emerson, referred to a purely esthetic type. In
reality the Boston esthetes were far from being prepared to
understand an actual person who was truly as free "as the
clear northwestern wind" or who seriously declared himself
brother to "the evil-doer." Lowell, who was never quite reconciled to Thoreau, was always sharply opposed to Whitman. He
had described the contemporary poet as "an empty rhymer who
lies with idle elbow on the grass," and we can easily imagine
what must have been his opinion of Whitman's baffling introduction to his collection.

> I celebrate myself,
> And what I assume you shall assume,
> For every atom belonging to me as good belongs to you.

I loafe and invite my soul,
I lean and loafe at my ease . . . . observing a spear of summer
    grass.[2]

Emerson, whose sentiments toward Whitman underwent constant oscillation, as late as 1874 had not included a line from
Whitman in his American anthology, *Parnassus;* and Lowell,
on becoming Longfellow's successor at Harvard, likewise omitted
Whitman from his Parnassus by striking him from the list of
American poets whose names should adorn the façade of the
library in Boston. Carpenter, in *Days with Walt Whitman*, has
preserved the following extremely characteristic observation of
Lowell's made in the seventies: "I can't think why there is all
this stir about Whitman; I have read a good deal of his poetry,
but I can't see anything in it—*I can't see anything in it.*" [3]
There is something very significant in the attitude of these two
American intellectual leaders who had invoked the future poet
and predicted his early appearance. Obviously they did not
understand him.

The failure in 1855 of *Leaves of Grass* to produce the expected effect may be accounted for by the fact that this was only
the first edition of the famous book, which went through many
stages, with important additions in 1856, 1861, 1871, and
1881, all of which were finally welded into one whole. The great
poems "Salut au Monde," "Song of the Open Road," and "Crossing Brooklyn Ferry" first appeared in 1856. Two of the most
important sections of the present *Leaves of Grass, Children of
Adam* and *Calamus*, first appeared in the 1860 edition, and
Drum-Taps was added after the Civil War, 1865. Nevertheless, the 1855 edition is naturally of great and very special interest. With its theoretical Preface and its twelve untitled
poems—(the world-famous titles "Song of Myself," "The Sleepers," and so forth, came gradually as the great amalgamation
took place in the course of the years)—the young poet is revealed in all his first spontaneous and confident impetuosity. In
the individual poems and episodes of this first edition we can
discern with remarkable clarity the basic features of his poetic
physiognomy.

The well-known Preface, the renowned ten-page manifesto

with which Whitman introduced his book, appeared in an abbreviated form in the *Complete Prose*, and is in itself of importance only in literary history. Its prose style is entirely consistent with the groping, uncertain fragments of the notebooks during the years when the poet was still experimenting with his form, and its undigested content is made up of the most essential ideas which he had derived from Carlyle, Emerson, or his own turbulent soul, but which he had not yet utilized in poetry. Even in the second edition Whitman transferred part of the Preface into "The Poem of Many in One." Before its final version in 1871 this composition went through four revisions and became the great program poem, "By Blue Ontario's Shore," which is actually nothing more than the 1855 Preface written in prose-verse and prosodically arranged.

Nevertheless, the original form of this Preface is important. There for the first time Whitman defined his vision of America and the American poet. From Emerson he got the idea of America herself as "the greatest poem." [4] But for Whitman, unlike Emerson, this meant particularly the common people, "south, north, west, east—through all its mighty amplitude." They should disregard the past and relying only on themselves:

re-examine all you have been told at school or church or in any book, dismiss whatever insults your own soul, and your very flesh shall be a great poem and have the richest fluency not only in its words but in the silent lines of its lips and face and between the lashes of your eyes and in every motion and joint of your body.

America is the great source of inspiration, and in the first communication Whitman defines his book as an *American* phenomenon—the international emphasis came much later, after recognition in Europe began to manifest itself. The new poet shall be natural and popular, his form shall be understood by all: "The great poets are also to be known by the absence in them of tricks," and "Who troubles himself about his ornaments or fluency is lost." The new poet stands in the midst of today and looks toward the future. "The greatest poet forms the consistence of what is to be from what has been and is." The poet shall know all classes and be abreast of the knowledge of his time. "The sailor and traveler . . . the anatomist chemist astronomer geologist phrenologist spiritualist mathematician historian and lexicographer are not poets, but they are the lawgivers of poets and their construction underlies the structure of every perfect poem . . . If there shall be love and content between the father and the son and if the greatness of the son is the exuding of the greatness of the father there shall be love between the poet and the man of demonstrable science. In the beauty of poems are the tuft and final applause of science." And above all the poet shall awaken men, not lull them to sleep; he shall open their eyes to the endlessness of eternity. "A great poem is no finish to a man or woman but rather a beginning." Finally the startling climax of the Preface is the strong assertion: "There will soon be no more priests. Their work is done." Poets are the priests of the future. "A new order shall arise and they shall be the priests of man. . . . They shall arise in America, and be responded to from the remainder of the earth."

We find these themes in "Song of Myself" and the other great poems in *Leaves of Grass*. Some of the themes in the Preface are obviously worked out carefully in the poems, such as the older man as protective guide and teacher of the young—that is the Socratic theme. Whitman reveals that his task is, not to shape ideas, but to awaken independent thought—that is the Socratic "midwifery." In another place the poet is indomitably optimistic when he looks at the stars at night. These passages make up the "great episodes" in "Song of Myself." Also the language in the Preface now and then breaks out into proseverse: Will the poet of today survive beyond his life-time? Will he be read centuries ahead?

Will the same style and the direction of genius to similar points be satisfactory now? . . . Have the marches of tens and hundreds and thousands of years made willing detours to the right hand and the left hand for his sake? Is he beloved long and long after he is buried? Does the young man think often of him? and the young woman think often of him? and do the middleaged and the old think of him?

The rhythm is gradually being born here in the Preface. If we break this passage into lines of verse we have a typical Whitman poem.

At the conclusion of the Preface there is a eulogy of the English language which Whitman later reworked into verse ("Poem of Many in One") as early as 1856, but for patriotic reasons deleted it from the collection in 1860:

The English language befriends the grand American expression . . . . it is brawny enough and limber and full enough. . . It is the powerful language of resistance. . . . It is the dialect of common sense. It is the speech of the proud and melancholy races and of all who aspire. It is the chosen tongue to express growth faith self-esteem freedom justice equality friendliness amplitude prudence decision and courage. It is the medium that shall well nigh express the inexpressible.

In 1856 this became in poetic form:

Wonderful is language!
Wondrous the English language, language of live men,
Language of ensemble, powerful language of resistance,
Language of a proud and melancholy stock, and of all who aspire,
Language of growth, faith, self-esteem, rudeness, justice, friend-
     liness, amplitude, prudence, decision, exactitude, courage,
Language to well-nigh express the inexpressible,
Language for the modern, language for America.[5]

Here again it is interesting to follow the development of Whitman's style in its actual transition from prose to poetry. No less interesting is the refinement of the repetition, the catalogue, with only a few reminiscences of the prose in the verse. The whole 1855 Preface, sketchy, chaotic, but strikingly effective as it is, can be studied as the last step on the way before the journalist Whitman actually developed into the poet Whitman. The poet first really became vocal in the twelve poems following this Preface in the first edition.

In the original order of publication the twelve poems of the 1855 edition are (using the later titles): "Song of Myself," "Song of Occupations," "To Think of Time," "The Sleepers," "The Body Electric," "Faces," "Listen to My Morning's Romanza" (later expanded into "Song of the Answerer"), "Europe," "A Boston Ballad," "There Was a Child Went Forth," "Who Learns My Lesson Complete," and "Great Are the Myths" (later "Youth, Day, Old Age, etc."). Of these "A Boston Ballad" and "Europe" are the oldest—I have mentioned already [6] that "Europe" (originally "Resurgemus") was written in 1850—"A Boston Ballad" was written in 1854, the year of the famous slave delivery in Boston, a result of the Compromise of 1850. These two poems are the earliest examples of the new rhythm in Whitman's verse—therefore he included them in the collection. But they are of very doubtful value; essentially historic in subject, they were accordingly foreign material in his book.[7]

The chief poem in the collection is "Song of Myself," and today it is the poem in which Whitman's lyric originality reveals itself most distinctly and in greatest variety. "Song of Myself" underwent only minor changes in the later editions, a strengthening of the framework and a tightening of the connection between the fifty-two separate sections. In this, Whitman's first great and justifiably ranked as his most famous poem, we have the bulk of the material for an accurate characterization of the new lyricist in world literature, in all his peculiarity and individuality.

The reader's first impression of the whole 1855 edition is based on the joy, confidence, and optimism in this poem. Whatever of despair or pessimism may be found in the book is completely overshadowed at first by the poet's elemental joy in appearing as the self-appointed and confident representative of his country and his age. It is characteristic of the "I," which is such an important word in "Song of Myself," that it is constantly changing from the personal pronoun to the vicarious representation of each reader, of democracy, of mankind, of America, or of the great procession of poets and prophets down through the centuries. There is something sublime about that "I," and the way in which Whitman expands it to include all in one is impressive. His method of using contemporary America as his theme is admirable, the America of the Transcendentalists, of De Tocqueville, of democracy. He gave the "pass-word of democracy" in his poem; he sang, not of acquired or preserved wealth, but about what will become a heritage through freedom and progress. Twice in the poem he formulates his own fundamental democratic creed, first in Section 24:

By God! I will accept nothing which all cannot have their counterpart of on the same terms.

Again toward the end of the poem, in Section 48, where the poet
asserts:

And whoever walks a furlong without sympathy walks to his own
funeral, dressed in his shroud,

.   .   .

And there is no trade or employment but the young man following
it may become a hero,
And there is no object so soft but it makes a hub for the wheeled
universe, . . .

This leads, however, directly away from the "political" concept of democracy—which never interested Whitman as much
as people were once inclined to think—and toward transcendental, pantheistic democracy, which was always the poet's
main subject. The basic emotion in Whitman's lyricism is a feeling of kinship with all creation, evidenced in the very title
Leaves of Grass. The grass is the great democratic symbol in
nature, and it is by lying on it and "observing a spear of summer grass" that the whole great motif is set in motion. The
poem holds firmly to that idea throughout all fifty-two sections.
Each for himself searches in the remotest corner of the human
throng and in every paradox of existence for the kinship.

Do I contradict myself?
Very well then . . . . I contradict myself;
I am large . . . . I contain multitudes.

But the whole poem concludes with the image of the poet as
he departs bequeathing himself "to the dirt to grow from the
grass I love, If you want me again look for me under your
bootsoles." The "I" which vanishes in the metamorphoses, into
the all-embracing realm of evolution, is such an important feature of Whitman's world concept that it is necessary to grasp
it at the very beginning of a characterization of him. In "Song
of Myself" the image of the grass is more basic and fundamental than it appears at first reading.[8] Primarily the image
reflects the essentially pantheistic feeling of the poet.

Tenderly will I use you curling grass,
It may be you transpire from the breasts of young men,

It may be if I had known them I would have loved them;
It may be you are from old people and from women, and from off-
    spring taken soon out of their mothers' laps,
And here you are the mothers' laps.

This grass is very dark to be from the white heads of old mothers,
Darker than the colorless beards of old men,
Dark to come from under the faint red roofs of mouths.

O I perceive after all so many uttering tongues!
And I perceive they do not come from the roofs of mouths for
    nothing.

I wish I could translate the hints about the dead young men and
    women,
And the hints about old men and mothers, and the offspring taken
    soon out of their laps.

What do you think has become of the young and old men?
And what do you think has become of the women and children?

They are alive and well somewhere;
The smallest sprout shows there is really no death,

All goes onward and outward . . . . and nothing collapses,
And to die is different from what any one supposed, and luckier.

Section 6.

This passage follows Section 5, in which the cosmic experience is described in detail:

Swiftly arose and spread around me the peace and joy and knowl-
    edge that pass all the art and argument of the earth; etc.

These two sections are closely linked in the framework of the
poem. Together they reveal the actual emotional origin of the
powerful vision; Section 1, in which the poet lies on the grass,
only shows us the purely material situation.

The cosmic-pantheistic emotion so significant in Whitman's
poetry is conspicuous throughout the many sections of "Song
of Myself." Like Wordsworth, Coleridge, Shelley, Almquist,
Hugo, Carducci, and Johannes V. Jensen, the poet pauses before the animals.

Oxen that rattle the yoke or halt in the shade, what is that you
    express in your eyes?
It seems to me more than all the print I have read in my life.

My tread scares the wood-drake and wood-duck on my distant and
    daylong ramble,
They rise together, they slowly circle around.   Section 13.

And as in the old pantheistic nursery-tales of "the youth,"
"the traveler," or "the monk," suddenly, as if by a miracle,
he understands their language.

The wild gander leads his flock through the cool night,
Ya-honk! he says, and sounds it down to me like an invitation;
The pert may suppose it meaningless, but I listen closer,
I find its purpose and place up there toward the November sky.
       Section 14.

This passage is of basic importance. Whitman returns to it
in Section 52, where it is the poet himself who, like a bird, sounds
his "barbaric yawp over the roofs of the world" in order to
persuade humanity to follow him. The startling effect of the
concluding passage is prepared for in this little scene in Section 14. This illustration throws light on the composition of
the poem. The poet's identity with all creation, an important
phase of his pantheistic feeling, naturally leads to his merging
with the hunted slave, the heroic sea captain, the Arctic explorer,
the gallant dying fireman, and so forth, in the many episodes of
the poem, and also to the search into the lower stages of evolution. There a blade of grass becomes fully as important as the
planetary system, and he proudly and contentedly incorporates
in himself the most ancient of geological epochs.

I find I incorporate gneiss and coal and long-threaded moss and
    fruits and grains and esculent roots,
And am stucco'd with quadrupeds and birds all over,
And have distanced what is behind me for good reasons,
And call anything close again when I desire it.   Section 31.

He can turn back at will. In vain the mastodon retreats beneath its own powdered bones, in vain the snake tries to slide
away, the elk to hide in the inner passes of the woods, and the auk

to escape to the far North—the poet follows and joins them at will. That is one of the most baroque examples of the identification which plays such a significant role in all Whitman's poetry.

In me the caresser of life wherever moving . . . . backward as
    well as forward slueing.   Section 13.

In Section 39 he suddenly presents the savage as the model of the perfect man, and the poet asks:

Is he waiting for civilization or past it and mastering it?

.   .   .

Behaviour lawless as snow-flakes . . . . words simple as grass . . .

This is a very Rousseauistic sentiment shared by Whitman with his contemporary Melville, revived in later American literature by Jack London and Sherwood Anderson. We can see that this is an inconsistent point of view for a singer of modern Democracy, but the idea persists in Whitman and is of vital significance in the development of his 1860-theory of "the divine average" which was to rescue the States from the political quagmire.

The natural, the animal, is in any case an ideal, and with pride the poet assumes animal forms in the series of his identifications. Even in Section 3 he stood

    Stout as a horse, affectionate, haughty, electrical,

prepared to take possession of the earth; and in Section 32 the image is repeated in the description of the "gigantic stallion" with which Whitman instantly identifies himself in his gallop through the farflung realm of evolution. In more recent literature D. H. Lawrence emphasized the significance of this image by using a horse to symbolize "the life-force" in his novel *St. Mawr*, 1905, just such a horse as exactly fits Whitman's almost passionate description. As a whole, Section 32 is significant in this phase of the pantheism in *Leaves of Grass*. It contains one of his most sublime pictures of the relationship between animals and man, between past and present, and his own personal share in evolution.

I think I could turn and live awhile with the animals . . . . they
    are so placid and self-contained,
I stand and look at them sometimes half the day long.

They do not sweat and whine about their condition,
They do not lie awake in the dark and weep for their sins,
They do not make me sick discussing their duty to God,
Not one is dissatisfied . . . . not one is demented with the mania
of owning things,
Not one kneels to another nor to his kind that lived thousands of
years ago,
Not one is respectable or industrious over the whole earth.

So they show their relations to me and I accept them;
They bring me tokens of myself . . . . they evince them plainly
in their possession.

I do not know where they got these tokens,
I must have passed that way untold times ago and negligently dropt
them,
Myself moving forward then and now and forever.

Here he uses two themes of major importance in the poem,
the wander motif and the religious motif, which occasionally
become so closely interwoven that they are one, for if the poet
is today the wanderer, with his staff and his rain-proof coat,
he is also the wanderer throughout the centuries. Therefore he
is also Christus, to whom he refers so disrespectfully. The theme
is developed in Section 38. He is on the point of making "the
usual mistake" of denying Him— Yet He was also in a way a
part of himself. The poet's sight is strangely obscured—then
suddenly he plainly recognizes his "own crucifixion and bloody
crowning" and remembers the trickling tears and blows of clubs
and hammers.

I remember . . . . I resume the overstaid fraction,
The grave of rock multiplies what has been confided to it . . . .
or to any graves,
The corpses rise . . . . the gashes heal . . . . the fastenings roll
away.

I troop forth replenished with supreme power, one of an average
unending procession,

.   .   .

Inland and by the seacoast and boundary lines . . . . and we pass
the boundary lines.

Our swift ordinances are on their way over the whole earth,
The blossoms we wear in our hats are the growth of two thousand
years.

Eleves I salute you, . . .

In this passage, in which the mystic note is so surprisingly
blended with Whitman's peculiarly florid diction, we find ar-
ticulated for the first time this modern American's attitude
toward the Christ-figure. Strongly influenced by Elias Hicks
and his Quakerism, he pictures the *human* Christ and confi-
dently places himself at His side. The idea was important in
later American literature. Whitman risks the most daring expression to clarify his idea: He accepts the gods of the various primitive religions as "rough deific sketches," but sees "as
much or more in a framer framing a house."

The bull and the bug never worshipped half enough,
Dung and dirt more admirable than was dreamed,
The supernatural of no account . . . . myself waiting my time
to be one of the supremes,
The day getting ready for me when I shall do as much good as the
best, and be as prodigious,   Section 41.

And with a daring expansion he develops the idea in the famous section toward the end of the poem, Section 48.

And I call to mankind, Be not curious about God,
For I who am curious about each am not curious about God,
No array of terms can say how much I am at peace about God and
about death.

.   .   .

Why should I wish to see God better than this day?
I see something of God each hour of the twenty-four, and each
moment then,
In the faces of men and women I see God, and in my own face in the
glass;
I find letters from God dropped in the street, and every one is
signed by God's name,
And I leave them where they are, for I know that others will
punctually come forever and ever.

Here his identification with the divinity is complete and parallels the situation in which the poet finds in the animals marks of himself which he lost untold ages before; the poet and the divinity go through the world in the same fashion and leave letters and tokens which the human race can gather up and marvel at. Just as the grass and green turf is "the handker-chief" the Lord has dropped, so the poet's book, *Leaves of Grass,* is the same thing with his signature in one corner that mankind may pause, wonder, and ask "Whose?"

But along with the boldness and arrogance in these lyric metaphors we must not forget that the poet also puts himself in the great procession of gods, poets, and thinkers of the ages. He recognizes his connection with them and, more important, his dependence on them.

> The blossoms we wear in our hats are the growth of two thousand
>   years.   Section 38.

Here Whitman has a counterbalance for his self-worship—and the readers who have hitherto felt repelled by him should feel so no longer when they hear why he is so proud, that it is entirely on their account. In later poems Whitman often returned to the image of the modern man who appears in this poem as "an acme of things accomplished . . . an encloser of things to be," and to the procession down through the centuries. In "Song of Myself" this image is used again in Section 41, when the poet enumerates the earlier primitive religions, recognizing their value in their time and place.

> Admitting they bore mites as for unfledged birds who have now
>   to rise and fly and sing for themselves,

but the poet of modern times comes "magnifying and apply-ing"; embodying the old religions in himself, but magnifying and enlarging them. Here the wander motif in Whitman's poetry becomes sublime, though occasionally it seemingly degenerates into a vagabond- and idler-theme. It is the *leit-motif* of *Leaves of Grass,* and in "Song of Myself" it is combined with religious purpose in a pre-view of the themes which Whitman was to work out further and make into separate poems in later editions. The wander motif afterwards inspired two famous poems: "Song of the Open Road," with its purely Rousseauistic theme of wandering in nature, and "Pioneers! O Pioneers!" (1865), which, contrary to the usual interpretation, is not an American "genre piece," but a mystical, pantheistic vision on the theme of the succession of the generations.

Continuity, development, evolution receive homage in Section 44:

> It is time to explain myself . . .

in which the poet philosophically looks back throughout the epochs to the first, infinite Nothing, where his wandering began.

> . . . I waited unseen and always,
> And slept while God carried me through the lethargic mist,
> And took my time . . . . and took no hurt from the foetid carbon.
>
> .   .   .
>
> Immense have been the preparations for me,
> Faithful and friendly the arms that have helped me.
>
> .   .   .
>
> Before I was born out of my mother generations guided me,
> My embryo has never been torpid . . . . nothing could overlay it;
>
> .   .   .
>
> Monstrous sauroids transported it in their mouths and deposited it with care.
>
> All forces have been steadily employed to complete and delight me,
> Now I stand on this spot with my soul.

And immediately following the backward glance, in Section 45, is one of the poet's most powerful lyric flights, in which after having talked so long in the role of humanity he suddenly becomes himself, positively and definitely—the personal Ego takes possession in a lyrical, musical, erotic hymn which introduces the poem's finale. Here again, as in the opening section, it is the poet personally and only he who speaks of himself and his book and defines precisely its nature and significance. The wanderer through the geological epochs and the centuries appears as a human being on the highway with his staff and rainproof coat, who can be seen for what he is.

But the religious, pantheistic reflections are carried on and completed in this last personal section of the poem. The poet opens his hatch at night and looks up toward the distant, shining constellations. Or early in the morning, while his young disciple sleeps, he climbs a hill and looks at the paling stars and asks his soul the significant question:

> . . . When we become the enfolders of those orbs and the pleasure and knowledge of every thing in them shall we be filled and satisfied then?

And my spirit said No, we level that lift to pass and continue beyond.   Section 46.

The wandering will never cease, but continue to go on and on. The pantheistic idea of continuity and joy is behind these images and visions. To Whitman any moment seemed as little worthy of the plea, "Verweile doch, du bist so schön," as to Faust; there is immeasurable space, unmeasured time, and infinite joy beyond each instant. And to one he loves the poet says, "speak before I am gone," "I stay only a moment." As with Goethe, the wanderer can never pause for a permanent love affair. The culmination for the pantheistic poet is the idea of death, which frightens him as little as does the idea of God.

And as to you death, and you bitter hug of mortality . . . . it is idle to try to alarm me.

To his work without flinching the accoucheur comes,
I see the elderhand pressing receiving supporting,
I recline by the sills of the exquisite flexible doors . . . . and mark the outlet, and mark the relief and escape.

And as to you corpse I think you are good manure, but that does not offend me,
I smell the white roses sweetscented and growing,
I reach to the leafy lips. . . . I reach to the polished breasts of melons.

And as to you life, I reckon you are the leavings of many deaths,
No doubt I have died myself ten thousand times before.

I hear you whispering there O stars of heaven,
O suns. . . . O grass of graves. . . . O perpetual transfers and promotions. . . .   Section 49.

The real content of the poem is the great acceptance of life as it is, with all its contrasts and contradictions, soul and body equally good, youth and old age, man and woman equally good.

Maternal as well as paternal, a child as well as a man,   Section 16.

the poet stands and encompasses all creation in himself. In the concluding section he tries to find the ultimate form through his faith and his knowledge. The cosmic vision which was the point of departure has expanded in the whole poem and is described as a great struggle, a wonderful ecstasy.

Wrenched and sweaty . . . . calm and cool then my body becomes;
                              Section 50.

and now there is left only the discovery of the final, concluding phase which will embrace and express the whole. But in vain!

> Something it swings on more than the earth I swing on,
> To it the creation is the friend whose embracing awakes me.

At the end of the road, as the conclusion of all the wandering, the transformations and visions, there stands The Great Camerado whom Whitman mentioned in Section 45. We cannot fail to recall the Persian Rumi who also described his reunion with a friend (his real friend Shamzi Tabriz) as symbolic of his union with God. By a coincidence in world literature, the result of a similarity in disposition and way of thinking which is extremely noteworthy in the "connecting links of literary history," Whitman used as a conclusion for his pantheistic vision the very same lyrical imagery as the Persian poet, that of a friend into whose arms he falls to be united finally and completely with the Infinite and Whole.

No less interesting than these abstract mystical passages, which in a great measure establish Whitman's similarity to other famous mystical poets in world literature, are the more specific —one is tempted to say material or realistic—expressions of what he thinks of his book and intends to accomplish with it. His democracy is unbounded.

This is the meal pleasantly set . . . . this is the meat and drink
     for natural hunger,

It is for the wicked just the same as the righteous. . . . . I make
  appointments with all,
I will not have a single person slighted or left away,
The keptwoman and sponger and thief are hereby invited . . . .
  the heavy-lipped slave is invited . . . . the venerealee is invited,
There shall be no difference between them and the rest.
                                                 Section 19.

And he seeks his audience preferably among the masses of common people.

I am enamoured of growing outdoors,
Of men that live among cattle or taste of the ocean or woods,
Of the builders and steerers of ships, of the wielders of axes and
  mauls, of the drivers of horses,

                  .   .   .

What is commonest and cheapest and nearest and easiest is Me,
                                                 Section 14.

My face rubs to the hunter's face when he lies down alone in his
  blanket,
The driver thinking of me does not mind the jolt of his wagon,
The young mother and old mother shall comprehend me,
The girl and the wife rest the needle a moment and forget where
  they are,
They and all would resume what I have told them.   Section 47.

   For what he says is not special truth, but universal truth.
These are not his own thoughts; he is only appointed to express
them.

These are the thoughts of all men in all ages and lands, they are
  not original with me,
If they are not yours as much as mine they are nothing or next to
  nothing,

                  .   .   .

This is the grass that grows wherever the land is and the water is,
This is the common air that bathes the globe.   Section 17.

   But spoken by a poet, their power is limitless. In the baroque
Section 40 he reveals this power in the two grotesque images of

the person "impotent, loose in the knees" into whose jaws the poet blows strength, and of the dying man into whose room he pushes and sends away the physician and priest.

I seize the descending man . . . . I raise him with resistless will.

. . .

I dilate you with tremendous breath. . . . I buoy you up;

. . .

Not doubt, not decease shall dare to lay finger on you,
I have embraced you, and henceforth possess you to myself.

In the same section we find the striking sexual description of the poet's idea of the effect of this book on the public.

On women fit for conception I start bigger and nimbler babies,
This day I am jetting the stuff of far more arrogant republics.

This passage is important for an understanding of the extent to which sexual imagery impregnates Whitman's form of expression. In the next section of the poem appeared a similar passage which aroused such a storm of protest that he omitted it after the third edition. The poet is exulting over the cautious old "hucksters" of religion and says of them:

The most they offer for mankind and eternity less than a spirt of
my own seminal wet, . . .

Since his own mystical experience resembled a sexual ecstasy, he wants to achieve a similar effect.

Whitman's primary intention is to bring humanity something real, necessary, and indispensable.

I am he bringing help for the sick as they pant on their backs,
And for strong upright men I bring yet more needed help.

Section 41.

Above all, he wants to awaken each individual to independent thinking, to give him to himself. He says this outright.

You shall no longer take things at second or third hand . . . .
nor look through the eyes of the dead . . . . nor feed on the
spectres in books,
You shall not look through my eyes either, nor take things from me,
You shall listen to all sides and filter them from yourself.

Section 2.

The poet appears almost like a seducer to drag humanity away from prayer-stools, churches, philosophy, meals, libraries, banks—just like the Biblical tempter.

But each man and each woman of you I lead upon a knoll,
My left hand hooks you round the waist,
My right hand points to landscapes of continents, and a plain
    public road.

Not I, not any one else can travel that road for you,
You must travel it for yourself.   Section 46.

The passage is magnificent. Each must find and travel the road alone (and alone assume the responsibility for it). This is not a new theme in literary history, but Whitman's treatment of it is a classic in nineteenth century poetry. In *Zarathustra* Nietzsche later said the same thing in his own way. The teaching of Whitman and Nietzsche was instilled in the poetic ethics of modern literature by two modern writers who were both, and at the same time, disciples of Nietzsche and Whitman: André Gide, in France, and Herman Hesse, in Germany. In the work of both of these important writers the major theme is "the way to thy self."

In "Song of Myself" the theme is sounded in the wander motif. The poet and his disciple journey together on the great highway, "wonderful cities and free nations we shall fetch as we go"—a motif which has poetic significance because it has been a model for imitators in later poetry. Whitman himself was fully conscious of his significance as a perfect prototype, and formulated it in this disarming way.

Long enough have you dreamed contemptible dreams,
Now I wash the gum from your eyes,

.   .   .

Long have you timidly waded, holding a plank by the shore,
Now I will you to be a bold swimmer,
To jump off in the midst of the sea, and rise again and nod to me
    and shout, and laughingly dash with your hair.   Section 46.

It is most disarming, however, when Whitman admits that he is also only one stage in the journey, a courier in the race

which began once interminable ages ago and will never end.
And he hopes to live to see others go further than he and leave
him behind. He even teaches them to do so; he says this flam-
boyantly.

He that by me spreads a wider breast than my own proves the
　　width of my own,
He most honors my style who learns under it to destroy the teacher.

．　　．　　．

I teach straying from me, yet who can stray from me?
I follow you whoever you are from the present hour;
My words itch at your ears till you understand them.

Section 47.

That is the essence of the poem and its magic, that confidential
tone of direct conversation establishing personal communication
between the poet and the reader, which more than anything else
is responsible for the peculiar effect of "Song of Myself," an
effect that even the unsympathetic reader finds almost irresistible.

　The effect of the poem! Having considered the content of
the poem, let us now survey the task the poet set for himself.
The style is still to be considered. What method has Whitman
used in the successful completion of his undertaking, and what
poetic and technical defects characterize this lyric masterpiece
of American literature?

　The defects of the poem lie in its loose, confused organization;
in the "catalogues" and "litanies," the long reiterations in
which Whitman did not succeed in animating his phrases, so
that they are no more than cold, uninspired prose; and finally
in the passages of the poem where there is a multiple use of the
"I," an involuntary but highly significant division which shows
us a side of the poet that Whitman did not intend to reveal: at
such times there is duality and ambiguity in the phrasing which
weakens the poetic unity, but often makes an interesting and
valuable contribution to the understanding of Whitman's personality.

　Whitman attempted to keep a firm hold on the thread of his
composition throughout the fifty-two sections by allusions to

the starting point, that is, the poet's contemplation of the grass, as in Section 6: "What is the grass?" and so forth, in Section 17, "the grass that grows," and so forth; or by the assurance that the poet knows where he is going, as in Section 33, "I am afoot with my vision!" Or the poet seems to collect all the themes and prepare for a conclusion as in Section 44: "It is time to explain myself"—but his ideas flit far and wide and often seem to desert the original theme completely, especially in the catalogue passages. In later editions Whitman tried to correct this fault and to improve the organization, but, characteristically, by an addition as late as in 1881. After the weakest and most heterogeneous of the catalogues, that of Section 15, he added the line:

And of these one and all I weave the song of myself.

The poem was thus suddenly brought into focus again.

The inserted stories are also detrimental to the composition—least so when the poet identifies himself with the chief character in the anecdote, as in the famous snapshot of the fugitive Negro slave in Section 33. Here the identification is so impassioned that we feel as if it is the poet's personal "I" that appears, and the description evolves smoothly into a series of accounts of other human suffering. More awkward are the snapshots of American history, especially of the American Revolution, which Whitman always liked to introduce into his poetry and which did add a patriotic note. But in the reading the stories come in as characterizations of the "I." They are childish recollections that entered into the poet's consciousness to such an extent that, as he himself described it in "There Was a Child Went Forth," they became a part of him. But the long anecdotes are entirely outside the design or framework of the poem. Without any particular explanation they completely fill Sections 11, 34, 35, and 36. They are the accounts of the woman and the young men bathers, the battle in Texas, and the almost Cooperesque description of the "old-fashioned frigate-fight." Considered separately, these narratives have real value, especially the anecdote of the battleship sinking after the battle, which reveals Whitman's remarkable talent for description. He anticipates his own later hospital sketches of the Civil War; the picture he gives is fully as genuine and vivid before he had lived through the horrors of war as afterward. But significantly, these narratives are most effective when printed out of their context, as they have been from time to time in English and American anthologies. Whitman himself realized that the framework went to pieces and tried to remedy it in 1867 by an addition to Section 36.

O now it is not my grandmother's father there in the fight;
I feel it is I myself.

But this addition was omitted after 1871. Actually it would have been more consistent to take the last two stories out of the poem. Another difficulty arises over the narrative in Section 11 about the lonely woman and the twenty-eight young men. This lacks any connection with what has preceded it other than that the poet has told of an Indian girl's wedding—and of the white woman who has had no wedding—; then follows the remarkable and daring description of the young woman who in imagination joins the young men bathers.

The young men float on their backs, their white bellies swell to
    the sun . . . . they do not ask who seizes fast to them,
They do not know who puffs and declines with pendant and bending
    arch,
They do not think whom they souse with spray.

There is no questioning the remarkable force and clarity almost of a mystical sort of the episode, supported by the occult numbers (twenty-eight young men and her twenty-eight years) to which Whitman was now and then partial; and the account could be spared with difficulty because it immediately arouses and stimulates the reader's interest at a point where, otherwise, it would be lost in abstraction.

To what extent did Whitman consciously work out the framework and outline of the poem? The preliminary drafts (in *Uncollected Prose and Poetry*) give no guidance; they contain incomplete, sketchy details, but no plan. Probably the prepared outline was the loosest possible. The coherence in this poem, as in Whitman's poetry in general, is a stream-of-consciousness-association. One image introduces the next. The poet is in the power of his material; he writes under inspiration.[9] And when it is spent the poem is finished. The flow of ideas provides order and emphasis, but makes revision difficult. (In later poems we can trace the inspiration in detail and often discern the lack of a plan by observing that the poem begins very forcefully, but gradually "runs down." Many of the great hymns have no goal or point; they gradually decline from the strong introductory image to weaker variants until no more associations suggest themselves and the poem ends.)

In order to understand "Song of Myself" we must get this stream-of-consciousness method clear. In *Whitman, an Interpretation in Narrative* [10] Holloway comments in passing on Whitman's inspiration and method of composition. He says that "The Sleepers," in the first edition, is the poet's attempt to reproduce "the strange but never incongruous succession of images in the mind of the sleeper"; and that is the essence of Whitman's poetry as a whole. I do not feel that this interpretation should be limited to "The Sleepers"; it applies to Whitman's poetic inspiration in general. The stream of imagery, of associations, in his poetry, and particularly in "Song of Myself," many times has the appearance of being unconscious, of the subconscious acting on its own. As often happens in dreams, the poet, without realizing it, betrays himself in this imagery. In fortunate ignorance of modern dream interpretation he records this struggle with his consciousness in the texture of the poem. If the poetic value is sometimes weakened by this omnivorous and unselective method, the psychological interest is undeniably heightened. Besides, there is in this almost continuous succession of associations with the given cue word something which points toward the modern literary movement, toward surrealism and James Joyce, whose "stream-of-consciousness" flows in an absolute parallel with Whitman's, though in a really less poetically inspired manner.

Here also Whitman has been the literary pioneer, in each case the forerunner. In "Song of Myself" the stream of associations usually flows naturally. If we once get the thread, we need not let go—aside from the three stories which possibly were interpolated later, and the great lyrical "Hymn to the Earth and

Ocean" at the conclusion of Section 21 and the beginning of
Section 22. In spite of its poetic beauty the latter seems to be
foreign matter in its context. Probably it is a poetic fragment
which Whitman was only able to use by introducing it into
"Song of Myself"—that is, as "a part of himself."

The best example of the effective use of stream-of-consciousness in the poem is in the great catalogue of Section 33, the best
of all the catalogues (or litanies, as Catel terms this detailed
reiteration in contrast to those in which Whitman uses only
lists of substantives without descriptive adjectives)—and its
colorful, glittering crescendo disarms all the attacks on this
genre in Whitman's poetry.

Section 33 in "Song of Myself" naturally divides into three
parts: first, an introduction of eight lines in which the poet, we
might say, takes off in his vision; then the course itself over the
changing landscapes of the globe, throughout centuries and
spheres; and finally, inspired by all the joyous and mighty
scenes and using the technique of variety and contrast so characteristic of Whitman, the conclusion is a pilgrimage through
the varied forms of human misery which the poet takes on himself and with which he identifies himself. For us the chief interest
is in the route itself: from "the city's quadrangular houses," his
starting point, to his visit to "the orchards of God," and then
the momentary pause, as if to catch his breath, but with the assurance that he anchors his ship "for a little while only."

The description of where he has traveled is as follows.

Where the quail is whistling betwixt the woods and the wheatlot,
Where the bat flies in the July eve . . . . where the great goldbug
    drops through the dark;
Where the flails keep time on the barn floor,
Where the brook puts out of the roots of the old tree and flows
    to the meadow,
Where cattle stand and shake away flies with the tremulous shud-
    dering of their hides,
Where the cheese-cloth hangs in the kitchen, and andirons straddle
    the hearth-slab, and cobwebs fall in festoons from the rafters;
Where triphammers crash . . . . where the press is whirling its
    cylinders;

Wherever the human heart beats with terrible throes out of its ribs;
Where the pear-shaped balloon is floating aloft . . . . floating in
    it myself and looking composedly down;
Where the life-car is drawn on the slipnoose . . . . where the heat
    hatches pale-green eggs in the dented sand,
Where the she-whale swims with her calves and never forsakes them,
Where the steamship trails hindways its long pennant of smoke,
Where the ground-shark's fin cuts like a black chip out of the
    water,
Where the half-burned brig is riding on unknown currents,

.   .   .

Upon the race-course, or enjoying pic-nics or jigs or a good game
    of base-ball,
At he-festivals with blackguard jibes and ironical license and bull-
    dances and drinking and laughter,
At the cider-mill, tasting the sweet of the brown sqush . . . . suck-
    ing the juice through a straw,
At apple-pealings, wanting kisses for all the red fruit I find,
At musters and beach-parties and friendly bees and huskings and
    house-raisings;
Where the mockingbird sounds his delicious gurgles, and cackles
    and screams and weeps,
Where the hay-rick stands in the barnyard, and the dry-stalks are
    scattered, and the brood cow waits in the hovel,
Where the bull advances to do his masculine work, and the stud to
    the mare, and the cock is treading the hen,
Where the heifers browse, and the geese nip their food with short
    jerks;
Where the sundown shadows lengthen over the limitless and lone-
    some prairie,
Where the herds of buffalo make a crawling spread of the square
    miles far and near;
Where the hummingbird shimmers . . . . where the neck of the
    longlived swan is curving and winding;
Where the laughing-gull scoots by the slappy shore, and laughs
    her near-human laugh;

.   .   .

Where the splash of swimmers and divers cool the warm noon;
Where the katydid works her chromatic reed on the walnut-tree
    over the well;

Through patches of citrons and cucumbers with silver-wired
leaves,
Through the salt-lick or orange glade . . . . or under conical
furs [*sic*];

.   .   .

Looking in at the shop-windows in Broadway, the whole forenoon
. . . . pressing the flesh of my nose to the thick-plate glass,
Wandering the same afternoon with my face turned up to the
clouds;
My right and left arms round the sides of two friends and I in the
middle;

.   .   .

Hurrying with the modern crowd, as eager and fickle as any,
Hot towards one I hate, ready in my madness to knife him;
Solitary at midnight in my back yard, my thoughts gone from me
a long while,
Walking the old hills of Judea with the beautiful gentle god by
my side;
Speeding through space . . . . speeding through heaven and the
stars,
Speeding amid the seven satellites and the broad ring and the
diameter of eighty thousand miles,
Speeding with tailed meteors . . . . throwing fire-balls like the
rest,
Carrying the crescent child that carries its own full mother in its
belly:
Storming enjoying planning loving cautioning,
Backing and filling, appearing and disappearing,
I tread day and night such roads.

We see the whole crescendo massed and climaxed in this final
line, which is a natural culmination for the series. The presentation is remarkably effective, with each organic image linked to
the next, association to association, every detail with its own
well-defined and strikingly colorful characteristic. The coherence and lucidity is continued throughout the remainder of this
section, which, on the whole, is to a greater degree than "The
Sleepers" the most typical example of Whitman's peculiar

vigor and integration in his early poetry. Besides the vocabulary (which is strongly Whitmanesque, especially in the use of numerous present participles) it is for the catalogue itself that the passage quoted above is important, because it throws light on what Whitman intended to do when he wrote his other, weaker catalogues.

The danger of the catalogues is that they easily become too much like prose, mere dry repetitions, lacking the power to awaken the intended associations for the reader. And that was their effect upon his contemporaries. Clara Barrus quotes a comment Emerson made in 1871 when sending Whitman a message that he was dissatisfied with him. "I expect him to make the songs of the nation, but he seems to be contented to make the inventories." [11] And Knut Hamsun, whose well-written and impassioned youthful work *Fra det moderne Amerikas Aandsliv* [On the Intellectual Life of Modern America], contained one of the most savage assaults on Whitman in world literature, said on this subject:

His tabulated poetry, those impossible reiterations of persons, states, household furniture, tools, articles of dress . . . reveal not a spark of poetic talent. When Whitman celebrates a thing he says right in the first line that he is celebrating that thing—in order to say in the next line that he celebrates a second thing, in the third line a third thing—without celebrating it in anyway except by naming it. He does not know more of anything than its name, but he knows many names. [12]

We see plainly how unjust and exaggerated this characterization is by looking at the recently quoted section in which there was not a single "name" of which Whitman did not reveal his intimate knowledge by a characterizing adjective. Still, there is in Hamsun's interpretation of Whitman something which is apropos. His main thesis is that Whitman is a "savage." The Indian traits in his poetry are emphasized, and among them his fondness for the old Indian names (for example, Paumanok for Long Island) : "He is influenced by the primitive music of these place names to such an extent that he sticks whole lists of them on his pages, where they have no connection whatsoever with the text." On page sixty-five we find Hamsun's chief, witty criticism of Whitman as a poet: "It needs at least twice as much inspiration to read such verse as to write it." Without a doubt he touches on something fundamental in Whitman's poetry, and especially in its early form. Whitman really cherished an almost Indian-like enthusiasm for words, for the vocable itself. (In this connection note particularly in his drafts the long lists of words with which he obviously expected to produce special effects in his poems.) It is as if he attributed to words a sort of primitive magic, corresponding to the attitude of primitive peoples, who think that they possess a thing if they can call its name. Michaud characterizes Whitman's peculiar form of expression by saying: "A sign for an idea, a word for a world." [13] He depends on the reader to have the same associations, the same inspiration which moved him when he wrote the sign for the thing. For Whitman a catalogue of words was as vivid as a net full of sprawling, shining fish, but time after time he must have found they were stiff and cold by the time the reader saw the net. He gradually realized the danger in his repetitions and abbreviated them in his later poetry. The long catalogues belong to the first period.

But even in "Song of Myself" Whitman had a very good idea of what critics would hold against him. As a motto for his expansive poetry he introduced in Section 23 a typically Whitmanesque Gallic word, *"en masse,"* to express what he hoped to gain by his elaborately contrived style, and in Section 42 he himself put his finger on his long lines and his self-esteem.

I know perfectly well my own egotism,
And know my omnivorous words, and cannot say any less, . . .

Finally, in Section 51, he anticipates the accusation of contradicting himself and makes a last allusion to the motto *en masse.*

> Do I contradict myself?
> Very well then . . . . I contradict myself;
> I am large . . . . I contain multitudes.

He worked hard to perfect his style. The "omnivorous words" became less omnivorous in his later poems; the reiterations were discontinued, the use of dots decreased, and it was his constant

aim to improve the unmistakable rhythm which he attained in
his best prose-verse. "Make this more rhythmical" is a typical
memorandum in the notebooks of this period, and from the notebooks we learn how the rhythm was born in the prose fragments which later became the most famous passages in his poems.
He worked to produce "liturgic prose" in the same way that
Paul Claudel has done in our day. He continued to polish single
lines throughout successive editions until the result satisfied him.
For example, the opening line of Section 24 of "Song of Myself":

1855: Walt Whitman, an American, one of the roughs, a kosmos,

1867: Walt Whitman, am I, of mighty Manhattan the son,

1871: Walt Whitman am I, a Kosmos, of mighty Manhattan the
son, . . .

Thus came into existence many of the lines about which
Adolf Hansen said in 1901 that they are so long that we "inevitably strangle on them," [14] and which prompted Johannes
V. Jensen to speak of "the fervid mysticism in these wild rhymes,
all straining the reader's breath in accordance with the vitality
the poet had breathed into them." [15]

Bliss Perry was one of the first clearly to recognize that
Whitman's prose-verse was not, as popularly supposed, merely
scribbled down and put together casually, without revision,
but, on the contrary, in many instances "had been constructed
with the utmost care." [16] He was the first in America to make it
a subject of metrical study. In "Song of Myself" he found,
besides dactylic hexameters now and then, the six-footed anapest
which Tennyson often used and the free blank verse of the older
English dramatists. This record is only of academic interest,
since Whitman used none of these meters consciously, having
worked them out only casually, but they are found mingled
with the special Whitmanesque prose line which Bliss Perry
characterizes by quoting from a study by Professor F. N. Scott;
"The Whitmanian line consists, like the prose sentence, of an
advancing and retreating wave. He varied the length of these
waves, varied the speech rhythm to coincide or conflict with the

routine scansion, introduced minor waves and impulses and used alliteration and refrain." [17] This explanation is unusually precise. Bliss Perry's chief point, and one most fundamental to the understanding of Whitman's style, is that the poet intended to create a spoken rather than a written poem. "Not to apprehend *Leaves of Grass* as a *man speaking* is to miss its purport." [18]

That is the main clue to an understanding of Whitman's special diction; the peculiarities and oddities can almost all be explained in this way. The poet's first impression of the art of words had come through two speakers, Elias Hicks and Booth. His early desire to become an orator was still vital while he was writing the first draft of "Song of Myself," and probably he at first intended it for a formal declamation, which he preferred to reading. Gradually, as the poem grew, he declaimed it to himself on his walks along the beach. In the notes about the art of reading aloud and speaking which he wrote down in the following year, now to be found in Furness's *Workshop*,[19] it is plainly evident that many of the themes later used in poems were originally thought of for lectures, and the form of expression was essentially affected thereby. "We need somebody or something whose utterance were like an old Hebrew prophet's." [20] Whitman developed in detail what he thought this modern oratorical style should be:

. . . a stern and harsh passage, crackling and smashing like a falling tree, many other passages of many different tones, but all converging sooner or later into the clear, monotonous voice, equable as water—sometimes direct addresses made to you, the hearer, with a pause afterwards, as if an answer were expected, then perhaps for many minutes total abstraction and travelling into other fields . . . vocalism limpid, inspired [21] . . . besides direct addressing *to You*, another leading trait of Lectures may well be— strong assertion—("I say"—it is so?)—launched out with fire, or emphasis, or enthusiasm, or anger . . .[22]

And again:

Practise and experiment until I find a flowing, strong, *appropriate speaking, composition style* . . .[23]

It is impossible not to see the connection between this essay on the theory of speaking and the style of "Song of Myself," which Whitman himself later characterized as "a new and national declamatory expression." [24] The spoken word was always his ideal. "A vocal style" and "vocalism" are frequent terms in his work, in which the "orator" always appears as a sort of idealized figure. Since he associates a kind of magic with words, he shows the same attitude toward the voice: "the divine power to speak words" is the famous refrain in the poem "Voices" (later expanded into "Vocalism"), in which in 1860 he expressed his intense admiration for human voices.

O what is it in me that makes me tremble so at voices?

Surely, whoever speaks to me in the right voice, him or her I shall
    follow, as the waters follow the moon, silently, with fluid steps,
    any where around the globe.[25]

It is likewise an orator who composes "Song of Myself," and an essential share of the effect of the poem depends on that fact. It is full of rhetorical tricks, first the direct address, which is not merely oratorical, but conversational.

Section 23: Gentlemen I receive you . . .

Section 40: Man or woman! I might tell how I like you, but cannot,

Section 42: Come my children,
            Come my boys and girls, and my women and house-
                hold and intimates, . . .

Or

Section 43: I do not despise you priests; . . .

Even more effective than these collective addresses are the personal; the poet addresses his reader directly with a question.

Section 2: Have you practiced so long to learn to read?

Section 35: Did you read in the seabooks of the oldfashioned
            frigate-fight?

Or with the assurance in Section 2.

You shall not look through my eyes either, nor take things from me,
You shall listen to all sides and filter them from yourself.

And he constantly keeps the illusion that it is a conversation, a personal experience, not something read in a book. Whitman continually used the words "to hear" instead of "to see," for example:

Section 25: . . . whoever hears me let him or her set out in search of this day.

Section 47: The farmboy ploughing in the field feels good at the sound of my voice.

The greatest force is exerted when the poet speaks to his reader as if he were the one person in the world in whom the poet prefers to confide and suggests to the individual reader that they are entirely alone.

> This hour I tell things in confidence,
> I might not tell everybody but I will tell you.
>
> Section 19

This strangely engrossing conversational style, in which the poet seems to look up from the book at his reader or to leap from the page into his arms, later became a mannerism of Whitman's. We are scarcely speaking too strongly if, after *identification*, we put *suggestion* as one of Whitman's most definite poetic devices in *Leaves of Grass*.

Another characteristic of the oral style is the parenthesis so numerous in the poem, mostly in the later editions, less so in the first version. It is appropriate to deal with it here because it is so essential in the finished poem. The final version of this particular poem has no less than forty parentheses, and in my opinion they should be regarded as part of Whitman's rhetoric, for example:

The regatta is spread on the bay . . . . (how the white sails sparkle;)

.   .   .

The prostitute draggles her shawl, her bonnet bobs on her tipsy and pimpled neck,
The crowd laugh at her blackguard oaths, the men jeer and wink to each other,

(Miserable! I do not laugh at your oaths nor jeer you,)

Section 15.

The insignificant is as big to me as any,
(What is less or more than a touch?)   Section 30.

. . . . I keep no account with lamentation;
(What have I to do with lamentation?)   Section 44.

Is it not obvious that these parentheses are a purely rhetorical indication of tempo and inflection? Instead of parentheses he could just as well have used the "aside" found in the old plays. Thus, the peculiarities of diction and style in "Song of Myself" can be explained by Whitman's desire to create a "vocal style."

The present participles, which play such an important role in Whitman's diction, are more difficult; often they form the major obstacle in translation. In the two standard German translations, those of Johannes Schlaf, in 1907, and Hans Reisiger, in 1922, Schlaf consistently chose to translate the participles into the ordinary present tense, while Reisiger, in so far as possible, tried to create a corresponding participial form in German. The conclusion of the long catalogue quoted above ("Storming loving enjoying planning cautioning") is an excellent example of the extent to which it is characteristic of Whitman's whole diction. Of course this participial form is more common in English, especially in poetry, than in the other major languages. One reason for Whitman's use of this form was to avoid the usual present tense of the verb: *I storm, I love,* and so forth, and the ordinary verbs to which he seems to have had such an aversion that he often omitted them altogether, as in the introduction to Section 42.

. . . . A call in the midst of the crowd,
My own voice, orotund sweeping and final.

Here the verb is omitted in both sentences. However, the use of the participial form becomes a dangerous mannerism for Whitman. How unfortunate we can best see in another quotation from Section 42.

Here and there with dimes on the eyes walking,
To feed the greed of the belly the brains liberally spooning,
Tickets buying or taking or selling, but in to the feast never once
    going;
Many sweating and ploughing and thrashing, and then the chaff
    for payment receiving,
A few idly owning, and they the wheat continually claiming.

That is a complete sentence in the poem, not a disconnected
quotation, and it is really untranslatable into a parallel form.
Even Reisiger gave up translating participles in this passage,[26]
where they do quite as much to obscure the meaning and the
coherence as they add to the vigor of the lines. The participial
mannerism reached its climax and conclusion in the *Calamus*
poem: "We two boys together clinging," also in "So Long" in
1860 and the Lincoln memorial poem, "When Lilacs Last . . ."
of 1865.

Whitman's vocabulary, his use of words in "Song of Myself" especially, is most interesting. In the Preface he had
already reminded himself to omit all the traditional ornaments
of poetry which only tended to separate the poet from his reader.
"I will have nothing hang in the way, not the richest curtains.
What I tell I tell for precisely what it is." And Bliss Perry has
printed some quotations from the "Rules for Composition" which
Whitman wrote down for his own use at the beginning of the
fifties: "Common idioms and phrases—Yankeeisms and vulgar-
isms—cant expressions, when very pat only." [27] It was primarily the commonplace speech that interested him. (Afterwards, in *November Boughs*, he published an article on "Slang
in America.") And he introduced everyday turns of phrase and
expressions into his poetry, mingled with Americanisms, professional jargon, Italian, Spanish, and French words, along
with various home-made expressions. We have suggestive examples of all these in "Song of Myself." Reminiscent of conventional poetry are his many alliterative pairs: to "lean and loafe"
(Section 1), "cipher and show" (Section 3), "piddle and pat-
ter" (Section 42), "no chair, nor church" (Section 46), "filter
and fibre" (Section 52). Occasionally he succeeds in coining an
expression by an unexpected paralleling, as in Section 20 "a

suck and a sell" for delusion and farce; by juxtaposing the two Americanisms he gains a new and characteristic effect in his diction. As an example of his home-made substantives there is "an encloser," in Section 44. But it is ordinarily by the use of foreign words that he obtains his most distinctive effects; naturally we must distinguish between anglicized French words (*villain, enamoured, unique,* and *ennui,* which he used) and those he took over on his own account, like *eleves* in Section 38 and *en masse* in Section 23. *Children of Adam* was first called *Enfans d'Adam* and "Poem of Salutation" was later changed to "Salut au Monde."

He used "contralto," "regatta," and "piazza," in Section 15, and "vivas," in Section 18, from Italian,[28] and *Camerado* from Spanish became one of his favorite expressions.[29] Besides the peculiarly American terms "squatter" and "trapper" in Section 15 and "Hoosier" in Section 16, he used four noteworthy Americanisms: "toting," in Section 15, for carrying; "turn" in Section 22, for contest (inning or round in sporting terms); "grit" in Section 40, for determination and strength; and finally "dicker" in Section 33, for bargaining. "Katydid," also in the long catalogue of Section 33, is the name of several species of grasshoppers peculiar to America, and the word "scuttle" for small opening, in Section 45, comes from astronomer's terminology (sliding door on top of observatory). Whitman took his names and designations from everywhere: one of his favorite words, *adhesiveness* for comradeship, union, a word which later came to have the greatest significance for him as the designation of the emotion on which his whole new democracy was to be built, comes from the phrenological jargon. Three of the other expressions in his ideology: "nativity," "amativeness," and "suggestiveness," are not found in "Song of Myself"; the more arresting word "identity," in Section 3 and Section 28, is used in a way which leaves no doubt that to Whitman it meant something essential and special.

Thus, we have returned to that important point in "Song of Myself," the duality of the "I," the split, the ambiguity which was almost overcome by this theory of identity. The duality in the poem is primarily in the "I," which is presented now as the poet himself with his personal identification, now as "the general human personality, typified in myself." Whitman thus strove first to establish an identity between himself and the whole universe. Then comes the identity between male and female when they meet in procreation. As in Section 3:

Out of the dimness opposite equals advance . . . . Always substance and increase,
Always a knit of identity . . . . always distinction . . . . always a breed of life.

"Always a knit of identity" is the first use of the word in "Song of Myself." The third and most important identity is that between soul and body, one of Whitman's most fundamental dogmas—their complete, indissoluble union being one of the poet's most passionate desires.

Clear and sweet is my soul . . . . and clear and sweet is all that is not my soul.

Lacks one lacks both . . .   Section 3.

And in Section 5 he says:

I believe in you my soul . . . . the other I am must not abase itself to you,
And you must not be abased to the other.

These two sentences in the very beginning of the poem leave no doubt of the intention, an idea which was developed throughout Whitman's work, even into old age. But in the beginning the expression is either mystical or ambiguous. In the fourth line of the poem he says:

I loafe and invite my soul.

Therefore the soul is a person who can be "invited" and spoken to, and the "You" who appears in the poem suddenly seems in several instances to be this soul, not the reader, as we might suppose. In Section 5, for example, in the cosmic vision, it is the soul who accepts the poet's invitation and lies with him and looses "the stop from your throat." But the poem continues:

I mind how we lay in June, such a transparent summer morning;
You settled your head athwart my hips and gently turned over upon me,

And parted the shirt from my bosom-bone, and plunged your
    tongue to my barestript heart, etc.

It is quite shocking that it is the soul who does this. The expression is ambiguous; we see there is a mystery, perhaps a
veiled erotic situation similar to that in "Once I Pass'd." But
this, of course, does not detract from the strange beauty of the
situation. The second point about the scene is splendid and noteworthy: the repose and unity which is attained between soul
and body in this cosmic vision out of which the whole poem
grew.

How important a role is ascribed to the unity of body and
soul that he proclaimed is most obvious in the motto written for
Leaves of Grass, in 1876, which now appears just after the
title-page of the collection.

Come, said my Soul,
Such verses for my Body let us write, (for we are one,)
That should I after death invisibly return,
Or, long, long hence, in other spheres,
There to some group of mates the chants resuming,
(Tallying Earth's soil, trees, winds, tumultuous waves,)
Ever with pleas'd smile I may keep on,
Ever and ever yet the verses owning—as, first, I here and now,
Signing for Soul and Body, set to them my name, Walt Whitman.

Soul and body are one, and they are both called Walt Whitman, but the soul is immortal and is not, like the body, subject
to the law of transmutation. The soul signs its name to this poem
in order to have some identification if it should return—and
will always "own" these poems and could continue the work on
them. That is approximately the idea; it is not without beauty,
but far from clear and consistent, and does not give a very
convincing picture of the identity.

Moreover, the phrases in the many poems on the same theme
between "Song of Myself" and this motto, written twenty-one
years later, are always wavering and uncertain. An excellent
example is Section 12 of "Song of Joys" (1860).

O Death!
O the beautiful touch of Death, soothing and benumbing a few
    moments, for reasons;

O that of myself, discharging my excrementitious body, to be
    burned, or rendered to powder, or buried,
My real body doubtless left to me for other spheres,
My voided body, nothing more to me, returning to the purifications,
    further offices, eternal uses of the earth.

Here the concept of the soul has suddenly become "my real
body," and the phrase is also used in Section 48 of the 1860
"Proto-Leaf" [Section 13 of "Starting from Paumanok"],
probably to designate unity between the two, but only making
it doubly questionable by the duality of the phrase.[30] The climax
of this remarkable identity of soul and body is in "Pioneers! O
Pioneers!" (1865), where the "I" is included in the long procession.

> I too with my soul and body,
> We, a curious trio, picking, wandering on our way.

The change is erratic and very significant. W. S. Kennedy, a
zealous Whitman champion and one of "the hot little prophets,"
in *The Fight of a Book for the World*, 1926, interpreted the
enigmatic passage thus: the "I" in the poem is not a reference to the poet himself but to the divine principle, the "underlying Will, or Absolute Being," [31] of which both soul and
body are functions. This explanation seems the only possible
one. The Whitmanesque "I" is really momentarily a third division of the duality of soul and body in one person; it is the world-
soul, the Emersonian Oversoul, of which not only the poet, not
only humanity, but also the grass, grains of sand, the ant, the
tree-toad, the blackberry bramble ("Song of Myself" Section
31) are form and function. And this identity extends to include
every living thing, all the diversities mentioned in "Song of
Myself" which the poet hopes will sing together in one grand
harmony. The influence of Hegel and the Hegelianism which
Whitman frequently emphasized in himself can unmistakably
be detected here. Hegel's idea of the progress of the world as a
continual advance toward greater unity is shared by Whitman,
but he did not get it from Hegel. Thesis, antithesis, synthesis
are also Whitman's plan for the union of all the multiplicities,
identity in opposition to all diversities. In any event it is obvious

that the very word "trio" for this identity is from the famous Hegelian "triad," an influence that Whitman revealed by various phrases in later poems.[32]

The elimination of conflicts by synthesis and identity are the hope, the goal of "Song of Myself." Nevertheless, it is impossible for the reader not to see that the duality interferes in various ways and that Whitman himself at that period was conscious of the fatal duality. In Section 16 he speaks of "my own diversity" (in "Starting from Paumanok" it becomes the baroque expression "Mélange my own!"), and from time to time the personal, lyrical emotion in the poems conflicts with the pose of conqueror and prophetic majesty which the poet planned for himself. Even in Section 4 of "Song of Myself" Whitman betrays the duality when he talks of the "I," the chief narrator and declaimer of the poem, and then in contrast to that, a second "I," the "me myself," who is neither the narrator nor the great "I" of Nature, but, on the contrary, a third, an uncertain, passive and watchful "I" who

Looks with its sidecurved head curious what will come next,
Both in and out of the game, and watching and wondering at it.

For the initiated there is no doubt that here the real, personal, Walt Whitman is introduced into the poem—not the cosmic "I," not the prophet, world-traveler and vagabond, the confident, grandiloquent "I," but the actual, existent young American whom we also knew before the book came into existence, contemplative, expectant, "both in and out of the game" (in real life usually out of it), who often betrays himself in the poem in a characteristic fashion, and in a voice widely at variance with the voice of the confident, masculine braggadocio in which the poem is otherwise written. By the side of the "I," who, "stout as a horse, affectionate, haughty, electrical," dares take up life's greatest mysteries, there is a second "I," strangely young and uncertain, strangely groping, strangely feminine in his emotions.

At the side of him who turns "the bridegroom out of bed" and stays with the bride all night and presses her to his lips and thighs, at the side of him who "on women fit for conception" starts bigger babies ("This day I am jetting the stuff of far more arrogant republics"), is this other more real Whitman "going in for my chances, spending for vast returns" (Section 14), he who as a wistful adolescent youth is adorning his person to bestow himself on the first that will take him.

The divergence in emphasis is extraordinary, and the "identity" is indiscernible. In Section 19 the poet says of his verse:

This is the press of a bashful hand . . .
This is the touch of my lips to yours . . . . this is the murmur
   of yearning.

But in Section 18:

This is the trill of a thousand clear cornets and scream of the
   octave flute and strike of triangles.

There is something here out of harmony, something defiant, forced, an assumed superiority and unity, an identity which, to the detriment of the composition, is revealed at a moment when the poet is most sincere and true to his own nature.

The most remarkable divergence from the "I" elsewhere set up and extolled appears in Section 27—at first glance one of the most puzzling sections of the poem. On close inspection it is one of the most interesting parts, but quite outside the pattern of the poem, and it gives the poet away. It makes an important contribution to the understanding of Whitman's peculiar idea of identity. The association, the connection, is erotic. The cue-word is "touch" in a sexual sense:

Is this then a touch? . . . . quivering me to a new identity,
Flames and ether making a rush for my veins,
Treacherous tip of me reaching and crowding to help them,
My flesh and blood playing out lightning, to strike what is hardly
   different from myself,
On all sides prurient provokers stiffening my limbs,
Straining the udder of my heart for its withheld drip,
Behaving licentious toward me, taking no denial,
Depriving me of my best as for a purpose,
Unbuttoning my clothes and holding me by the bare waist,
Deluding my confusion with the calm of the sunlight and pasture
   fields,
Immodestly sliding the fellow-senses away,

They bribed to swap off with touch, and go and graze at the edges
    of me,
No consideration, no regard for my draining strength or my anger,
Fetching the rest of the herd around to enjoy them awhile,
Then all uniting to stand on a headland and worry me.

The sentries desert every other part of me,
They have left me helpless to a red marauder,
They all come to the headland to witness and assist against me.

I am given up by traitors;
I talk wildly . . . . I have lost my wits . . . . I and nobody else
    am the greatest traitor,
I went myself first to the headland . . . . my own hands carried
    me there.

You villain touch! what are you doing? . . . . my breath is tight
    in its throat;
Unclench your floodgates! you are too much for me.[33]

    This is a lyrical account of an unmistakably auto-erotic sexual experience. It was faintly anticipated by the picture of a similar physical emotion in the cosmic experience in Section 5, in the musical trance in Section 26, and in the episode in which the poet, while swimming, takes a "turn" with the sea in Section 22. All are descriptions of emphatically accented auto-erotic emotions. In the passage quoted above they escape under full sail in intentionally suggestive imagery. Its poetic quality is undeniable. It is unique of its kind in world literature, but it certainly unveils the "I" who wrote "Song of Myself."

    The first edition of *Leaves of Grass* betrays the strange adolescence of Whitman's whole attitude, which of course showed itself primarily in the erotic descriptions. Later, in *Calamus*, he needed only to sit near the one he loved and hold him by the hand to be content and happy; this is anticipated in these earlier poems: an uncertain, experimental, yearning voice that Whitman later made every effort to conceal or erase entirely from his book, because it was so incompatible with the role of erotic confidence and superiority which he had set himself to play. In this connection there is a highly significant passage in

"The Sleepers" which was deleted in 1856. It closes Section 1 and very effectively expresses the erotic feeling of a youth divided between hot longing and scorching shame.

O hotcheeked and blushing! O foolish hectic!
O for pity's sake, no one must see me now! . . . . my clothes were
    stolen while I was abed,

           .   .   .   .

I feel ashamed to go naked about the world,
And am curious to know where my feet stand . . . . and what is
    this flooding me, childhood or manhood . . . . and the hun-
    ger that crosses the bridge between.

The passage is almost sublime in its description of the adolescent youth's uncertainty as to "where he stands," "child or man," and of the gnawing hunger which fills him on the bridge between. But Whitman himself clearly felt that this was too intimate, and therefore he later deleted it. For a complete understanding of the peculiar erotic emotion of the first edition this revelation is indispensable, and it is doubly remarkable that it has not been used in earlier interpretations.

Another trait revealed in the first edition is that the narrative episodes have a tendency to take the feminine point of view. The poet himself is the old mother, the widow in the night, the deserted wife,[34] and in the baroque but unforgettable passage in Section 11 he is in reality the lonesome young woman watching the young men bathing—just as in the famous section of "The Sleepers" he is the woman who masturbates ("Double yourself and receive me darkness"). In its daring this is one of Whitman's strangest, cleverest descriptions, and it has remained in all the editions. Considered in connection with the auto-erotic incident in Section 28 of "Song of Myself," it gives its own picture of Whitman's personal experience. At any rate, Catel has based his whole definition of Whitman's sexual pathology on these apparently auto-erotic tendencies as revealed in the first edition. Thus, when Whitman says of the young woman in the window that she is twenty-eight years old "and all so lonesome" we cannot avoid feeling that it is a most deeply personal confession and think of Whitman's own first twenty-

eight years, 1819–1847. "Song of Myself," besides being a very
impressive self-expression, is also a moving and sublime self-
revelation.

In his erotic descriptions in "Song of Myself" Whitman
plainly gives evidence that he is the poet who five years later
will write the notorious *Children of Adam* poems. From the beginning it was his program to proclaim "the illustriousness of
sex." And the erotic descriptions are more than a program. The
purely physical side of human nature stimulated and inspired
his fantasy in a special way. In Section 24 of "Song of Myself"
he says:

If I worship any particular thing it shall be some of the spread
    of my body;
Translucent mould of me it shall be you,
Shaded ledges and rests, firm masculine coulter, it shall be you,
Whatever goes to the tilth of me it shall be you,
You my rich blood, your milky stream pale strippings of my life;
Breast that presses against other breasts it shall be you,
My brain it shall be your occult convolutions,
Root of washed sweet-flag, timorous pond-snipe, nest of guarded
    duplicate eggs, it shall be you,
Mixed tussled hay of head and beard and brawn it shall be you,
Trickling sap of maple, fibre of manly wheat, it shall be you; . . .

It is not to be denied that this is both poetic and characteristic, and we understand why Frank Harris and D. H. Lawrence have regarded it as a basis for a completely frank modern erotic poetry.

But if "Song of Myself" holds the germ of *Children of Adam*,
it also contains the seeds of *Calamus.* An actual, detailed Calamus situation hardly exists apart from the famous arsis of Section 45.

My lovers suffocate me!
Crowding my lips, and thick in the pores of my skin,

which introduces the mighty lyrical crescendo of the conclusion.
But at the same time it should be noted that on many occasions
we must be on guard against Whitman's use of the word "lover."
Previously Emerson (in "Friendship") used the term "lover"
interchangeably for friend, meaning intimate friend or com-

rade. And so it must often be understood in Whitman even though on many occasions he consciously played on the double usage. If there are no particular Calamus-episodes which can be pointed out in "Song of Myself," there are still places where the peculiar erotic inclination asserts itself. So it did, perhaps unconsciously, in the poet's emotion breaking through the descriptions of the young man who drives the express wagon in Section 15, of the lads on the fire engine, Section 41, and of the young mechanic in Section 47 who understands him so well. In his notebooks there is a passage that is especially pertinent in this connection:

Understand that you can have in your writing no qualities which you do not honestly entertain in yourself. . . If you love to have a servant stand behind your chair at dinner, it will appear in your writing; if you possess a vile opinion of women, or if you grudge anything, or doubt immortality, these will appear by what you leave unsaid more than by what you say. There is no trick or cunning, no art or recipe by which you can have in your writing that which you do not possess in yourself.[35]

More than in any other way, Whitman betrays himself by the double expression "him or her," which after "Song of Myself" became so characteristic of his diction. ("The real or fancied indifference of some man *or* woman I love," Section 4. "Man or woman! I might tell you now I like you . . . ," Section 40.) There is in this designation a doubt about the choice, a doubt which for a normal man would never arise, and it is very characteristic of Whitman's feeling of insecurity and vacillation on the bridge between childhood and manhood.[36] But primarily we are aware of the unsatisfied yearning. It is a lonely man who speaks. He is filled with a longing to see "Faces, faces, faces." His inspiration is fed by strangers whom he passes in the street and whom he will never know. "Wherefore is there no response?" The sea and the grass are his friends in whose arms he must rest, the Great Camerado of all creation for whom he yearns so despairingly.

"Song of Myself" is a long ecstatic declaration of love for the whole world and all humanity, but at the same time it is partly a sermon. The poem has many of the singular character-

istics of the earlier mystics and the older pantheistic poets in
literature which Whitman had not read at that time. Grass,
with its roots in the hearts of young men, is one of the metaphors found in the Persian poets, especially Omar Khayyám.
Tree frogs, which fascinated Whitman, aroused no less enthusiasm in Angelus Silesius ("The frog is as beautiful as the
seraphim").[37] To both Blake and Whitman the creation of a
tiny flower was "the work of the ages." [38] And finally there is
the image of the grass as the child of vegetation. We cannot
help remembering the familiar lines from Goethe's on metamorphosis of the plants: "yet indivisible the form of its first
appearance remains and so the child appears among the
plants." [39]

This similarity in expression and poetic experience is only
one of many qualities of Whitman's poetry, in which the interpretation of nature is otherwise indisputably original, but it
is stimulating for the reader to note these traits that he shared
with the greatest writers. The personification of nature, more
fully developed later, is found even in "Song of Myself." The
sea calls the poet with "crooked inviting fingers," and he plunges
in to have a "turn" with it (Section 22). And the surprising
clarity and lucidity of the nature imagery which afterwards
made E. C. Stedman call Whitman "the finest word-painter of
open nature who has ever lived" [40] are obvious in the first edition, especially in the long catalogue. But Whitman's emotion
was deeper than that of a nature lyricist; he felt himself to be
an evangelist of nature, and this conviction determined the whole
atmosphere of the poet. To Whitman the poet is a prophet, a
seer, who is charged with telling mankind these things. The close
connection between this call, as Whitman interpreted it, and
his Quaker leanings cannot be doubted. Just as someone arose
to speak in the Quaker meetings because inspiration suddenly
came to him, so did Whitman rise up in his age because the "inner light" filled him. He is as direct as they are; he keeps his
hat on as they do ("I cock my hat as I please indoors or out,"
Section 20), he says "thou" and "brother" to everyone he
meets, like them he breaks with the official clergy and despises
the divine services and ceremonies. And all the passages about

the sick, the wound-dresser motif in "Song of Myself," which so strangely anticipate his own later experiences during the Civil War, are related to the Quaker teachings. The influence of Elias Hicks on his earliest childhood is evident. Whitman was fully conscious of his Quaker traits, and in the third edition emphasized them by introducing the Quaker nomenclature for the months, using "third month," "fourth month," and so forth, instead of March, April, and so forth (even in the revised "Song of Myself"), as a definitive characteristic of his poetic diction, as in the present reading of Section 19:

Do you guess I have some intricate purpose?
Well I have, for the Fourth-month showers have and the mica on
    the side of a rock has.

Originally it read "April-rain." This use of the Quaker names for the months was a poetic quality in "Song of Myself" rather than a mannerism.

    The other poems in the 1855 collection are mostly commentaries on or cuttings from "Song of Myself." In "Song of Occupations" and "To Think of Time" he addresses the "American Masses," the common people, each individual, "Workman, whoever you are!" with assurances of the importance and nobility of each person. And the cue words, "Camerado," "identity," "the mystic unseen soul," are used again and again. But the poems are weak and prosaic, with catalogues blooming wildly.[41] "I Sing the Body Electric" is more interesting as the first of the poems which later formed the *Children of Adam* group. It offers many valuable contributions to the understanding of Whitman's interpretation of the right attitude toward the body. As in "Song of Myself," he reiterates all parts of the body in an enthusiastic catalogue. To him the human body is a poem which he cannot approach without emotion.

To be surrounded by beautiful curious breathing laughing flesh is
    enough,
To pass among them . . . . to touch any one . . . . to rest my
    arm ever so lightly round his or her neck for a moment . . . .
    what is this then?
I do not ask any more delight . . . . I swim in it as in a sea.

The strongly sexual emphasis in Whitman's frequent use of "swimmers" in the poems is clear in this quotation. But at the same time there is also an obvious adolescent characteristic in his eroticism, especially in the concluding lines of the section, in which he describes the various kinds of physical beauty: women at their work, firemen, the reaper as he mows.

Suchlike I love . . . . I loosen myself and pass freely . . . . and
    am at the mother's breast with the little child,
And swim with the swimmer, and wrestle with wrestlers, and march
    in line with the firemen, and pause and listen and count.

"The Sleepers" has a unique position as one of Whitman's most remarkable poems, so skillfully executed that we are inclined to place it much later in his poetic evolution. Whitman himself realized this and put it toward the end of the book (after "Sea-Drift," 1860, after "Drum-Taps," 1865, after "Passage to India," 1871, and even after "Autumn Rivulets," 1882). This shifting of "The Sleepers" is a typical example of the amalgamation that took place in *Leaves of Grass*. We have noticed that Holloway used this poem as an example of the notably dream-like but irresistible stream of associations in Whitman's poems. And I have already mentioned the contribution it makes to our understanding of Whitman's erotic psyche. But it is primarily the emotion itself in the poem which is of a peculiarly suggestive nature, a tone and feeling attained later only in his most melodic poems, "Out of the Cradle" and "Passage to India." What Whitman aimed for in "Salut au Monde," 1856, but almost smothered in too many conspicuous foreign words and names, he achieved here in the great fellowship of sleep, that is, the expansion and encompassing, the synthesis of all animate things into one. The poet goes from bed to bed and in his vision shares the dreams of all the other dreamers—he actually *is* all the other dreamers.

The sleepers are very beautiful as they lie unclothed,
They flow hand in hand over the whole earth from east to west as
    they lie unclothed;

The Asiatic and African are hand in hand . . . . the European
    and American are hand in hand,
Learned and unlearned are hand in hand . . and male and female
    are hand in hand;

.   .   .

The father holds his grown or ungrown son in his arms with meas-
    ureless love,

.   .   .

The scholar kisses the teacher and the teacher kisses the scholar
    . . . . the wronged is made right,
The call of the slave is one with the master's call . . and the master
    salutes the slave,

.   .   .

They pass the invigoration of the night and the chemistry of the
    night and awake.

The vision is beautiful and is worked out and adhered to throughout the whole poem with great poetic force. Interspersed are some of Whitman's most famous episodic narratives, motivated as pictures in his dream: the picture of the swimmer who is battered against the cliffs, the picture of the wreck at Hempstead Beach, Washington's Farewell to his army, and finally the story of his mother and the red squaw who once came to the Van Velsor farm and how his mother fell in love with her.

She remembered her many a winter and many a summer,
But the red squaw never came nor was heard of there again.

They are all memories and tales from his childhood. The poet becomes a child again and like all the other dreamers goes home in his dreams. The conclusion of the poem emphasizes this in mystical symbolism.

I stay awhile away O night, but I return to you again and love you;

.   .   .

I will duly pass the day O my mother and duly return to you.

The night is the great mother to whom the poet wants to return. The mother figure, who earlier in the poem and in other poems of the collection ("Song of Myself," "Faces," "There Was a Child Went Forth") had been his own mother, Louisa Van Velsor, here suddenly assumes mythical proportions. The Whitmanesque Mother-worship, in which America, the earth, night, and then the sea are in turn the great mother, here first sounds the minor chord as a prelude to "Out of the Cradle." Also the purely mystical characteristics of "Song of Myself" are repeated in "The Sleepers." The poem begins in a trance, an ecstasy, here indicated by the oriental imagery of a dancer and his dance, an image that often recurs in pantheistic poetry.

I am a dance [*sic*] . . . . Play up there! the fit is whirling me fast,[42]

I am the ever-laughing . . . . it is new moon and twilight.

Viewed as a unit, this first edition of *Leaves of Grass* is a powerful and astonishing poetic achievement. On first reading the poems we feel their originality and overwhelming forceful-ness. A note of buoyancy and arrogance is dominant, in spite of the passages in which we can hear hints of different tones to appear in future work. The large new land victoriously makes its appearance in world literature, singing in its own strong, self-confident voice. The famous letter which shortly after the publication, in July, Emerson impulsively sent to the unknown writer now seems the completely natural expression of the effect the book was intended to create in world literature.

Concord, Massachusetts, 21 July, 1855

DEAR SIR—I am not blind to the worth of the wonderful gift of "Leaves of Grass." I find it the most extraordinary piece of wit and wisdom that America has yet contributed. I am very happy in reading it, as great power makes us happy. It meets the demand I am always making of what seemed the sterile and stingy nature, as if too much handiwork, or too much lymph in the temperament, were making our western wits fat and mean.

I give you joy of your free and brave thought. I have great joy in it. I find incomparable things said incomparably well, as they must be. I find the courage of treatment which so delights us, and which large perception only can inspire.

I greet you at the beginning of a great career, which yet must have had a long foreground [N.B.] somewhere, for such a start. I rubbed my eyes a little, to see if this sunbeam were no illusion; but the solid sense of the book is a sober certainty. It has the best merits, namely, of fortifying and encouraging.

I did not know until I last night saw the book advertised in a newspaper that I could trust the name as real and available for a post-office. I wish to see my benefactor, and have felt much like striking my tasks and visiting New York to pay you my respects.

R. W. Emerson.

The impression the book had made on Emerson is plainly evident in every line of this letter. The philosopher in Concord spontaneously felt the connection between his own work and this verse—and with complete clarity recognized its significance. The extreme narrowmindedness and many misgivings of his family and acquaintances were responsible for making him retract little by little until his frank declaration in the letter was gradually displaced by something weaker and less clear, and as Whitman's reputation grew and spread Emerson could bring himself to say and believe, in all seriousness, that Whitman was losing ground. We are indebted to Frank Sanborn, a close friend of Emerson's but also an early and loyal Whitman disciple in hostile Boston, for the report of the pressure Emerson's family, and especially his daughters, exerted to get him to give up his original opinion of *Leaves of Grass*.[43] This is highly indicative of how the first unbiased view of an important man can be swayed by what others think. Bostonians turned whatever criticism they could against Whitman. Emerson's first letter to him was the frankest and most truthful recognition of his work and its significance, and the most forthright, that Whitman received during his lifetime from the recognized intelligentsia of his country. Very interesting is Emerson's perception of "the long foreground" which must necessarily have preceded the writing of such a book.

But Emerson was unique in his momentary clarity of insight and appreciation. There were a few favorable criticisms and a long list of antagonistic ones, especially in the New York *Criterion,* which described the book as "bombast, egotism, vulgarity, obscenity and nonsense." And in the English papers the reaction was the same. The London *Leader* called the work "This strange, grotesque and bewildering book." The London *Critic* called the author a Caliban who, for certain passages in the book, "deserves nothing so richly as the public execution- er's whip." Whittier, like Emerson, had received a copy from the author, but he is said to have thrown it into the fire. And the book did not sell at all. But Whitman's self-confidence and obstinacy were not destroyed by such unexpected results. Within a few months after its appearance he began the practice of writ- ing laudatory reviews of his own work, a practice he continued even in his old age, to the surprise and disgust of his European admirers. A remarkable number of reviews, reprinted in good faith and quoted in Europe by Rudolf Schmidt among others, later proved to be Whitman's own. It required enormous and naïve self-confidence, entirely without scruples, to be able to do that, but Whitman had it; this was all of a piece with the psychology that produced the book. The reasoning which could regard this procedure as legitimate was primarily "American" —that is the only explanation and apology.

The Americanism in *Leaves of Grass* is exactly what Whit- man emphasized in three notorious accounts of himself that appeared in the autumn of 1855, one in Fowler and Wells's *Phrenological Journal*, another in the Brooklyn *Times*,[44] and the third in *The United States and Democratic Review*, in which Whitman gave the report the following grandiose head- ing: "An American Bard at Last!"

There was a sincere fervor in Whitman's advertisement of himself and his work. His self-confidence was so great that the limited sales did not depress him at all. He had Emerson's letter and he had visits from people interested in literature to stimu- late and inspire him. Among the visitors were Henry Ward Beecher, Thoreau, Moncure D. Conway, and the prominent English politician and democrat Lord Houghton, whose con- cern with social problems gave him a special interest in Whit- man's poetry. Thoreau's visit is of particular interest. This contemporary American author, whose work had been inspired and called forth by Emerson in much the same way as had Whitman's, went with Bronson Alcott to Brooklyn, impelled only by curiosity to "see the animal," and was unexpectedly fascinated by the poet. Instead of "the New York rowdy" that he expected after reading the poems and notices, he found a clean, wholesome man with great personal charm. "Since I have seen him, I find I am not disturbed by any brag or egoism in his book," Thoreau wrote Harrison Blake.[45] Though in their poetry they had so much in common and in their private lives took the same attitude toward the burning questions of the day, such as Women's Rights and slavery, yet any real intimacy between these two men was unthinkable. Temperamentally they were too far apart. They were both nature lovers, but Thoreau was a recluse, did not believe in democracy, and was by education an esthete, and academician. The oriental quality of Whitman's poetry had first attracted him, and naturally he mentioned the subject during their talk. In reply to a question as to whether he had read the Indian or Persian poets, Whitman answered, "No; tell me about them!" It is from the edition of *Thoreau's Familiar Letters,* edited by Harrison Blake,[46] that we know the exact details of their meeting. Two of Thoreau's letters in this book were about Whitman. The most important passages have been quoted by Bliss Perry: "We ought to rejoice greatly in him. He occasionally suggests something a little more than human." Of all the Bostonians, Thoreau was, perhaps, the one who understood Whitman best and remained most loyal to him until his death—even in his discussions with Emerson, who jestingly referred to *Leaves of Grass* as "a mixture of Bhagavad-Gita and the New York Herald." [47]

Still another of the early visitors deserves notice, the young intellectual and literary-minded minister, Moncure D. Conway, whom Emerson sent to Whitman. He visited Whitman in September, 1855. His account of the visit, first published eleven years later in the *Fortnightly Review* for October, 1866, has in the course of time been accepted as the basis for the standard description of Whitman's appearance at that time. In Scandinavia it was quoted at length by Rudolf Schmidt, and some details in it have obviously been used by both Knut Hamsun and Johannes V. Jensen. Conway, who throughout his life was one of Whitman's loyal champions, found him on this first visit lying on his back on the beach "in the place where he preferred to compose his poems." They went swimming together and later took a long walk through Brooklyn and rode the ferry to New York. On the ferry and buses Conway noted the familiar and friendly intercourse between Whitman and the common people, who, further investigation revealed, had no suspicion that Whitman was a "poet" or that he had published a book. Also in Whitman's room he saw notes and rough drafts of a new edition lying about.

For Whitman now devoted himself exclusively to a new and larger edition of *Leaves of Grass*, which would finally and decisively crush all opposition. He had entirely given up all other occupations in order to concentrate on writing, and exactly a year after the first edition he placed with Fowler and Wells the second edition, this time a thick volume of 384 pages, with nineteen new poems added to the original twelve. The poems in this book had titles for the first time, long inconvenient titles, all containing the word "poem": "Poem of the Heart of the Son of Manhattan Island," "Liberty Poem for Asia, Africa, Europe, America, Australia, Cuba [!], and the Archipelagoes of the Sea," "Poem of the Daily Workmen and Workwomen of These United States," and so forth, and so forth. Under the later titles there were the following new poems, many of them among Whitman's most famous work: "Salut au Monde," "Song of the Open Road," "Song of the Broad-Axe," "Song of the Rolling Earth," "Crossing Brooklyn Ferry," "Unfolded out of the Folds," "This Compost," "To You," "On the Beach at Night Alone," "Excelsior," "Assurances," "To a Foil'd European Revolutionaire," "Miracles," "Respondez," "Mannahatta's Streets I Saunter'd," "Poets to Come," and two later included in the *Children of Adam* group, "Spontaneous Me," and "A Woman Waits for Me," and the first poetic version of the 1855 Preface, here called "Poem of the Many in One." The engraving of the poet from the first edition was retained, and on the back-strip was printed in gold letters a sentence from Emerson's letter: "I greet you at the beginning of a great career, R. W. Emerson." [48]

THE SECOND EDITION

We shall now consider a powerful and significant expansion of the collection. The melody is played by the full orchestra, whereas, especially in "Song of Myself," it was only warbled and "played on a shepherd's flute." In "Poem of Salutation" ("Salut au Monde") the growth is absolutely overwhelming. The poet's "I" has expanded to embrace the whole earth.

> Within me latitude widens, longitude lengthens.

Within the poet are cities, lakes, mountains and rivers; within him are railroad lines over the continent and the strange web of electric telegraph wires covering the globe! The first tentative "Whoever you are" of the earlier edition has now reached the utmost boundary where practically all the inhabitants are named and greeted from

> You Norwegian! Swede! Dane! Icelander! you Prussian!
> You Spaniard of Spain! you Portuguese!
> You Frenchwoman and Frenchman of France!   Section 11.

to

> You Hottentot with clicking palate!   Section 12.

> Each of us inevitable,
> Each of us limitless— . . .
>
> .   .   .
>
> Each of us here as divinely as any is here.

Whereas in "Song of Myself" the poet sang lyrically:

> In vessels that sail my words must sail . . .   Section 47.

the words are more violent and more majestic in "Salut au Monde" (the first title of which was "Poem of Salutation"):

> I think I have risen with you, you vapors, and moved away to distant continents, and fallen down there, for reasons,
> I think I have blown with you, you winds,
> I think, you waters, I have fingered every shore with you,
> I think I have run through what any river or strait of the globe has run through,
> I think I have taken my stand on the bases of peninsulas, and on imbedded rocks.

What cities the light or warmth penetrates, I penetrate those cities
    myself,
All islands to which birds wing their way, I wing my way myself.
                                                        Section 13.

In "Crossing Brooklyn Ferry" (originally "The Sun-Down
Poem") Whitman developed a theme Bryant had also used in
his "Flood of Years." Its wild emotional intensity affected Thoreau more than did any other poem in *Leaves of Grass.* Here
Whitman spoke for the first time to future generations, who
could look back to him because he had looked forward to them.
And he continued the magic of personal conversation with which
he had experimented earlier, in "Song of Myself."

Typical of the latter is also the "Poem of You, Whoever You
Are," in which the reader is identified with the one of whom the
poet is thinking.

Whoever you are, now I place my hand upon you, that you be my
    poem,
I whisper with my lips close to your ear,
I have loved many women and men, but I love none better than you.

In "Poem of the Road" ("Song of the Open Road") the
wander motif has developed into a powerful, swelling composition of traveling through natural scenes, then of journeying
through time and space. The poet tells humanity to think of
"the universe itself as a road, as many roads—as roads for travelling souls." As in "Song of Myself" here he "beat the gong of
revolt"; now his call is "The cry of battle." Those who would
be his companions must leave everything for the open road.

Mon enfant! I give you my hand!
I give you my love, more precious than money,
I give you myself, before preaching or law;
Will you give me yourself? Will you come travel with me?
Shall we stick by each other as long as we live?   Section 15.

In the "Poem of the Road" Whitman first uses the word
"adhesiveness" to designate the love between men for which he
himself was such a perfect medium.

Here is adhesiveness . . .
Do you know what it is as you pass to be loved by strangers?
                                                        Section 6.

And then he gives a vivid description of his own emotions.

Why are there men and women that while they are nigh me the
    sun-light expands my blood?
Why when they leave me do my pennants of joy sink flat and lank?
Why are there trees I never walk under but large and melodious
    thoughts descend upon me?
(I think they hang there winter and summer on those trees, and
    always drop fruit as I pass;). . .

The phrases of this second edition are often consciously mystical in a sort of modern Biblical style. It was always difficult for Whitman to find a word for his own peculiar affection, and in "Poem of the Road" he tried out "efflux of the soul" (Section 7), which he repeats so frequently that it acquires a certain significance. In "Poem of the Sayers of the Words of the Earth" ("Song of the Rolling Earth") the symbolic wording is completely characteristic of Whitman: every phrase is intentionally vague. He refers to the earth as the old mother with unfailing words who sits day and night with a mirror in her hand "inviting none, denying none," while the four and twenty [hours] appear each day and the three hundred and sixty-five tread their dance around the sun.

Looking from no countenances of their own, but from the countenances of those who are with them,
From the countenances of children or women, or the manly
    countenance,
From the open countenances of animals, from inanimate things,
From the landscape or waters, or from the exquisite apparition
    of the sky,
From our own countenances, mine and yours, faithfully returning
    them.

Because of the strident conflicts and contrasts in his own soul in "Crossing Brooklyn Ferry," he seeks new and bold expressions.

I too knitted the old knot of contrariety,

he says of himself. Like the romantic mystics Novalis and Hoffmann, and the more recent mystic Hermann Hesse, he finds various characteristics of the animal kingdom in himself.

The wolf, the snake, the hog, not wanting in me, . . .

But he feels that the identity which he gets through his body takes up and unites all these contradictions and potentialities in itself.

The mystic "I" is far more dominant in this second edition than in any later editions. In "Song of Myself" (Section 45) Whitman praised the various ages of man in their succession as equally honorable. Here, in "Poem of the Road," it becomes a bold identification of all ages simultaneously in one person. The followers of the poet on the great journey are "swift and majestic men! they are the greatest women!" And he continues:

Committers of crimes, committers of many beautiful virtues,

.   .   .

Journeyers over consecutive seasons, over the years—the curious
    years, each emerging from that which preceded it,
Journeyers as with companions, namely, their own diverse phases,
Forth-steppers from the latent unrealized baby-days,
Journeyers gaily with their own youth—journeyers with their
    bearded and well-grained manhood,

.   .   .

Journeyers with their sublime old age of manhood or womanhood.

The picture is both baroque and sublime; I know of only one comparable passage in world literature, and that is by the noteworthy German romanticist, Leopold Schefer, whose *Laienbrevier*, 1834, a German pantheistic "Bible" much like *Leaves of Grass* in America, asserts that man is only complete when all ages are united in one whole.[49] The confidence and assurance that permeates Whitman's lyricism is entirely unrestrained in this edition of *Leaves of Grass*. The grandioseness and aggressiveness, which so many people find disgusting, appear primarily, in fact almost exclusively, in the poems written in this year. The prophet Walt Whitman reached a climax in "Poem of Salutation" and "Poem of the Road." He is the founder of a religion and is filled with a divine arrogance. The official priests who were mentioned somewhat tolerantly in "Song of Myself" ("I do not despise you, priests," and so forth, Section 43) are now deserted in the mighty crescendo of the Open Road and left scornfully behind.

Allons! From all formulas!
From your formulas, O bat-eyed and materialistic priests!

Instead, Biblical phraseology and imagery are used to present Whitman's new pantheistic religion. In "Song of Myself" he had a short passage about the body as manure for new bodies. Here in this second edition appears the famous poem, "Poem of Wonder at the Resurrection of Wheat" (later "This Compost").

It grows such sweet things out of such corruptions, . . .

The grave and manure are for Whitman heathen and natural images of the resurrection.

Yet Behold!

. . .

The bean bursts noiselessly through the mould in the garden, . . .
The resurrection of the wheat appears with pale visage out of its
    graves, . . .

To the Puritans this was blasphemy. But the poem is both powerful and delicate. The alliteration and refinement in style, which had already begun in this second edition, is interesting. Now, more than in the first edition, there is reason to mention rhythm, certainly in the great "Broad-Axe Poem" ("Song of the Broad-Axe"). This poem is chiefly a catalogue and association of ideas, all associations being based on the word axe, from the wood-cutter's, the carpenter's, and the fireman's, to the modern executioner's axe and the battle axe of the knight. But the introduction is a musical piece of prose-verse in trochaic meter.

Broad-axe, shapely, naked, wan!
Head from the mother's bowels drawn!
Wooded flesh and metal bone! limb only one and lip only one!
Gray-blue leaf by red-heat grown! helve produced from a little
    seed sown!
Resting the grass amid and upon,
To be leaned, and to lean on.

In these lines we can almost hear the harsh music of the axe stroke. That was a new note in Whitman's verse. But in this collection, for the last time, the catalogue breaks out, luxuriant and dominating. Full of repetitions are: "Poem of Salutation," "Broad-Axe Poem," and "Poem of You, Whoever You Are," and even the sexual program poem, "Poem of Procreation" (later "A Woman Waits for Me").

Sex contains all,
Bodies, souls, meanings, proofs, purities, delicacies, results, pro-
    mulgations,
Songs, commands, health, pride, the maternal mystery, the semitic
    milk,
All hopes, benefactions, bestowals, etc.

One poem seems to herald the new attitude of the later edi-tions: "Poem of the Proposition of Nakedness," later called "Respondez," in which Whitman ironically gives vent to his dissatisfaction with the state of politics in the fifties. This poem is a sort of negation of "The Sleepers." Everything good reach-ing fulfillment, in the latter poem, fails and is destroyed in the former; everything which is united in the one is separated in the other.

Let books take the place of trees, animals, rivers, clouds!

But Whitman sensed the conflict between this poem and the whole tone of his book, and in the final edition he split it into two meaningless fragments, with the titles "Reversals" and "Transpositions"—two typical examples of what can happen when a poet outgrows his verse or comes into conflict with his own program.

Otherwise this edition expresses only overwhelming joy, strength, arrogance.

And who has made hymns fit for the earth? For I am mad with
    devouring ecstasy to make joyous hymns for the whole earth!
                    ("Poem of the Heart of the Son of Man-
                    hattan Island," afterwards "Excelsior.")

Confidence can be strengthened by repetition. The "Faith Poem" ("Assurances") is like a series of corroborations of what we already know from reading other poems. And "Poem of Procreation" is a decidedly dull and programmatic repeti-tion of what had been said more effectively in "Song of My-self." But there is also Whitman's sex program, which is pre-

sented without comment in "Poem of Many in One" ("By Blue
Ontario's Shore").

I swear I have had enough of mean and impotent modes of ex-
    pressing love for men and women,
After this day I take my own modes of expressing love for men
    and women.

The soberness of the expression is in contrast to its unparalleled boldness, as in "Poem of Procreation":

I pour the stuff to start sons and daughters fit for These States—
    I press with slow rude muscle,

.   .   .

Through you I drain the pent-up rivers of myself,

.   .   .

The drops I distil upon you are drops of fierce and athletic girls,
    and of new artists, musicians, singers.

Poetically this is just so much repetition. But in the "Bunch
Poem" ("Spontaneous Me") it is possible to trace development.
This is probably Whitman's most inspired erotic poem, and
naturally it later became the chief poem in *Children of Adam.*
In much of Whitman's erotic poetry it is impossible not to notice an exaggerated expression probably resulting from a too-
conscious straining for effect. Yet there are some poems in this
group indisputably among his most outstanding lyric pro-
ductions, especially those in which his pantheistic and erotic
emotions are fused, as in the "Bunch Poem," where his own
personally confused and shy eroticism finds expression in single
lines of convincing sincerity and simplicity. Certain passages
of "Song of Myself" must be mentioned along with the "Bunch
Poem" as offering the most significant specimens of Whitman's
erotic lyricism. Nature in spring and harvest, grass, birds, trees,
apples, the damp fragrance of woods in early morning, falling
leaves, to the poet all these are the poetry of love.

Beautiful dripping fragments—the negligent list of one after
    another, as I happen to call them to me, or think of them,
The real poems, (what we call poems being merely pictures,)
The poems of the privacy of the night, and of men like me.

This changes to pathos in the imagery of the wild bee that finds satisfaction on the lady flower, "curves upon her with amorous firm legs," or in the final variation of the recurring image of the sea as the powerful violent lover of the poet.

The souse upon me of my lover the sea, as I lie willing and naked.

We recall the emotion of Section 28 of "Song of Myself" when he again speaks of "The curious roamer, the hand, roaming all over the body" and "the irritable tide that will not be at rest." The auto-erotic feeling is not to be mistaken, but the specific erotic expression does not intrude on the reader in this remarkable and suggestive poem. Instead, it is a poem of the erotic emotion in general, unisexual and polysexual—unique in the lyricism of world literature. It is part of Whitman's talent to reveal for us even the feeling of erotic submission. In his introduction to the 1919 translation, Johannes V. Jensen expressed it thus:

[In Whitman's poetry we have] the key to the feminine emotion itself, which it is not possible otherwise to look into. Women cannot and will not go into it, and those who have done it have not been real women. Whitman's erotic confession sounds as if it came from an instrument tuned in the womanly key; like a girl's, his soul is just beneath the skin, everywhere and nowhere, he is vasomotorly prompted whether in the bath or before the fire; like women he feels the tension in all sorts of places. Beauty is present, as always when we meet femininity, so long as you forget while you read that it was a big bearded, lubberly fellow who wrote it.[50]

In his book Whitman includes the whole world in his great emotion. "Here is the profound lesson of reception," he exclaims in the "Poem of the Road," and he does not doubt that everyone will accept him as he accepts them.

To gather the minds of men out of their brains as you encounter them! to gather the love out of their hearts!

This is a new variation of "Song of Myself," Section 45, and the *Calamus* and *Children of Adam* motifs ring out as clearly as a Wagnerian *leit-motif*. The poet calls a meeting. The new community, the new democracy, is made up of the comrades and wanderers he has gathered about him.

The place where the greatest city stands is not the place of
stretched wharves, docks, manufactures, deposits of produce,

. . .

Nor the place of the best libraries and schools, nor the place where
money is plentiest,

. . .

Where the city of the faithfulest friends stands,
Where the city of the cleanliness of the sexes stands,
Where the city of the healthiest fathers stands,
Where the city of the best-bodied mothers stands,
There the greatest city stands.   "Broad-Axe Poem."

That is a bold proclamation. It is the race he inaugurates,
the race whose representative he professes to be. He is the beginning and the salvation. The poetic gist of the second edition
of *Leaves of Grass*, 1856, is in Section 6 of the "Broad-Axe
Poem."

All waits, or goes by default, till a strong being appears;
A strong being is the proof of the race, and of the ability of the
universe, . . .

That Whitman regarded himself as this strong being is
amply confirmed in the notorious letter to Emerson which he
printed in an appendix to the new edition in answer to Emerson's
letter to him. In it Whitman assured Emerson of the debt he
felt he owed him. "Those shores you found. I say you have led
The States there—have led Me there." And in the following
high-flown words he declared:

The first edition, on which you mailed me that till now unanswered
letter, was twelve poems—I printed a thousand copies, and they
readily sold; these thirty-two Poems I stereotype, to print several
thousand copies of. I much enjoy making poems . . . the work of
my life is making poems. I keep on till I make a hundred, and then
several hundred—perhaps a thousand. The way is clear to me. A
few years, and the average annual call for my Poems is ten or
twenty thousand copies—more, quite likely. Why should I hurry
or compromise? In poems or in speeches I say the word or two that
has got to be said, . . . Master I am a man who has perfect faith.

That is a brief prose epitomization of the spirit of *Leaves of Grass* in its earlier stages, and can be inspiring or infuriating, depending entirely on the individual reaction to the book. But in this optimism there is confidence and assurance that commands admiration.

The effect of the second edition on contemporary readers was repelling, mainly, of course, because of the new sex poems, whose meaning was only too clear. The critics kept coldly aloof, and even Thoreau, in what was otherwise an approving letter, wrote to Harrison Blake that in these poems

He does not celebrate love at all. It is as if the beasts spoke.[51]

Fowler and Wells were so horrified that they refused to handle the book, and Emerson's reaction when he received the new volume with his comment about the older edition blazoned on the back-strip we have from an eyewitness, Josiah Quincy, whom Bliss Perry has quoted.

Mr. Emerson came into his study at Concord where I was sitting, bearing in his hand a book which he had just received. This was the new edition of Whitman's book with the words "I greet you at the beginning of a great career. R. W. Emerson," printed in gold letters upon the cover. Emerson looked troubled, and expressed annoyance that a sentence from a private letter should be wrenched from its context and so emblazoned. . . I noted the incident because at no other time had I seen a cloud of dissatisfaction darken that serene countenance.[52]

In *The Conservator*, May, 1897, F. B. Sanborn recorded that Ellery Channing visited Emerson on the day he received the second edition of *Leaves of Grass* and that he "never saw Emerson so angry in his life."

"The proof of a poet is that his country absorbs him as affectionately as he has absorbed it," thus had Whitman concluded the 1855 Preface. The irony is cruel and devastating. Whitman deleted this line from later versions of the Preface, and in the passage of "By Blue Ontario's Shore" which corresponded to it he added the words "in the long run." [53] The disappointment at not finding the audience for which he had hoped must have been crushing. As usual he got no sympathy from his family. There are two frequently quoted remarks by

George Whitman which show that neither his mother nor his brothers and his sisters regarded Walt's poetry as anything except nonsense: "I saw the book—didn't read it at all—didn't think it worth reading—fingered it a little. Mother thought as I did—did not know what to make of it . . . I remember mother comparing *Hiawatha* to Walt's, and the one seemed to us pretty much the same muddle as the other." [54] He had failed to reach those he had hoped would listen. His book did not sell; indeed, who would buy it? He had written:

The young mechanic is closest to me, he knows me pretty well,
The wood-man that takes his axe and jug with him, shall take me
    with him all day,
The farm-boy ploughing in the field feels good at the sound of my
    voice . . .   Section 47 of "Song of Myself."

—but the words turned ironically against him, because Whitman as a poet never managed to get on speaking terms with the common people to whom primarily he wanted to address himself. "Wherefore is there no response?" "In poems or in *speeches* I say the word that has got to be said," he had written Emerson. It is only natural, then, that after his failure as a poet the idea of becoming an orator occupied him. All his plans and drafts for addresses and lectures, of which Furness has preserved a part, date from the period just after the fiasco of the second edition. Then, for the first time, he heard the two lecturers whom in his old age he mentioned as having been particularly inspiring. They were Theodore Parker and Father Taylor. Just at that time Melville made a lecture tour of the United States, and the increasing political confusion and unrest of the period would have been favorable for a folk orator and preacher like Whitman with his opinions. But for one reason or another the ambition never amounted to anything. The most probable explanation is that in reality Whitman had no ability as a speaker, that his voice was weak and thin. This seems to have been the almost unanimous opinion of friends and enemies, and contrasted strangely with his majestic appearance. And as to his lectures, Bliss Perry relates that his friends O'Connor and Swinton jokingly teased him about his mannerisms when declaiming.[55]

Whitman was a poet and that was his destiny. "The work

of my life is making poems!" But the next edition of *Leaves of Grass* did not appear until 1860. What did he do? What was happening in those four years? *In contrast to all the earlier biographers I consider these years the most important in Whitman's life because of the immense and major change in the spirit of the new poems in 1860.* Something developed or something was defeated—exactly what we do not know, because Whitman never discussed it, but from the result we can surmise a crisis of momentous significance, the real crisis of Whitman's life.

Biographical information is almost nonexistent. Whitman himself destroyed *everything*—a fact which is in itself significant. And the notebooks which run in unbroken succession from 1847 to this period, have been removed and possibly burned for the years between 1855 and 1859. We know that between 1857 and 1859 he had an editorial job, his last, with the Brooklyn *Times*, and in Holloway's *Uncollected Poetry and Prose* we find from this period a few articles on prostitution, the courts, and Dickens, whose unhappy domestic situation Whitman described with a sympathy in which Holloway traces "the unmistakable note of personal experience, even though we cannot know the details of that private pain." [56] During these years he frequented Pfaff's German Restaurant and was associated with journalists, poets, loafers, and Bohemians. At one time he, among others, belonged to the circle around the famous Ada Clare, "The Queen of Bohemia," a highly gifted woman who had a little son [illegitimate], and had really achieved for herself "the emancipation of woman." She probably made somewhat the same impression on Whitman that Margaret Fuller had made ten years earlier. He saw in her the type of "a New Woman born too soon." [57] But otherwise the milieu does not sound attractive, in spite of the legends which sprang up in the course of time (as they always do about that sort of setting). Emerson's remark "I had great hopes of Whitman until he became a Bohemian" [58] refers to these years of defeat and ruin, when it was an accepted fact that anyone who wanted to see Whitman would find him at Pfaff's. Young William Dean Howells, who was collecting material for a realistic picture of American everyday life, looked there for Whitman and found him

presiding at one end of a large table, surrounded by a group
of highly disreputable characters. Whitman apostles have since
tried unsuccessfully to protest against the reports that he led
a "wild life" during these years—although the meaning of the
term "wild life" is naturally always changing. But we have a
portrait, a full-figure photograph (taken in 1859), which was
reproduced by Henry Bryan Binns with the following comment: "The pose . . . is unstudied and a little awkward; one
cannot help feeling that the man ought to loaf a little less. The
head is magnificent but the knees are a little loose." [59] And
in *Uncollected Poetry and Prose* [60] Holloway reproduced a drawing Whitman made of himself one day at Pfaff's, with a red
nose and accompanied by some enigmatical phallic additions.
Holloway himself makes no comment, but it gives a tragic impression of dissolution and decay. Is it farfetched to connect
this entirely new attitude of Whitman's, who before 1855 "never
smoked and seldom drank," with the fiasco of 1856, and even
more with a disturbed and unhappy private life? We have heard
of such things before. I suspect that at this time Whitman drifted
aimlessly, perhaps would never have reformed if the Civil War
had not begun and given him a new field of activity, a new
atmosphere, where new horizons opened for him. The life at
Pfaff's ended suddenly one day in 1861, just after the outbreak
of the war, when one of the group stood up and proposed a toast
to the Southern cause (a great many New Yorkers were on the
side of the South). Whitman abruptly got up and left, not to
return for twenty years. In connection with this dramatic conclusion of a period of confusion and despair, it is impossible
not to think of the famous fragment from the notebook dated
April 16, 1861, three days after war was declared.

*I have this day, this hour, resolved to inaugurate for myself a pure,
perfect, sweet, clean-blooded robust body, by ignoring all drinks
but water and pure milk, and all fat meats, late suppers—a great
body, a purged, cleansed, spiritualized, invigorated body.*[61]

In this I can see only a frank admission, and proof for us, that
he had been sinking downward and resolved again to seek the
"Open Road."

If there is any period in Whitman's life to which the heading "Romance" can be applied, as most biographers have continually tried to do for the relatively insignificant New Orleans period, it must be the years between the second and third editions of *Leaves of Grass,* during which Whitman had a love affair, the details of which we shall never know, a defeat, the mark of which we can clearly see in the 1860 edition, and the results of which were his dissolute and disgraceful saloon life, which lasted until the outbreak of the war in April, 1861.

We know that immediately after the fiasco of 1856 Whitman was definitely continuing work on the expansion and revision of his book. On one page of a notebook Holloway found this memorandum: "The Great Construction of the New Bible. Not to be diverted from the principal object—the main life—the three hundred and sixty-five.—It ought to be ready in 1859." [62] The book was certainly the anchor of his existence, even though it took a year longer than expected. When the notebooks again take up the subject of the third edition, we immediately find a sketch in which Whitman sought to characterize and orient the new form of *Leaves of Grass.*[63] His "new Bible" was to supersede Plato and Jesus (!) :

now a third religion I give . . . . I include the antique *two* . . . .
I include the divine Jew, and the Greek sage. . . More still—
that which is not conscience, but against it—that which is not the
Soul, I include. These, whatever exist, I include—I surround all,
and dare not make a single exception.

But already there is a trace of the *new tone.* What is that "which is not the soul"? There was nothing which was not the soul in the first two editions. The expression refers to one of Whitman's most ambiguous ideas, the evil principle, negation.

I am the poet . . .
And am not the poet of goodness only—I do not decline to be the
    poet of wickedness also.

This idea from Section 22 of "Song of Myself," comes out strongly in the third edition and harmonizes with the events of a private nature which form the background for all the new poems added in this edition.

That there had been a change in the grandiloquent, conquering, primitive but charming "rowdy" of the 1855 portrait is
obvious in the two great poems published before the edition appeared: "A Child's Reminiscence" (later "Out of the Cradle
Endlessly Rocking"), in the New York *Saturday Press* on
December 24, 1859, and "Bardic Symbols" later "As I Ebb'd
with the Ocean of Life"), in the *Atlantic Monthly*, April, 1860.
Both poems have the sea as somber motif.

"Out of the Cradle Endlessly Rocking" is justifiably one of
Whitman's most admired poems for its beautiful theme and
musical form no less than for the human note of sorrow and
grief which is so truly and intimately felt in it. The simple
story [64] is a supposed childish memory of the Paumanok coast,
two birds "from Alabama" which nest at the edge of the beach
and which the boy watched until one day the she-bird was gone
("May-be killed, unknown to her mate,") and the he-bird was
left alone.

> And thenceforward, all summer, in the sound of the sea,
> And at night, under the full of the moon, in calmer weather,
> Over the hoarse surging of the sea,
> Or flitting from brier to brier by day,
> I saw, I heard at intervals, the remaining one, the he-bird,
> The solitary guest from Alabama.

In a marvellous way the child understood what the bird sang:
"The rest might not—but I have treasured every note," and
now the poet produces the song of "Two together," as if he
himself were the lonely bird.

Whitman's often-used erotic motif of the eternal embrace and
union of the sea and the waves here suddenly becomes a tragic
motif. The crooked beckoning fingers which in "Song of Myself" were so provocative and irresistible now become helpless
white arms "out in the breakers tirelessly tossing," while the
sad whisper of the surf-beat is reproduced in the rhythm.

Soothe! Soothe!
Close on its wave soothes the wave behind,
And again another behind, embracing and lapping, every one close,
But my love soothes not me.

The lament mounts and mounts.

O throat!
Sound clearer through the atmosphere!
Pierce the woods, the earth,
Somewhere listening to catch you must be the one I want.

Shake out, carols!
Solitary here—the night's carols!
Carols of lonesome love! Death's carols!
Carols under that lagging, yellow, waning moon!
O, under that moon, where she droops almost down into the sea!
O reckless, despairing carols.

Could that be regarded as anything except a personal outcry of Whitman? In any case he never attained a greater degree of lyrical warmth and concentration. The bird's song ends with a hopeless:

> *Loved—but no more with me,*
> *We two together no more.*

And in conclusion the famous and grand apostrophe to the sea, "the fierce old mother incessantly moaning," in Whitman's peculiarly mystic style, and once more a hint of the Hegelian Triad is graphically introduced.

The colloquy there—the trio—each uttering,
The undertone—the savage old mother, incessantly crying,
To the boy's Soul's questions sullenly timing—some drowned
    secret hissing,
To the outsetting bard of love.

All his poetry has its source in this old experience.

Now that I have heard you,

        .   .   .

And already a thousand singers—a thousand songs, clearer,
    louder, more sorrowful than yours,
A thousand warbling echoes have started to life within me,
Never to die.

        .   .   .

O you demon, singing by yourself—projecting me,
  . . never more shall I cease imitating, perpetuating you,

. . .

Never more the cries of unsatisfied love be absent from me,
Never again leave me to be the peaceful child I was before . . .

And in the night on the shore he begs the wild old mother for the word which will be a clue to "the destiny of me."

The word final, superior to all,

. . .

Answering, the sea,
Delaying not, hurrying not,
Whispered me through the night, and very plainly before day-
    break,
Lisped to me constantly the low and delicious word DEATH,
And again Death—ever Death, Death, Death,
Hissing melodious, neither like the bird, nor like my aroused child's
    heart,
But edging near, as privately for me, rustling at my feet,
And creeping thence steadily up to my ears,
Death, Death, Death, Death, Death.

The unspoken word, "the word" which Whitman sought so zealously and so arrogantly in Section 50 of "Song of Myself" and of which he said:

It is not chaos or death—it is form, union, plan—it is eternal life—
    it is HAPPINESS.

—that word Whitman found in the years between 1856 and 1860, and it was both death [65] and chaos—but primarily death.

The whole change, the complete reversal, of Whitman's tone is obvious. *But all the earlier biographers have only touched very negligently on this change.* Holloway was the first to consider it, but remarks half indifferently: "Had his lover died? Surely some lover had died and he could find solace only in song." [66] Without a doubt it refers to an experience of the most personal kind. It is evident in all the minute textual changes Whitman later undertook with the final edition in mind, and in the fact that he tried to conceal it. The real theme of the poem is the simple "Two Together," which was emphasized in the first

strophe of the bird's song, and which in the first version in the
Saturday Press, as later in the 1860 edition, was not limited to
the bird's song but also referred to the poet's sympathy with and
participation in it. Instead of the abstract conclusion of the
present text:

> Which I do not forget,
> But fuse the song of my dusky demon and brother,

in 1859 and 1860 it read:

> Which I do not forget,
> But fuse the song of two together,

with the words "two together" italicized in the 1859 text, showing that it was *the theme* and that he sang it for the same reason.
Whitman wanted to expand the motif of the poem from the
simple, personal one of having lost someone he loved to mean all
separation and death. Hitherto no attention has been paid to
this, although it is of the utmost importance in Whitman's organization of the whole book. The italicizing of the theme in
the last lines of the first text shows how individual and personal
it had originally been to him, and the alteration is indicative
that his "caution," his prudence (which phrenologists put at 7),
asserted itself lest the poem should be felt as too personal. Exactly the same effect results from two other minor changes in
the text: an unimportant one in the bird's first joyous song,
where "If we two but keep together," which was characteristic
of Whitman's mood in 1860, became a neutral "While we two
keep together," and finally a very significant revision in the section at the beginning of the bird's lament. The boy glided down
in the evening darkness while the white arms tossed tirelessly
out in the breakers, imprinting the song of lamentation on his
mind. In the *Saturday Press,* and only there, this read:

> *Which I now too sing, repeating, translating the notes,*
> Following you my brother.[67]

But in *Leaves of Grass* it was changed to

> Listened, to keep, to sing—now translating the notes,
> Following you, my brother.

Here the idea of following his brother is stripped of its original significance, which was that he did it because he himself was in the same situation, whereas the final version says no more than that he, as a poet, *repeats and translates* the bird's song. Even that has so far passed unnoticed.

As a result of the way in which it is handled, the sorrowful, painful motif in this poem leaves an impression with the reader of emancipation and hope, but the impression left by the other of the two great night poems of the Paumanok shore, in which the wild old mother plays the chief role, is entirely gloomy and depressing. In "Bardic Symbols," "Elemental Drift," or "As I Ebb'd with the Ocean of Life," as its three different titles have read,[68] the poet walked on the shore one autumn afternoon

> . . . where the sea-ripples wash you, Paumanok,
> Where they rustle up, hoarse and sibilant.

The mother motif from the earlier poem rings out suddenly, not sorrowful and moody as before, but dark and despairing. He no longer walks where an old mother quietly rocks her cradle, but where "the fierce old mother endlessly cries for her castaways." And as he looks at the wreckage and driftwood on the shore the poet feels like a wrecked ship himself—or even worse.

> As I wend the shores I know not,
> As I listen to the dirge, the voices of men and women wrecked,
> As I inhale the impalpable breezes that set in upon me,
> As the ocean so mysterious rolls toward me closer and closer,
> At once I find, the least thing that belongs to me, or that I see or
>   touch, I know not;
> I, too, but signify, at the utmost, a little washed-up drift,
> A few sands and dead leaves to gather,
> Gather, and merge myself as part of the sands and drift.

> O baffled, balked,
> Bent to the very earth, here preceding what follows,
> Oppressed with myself that I have dared to open my mouth,
> Aware now, that, amid all the blab whose echoes recoil upon me,
>   I have not once had the least idea who or what I am, [N.B.]
> But that before all my insolent poems the real ME still stands un-
>   touched, untold, altogether unreached,

Withdrawn far, mocking me with mock-congratulatory signs and
    bows,
With peals of distant ironical laughter at every word I have written
    or shall write,
Striking me with insults till I fall helpless upon the sand.

The tone is disconsolate. Not only is he disgusted by his
writing, but the whole of *Leaves of Grass* has become "a few
sands and dead leaves" fleeting like sand, because not once has
he been able fully to express himself in his poetry. The motif
from Section 4 of "Song of Myself" with the "I," "the Me Myself" who stood beside the poet "looking with side-curved head,
both in and out of the game," has here become a nihilistic criticism without any consoling moments. "The real ME" he has not
been even remotely successful in putting into his book.

Toward the end of the poem is the memorable and affecting
apostrophe to the father, figuratively called Paumanok (if the
sea was his mother then the island was his father), but there
is clearly an undertone of personal application to his real father,
with whom, for the first and only time he feels a kinship in this
moment of shipwreck.

> I throw myself upon your breast, my father,
> I cling to you so that you cannot unloose me,
> I hold you so firm, till you answer me something.

The poem closes with a prayer to the wild old mother, who
grieves over her lost children, not to deny him or his—the image
is ambiguous. Does he mean himself and those like him, or does
he mean himself and all his various aspects and qualifications,
"one contradicting another"? Humanity cannot help itself.

Just as much for us that sobbing dirge of Nature,
Just as much, whence we come, that blare of the cloud-trumpets;
We, capricious, brought hither, we know not whence, spread out
    before You, up there, walking or sitting,
Whoever you are—we too lie in drifts at your feet.

The arrogant pantheism of the earlier editions has become a
hopeless pantheism. Whitman makes a wry face at his own proud
hail, "Whoever you are," and unmercifully evokes a cruel contrast to the imagery of seeking him under the boot soles at the

end of "Song of Myself"; he is still there, but no more as the sprouting grass at the reader's feet, now only a chance bit of wreckage thrown up on the shore of existence.[69]

These two poems were the forerunners of the new edition of *Leaves of Grass.* A fact which is very well worth noticing. And it is characteristic that through these poems two of his later most loyal friends were first attracted to him. John Burroughs read "Out of the Cradle" in the *Saturday Press,* and while Whitman was in Boston arranging with Thayer and Eldridge to publish his book he was sought out by the young author William D. O'Connor who was connected with the firm and eager to meet him after having read "As I Ebb'd" in the *Atlantic Monthly.* It was Whitman's first visit to Boston (February–March, 1860). He had naturally immediately looked up Emerson and had the famous talk which he mentions in *Specimen Days* ("Boston Common—More of Emerson"). While they walked up and down Beacon Street in the two-hour-long conversation, Emerson discussed with Whitman the sex poems, which more than anything else separated Whitman from the Bostonians in American intellectual circles. Rather than make Whitman less confident, it is probable that the argument strengthened his determination on this point. His account of it is not without humor.

. . . each point of E.'s statement was unanswerable, no judge's charge ever more complete or convincing, I could never hear the points better put—and then I felt down in my soul the clear and unmistakable conviction to disobey all, and pursue my own way. "What have you to say then to such things?" said E., pausing in conclusion. "Only that while I can't answer them at all, I feel more settled than ever to adhere to my own theory, and exemplify it," was my candid response. Whereupon we went and had a good dinner at the American House.

THIRD EDITION

The new Bible, the third edition of *Leaves of Grass,* with its 456 pages and 122 new poems, appeared in Boston in May, 1860, and sold about 5,000 copies. The old rowdy portrait of the author was replaced by a poor and fatuous "official" portrait, a reproduction of a painting by Charles Hines.[70] This edition is most important because through it Whitman got the attention of his future public. It was the 1860 edition that determined his fame in England and thereby his world renown.[71] The new note, the celebration of the mystic third "which is not the soul," and his disappointment and despair, did not impress his new readers as strongly as it does the literary historian examining the sequence of the editions, because the new poems were scattered through the old, arrogant poems which the ordinary reader naturally regarded as the most characteristic. "Song of Myself" will always dominate every edition of *Leaves of Grass*.

The first poem of the new edition was called "Proto-Leaf," later, in 1867, "Starting from Paumanok," and in all later editions was placed in the book before "Song of Myself." Whitman had found a poetic form for the ideas of the 1855 Preface, and all the new, clearly formulated subject matter of the poet's "proclamation." If one has read the two earlier editions, the poem naturally seems to be repetitious, but if one first meets *Leaves of Grass* in its final form and reads the poem in its place at the very beginning, "Starting from Paumanok" is really the best imaginable introduction and preparation for the collection. Its lyrical soaring and high-pitched eloquence make it one of Whitman's most finished, most rhetorically successful long poems. The words "union," "identity," "libertad," "democracy," "adhesiveness" are presented one after another and commented upon. Short sentences in the poem emphasize the poet's intention. He wants to write for America, to collect all the states, with all their contradictions, into one identity ("I strike up for a new world," Section 1). North and South, man and woman, all shall be united in the great democracy of his poem.

Democracy!

. . .

Ma femme!
For the brood beyond us and of us,

. . .

I, exultant, to be ready for them, will now shake out carols stronger
      and haughtier than have ever yet been heard upon the earth.
                                                    Section 12.

But that is only the beginning:

> O expanding and swift! O henceforth, . . . Section **17**.

There shall be a completely new and spring-fresh world,

> A new race, dominating previous ones, and grander far,

> . . .

> These! these, my voice announcing . . .

That is to be the result and consequence of his book—an exalted program. And in the magnificent culmination he celebrates the *identity* his book is to have. It passes beyond the national boundaries; even the strange and disjoined shall be united and reconciled. This is a combined social and religious proclamation of a religion of the future.

> O I see the following poems are indeed to drop in the earth the germs of a greater Religion.
> [1860 reading of what is now opening line of Section 10.]

In the framework of this poem he has brilliantly succeeded in giving a résumé of the main themes of *Leaves of Grass*. They are all mentioned and all prepared for, so that the poem is almost like a poetic table of contents for the book. That is its function in the collection. There is, for example, the theme of future generations, the "Salut-au-Monde" of Section 6.

> I will trail the whole geography of the globe, and salute courteously every city large and small; . . .

Then the theme of "the poem of evil," the theme of the great highway with the creation mystically described in Section 10, the theme of the bird from Alabama in Section 11, the criminal whose guilt the poet shares in Section 12, "whoever you are," and the question of women's rights in Section 14. It is really an admirable summing up and preparation. Naturally, it emphasizes particularly the two splendid new sections of the book: *Children of Adam* and *Calamus*. Of *Calamus* he says:

> I will sing the song of companionship,

> . . .

> I will write the evangel-poem of comrades and of love,
> (For who but I should understand love, with all its sorrow and joy?
> And who but I should be the poet of comrades?) Section **6**.

And then almost polemically and ironically taking into consideration the conversation with Emerson, the scandalous *Children of Adam* poems are announced.

And I will show of male and female that either is but the equal of
the other,

.   .   .

And sexual organs and acts! do you concentrate in me—For I am
determined to tell you with courageous clear voice, to prove
you illustrious.   Section 12. [Originally in Section 6.]

With this opening poem in 1860 Whitman began for the first time the conscious integration of all the poems in Leaves of Grass *into a unit, which he afterwards continued incessantly to improve until his death.* Thus, this edition is particularly significant. There is something extremely interesting, something humanly moving, in the fact that during those years, when contradictions were pulling and contending within him and he probably found it difficult to "unite them in one person," he strove to overcome all the difficulties in his book. The first title of "By Blue Ontario's Shore" was "Poem of Many in One," one of Whitman's most characteristic titles, and the wording was repeated in "Proto-Leaf" in a passage concluding Section 2, which was afterwards deleted.

Chants inclusive—wide reverberating chants,
Chants of the Many In One.

The great "melange," the great "diversity" has to be settled. The conflicts in his own soul have to be conquered, because they are found in one body as the many poems are collected in one book. A reminder of the personal situation he was in as poet and human being, while in a strain of optimism he prepared his new Bible for publication, is still to be found in the concluding line of Section 1 of "Proto-Leaf."

Solitary, singing in the west, I strike up for a new world.

The emphasis on the word solitary makes us recall the bird in "Out of the Cradle," the solitary guest from Alabama, and this reveals a state of mind in the poet far different from his mood when he wrote the poems of the earlier editions.

The new introductory poem brought order to *Leaves of Grass*. We shall see how the order is revealed in this edition. There is more strength and consistency than we are inclined to believe beforehand. Just as "Proto-Leaf" introduced the collection, "From Pent-up Aching Rivers" similarly introduced the *Enfans d'Adam*. It résuméd the themes of the sections as "Proto-Leaf" summarized the themes of the whole collection. The poem stressed the controversial sex material (again directed at Emerson), and emphasized that the poet wished to celebrate freely the impulses in himself and "the phallus," "That of myself without which I am nothing." The erotic themes enumerated are: the swimmers, the mating of the birds, the lovers-meeting between the sea and the shore ("the mad pushes upon the land"), and finally the two poems, "Native Moments" and "We Two How Long We Were Fool'd." The latter is one of Whitman's finest erotic poems and is forecast in the introductory poem by:

O I wish that you and I escape from the rest, and go utterly off—
    O free and lawless,
Two hawks in the air—two fishes swimming in the sea not more
    lawless than we; . . .

It was highly typical of Whitman's lyricism as a whole to repeat in one poem a whole series of themes instead of celebrating a single one of them. That was what Hamsun mentioned as a fundamental defect in Whitman's poetry. But we see here that it was true only of the first step. *The single catalogue poem or program poem was now placed at the head of a section in which the individual themes were used, and it was employed in a completely artistic way.* Significantly, there is one of the themes of Whitman's sex gospel in the program poem.

Singing . . . the prostitute, who detained me when I went to the
    city,
Singing the song of prostitutes.

When in 1881, with his future reputation in mind, Whitman completed his greatest revision, this was deleted, both because he carefully tried to eliminate the most conspicuous repetitions in the text and probably also because the theme was one of the most controversial in the book.[72] In other respects the program poem frankly proclaims Whitman's whole gospel of erotic emancipation; consideration of the sex question today, he argues, ought to be brought forward (or backward) to the purely Adamic standpoint, a natural state of innocence must again arise. We are all children of Adam. Sex must be freed from the puritanical system of repression and opposition. Thus, the poet now comes to

> Celebrate you, enfans prepared for,
> And you, stalwart loins.

This erotic freedom is one of the most important links in Whitman's whole plan for a "new race" and new democracy, and was later in modern American literature of decisive importance to the anti-puritan authors at the beginning of the century. In this part of his program Whitman was far ahead of his time, but in the 1860 edition it was clearly obvious that it was only a *program*. The new *Children of Adam* poems were too impersonal to be anything but program poetry. The boastful lyric theme in "Song of Myself" of "jetting stuff for bolder more arrogant babies" had become a *social function and plan*, and was celebrated as such. And the three earlier poems, "I Sing the Body Electric," "A Woman Waits for Me," and "Spontaneous Me," fall into this category and must be considered from this point of view. They are not personal expressions—only a program. The Adamic theme is oriented by an unimportant little poem, almost an "Inscription," with which Whitman opens and closes the section. These short poems used as prologue and epilogue, both for individual sections and for the whole collection, are a mannerism of Whitman's. Before "Starting from Paumanok," the introductory poem to the final edition of *Leaves of Grass*, there are no less than twenty-four so-called "Inscriptions," distinct fragments, aphorisms, or epigrams, many of them from his later years. *Children of Adam* was introduced by a little snapshot of Adam followed by Eve (or following her) taking possession of the great paradisical garden of the earth, and the section ends with a still shorter poem in which Adam presents his nakedness before the world (and Whitman his before his readers).

Touch me—touch the palm of your hand to my body as I pass,
Be not afraid of my body.

The *Children of Adam* poems tell us nothing personal about Whitman or about the crisis in his life during these years. The most important of them were not written at that time, but, as the arrangement of the book proceeded, were added in the context of his new doctrine. Far stronger and more vital are the poems in the completely new *Calamus* section of the 1860 edition, the most difficult, the most disputable, and the most misunderstood section of *Leaves of Grass*, but in it we must search for, and can be sure of finding, clues to the understanding of Whitman's unfortunate situation—and his shipwreck.[73] So much has been said, pro and con, as to how much private and personal interpretation can be read into these poems that the general reader is naturally uncertain of the intention of the Calamus poetry. The whole question has been so confused and muddled, not only by the little prophets but also by Whitman himself when, late in life, he became cautious and deleted some of the most personal and most revealing poems, that what on first reading seems clear and obvious must now be closely examined. What should be obvious from the poems themselves will now have to be proved.

Whitman emphasized the section until no one could be in doubt about how personal was the confession that followed. The introductory "Inscription," later called "In Paths Untrodden," followed the custom of the third edition of preparing for the program poem (later entitled "Scented Herbage of My Breast"). The erotic significance is unmistakable. The poet comes forward in the lines:

Escaped . . .
From all the standards hitherto published . . . ,

and wants to explain what is the basic reality in him, what is the secret of his poetry, "for in this secluded spot I can respond as I would not dare elsewhere." [74] And "the secret" is the poet's firm belief in "manly attachment," in "athletic love." Whitman appears in *Calamus*, like Adam in the earlier section

> To tell the secret of my nights and days,
> To celebrate the need of comrades.

The phrase, "The need of comrades," may in this case be regarded only as a parallel to the need for magnificent wives who can bear a new race for a new world, a purely social requisite. That is the social theme in "The Song of the Broad-Axe," in which the greatest city is found.

> Where the city of the faithfulest friends stands,
>
>   .   .   .
>
> Where the city of the healthiest fathers stands,
> Where the city of the best-bodied mothers stands,
> There the greatest city stands.

This has become a democratic program for masculine society. But only in one of the *Calamus* poems is the program emphasized. In No. 5, later called "For You, O Democracy," which contains some undisputably sublime lines:

> I will plant companionship thick as trees along all the rivers of America, and along the shores of the great lakes, and all over the prairies,
> I will make inseparable cities, with their arms about each other's necks.

Otherwise it is impossible to see any "program," much less a social program, in *Calamus*. This is really a collection of love poems, the only ones Whitman wrote. When in 1856 Thoreau justifiably said of the first *Children of Adam* poems, "He does not celebrate love," his comment was entirely consistent with the fact that in *Children of Adam* there was really nothing of love as an emotion, but only as a program.[75] In *Calamus* Whitman first celebrated the emotion of love in all its phases. In *Children of Adam* he was confident and masterful; in *Calamus* he was shy, hesitant, and wistfully stammering. In that, too, he betrayed himself. The 1860 edition was a shocking but inevitable unmasking.

The glaring incongruity between these poems and the "new Bible" in which they appeared was doubly conspicuous because of the tragic tone which ran through them. The program poem repeats the theme of death which we remember from "Out of the Cradle." The individual Calamus leaves which are first the hairs on his breast ("Scented Herbage of My Breast"), then the grass on the rolling earth, then the poems in his book, all make him think of death. "Body leaves, *tomb leaves*," he called them later and:

I am not sure but the high soul of lovers welcomes death most.

That is an unusual starting point for a democratic program. On the other hand, regarded as the entirely personal expression of disconsolate love, it acquires positive meaning. A collection of *love poetry* might well be prefaced with these lines:

O slender leaves! O blossoms of my blood! I permit you to tell, in
    your own way, of the heart that is under you,
O burning and throbbing—surely all will one day be accomplished;
O I do not know what you mean, there underneath yourselves—
    you are not happiness,
You are often more bitter than I can bear—you burn and sting me.

This intensely personal note is repeated again in a stronger poem, No. 15 in the 1860 edition (now called "Trickle Drops"). Here the individual poems are no longer blades of grass or leaves, but drops of blood which fall

From wounds made to free you when you were prisoned.

It is audacious to try, as Henry Bryan Binns and Bazalgette have tried, to regard that as the inauguration of a social program. Their attempt to interpret it symbolically is forced. And why the attempt? The *Calamus* poems are all love poems. They express a homosexual emotion in all its nuances, from yearning and personal attraction to happy union, envy, and jealousy. More than once they recall the Persian love-poets Hafiz and Sadi and the Greek Sappho in the emotions and form of expression, most clearly, perhaps, in No. 43 ("O you whom I often and silently come"), in which he describes his feelings when the loved one is near, paralleling Sappho's famous poem to a young girl [76] ("That man whoever he may be," etc.) Involuntarily we recall Johannes V. Jensen's characterization of Whitman's "key to the feminine emotion itself." That is marvelously revealed in these very poems. But at the same time *Calamus* is a tragic group of poems—Whitman probably wrote these verses quite innocently and published them without considering how he exposed himself—because they spring from unrequited love; they are "tomb leaves" about something which he had struggled for in his life, but which is now no more. Thus, they are the proclamation of a whole new attitude in his poetry, and as he himself says, "You are *not* happiness."

There is something revealing and sensational in the fact that the tragedy of these *Calamus* poems lies, not in the abnormal character of the emotion, as we might be inclined to believe, if only for historical reasons, but because his love is not reciprocated. Whitman openly mentions the importance of this for his poetry in No. 39 ("Sometimes with one I love").

Sometimes with one I love, I fill myself with rage, for fear I effuse
  unreturned love;
But now I think there is no unreturned love—the pay is certain,
  one way or another,
Doubtless I could not have perceived the universe, or written one
  of my poems, if I had not freely given myself to comrades, to
  love.

In 1867 the last line was altered to read:

(I loved a certain person ardently, and my love was not returned,
Yet out of that, I have written these songs.)

That is clearly a confession and a declaration which there is no reason to doubt.[77]

In *Children of Adam* Whitman had already introduced a theme and motif which, entirely contrary to the plan, betrayed the fact that his song grew out of an unhappy love affair. "We two how long we were fooled"—about the happiness which awaits him and his lover when they meet again in the world of transmutation as two birds in the air, two fish in the sea, or two waves which break over each other in foam—really belongs in the *Calamus* section because of the mood. It has nothing to do with

the triumphant physical lover of *Children of Adam.* In effect the
program poem of *Calamus* refers to it in the theme "surely all
will one day be accomplished." But in the program poem of
Children of Adam there is nothing to introduce it. Furthermore,
it is the same theme as "Out of the Cradle Endlessly Rocking."
"The unsatisfied love," whose song and echo will always live in
the poet's heart, is exactly that to which he now gives expression.
The connection is doubly clear because the theme of "We two"
from the bird song is repeated so emphatically in the shorter
poem. The two who were separated have finally found each other.

We have circled and circled till we have arrived home again—we
two have.

But that is only wishful thinking. It does not come true in real
life; it has nothing to do with reality. The tragic introductory
strophe of the poem

You and I—what the earth is, we are,
We two—how long we were fooled!

is based on reality and facts.

Though we are so decidedly lacking in biographical information about Whitman, though he has himself cleverly and consistently destroyed every trace which could help with a historical
explanation, nevertheless we have in the *Calamus* poetry—from
which he himself said that we must get clues for a real understanding of him—plain evidence of a tragic love affair, probably
about 1859, when, according to Holloway's statement, the poems
were written. If, therefore, we used the term "Romance" for any
part of his life, it must be this. By studying the book alone, in its
changing phases, it becomes clear and obvious that it was between the second and the third editions that the crisis in his life
took place. Holloway and Catel have exploded the New Orleans
myth, but neither of them was concerned with a closer investigation of this second and more decisive period. Holloway makes the
laconic concession that "surely some lover had died," and afterwards talks of Whitman's love affair as "a passion so tragically
powerful" and of *Calamus* as "born out of a mood . . . but it is
an unhealthy mood." [78] He does not engage in a more careful
definition of Whitman's personality as it is here revealed.

Earlier I mentioned the adolescent and effeminate traits in Whitman's erotic psychology. At the climax of the first and second editions his eroticism merges with his religious emotion in a fashion not unfamiliar in world literature. Certain effeminate medieval mystics such as Heinrich Suso and the Persian poet Rumi expressed themselves in similar fashion. Divinity and the longed-for beloved are one and the same person. The theme is developed in the third edition in "Proto-Leaf."

Not he, adhesive, kissing me so long with his daily kiss,
Has winded and twisted around me that which holds me to him,
Any more than I am held to the heavens, to the spiritual world.

In *Tilskueren*, January, 1919, a Danish translator rendered "he" as "nogen" (some one), and later as "ham eller hende," Whitman's peculiar dual "him or her," which significantly enough is *not* found in this passage. It is important that Whitman's whole concept of the divinity is so closely united to his ideal of "manly attachment." We have seen how his great longing for an answer, an echo, a release, was not satisfied by his reception as a poet. Thus, on the *first* attempt his verse was no emancipation, it was just "cries of unsatisfied love," it was the old question of his youthful story, "Wherefore is there no response?" Therefore, in the years immediately after 1856, everything was stored up and waiting for a *personal* outpouring of his need for love. We see what kind of outcry it was, but it comes out more clearly in the 1860 edition, because there it was not impeded. Afterwards Whitman deleted the two poems which disclosed most intimately and most personally what had happened to him. Since they are not in modern editions of *Leaves of Grass*, I quote the complete poems.

In the introduction to the first (No. 8 of the *Calamus* group) Whitman describes the various stages of his development.

Long I thought that knowledge alone would suffice me—O if I
    could but obtain knowledge!
Then my lands engrossed me—Lands of the prairies, Ohio's land,
    the southern savannas, engrossed me—For them I would
    live—I would be their orator;

Then I met the examples of old and new heroes—I heard of war-
riors, sailors, and all dauntless persons—And it seemed to me
that I too had it in me to be as dauntless as any—and would
be so;

And then, to enclose all, it came to me to strike up the songs of the
New World—And then I believed my life must be spent in
singing; . . .

Then he continues by telling what happened.

But now take notice, land of the prairies, land of the south savan-
nas, Ohio's land,

Take notice, you Kanuck woods—and you Lake Huron—and all
that with you roll toward Niagara—and you Niagara also,

And you, Californian mountains—That you each and all find
somebody else to be your singer of songs,

For I can be your singer of songs no longer—One who loves me
is jealous of me, and withdraws me from all but love,

With the rest I dispense—I sever from what I thought would
suffice me, for it does not—it is now empty and tasteless to me,

I heed knowledge, and the grandeur of The States, and the example
of heroes, no more,

I am indifferent to my own songs—I will go with him I love,

It is to be enough for us that we are together [N.B.]—We never
separate again.

This poem is absolutely astounding. We cannot question the
beauty and vigor of the contents and treatment; its genuine
passion is unmistakable. More arresting is *its complete dis-
agreement with the program of the volume in which it appears.*
Suddenly the poet no longer cares for his land, his poetry, the
greatness of which was a fixed belief, his hold on existence. Now
he celebrates something entirely different, which makes other
interests superficial, because his passion does not need any outlet except the natural one.

This poem with its pretended contents of passionate happiness is beyond analysis, because we are left with no evidence except the poem itself. But it is supplemented immediately by the
second poem, No. 9, which is, perhaps, the most poignant of the
Calamus poems. It is impossible to misunderstand the note of
despair.

Hours continuing long, sore and heavy-hearted,

Hours of the dusk, when I withdraw to a lonesome and unfrequented
   spot, seating myself, leaning my face in my hands;

Hours sleepless, deep in the night, when I go forth, speeding swiftly
   the country roads, or through the city streets, or pacing miles
   and miles, stifling plaintive cries;

Hours discouraged, distracted—for the one I cannot content myself without, soon I saw him content himself without me;

Hours when I am forgotten, (O weeks and months are passing,
   but I believe I am never to forget!)

Sullen and suffering hours! (I am ashamed—but it is useless—
   I am what I am;)

Hours of my torment—I wonder if other men ever have the like,
   out of the like feelings?

Is there even one other like me—distracted—his friend, his lover,
   lost to him?

Is he too as I am now? Does he still rise in the morning, dejected,
   thinking who is lost to him? and at night, awaking, think who
   is lost?

Does he too harbor his friendship silent and endless? harbor his
   anguish and passion?

Does some stray reminder, or the casual mention of a name, bring
   the fit back upon him, taciturn and deprest?

Does he see himself reflected in me? In these hours, does he see the
   face of his hours reflected?

This is probably the most poignant love poem in the whole
collection, and its omission in 1867 was an artistic loss. But from
Whitman's point of view it is clear why the omission was made.
The content of the poem could not be misunderstood. No explanation or misinterpretation is possible. The poet speaks
frankly of his shipwreck, his despair and loneliness. That gives
us the private foreground of all the *Calamus* poems. Like all love
poetry, they have come from loving another person in whom he
can see "his hours reflected." But in my opinion this poem is
also something like a rough draft or sketch for "Out of the
Cradle," in which the story of his lover having left him and
"contented himself with another" has been poetically trans-
muted into the lonely bird's song to the sea and the moon—
and the personal intimate pain has thus achieved a richer,

fuller tone. It seems to me that in the artistic shaping and artistic result these two poems parallel the real experience. The change of sex must be regarded as a far more innocent change of "he" and "she" than in the poem "Once I Pass'd," also originally a *Calamus* poem, but "for reasons" put under *Children of Adam.* At the same time, there are in the omitted poems the first traces in *Calamus* of a realization of the abnormality of the emotion. The question of whether "other men ever have the like" is an apprehensive development of the question asked in the first edition by the poet as a half-grown boy when in doubt as to "where he stood," childhood or manhood, and the gnawing hunger on the bridge between. We are repelled by it, and by the naïveté of the big "lubberly fellow," but we cannot deny that there is something sublime in its expression, as there always is when a real poet yields to a sincere emotion, whether it is love or wonder. Whitman's "wonder at the world," which Carpenter mentions, is nowhere more apparent than in his love poems.

Whitman's great emotion, his "manly attachment," his erotic burden, with its peculiar characteristic, influenced and colored his whole interpretation of the world around him, as we have observed in his earlier poetry. As Nietzsche says, "the degree and kind of a person's sexuality penetrates every corner of his being." [79] For a long time it was certainly Whitman's belief that it was a normal, healthy emotion which he nourished, although of abnormal warmth and strength; and in any case it was his dream to sanctify it in his poems.

You bards of ages hence! . . .

. . .

Publish my name and hang up my picture as that of the tenderest lover,
The friend, the lover's portrait, of whom his friend, his lover, was fondest,
Who was not proud of his songs, but of the measureless ocean of love within him—and freely poured it forth.

Instead he found his emotion was misunderstood, elicited scorn, and aroused opposition. Even he realized that there was a darker, more daemonic side, in No. 36 ("Earth! My likeness"), probably from the period of falling in love, and therefore in the chronology of the love affair it should be inserted between the two omitted poems.

Earth! my likeness!
Though you look so impassive, ample and spheric there,
I now suspect that is not all;
I now suspect there is something fierce in you, eligible to burst
    forth;
For an athlete is enamoured of me—and I of him,
But toward him there is something fierce and terrible in me, eligible
    to burst forth,
I dare not tell it in words—not even in these songs.

The blending of emotions and moods, of heedless confession and poetic interpretation, is extraordinary in this section of *Leaves of Grass.* It stretches from requited to unrequited love, from confidence and arrogance to insecurity and shame, from bold shout and frank courtship to a wondering desperate confession that love is a dangerous, inconstant passion which will not bring happiness, for example, No. 12.

> Are you the new person drawn toward me? . . .
> To begin with take warning, . . .[80]

Thus, in spite of the conflicting emotions, it is as tenderly expressed as any collection of love poetry in world literature. But we cannot deny that at times its diversity includes completely irreconcilable contradictions. Side by side with the bashful confessions of love and devotion, along with the poetically inspired expression of ideal friendship and comradeship, are poems suddenly and completely erotomaniac in character, in which the poet's insatiable longing for new faces, new experiences, makes us involuntarily doubt the sincerity and honesty of his experiences. As always when love becomes a purely lyrical emotion, it becomes universal, all-embracing, because it is directed at no one in particular—other than the poet himself. It is necessary to insist on the erotomaniac trait in Whitman's lyrics, because now and then we get the impression that, as he himself says, he is not capable of remaining long in one place, he must go on to new experiences, new sensations. If, therefore, Whitman in his own life did not establish a permanent love connection, he was prevented by his own nature; it would not have suited him. But as world literature has witnessed, this defect *was a part of his genius; the constant flitting and wandering of his emotion was all-pervading in his lyricism.* In modern literature we find the great German lyricist Richard Dehmel paralleling the erotomania of Whitman.[81] But this trait of volatility and insatiability does not make the tragedy in the poet's heart or the tragic personal experience of 1859 less bitter or less significant. The less that actually happened, the more clearly the secretly desired relationship was revealed as impossible and hopeless; then the more surely was the erotically aroused lover to believe that this was the only real love. To the erotic psyche mirrored in these *Calamus* poems it is really the unsuccessful love which will be transformed into the great love; whereas the successful love will last but a day or two and will then be displaced by a yearning for new faces, new experiences. All of this was revealed in the 1860 *Calamus*—a single experience and at the same time characteristic of his whole erotic type. *Calamus* is, therefore, the central nervous system of the book. In "Roots and Leaves," No. 13, Whitman says that only he who brings like emotions to the reading of these poems will see them unfold themselves as the sun and rain make flowers and leaves unfold. For all others they are the poet's avowals, a confession, and thus a clue to all *Leaves of Grass,* and at the same time a spectacular unveiling of a yearning, emotional man who has to sing the song of the passions to give vent to his own passion.

In spite of a few moments of happiness that Whitman may possibly have had in a love affair in the autumn of 1859, it is highly probable that after all *he was not talking of any erotic relationship,* that it never actually developed that far; moreover *I suspect that, after all, Whitman never actually had any such experience during his whole life, in spite of his homosexual bent.*[82] That is where the mistake in judging the homosexuals of world literature is always made. The question has always been an ethical one: How guilty is he? Never: To what spiritual or physical group does he belong? It is no longer a secret that just that dangerous blending of sex in human nature produces artists. Greater information and greater tolerance will probably result in a more open and frank discussion in literary history of this difficult subject. It will be to the advantage of the writers if it can be discussed with more freedom and sympathy. Many writers have undoubtedly produced their greatest work out of sublimated emotion, sublimated either voluntarily or because it was taboo. Just as in the work of Hans Andersen we can trace the artistic effects of an unexpressed sex life, so it is that Whitman's lyricism has gained in vigor and in emotional strength by his unfulfilled erotic longing. At the same time this unsatisfied yearning furnished an excellent excuse for his attitude when the Calamus question was brought up later in his life by Symonds. Hindered by the ignorance of the physiological and psychological aspects of the problem which prevailed until the beginning of this century, Whitman had a perfect right to deny his homosexuality if he had never indulged in homosexual practices. Probably he was totally unaware of the "type," though in old age he revealed a concern about this characteristic of his, by deletions and omissions in *Calamus.* As he expurgated his book he tried to expurgate his life. Such a statement may seem to be an impertinent intrusion into Whitman's privacy, but the literary historian will not so regard it. To the modern literary historian the intrusion is necessary if he does not content himself merely with the individual, but wants to get at the "type."

At the time of its appearance *Calamus* was intended as a program, a chapter in the new Bible; and it was a revelation, the frankest of Whitman's whole gospel. His "City of Friends" was not a new Philadelphia, with the motto, "City of Brotherly love," but a colony of homosexuals. As Holloway says,[83] his loudly proclaimed "Friendship" revealed itself to be "a jealous emotion." Whitman discovered that himself; therefore the deletions—he had to resume the prophet role and to emphasize it. In 1871, in *Democratic Vistas,* he tried to interpret all of *Calamus* in a social sense, to make the word "adhesiveness" into a democratic term, and in 1867 he deleted it from the Calamus

passage in "Starting from Paumanok." The comparisons of
Whitman with Christ which with such bad taste abounded in
the early little tracts about him served the same purpose. But
such efforts were useless; events took another course. Whitman's place in world literature did not depend on that and the
question is now settled. Whitman is generally recognized as an
American lyricist, as one of the unique and original lyricists
in world literature, whose influence has reached literary circles
in every country. He is not taken seriously as a prophet or social
reformer. Bertz first formulated the complaint against him in
introducing and defending his physiological study of Whitman
in 1905. "The right of the scientific critic to examine the sex-
life of an important man is never more obvious than when abnormal emotion is proclaimed as normal and a gospel, even a
religion made of it." [84] Holloway, whose great admiration for
Whitman as a poet has made him the best known Whitman
scholar in the States, says of the proclamation in *Calamus:*
"Here . . . a man yields to an impulse which, were it common,
would soon reduce the world to chaos." [85] Even the early
twentieth-century Whitman scholars, such as Henry Bryan
Binns, Johannes Schlaf, and Bazalgette, tried in spite of everything to proclaim Whitman as a religious prophet and reformer,
with a message for humanity of more than literary interest.
This point of view was insupportable, and Americans realized
it sooner than Europeans. The two highly gifted thinkers George
Santayana and William James discussed it at the turn of the
century in *Interpretations of Poetry and Religion* (1900) and
Varieties of Religious Experience (1902). Santayana was
harsher, because he did not take Whitman seriously; James, on
the other hand, found valuable examples of religious experience in *Leaves of Grass*, and on the whole seems to have had a
real appreciation of Whitman as a great poet. He objected only
to the blind idolatry of the religious proclamation; he was
tolerant of its double-toned volition and defiance. With some
hesitation he included Whitman among the "healthy-minded":
"his gospel has a touch of bravado and an affected twist, and
this diminishes its effect on many readers." [86] The whole interpretation of Whitman has finally been clearly stated by Jo-

hannes V. Jensen in his introduction to Gelsted's translation
(1919) : "America has not pretended to follow Whitman as a
national spiritual leader. Probably it could not have done so.
Whitman towers among the great erratics, but not among the
harmoniously adjusted great, like Bjørnson, for example."

Johannes V. Jensen, in whose development Whitman has been
of great significance, as early as 1905 wrote a novel called
Hjulet [The Wheel], permeated with Whitman's poetry, both
consciously and in some instances unconsciously. He stressed
the importance and limitations of the great American. We can
almost say this is the *leit motif* of the book; paradoxical as it
may sound, *Hjulet* is, from a literary point of view, a discussion
of Whitman. The hero of the book, a young poet named Lee,
represents Whitman's value for the individual as an "introduction to America," as a celebration of modern reality, the
significance of his "new feeling," his great receptiveness, his
strong emotion in which even the *Calamus* poetry appears to
the poetically sensitive, normal man as "one of the letters
stamped with the great seal of nature." [87] Here Whitman is
an emotion, but not a program. Exercising near-genius in pre-
senting the duality and paradoxical quality of Whitman's work,
Jensen placed in the same chapter another leading character,
a homosexual swindler, Evanston, who exploited Whitman as
a prophet and his book as a Bible and creed. The new religion
that Evanston wants to establish in Chicago is literally a copy
and travesty of Whitman's "New Bible," the doubtful side
of his all-inclusive democracy turned into mob rule, his glorification of America perverted into stupid Yankeeism. Evanston
even made the poem "For You O Democracy" the *leit motif*
and motto of his preaching. "He used Whitman's soul like a
greasy masonic badge," Lee exclaimed. With admirable comprehension of all the potentialities of the new proclamation,
Jensen, in Chapters XIII and XV, has Evanston take advantage of the two most personal and dangerous aspects of Whitman's doctrine: Evanston's first victory travesties *the absorp-*
tion of all religions into himself. He invaded the city and
controlled its culture, having decorated himself with all the religious symbols, ready to receive genuflections from the entire

world. Finally he embraced *the union of evil and good*, of God and Satan in one person—an ancient mystical doctrine which Whitman probably seized upon just after the crisis in his life, but which it is absolutely impossible to advocate openly. Jensen has Evanston take up that theme also in the great outburst "Consider what God and Satan jointly could do . . . the good and evil turned into one channel." Whitman has suddenly become a demagogue—or an Oscar Wilde!—in any event an individual whose valuable poetic implications become dangerous and pernicious the instant they are taken as a rule and as a social program.[88]

This novel clearly illustrates the similarities between Whitman and Nietzsche as figures in the nineteenth-century drama of world literature, a similarity which was first perceived by Johannes Schlaf, though in an altogether different and more positive sense. We cannot deny either Whitman or Nietzsche the rank of eminent poetical preachers; the doctrines of both give negative results socially, just because neither of them belonged to the healthy-minded great, but with astonishing psychological resemblances and in spite of differences in milieu and intellect, both belonged to the erratic great of literary history.

Among the other poems in the new edition which it is necessary to discuss individually, there is the little-known *Chants Democratic* No. 4 (in 1867 called "American Feuillage"), one of Whitman's last but finest catalogues, in which he tries to collect into one poem everything in his country that he most loved. As civil war and disunion threatened, "These States" (Whitman's usual pompous designation for his country) were united in one identity.

Singing the song of These, my ever united lands—my body no more
inevitably united, part to part, and made one identity, any
more than my lands are inevitably united, and made ONE
IDENTITY.

It is also paradoxical that this edition, in which the poet tried to express a social and national optimism, appeared in perhaps the most fateful year of the history of the States, when the union artificially maintained for decades between the North and the South was visibly breaking up. Whitman saw the dissolution, but in his book refused to admit the desperate truth; hence the paradoxical tone of defiance and anxiety in the book. Spontaneous confessions of the real situation were made in several poems: "To a President," "To the States," a section of *Debris* which was afterwards renamed "Yet, Yet, Ye Downcast Hours," *Leaves of Grass* No. 17, which was later called "I Sit and Look Out," and also the shipwreck poem, *Thoughts* No. 5, afterwards "Thought." Later he tried to minimize these revelations by optimistic additions implying that things would soon be better. Typical of this attitude is *Chants Democratic* No. 9, later called "Thoughts of These Years," in which the conflict and the schism become only a link in certain progress.

How America illustrates birth, gigantic youth, the promise, the
    sure fulfillment, despite of people—Illustrates evil as well as
    good.

The last lines are especially interesting. For Whitman the great democratic fiasco of these years came to correspond to the fateful character of his love in the *Calamus* poems, and thus confirmed the duality of the book's proclamation of "evil as well as good!" But in *Democratic Chants* No. 11, now the second section of "Thoughts of These Years," Whitman made a characteristic shift. He turned to the West, to the young, unexploited mid-America, from which the glorious future should come with the new type, "the divine average." This expectation, a development of ideas in "Song of Myself," had now become the hope of America.

Of a free original life there . . .
                    .   .   .

Of immense spiritual results, future years, inland, spread there
    each side of the Anahuacs,
Of these Leaves well-understood there, (being made for that area).

Like De Tocqueville and Fredrika Bremer, Whitman now looked to the West. At that time the West was really coming to the fore historically. Abraham Lincoln was "The man from the West," and it was the Western states in the Civil War that would determine the superiority of the North and bring the final victory. But to understand the complete change in Whitman's attitude, it is important to note that the greatness of the States and the success of America was no longer a fact which could be celebrated, but a future hope of the poet, and his public was not his actual national contemporaries, but the *future race!* Behind this new point of view lay his painful disappointment over the 1856 fiasco.

Very conspicuous among the new poems is the famous "Poem of Joys," which it is difficult to fit into the scheme of the 1860 edition as I have here presented it. This is one of Whitman's most suggestive poems, one of the most modern, and one of his highly lyrical flights.

> O for the dropping of rain-drops in a poem!
> O for the sunshine and motion of waves in a poem.

In a series of isolated descriptions, in which the catalogue technique of the first edition is expanded to lyric soaring imagery without a suggestion of schematization, he celebrates all the longings and joys of his life, of childhood and youth, situations thought of, dreamed of, and wished for, memories of the sailor, the riverboat captain, soldier, fireman, whaler, farmer, orator.

O the orator's joys!
To inflate the chest—to roll the thunder of the voice out from the
    ribs and throat,

. . .

To lead America—to quell America with a great tongue.

Or a theme of joy from "Song of Myself":

O the old manhood of me, my joy!
My children and grand-children—my white hair and beard,

. . .

O the ripened joy of womanhood!
O perfect happiness at last!
I am more than eighty years of age—my hair, too, is pure white—
    I am the most venerable mother.

And a highly characteristic theme of the 1860 edition:

O something pernicious and dread!
Something far away from a puny and pious life!
Something unproved! Something in a trance!
Something escaped from the anchorage, and driving free.

The poem is written under a powerful inspiration; its lyrical sweep is phenomenal, its capacity for meeting and exhausting the description of a situation is overwhelming, as in his picture of youthful fishing trips on South Bay off Long Island. The whaling section was undoubtedly inspired by the episode in Melville's *Moby Dick* (Chapter XLVI), which on the whole must have been even more to Whitman's taste than *Omoo*, a book we know he rated very high. Nevertheless, the undertone of the poem is in harmony with the rest of the collection. The basic theme of the collection, death,[89] appears early in the poem and gives its own note, which we cannot catch without recognizing its importance. *Everything* in these passionate strophes about joy gives the impression of a wish, not a reality. It was never at any time Whitman's destiny really to know the joy of the sailor, soldier, or orator, because his talent, his limitations prevented it, but in places he does express a burning desire to know those joys, a desire which makes the poem a parallel to "We Two How Long We Were Fool'd," another song of joy, but only after all the obstacles, repressions, longings, and obligations of the present existence have been overcome and cast aside. These two poems of the 1860 edition stand as the two poetically complete expressions of the same painful ecstatic joy in the potentialities of creation, a pantheistic exaltation which is so characteristic of poets of Whitman's type. We have already met the yearning for other globes, spheres, ages in "Song of Myself," because it belongs to the cosmic emotion, but without this peculiar tone of bitter experience. The tone here is fuller and richer, as always in art which has an undercurrent of pain. The greatest songs of joy in literature have been written with a sob in the throat. We must regard in this light Whitman's poem of congratulation to a person dying. He congratulated him on the great possibilities that would be revealed when the "I" was conquered, when the struggling, headstrong individuality would expand like a thin stream of life in the vast distances which the "I" is never able to fathom and to become identified with, no matter how much it may desire to do so.

Finally, in this 1860 edition there are yet to be mentioned the poems about voices and oratory; *Chants Democratic* No. 12, later called "To Oratorists," and *Leaves of Grass* No. 21, afterwards renamed "Voices," in 1881 combined into one poem called "Vocalism," with the famous refrain (wishful thinking), "O the divine power to speak words," and the expressive poem from *Messenger Leaves* entitled "To Him That Was Crucified," the most direct of Whitman's Christ-poetry, in which the poet addresses himself on an equal footing to the crucified one.

> . . . O my comrade, . . .
> We few, equals, indifferent of lands, indifferent of times,
> We, enclosers of all continents, all castes—allowers of all theologies.

Naturally this has its source in Whitman's Quaker background, recognizable in so many ways in this edition, a democratic feeling even in religion; likewise it is a poetically sublimated link in the "new Bible," but a dangerous stage in Whitman's overvaluation of himself. With an extreme lack of taste this idea was later used by his admirers, especially in the interpretation of "To a Common Prostitute," which belonged to the same group of *Messenger Leaves* in the 1860 edition. The theme of the prostitute was one of Whitman's earliest proclamations and should never be omitted from his democracy—in 1860 there is a special emphasis on the fact that during these years he himself frequented dives and questionable associates. Many poems mention it, for example, No. 8 in *Enfans d'Adam* (afterwards "Native Moments") and even more emphatically No. 13 in *Leaves of Grass* (later "You Felons on Trial in Courts"). The poet identifies himself with the accused at the bar and with the prostitutes.

> . . . flaunting over the trottoirs, or obscene in your rooms,
> Who am I, that I should call you more obscene than myself?
>
> . . .
>
> Inside these breast bones I lie smutch'd and choked,

Beneath this face that appears so impassive, hell's tides continually
    run,
Lusts and wickedness are acceptable to me,
I walk with delinquents with passionate love,
I feel I am of them—I belong to those convicts and prostitutes
    myself,
And henceforth I will not deny them—for how can I deny myself?

The seriousness and bitterness of the tone is not to be misunderstood. During these years Whitman has felt the evil, the
negative principle in himself. His frequent association with
low company and his visits to the houses of correction, first in
New York and later in Washington and Philadelphia, to which
Conway and Dr. Bucke refer, have certainly impressed him
with the fact that he (like Alfred Noir in Edgar Lee Masters's
Spoon River Anthology) mingled with shipwrecked men in
whom he could see the shadow of himself. But later he tried to
raise the theme to a higher level, explaining away the prostitute
poems, which had naturally aroused the greatest sensation and
scandal in the States by saying about "To a Common Prostitute" what Kennedy later quoted in *The Fight of a Book for
the World*, "It is nothing but the beautiful little idyl of the New
Testament—about the woman taken in adultery." [90]

Here we have another example of the violently stubborn
conflicts in this edition between the completely personal intru-
sions and the themes which were used for general and religious
pronouncements. On one side is the book, on the other the man,
continually fighting, without ever being able to identify themselves with each other—one moment a Bible, the next instant a
vain, self-centered poet.

What am I after all, but a child, pleased with the sound of my own
    name? repeating it over and over.

This is one of the glimpses of self-understanding so surprisingly
and arrestingly scattered through the collection, never changed
or omitted despite his many revisions of the book. But these
examples give *Leaves of Grass* the impress of flux and uncertainty, which is at times one of its main points and special effects. Everything is relative—even reality. Out of the 1860

mentality there came such a dejected poem as *Leaves of Grass Number 18*, later called "All Is Truth," in which the poet declares that lies and truth, divinity and falsehood, are all relative concepts.

I feel in myself that I represent falsehoods equally with the
  rest. . . .

The theme is touched on in "Song of Myself," Section 24.

That I walk up my stoop, I pause to consider if it really be, . . .

This takes form in the *Calamus* poem No. 7, later given the very revealing title, "Of the Terrible Doubt of Appearances," which, more than any other, confesses the 1860 position. Here Whitman for the first time in the book goes so far as to express doubt of identity after death.

That may-be identity beyond the grave is a beautiful fable only,

but he finds comfort, support, or at any rate forgetfulness for his doubt in "my lovers, my dear friends." [91] His whole "City of Friends" becomes a Fata Morgana, an illusion, when his love suffers the fatal shipwreck. What then?

  Then all may arrive to but this . . .

he exclaims in "To My Soul," later called "As the Time Draws Nigh." Thus, there is nothing left except to write this book and let it go at that.

Evidence that Whitman attributed not merely decisive but also conclusive importance to the 1860 edition is found in the concluding "So Long," a poem of farewell, but in a very different key from the pathetic-pantheistic ecstatic ending of "Song of Myself." What his poem celebrates is now frankly revealed as being in the future, not the present; the time will come eventually when America will be what she promises to be, with great orators, great poets, great people, great mothers. The poem announces them. No longer is the poet the strong being who was needed; that person is yet in the future. Whitman announces the union just when the States are on the brink of a rupture. He announces adhesiveness even though he himself has not found it.

I say you shall yet find the friend you was [*sic*] looking for.
However, he has not found one and must now say farewell, or
"So long!" The poem as it now stands is comprehensible only
in the temper of 1860, when America's inner chaos exceeded the
worst expectation, and when Whitman himself realized that
he was not what he had claimed to be. The swimmer had been
driven hopelessly against the cliff and drowned; the proud ship
had foundered on a shoal in the Sound and ended as wreckage
—seaweed, driftwood, on Paumanok's shore. And as for a poet,
how does he differ from a meteor which gleams and vanishes in
the year of meteors? So Long! He turns to the future races.
They will understand him. He speaks to his distant reader in
the *Calamus* poem, No. 45, later "Full of Life Now!" He uses
the direct, personal address to his future readers.

> . . . Be not too certain but I am now with you.

The tone has gained in poetic richness what it has lost in joy and
happiness. So Long! It is a lonely man who sings, *solitary*, as
the whole collection is key-noted in "Proto-Leaf," or "Starting
from Paumanok"; lonely in the West, singing! The longing
for one, the right person, was forecast in the program poem
for the otherwise reticent *Enfans d'Adam* group as the motive
power of the whole, and also that this longing had so far been
excruciating and unfulfilled. "Yet the right person not near."
Therefore the poet projects himself out in time and space to
seek his camerado, his reader, his lover. So Long! To read this
poem as a program poem, a literary abstraction, is to deprive it
of its whole interest. In the midst of the parting the poet also
says that it is a person, not a book we should seek.

> This is no book,
> Who touches this, touches a man.

The note of departure is perfect. Farewell to his readers;
farewell to his poems!

> My songs cease—I abandon them.

Like an old traveler, he tried to "peal the old cry once more," the
old call of allurement which a wild bird once taught him. He
gives his reader, whoever he is, the last kiss, then projects him-

self into the world of metamorphoses, from which he will probably arise again, he knows not when or as what. In any event,
he is now free and emancipated, the one celebrated in "We Two
How Long We Were Fool'd" and "Poem of Joys"—"disem-
bodied, triumphant, dead."

This poem is one of Whitman's finest, most personal achievements, and is the richest imaginable conclusion for *Leaves of
Grass* because of its personal tone. Henry Bryan Binns, who
on the whole gives very superficial attention to the special character of the 1860 edition, comments on the concluding poem in
relation to the book. "The book is not only for the first time a
complete and living whole; it is a presence, a lover, a comrade,
and its close is like a death." [92] The expression "So Long" as a
word of parting is noteworthy as an example of Whitman's
power to stamp his language with freshness and appropriate-
ness by the use of an expression which seemed to him natural and
characteristic. The term was not in general use, but was first
accepted by Americans after this poem was published. Whitman himself had heard it used "among sailors, sports and prostitutes." [93]

This poem, "So Long," was one of Whitman's favorites, and
in the many succeeding editions it was always retained as the
conclusion of the book. It is a clear example of the complicated
integration which makes it impossible for the reader to follow
the different steps in the genesis of the book. This poem, though
written first, is now to be printed always as the last of the many
"Song of Parting" which Whitman wrote in the following years.

For more was to follow. The 1860 edition was not the *end*
and retirement. New poetic stimulation came. Abraham Lincoln, the War, the hospitals! As we observed earlier, there were
many indications that Whitman himself was losing his grip at
the very time when America was moving toward dissolution and
chaos. But so closely was this man's development and fate linked
to that of his country that the decisive historical events of
1860–61 were also crucial for him. We have already observed
in "To a President" from *Messenger Leaves* Whitman's position
on the political corruption and on Buchanan's wavering, ignoble
attitude on campaign issues. This poem, directed to Buchanan,

was an expression of the same pessimistic mood which had made Whitman compare himself to a meteor in a year of meteors. America had no leader. Whitman had dreamed of being one, but had given it up and relinquished hope of seeing anyone else in his place. Abraham Lincoln's appearance on the scene, his incomprehensibly bold attitude during the presidential election, his determination to fight for the preservation of the Union against any attempt to split it, changed the situation at once for the nation and also for Whitman. He had a peculiar understanding and admiration for Lincoln. The two men, Lincoln and Whitman, appear now—and for the future—as the most outstanding representatives of America of the 1860's. Whitman recognized Lincoln's great possibilities before others did in Brooklyn and New York, where, on his first official visit, he was very coolly tagged as "The Man from the West." The importance to Whitman personally of Lincoln's whole career can be seen not only in the poet's *Prose Works*, where he mentions Lincoln time after time, but also in the three great memorial poems in *Leaves of Grass*. Therefore it is doubly interesting to be able to record that Lincoln was one of Whitman's first readers and admirers in the States. Henry Bascom Rankin reports in his *Personal Recollections of Abraham Lincoln* (New York, 1916) that while Lincoln was a lawyer in Springfield he read *Leaves of Grass*, probably the 1856 edition, and jokingly told his friend how he had barely been able to rescue the book from the fury of the women. Lincoln would read aloud in the evening from "Song of Myself."

His rendering revealed a charm of new life in Whitman's versification. Save for a few comments on some broad allusions that Lincoln suggested could have been veiled, or left out, he commended the new poet's verses for their virility, freshness, unconventional sentiments, and unique forms of expression, and claimed that Whitman gave promise of a new school of poetry.[94]

In the portraits of Lincoln and Whitman during these years we cannot help noting a certain similarity, especially in their expression; in their blending of hardiness and sensitivity, of pathos and at the same time of strength of will. In any case, Whitman openly felt that Lincoln was a sort of confirmation of himself and of what he had celebrated and proclaimed in his book. To a considerable extent we can say that in Lincoln, Whitman found his *Great Camerado;* in the elegy he speaks of him as "my comrade departing." Certainly at this time there was a revolution in Whitman's inner life, a complete break with all the 1860 psychosis. He made a new beginning. We can say that for Whitman the war had somewhat the same significance as the First World War had for the young idealists and dreamers of French and German literary circles in 1914.

We can also say that psychologically there was a spiritual development, that his repressed emotional life found adequate expression in his hospital work, that there occurred the "sublimation" which for him, as for so many others of similar temperament, meant safety. Holloway has commented on this. He describes how "Whitman's hunger for emotional friendship" was transformed and purified by the hospital experiences, how he "learned the blessedness of those who give rather than receive." [95] The mother-instinct was released and utilized in his work among the hundreds of wounded young soldiers: "The very multitude of such contacts was the salvation of the author of *Calamus.*" We can confirm this in another way in the history of his book. In "Song of Myself," Section 40, he had described how he brought help to the sick.

> Behold I do not give lectures or a little charity,
> What I give I give out of myself.

Now he was actually living his ideal.

The result of this new and unexpected experience which came into Whitman's life was the little book *Drum-Taps*, of ninety-six pages, which he published in New York in 1865, after the War and his contribution to it were ended. It was as astounding as it was small. As an artistic achievement it marked an important and remarkable advance. In 1867 he added it to *Leaves of Grass* as an "annex," and when, in 1871, he included it in the main body of the book, it became one of the strongest, most effective parts of the whole work, along with *Children of Adam* and *Calamus*. It was a supplement and a fulfillment that probably first made the book the phenomenon and masterpiece of world literature that it is. The diffuse, all-embracing lyrical emotion was now unified by a definite theme. His ego-centric emotion became less arrogantly subjective; his feeling of comradeship was not an egotistic feeling, but was really democratic. This theme provided a basis for an interpretation of the Calamus sentiment. Many of the striking, earlier themes could fit into this new integration, thereby gaining in unity, especially the *Calamus* fragments which now became poems that could be immediately accepted by everyone, not only by those with peculiar qualifications. Whitman observed this fact with astonishment and delight. In a letter to O'Connor, which Bliss Perry quotes, he says: "Drum Taps has none of the perturbations of Leaves of Grass." [96] Note the word.

So much has been written in the many biographies about Whitman's work in the hospitals in Washington, with so much detail both factual and lyrical, that it is scarcely necessary to go into it here. The two main sources of our information about what really happened are Whitman's *Specimen Days*, 1882, his second book of prose, which consisted of extracts from his diaries, the most important part coming out of the Washington period, and the collection of letters to his mother published by Dr. Bucke in 1898 as *The Wound Dresser*. Actually the latter is not nearly so interesting as the diary, because, as Holloway commented,[97] in the letters to his mother Whitman was not completely himself, but deliberately appealed to her special limitations and emotions. Whether or not he kept his problems a secret from his mother during the crisis in his life we do not know; we can only draw conclusions from comparison with similar cases. Why else would he, for the first time in his life, live away from her for eleven years? In both his diaries and his notebooks, as well as in letters to his mother, we find many prose draughts which he later worked into poems. The whole motif of "A Sight in Camp in the Day-Break" is found in a letter to his mother. Holloway has found in the Library of Congress some letters to other people that he quotes in his book.[98] They give a remarkable picture of Whitman's characteristically sentimental relationship with his old New York associates, especially those at Pfaff's, "my darlings and gossips," as he called them.[99] As usual, however, we have the best source in *Leaves of Grass* itself; to some extent he was right in his widely practiced destruction of all his private papers, for here is really the complete man in the book, although certainly in a different light from that which he himself conjectured or wished.

It is an extremely noteworthy characteristic of Whitman's psychology that he did not enlist for military service during the intoxication and enthusiasm of the early days of the war, although Lincoln solemnly exhorted all citizens to volunteer, as Whitman's critics have always strongly emphasized. In 1882 one of his most zealous Boston enemies, Colonel T. W. Higginson, launched quite a campaign against Whitman with an article in *The Woman's Journal* about Whitman's presumed cowardice during the war. Was he effeminate, cowardly, weak? The "prophets" always answered these attacks by pointing out, among other things, that Whitman's contemporary Lowell did not enlist either and by reminders of the sacrifice and real heroism he exhibited in the hospitals. Nevertheless, the fact is significant. His poetry is illuminated in places by masculine enthusiasm, joy of conflict, and in the narrative episodes he likes to assume the soldier role and to fight where it is bloodiest. In other poems the mood is completely different, womanly, compassionate, gentle, horrified, or full of protest at the cruelty and meaninglessness of war. This is another conflict, another duality, one of many in Whitman's book. Some people have called it a typical Quaker trait, that he felt it wrong and sinful to bear arms [100]—and it is a real temptation to regard his hospital service in this light, because the Quakers have usually made such an important contribution by their ambulance work not only in the Civil War but also more recently in both world wars. But Whitman did not feel that it was a sin to bear arms. On the contrary, he expresses quite opposite sentiments. There has been talk that Whitman realized instinctively where he could give the best service—that despite his emphasis upon the athletic masculinity of his body, he understood with remarkable clarity that his was not a soldier's physique. We are reminded of Burroughs's characterization: "He was *not* an athlete, or a rough, but a great tender mother-man, to whom the martial spirit was utterly foreign!" [101] Coward or no coward, there was a lack of martial bearing. Whitman had pronounced moral courage, but about his physical courage we do not know.

However, Whitman waited, not enlisting, but staying at home with his mother for a full year while the support and mainstay of the family, George, was called into service. Walt supported the family as best he could by writing for the newspapers. During this period he wrote "Brooklyniana" for the Brooklyn *Standard*. Possibly he was fairly well paid for it. Perhaps he believed at first that the war would not last long. He mentions in his diary that at first it was the general opinion in New York "that it would blow over in sixty days." Instead, it was one of the bloodiest and most protracted wars in modern history. The first warning of what was to come was the report of the fatal defeat of the North at Bull Run, July 20, 1861. Whitman mentions it as one of the most catastrophic communications of his life—along with the news four years later of Lincoln's assassination. Then even Whitman awoke to a realization of the extent and import of the war, for the immediate cause of his leaving home was a message that George had been seriously wounded at Fredericksburg and was in a hospital in Washington. It was to nurse him that Whitman first left home, and this purely personal motive gradually expanded into the hospital work he undertook. He arrived in Washington without funds. He supported himself by writing articles for the New York papers, especially the New York *Times*, and later by positions he got for himself. First he was in the office of "the army paymaster," Major Hapgood, a position he secured because his former Boston publisher, Charles Eldridge, was employed there after his bankruptcy; later, through O'Connor, he found a place in the Indian Bureau of the Department of the Interior. Most of the money he used for gifts and nursing the wounded came from Emerson, Alcott, Wendell Phillips, or from friends in Brooklyn to whom he appealed.

The setting for these years of his life is well known to us from Dickens, whose satirical picture makes it very vivid.

Washington—It is sometimes called the City of Magnificent Distances, but it might with greater propriety be termed the City of Magnificent Intentions; for it is only on taking a bird's-eye view of it from the top of the Capitol that one can at all comprehend the vast designs of its projector, an aspiring Frenchman. Spacious avenues that begin in nothing, and lead nowhere; streets mile-long, that only want houses, roads, and inhabitants; public buildings that need but a public to be complete; and ornaments of great thoroughfares, which only lack great thoroughfares to ornament— are its leading features.[102]

Such, according to Dickens, was the appearance of the American capitol, scene of the two great conflicts and compromises of the preceding years. With its fourteen hospitals, it was the most important Northern headquarters behind the front. In *Specimen Days* the temper of the city during these years is clearly felt: Whitman's nocturnal wandering about the Capitol, the parades of soldiers, the transports of cattle and transports of deserters (a daily spectacle) through the city streets, his meeting with Lincoln, who saluted him and whom he saluted, although they never actually spoke to each other. (Lincoln's often quoted comment about Whitman, originally reported by O'Connor in *The Good Gray Poet*, dates from these years: "Well, he looks like a man!") Whitman's description of Lincoln's appearance: "I see very plainly Abraham Lincoln's dark brown face, with the deep-cut lines, the eyes, always to me with a deep latent sadness in the expression"—and his frequently reiterated statement that there is not a single good or well-drawn portrait of Lincoln: "None of the artists or pictures has caught the deep, though subtle and indirect expression of this man's face. There is something else there. One of the great portrait painters of two or three centuries ago is needed." [103] Then the famous passage on "Calhoun's Monument." One day in the hospital Whitman heard a soldier talking about a monument for the famous Southern leader in Charleston, and a second soldier dramatically interrupted with: "I have seen Calhoun's monument . . . It is the desolated, ruined south; nearly the whole generation of young men between seventeen and thirty destroyed or maim'd; all the old families used up . . . the name of southerner blacken'd with every shame—all that is Calhoun's real monument." [104] Finally there are Whitman's reflections on the remarkable mete-

orological phenomenon during these war years, "The Weather—
Does It Sympathize with These Times?" [105] or the peculiar
situation in world politics—that is, there was not one of the
European nations which did not wish misfortune for America
in the war "with the ardent prayer that the United States may
be effectually split, crippled and dismember'd by it." [106] Whitman seethed with the political furor of his country, and it is
an important link in understanding the other signals of his
future work. The fourth edition of *Leaves of Grass* was stamped
with violent nationalism. "We need this hot lesson of general
hatred, and henceforth must never forget it. Never again will
we trust the moral sense nor abstract friendliness of a single government of the old world." [107] Whitman became patriotic during these years, quite wholeheartedly nationalistic, and, as in
his youth, his patriotism found naïve expression—for example,
when he asserts that the army of the United States is the greatest, most intelligent, exhaustless, most reliable "in the world,
any land, perhaps all lands." [108] In his diaries Whitman tells
mainly of each day's "cases" among the wounded and dying,
young and old, fathers and sons, brothers and fathers. "I wonder if I could ever convey to another—to you, for instance,
reader dear—the tender and terrible realities of such cases." [109]
Here we find the seed of many of his most famous *Drum-Taps*
poems, for example, when he went with Major Hapgood and
Eldridge on an excursion into Virginia very close to the firing
line, he found there the inspiration for "As Toilsome I Wander'd Virginia's Woods," "Vigil Strange," and "A March in
the Ranks Hard-prest." The burden of all his prose pictures is
in the title of one of his latest, "The Real War Will Never Get
in the Books": "Future years will never know the seething hell
and the black infernal background of countless minor scenes
and interiors." What the war really meant to Whitman spiritually we see in his splendid poetry, not in *Specimen Days*,
valuable as that material is for the illumination of the relation
between theme and development.

The Washington period was a peak in Whitman's life, a great
strain, but also a great release and relief. At home in Brooklyn he had earlier made a practice of visiting his friends among

the bus drivers and ferry pilots when they were sick in hospitals, and that had been a sort of apprenticeship for his work
in Washington, which was not so much the usual duties of or-
derly or nurse as that of priest, physician, personal friend or
relative; it was the personal relationship with which he was
able to approach all these suffering men, the personal radiation
of interest and optimism toward the sick who loved and trusted
him—a great gift that hospital doctors knew how to value as
it deserved.[110] John Swinton's account of Whitman in the hospitals [111] gives us a vigorous and lively impression of his admirable work. Here his unused talents came into play. "He
had," writes Holloway,[112] "to cultivate that intuition which
makes women the best nurses." The feminine trait is overwhelm-
ingly apparent. Bliss Perry has preserved for us a characteristic passage in a letter to Eldridge during Whitman's hospital
years: "Charley I think sometimes to be a woman is greater
than to be a man." [113]

Almost equaling in importance his work or his mission were
the personal friends which Washington brought him, and the
fact that he became known to a part of the public which had
hitherto heard of him only as an obscene author. Many people
changed their opinions after meeting him face to face, especially women, whom the usual portrait of Whitman, the Christ-
portrait in particular, then, as now, repelled.[114] The most important friendships he had formed in Washington were with
Eldridge and the lawyer Hubley Ashton, who were of so much
help in the Harlan affair, and with O'Connor and Burroughs,
the first of the "prophets" for whom the spreading of Whitman's fame was in the future not merely a question of friendship but a life work. Both O'Connor and Burroughs were promising young authors who had jobs in government offices in
Washington, O'Connor in the Attorney General's Office and
Burroughs in the Treasury Department. W. D. O'Connor
(1832–89) had known Whitman in Boston, and immediately
after the poet came to Washington, O'Connor invited him to
his home. For awhile Whitman lived there and found a close
friend in Mrs. O'Connor. O'Connor was of Irish descent, with
a temperament of fire and flame, later a fanatical champion of

the Shakespeare-Bacon theory in a way that did more honor to his enthusiasm than to his intelligence. His constant haste prevented his being an author of any importance, even though two of his stories, *Harrington* and *The Carpenter*, evoked some interest at the time. He put his whole soul into Whitman's cause, and in the course of his life rendered invaluable service, even after a difference of political opinion, typical of his exuberant but honorable character, had put a stop to their friendly intercourse.

John Burroughs (1837–1921), who is best known as a nature writer in the style of Thoreau, was from a completely different mold. He was a young romantic dreamer, at that time strongly influenced by Emerson, and he had published a few short pieces. *Whitman and Burroughs Comrades*, by Clara Barrus, is an invaluable sourcebook for Whitman research and contains many enlightening details about Burroughs's first fanatical acceptance of Whitman, which could almost be characterized as falling in love, although Burroughs had been married since 1850. Like everyone for whom Whitman had an immediate appeal, Burroughs's manner of speaking and writing showed Whitman's influence for a long time. In a letter to a like-minded friend, E. M. Allen, he unbosomed himself in Whitmanesque phrases and quotations. For various contemporaries he cultivated a romantically exalted sentimental ideal of friendship more like Holderlin's *Hyperion* than *Calamus*. Especially after coming to Washington he became one of Whitman's most devoted disciples, largely because of his womanly way of feeling. Dr. Barrus, speaking of their friendship during these years, says:

Burroughs lived and moved and had his being in Whitman. . . One notes his unperturbed chronicling of the fact, "Walt kissed me like a girl." This act, which would have ruffled, perhaps estranged, most men, making impossible the bond of comradeship, found ready comprehension in Burroughs. His own large endowment of affection, amativeness, and potential "adhesiveness" was like a huge dynamo charging him and his associates.[115]

That during the 1860's he was like wax in the hands of the older man is particularly evident in his first book, *Notes on*

Walt Whitman as Poet and Person, which set forth not so much his own opinion of Whitman as Whitman's opinion of Whitman.[116] Later, in maturer years, he was one of the most intelligent and clearest-sighted of the prophets, the one in whom objective historians of literature could put their trust. Many of his observations, especially in the Barrus book, reveal how much more clearly than the other disciples he recognized Whitman's strength as well as his weakness.

In the summer of 1864 Whitman had his first warning that his health was not equal to the demands he was making on it. Letters to his mother are full of alarmed descriptions of his condition, "deathly faintness and bad trouble in my head." Doctors called it overwork and advised him to take a rest, and there is no doubt that Whitman had driven himself to great exertion, especially in those hot summer months of 1864, when the horrors of the Washington hospitals reached a peak. Nevertheless, it is certainly one of the myths that Whitman's later illness and paralysis were caused by his hospital work.[117] Bertz has plainly proved that in all probability the cause lay in inherited weakness. Whitman did not have a strong constitution and he had overestimated his strength. In any case, he had to leave Washington, and for six months went to live with his mother in Brooklyn. He collected his memoranda and his poems of the war. At this time he wanted to publish the hospital diaries, abstracts of which later appeared in *Specimen Days* (paralleling Duhamel's World War diary, *Vie des martyres*), but no publisher dared put money into such an unusual publication. Naturally *Drum-Taps* was more important to him, for he recognized its decisive significance in his literary production. In a letter to O'Connor written in January, 1865, there were a couple of sentences which he would scarcely have approved later: "It [*Drum-Taps*] is in my opinion superior to Leaves of Grass —certainly more perfect as a work of art . . . the true artist can see that it is yet under control." [118] The observation is correct, but must be understood to refer to *Drum-Taps* as it appeared in a separate book, not as a section in *Leaves of Grass,* which it later became.

The business of getting it published was not easy. Whitman's

friend Trowbridge took the book to Boston, but was not successful in finding a publisher there. Whitman returned to his position in Washington, though he had not fully recovered.[119] In
the fall of 1864 he decided to publish the poems at his own expense and for that purpose returned to New York during the
last months of the war. This was in April, and the book was
already in type—it was to be 72 pages; then on April 19 the
frightful and crushing announcement of Lincoln's death reached
Whitman. He immediately halted publication, and in the following weeks he wrote the great Lincoln elegy, "When Lilacs
Last in the Dooryard Bloom'd," which Swinburne pronounced
"the most sweet and sonorous nocturne ever chanted in the
church of the world"; [120] Bliss Perry, in his biography, classified it "with Lowell's *Commemoration Ode* as the finest imaginative product of the Civil War period." [121] This and a few
other Lincoln poems, along with later poems, became an annex,
"a sequel" of twenty-four pages in the book, which was first
printed in the fall of 1865. Thus, the great tragedy at the end
of the war, the historic close of a period that for Whitman, too,
had meant such a decisive release and catharsis, was, by a remarkable coincidence, marked by a poetic conclusion and climax
for the book which no prearranged plan, no artistic premedita-
tion, could have made stronger or more impressive.

DRUM-TAPS, 1865

The book divides itself naturally into four sections. First
are the poems written before the war, for example, "Years of
the Unperform'd," (later "Years of the Modern"), "Pioneers!
O Pioneers!" and "Broadway Pageant"; next poems dating
from the outbreak of the war, which were at his mother's home
in a little notebook that he often inquired about while he was
in Washington; then the main section of poems on the war and
the hospitals; and finally the poems in the *Sequel*, which form
a mighty crescendo, and also a résumé and conclusion, of the
emotional cycle through which Whitman had passed in the five
years since the publication of the Boston edition. The book is
important; with the exception of the 1855 edition it is the most
significant original contribution Whitman made to world litera-

ture, and for him personally, with the exception of the Boston edition, it represented the highest peak and expansion of his emotional and spiritual life.

The release and stimulation that the war meant for Whitman is easily recognized in the opening poems, "Eighteen-Sixty-One," "Beat, Beat Drums," and the impressive cantata "Song of the Banner at Day-Break," which strangely enough is frequently omitted from editions of the poems. In their excitement and joy in conflict, these poems clearly reveal the national significance Whitman attributed to the war. During the intoxication of the first months, without considering the future horrors, he regarded it as a holy war, a war for the ideal of the Union which the States in the years just past had forgotten and forsaken. And Whitman's whole fanatical, sentimental idea about a democracy that should be founded on the manly friendships, on the comradeship between men, got its confirmation at the outbreak of the war in the fellowship and generosity of the youth of America. Whitman transformed his Calamus idea into patriotism and enthusiasm for the war. "Affection shall solve the problems of Freedom yet," he says in "Over the Carnage Rose Prophetic a Voice," and continues:

One from Massachusetts shall be a Missourian's comrade;
From Maine and from hot Carolina, and another an Oregonese,
    shall be friends triune,
More precious to each other than all the riches of the earth.

That is the Calamus ideal in terms of real life. It is very interesting and significant that in reality this poem is an old *Calamus* poem, a continuation of "For You, O Democracy," which had acquired meaning for Whitman in *Drum-Taps*, and which he therefore used here, where its ecstatic climax:

I, extatic [*sic*], O partners! O lands! with the love of lovers tie
    you. . . .

could not be regarded as personal and thus be wrongly interpreted, but must be considered in the light of the existing military and political conditions which would explain it. This is a *transfer*, a *sublimation*, the meaning of which is not to be mistaken. Yet we cannot say that the remarkable duality found in *Calamus* is entirely lacking in *Drum-Taps*. The peculiar poem in *Calamus* about "the new person" who feels attracted to the poet, but will be disappointed—one of the erotomaniac poems—has a parallel in *Sequel to Drum-Taps* in "As I Lay with My Head in Your Lap, Camerado," in which Whitman confesses that he is unlike what people may believe, not so loyal or so honest.

I know I am restless, and make others so.[122]

He himself is a fighting man, a soldier, not in the war, but in life. He pays no attention to laws; threats of hell have no effect on him, nor promises of heaven. Those who follow him take a dangerous path and he himself is not certain where it leads, or whether he will be victorious or crushed and vanquished. The poem is a discordant note in the general tone of the collection. It was written after Lincoln's death.

The first poems of the collection picture the departure from home and the excitement of war. "Drum-Taps" describes the setting out from New York, "The Lady of Ships," as Whitman calls Manhattan, who like a proud old mother says farewell to her sons. The poem has one of Whitman's usual catalogues of all those who set off when they are called. This call to war corresponds to the tempting call of the wanderer in "Song of Myself." The mechanic leaves his tools, the lawyer his office, the driver his wagon, the salesman his store. This complete parallel to the older poem is very significant. It is as if Whitman himself were the personification of the war and calls to Americans— but this time he is heard. It is such a setting out as he had imagined. In the following poems he describes the sound of trumpets and drums, and "like a bird" flies over the Northern states calling the men to arms. The result, as indicated in the stately "Rise O Days from Your Fathomless Deeps," was nothing less than

Torrents of Men (sources and rills of the Northwest, are you indeed inexhaustible?)

This torrent of men was for Whitman the picture of the Democracy he had dreamed and proclaimed. In joy and pride he exclaims over it and over what the occasion signifies to him of fulfillment and confirmation.

Thunder on! stride on Democracy! strike with vengeful stroke!
And do you rise higher than ever yet, O days, O cities!
Crash heavier, heavier yet, O storms! you have done me good.

The expression is vigorous and effective, but otherwise these poems are almost without art. As far as the technique goes they might be from the 1855 edition. The real artistic achievement in the poems of the early days of the war is in "Song of the Banner at Day-Break," in which Whitman essayed a sort of dramatic cantata with four persons speaking, the poet, the banner and pennant (which are one), and a father with his child. In the poem the banner and pennant represent the sentiment at the outbreak of the war, the ideal of union which calls all its children to defend it. The banner is sometimes shaped like a sword, sometimes a snake, then a beckoning finger—and the child stands below and is drawn by it while the father timidly tries to hold the child back and wants it to be content with respectable wealth and humdrum peace. (Once more the Father-figure in Whitman's poem is the negative, restraining force.) The real lyricism is in the figure of the poet as he sings of the landscape and scenes in which the great new drama will be enacted. It is an idealized poet, a poet of the open air, such as Whitman always wanted to be.

My song is there in the open air—and I must sing.

The introduction is splendid, both simple and impressive:

POET

O a new song, a free song,
Flapping, flapping, flapping, flapping, by sounds, by voices
    clearer,
By the wind's voice and that of the drum,
By the banner's voice, and child's voice, and sea's voice, and
    father's voice,
Low on the ground and high in the air,
On the ground where father and child stand,

In the upward air where their eyes turn,
Where the banner at day-break is flapping.

The flag calls now to the others, and Whitman has it speak in one of the most clearly expressed rhythms in his book.

BANNER AND PENNANT

Come up here, bard, bard;
Come up here, soul, soul;
Come up here, dear little child,
To fly in the clouds and winds with us, and play with the measureless
    light.

The call of the flag excites the child and the poet, but it makes the father anxious. The child exclaims of the flag:

CHILD

O father, it is alive—it is full of people—it has children!
O now it seems to me it is talking to its children!
I hear it—it talks to me—O it is wonderful!
O it stretches—it spreads and runs so fast! O my father!
It is so broad, it covers the whole sky!

That is really an expression of the ideal declaration of war. Whitman emphasized and explained this ideal by the word "identity," which occurs no less than three times in the poem. In this we see what those days meant to him and his yearning for identity.

See the identity formed out of thirty-six spacious and haughty
    States, (and many more to come;)

He hailed the flag as the visible symbol of his great ideal and strong yearning.

Out of reach—an idea only—yet furiously fought for, risking
    bloody death—loved by me!
So loved! O you banner leading the day, with stars brought from
    the night!

The war gave him "a pleasure new and extatic," and he wanted to be like the banner which cracked and flapped over the children of the States and explain to them why they should fight.

The new musical note so strong in "Out of the Cradle" is completely dominant in this poem, not only in the rhythm or the many alliterations ("Demons and death then I sing" or "And banner so broad and so blue") but also in the choice of words, which is simpler than in some of the earlier poems. There is no vocal slag. The real and expressed emotions have become one, for example, when the poet sings of the sunrise over the sea, over the silk-white foam of the waves.

> But I am not the sea, nor the red sun;
> I am not the wind, with girlish laughter;
>
> .   .   .
>
> But I am of that which unseen comes and sings, sings, sings,
> Which babbles in brooks and scoots in showers on the land;
> Which the birds know in the woods, mornings and evenings,
> And the shore-sands know, and the hissing wave, and that banner
>   and pennant,
> Aloft there flapping and flapping.

In this passage Whitman's diction is so polished that we are reminded of Edgar Allan Poe.

This poem is long, but in general one of the characteristics of *Drum-Taps* is that Whitman has further improved the short form which he had used with such great success in the 1860 *Children of Adam* and *Calamus* sections. By concentrating on selecting the essential details he wrote his finest poems. In addition to the Washington poems and the memorial poems to President Lincoln, which are among the longest Whitman wrote, there are in *Drum-Taps* only two other long poems: "The Centenarian's Story" and "The Dresser." In "The Centenarian's Story" Whitman has an old man talk about the battle at Brooklyn, August 27, 1776. This is a typical example of Whitman's really fanatical devotion to Washington, expressed elsewhere in his poems, and was to some extent based on stories told in his childhood by his uncles. A prose sketch of the poem appears among Whitman's earliest work, "The Last of the Sacred Army." [123] "The Dresser" touchingly describes his own work during the war.

On, on I go—(Open, doors of time! open, hospital doors!)
The crush'd head I dress, (poor crazed hand, tear not the bandage
    away;)

. . .

These and more I dress with impassive hand—(yet deep in my
    breast a fire, a burning flame.)

And it concludes with these proud lines in parenthesis.

(Many a soldier's loving arms about this neck have cross'd and
    rested,
Many a soldier's kiss dwells on these bearded lips.)

Many of the familiar Whitman themes reappear in this poem,
such as "Whoever you are," the unknown hero who is greater
than the acclaimed hero, and finally the precious, irretrievable
blood which Whitman later in *Drum-Taps* used in a completely
pantheistic poem, "Pensive on Her Dead Gazing I Heard the
Mother of All." But the remarkable thing about this poem is
that under its later title, "The Wound-Dresser," it is accepted
as a picture of Whitman (in biographies it is frequently used
as a chapter heading for the period of the war years), but the
idea of Whitman's work in the hospitals was forecast in a vivid,
almost visionary way in Section 41 of "Song of Myself."

I am he bringing help for the sick as they pant on their backs.

From the Washington period came all the "occasional" poems
of the war, with the individual glimpses of "Cavalry Crossing
a Ford," "Bivouac on a Mountainside," and "An Army on the
March" in *Sequel to Drum-Taps*—which often remind us of
Liliencron's war lyrics—or the single short sentimental pictures: "O Tan-Faced Prairie Boy," or "Reconciliation" (also
in the *Sequel*), ". . . For my enemy is dead—a man divine as
myself is dead," in which the poet rises above reality and sees
everything from the vantage point of Eternity, where all things
merge.

. . . the hands of the sisters Death and Night, incessantly softly
    wash again, and ever again this soil'd world.

In these poems Whitman reveals the plasticity of his imagery
and his astonishing skill in epitomizing. First of all there are

five detailed, forceful descriptive poems that indisputably belong in the treasury of war lyrics of all time: "Come up from the Fields Father," "Vigil Strange I Kept," "A March in the Ranks Hard-prest," "A Sight in Camp in the Day-Break," and "As Toilsome I Wander'd Virginia's Woods," in which the Calamus motif is refined to a marvellously pure, clear, universal emotion. In a large measure this is because they all deal with death, Whitman's great new theme, the basis for both his description and his emotion.

These are all pure poetry, that is, they are not real, but fanciful occasions, which the poet develops with all the imaginative and emotional strength of which he is capable. Closest to actual experience is the poem about the long march over an unknown road, in which recollections of Whitman's own short excursion into Virginia is transformed into the dark and mystically inspired picture of the nocturnal hospital. Also from this short trip southward came the poem about the grave of the Unknown Soldier that the poet found,

> As toilsome I wander'd Virginia's woods,
> To the music of rustling leaves, kick'd by my feet, . . .

He finds the simple inscription on the board nailed to the tree:

> *Bold, cautious, true, and my loving comrade.*

That is like the mood of envy which came over him in *Calamus* when two friends met, but sanctified here because he stands in the presence of death.

> Long, long I muse, then on my way go wandering;
> Many a changeful season to follow, and many a scene of life;
> Yet at times through changeful season and scene, abrupt, alone, or
> in the crowded street,
> Comes before me the unknown soldier's grave—comes the inscription rude in Virginia's woods,
> *Bold, cautious, true, and my loving comrade.*

The most vigorous of these poems, but the most foreign to normal emotion, is the one about the strange vigil over the dead comrade on the nocturnal battlefield (". . . boy of responding kisses, never again on earth responding"). But at the same time there is a plastic clarity in this imaginary situation of the

soldier who kept watch over his dead friend as the night passed
and the constellations wheeled over his head until at dawn he
wrapped him in his blanket and buried him where he fell.

Ending my vigil strange with that—vigil of night and battlefield
    dim;
Vigil for boy of responding kisses, (never again on earth respond-
    ing;)
Vigil for comrade swiftly slain—vigil I never forget, how as day
    brighten'd,
I rose from the chill ground, and folded my soldier well in his
    blanket,
And buried him where he fell.

The frequent repetition of "vigil of night," "vigil for boy,"
"vigil I never forget," gives the poem a musical rhythm and
flow. Such reiteration used as an artistic device throughout
Drum-Taps becomes one of Whitman's established rhythmical
effects.

   There is something Grecian in Whitman's friendship poems,
as both Symonds and Havelock Ellis assert, though William
James says that it is "moral sophistry and strain" which most
definitely separates Whitman from the Greeks. Nevertheless
Homer's funeral of Patroclus and Whitman's "Vigil Strange"
are linked together by an affinity of feeling reaching across
three thousand years of literary history.

   The reckless and vaunting Christ motif of the 1860 edition
has in *Drum-Taps* been changed and sublimated into something
splendid, as in "A Sight in Camp in the Day-Break Grey and
Dim," when at dawn outside a hospital the poet sees three
covered stretchers and lifts the blanket from the face of one
after the other, an old man, a youth, and the third:

. . . —a face nor child, nor old, very calm, as of beautiful yellow-
    white ivory;
Young man, I think I know you—I think this face of yours is the
    face of the Christ himself;
Dead and divine, and brother of all, and here again he lies.

   The boastful "I," the defiant bragging "I myself" of the
earlier years has withdrawn from any implication in the poem.

The "I" is no longer he who "is" but he who sees and relates! This is one of the new signs of development in *Drum-Taps* and a natural result of the disappointment that Whitman had suffered, an essential link in the invariably painful process that makes poets out of people.

The finest of the five poems, "Come Up from the Fields Father," is wholly descriptive, and the "I" does not obtrude except in the parentheses, which, like a whisper in the reader's ear, add to the feeling of intimacy. It is probably the most masterly of all Whitman's short descriptive poems, and therefore, steeped as it is in poetry, merits quotation in full.

Come up from the fields, father, here's a letter from our Pete;
And come to the front door, mother—here's a letter from thy dear
  son.

Lo, 'tis autumn;
Lo, where the trees, deeper green, yellower and redder,
Cool and sweeten Ohio's villages, with leaves fluttering in the
  moderate wind;
Where apples ripe in the orchards hang, and grapes on the trellis'd
  vines;
(Smell you the smell of the grapes on the vines?
Smell you the buckwheat, where the bees were lately buzzing?)

Above all, lo, the sky, so calm, so transparent after the rain, and
  with wondrous clouds;
Below, too, all calm, all vital and beautiful—and the farm prospers
  well.

Down in the fields all prospers well;
But now from the fields come, father—come at the daughter's call;
And come to the entry, mother—to the front door come, right away.

Fast as she can she hurries—something ominous—her steps
  trembling;
She does not tarry to smooth her white hair, nor adjust her cap.

Open the envelope quickly;
O this is not our son's writing, yet his name is sign'd;

O a strange hand writes for our dear son—O stricken mother's
   soul!
All swims before her eyes—flashes with black—she catches the
   main words only;
Sentences broken—*gun-shot wound in the breast, cavalry skirmish,
   taken to hospital,*
At present low, but will soon be better.

Ah, now the single figure to me,
Amid all teeming and wealthy Ohio, with all its cities and farms,
Sickly white in the face and dull in the head, very faint,
By the jamb of a door leans.

Grieve not so, dear mother, (the just-grown daughter speaks
   through her sobs;
The little sisters huddle around, speechless and dismay'd;)
See, dearest mother, the letter says Pete will soon be better.

Alas, poor boy, he will never be better, (nor may-be needs to be
   better, that brave and simple soul;)
While they stand at home at the door, he is dead already;
The only son is dead.

But the mother needs to be better;
She, with thin form, presently drest in black;
By day her meals untouch'd—then at night fitfully sleeping, often
   waking,
In the midnight waking, weeping, longing with one deep longing,
O that she might withdraw unnoticed—silent from life, escape and
   withdraw,
To follow, to seek, to be with her dear dead son.

Without a superfluous word, simple yet exquisite in phrasing, the poem gives the most convincing example of Whitman
at his best as a poet. The emotion could not be more genuine.
It is characteristic of Whitman to assume the mother-role himself, as he has done before, but doubly so here because the poem
was so evidently conceived in a Calamus mood. If in no other
way this would be obvious from the description of the mother's
sorrow, her yearning "with one deep longing," a motif repeated
from the deleted *Calamus* poem, "Hours Continuing Long."

Does he still rise in the morning, dejected, thinking who is lost to
   him? and at night, awaking think who is lost?

Here, by a very important transposition, he has shifted his
own sorrow from 1859, the poignancy of his own loss, to this
mother-figure, and on that rests the poem's unforgettable au-
thenticity. At the same time it also indicates what happened
to Whitman spiritually during these years.

   The theme of death, the undertone linking all the poems of
this collection, was most explicitly and naturally developed in
the powerful composition in memory of President Lincoln, a
poem without description, without catalogues, without "action"
of any kind—pure music, full of alliterations, rhythms, and re-
frains, a poem in a minor key, worthy to be an example of how
far Whitman had now progressed in the art of lyrical selection
—and at the same time a valuable example in itself of "pure
lyricism."

   The lyrical images, the lyrical "properties," are three: the
lilac bush with its heart-shaped leaves from which the poet
breaks a sprig; the fallen star in the West which followed
Whitman through many nights and shone over his path, a
symbol of Lincoln; and finally the lonely bird with the bleeding
throat, the poet himself, who sings his lament among the cedars.

   In the swamp, in secluded recesses,
   A shy and hidden bird is warbling a song.

   Solitary, the thrush,
   The hermit, withdrawn to himself, avoiding the settlements,
   Sings by himself a song.

   Song of the bleeding throat!
   Death's outlet song of life—(for well, dear brother, I know,
   If thou wast not gifted to sing, thou would'st surely die.)

Here the personal association is not to be mistaken. This is
the grieving bird from "Out of the Cradle," [124] which reappears
and now has a deeper significance, for we must certainly accept
the line "If thou wast not gifted to sing, thou would'st surely
die" as a reference to all the old sentiments of the 1860 edition,
"to sing of his passions to give them their way." The progress

of the funeral train carrying Lincoln's body across the country is described, "With the show of the States themselves, as of crape-veil'd women standing," while he places his lilac sprig on the slowly moving coffin. Then follows a section about the great star in the West and what it meant to Whitman while it followed high above him "in the dark blue so mystic," full of meaning for him, full of a deeper significance, "As I saw you had something to tell, as you bent to me night after night."

The poet called his star "my comrade, departing," the final word to express his feeling for Lincoln. And the word which the star had for him was the same word which was once whispered to him on the Paumanok coast, the word "Death." At last the poet comprehended; but only after Lincoln's death did he completely and forever understand "the sacred knowledge of death." Then follows Whitman's greatest and most beautiful hymn to death, "Come Lovely and Soothing Death." (Shakespeare once sang something similar.) In Whitman's book the grand old mother becomes finally and significantly neither the earth, the night, nor the sea, but death, the "strong Deliveress," "delicate Death," the gentle mild pensive death, "O vast and well-veil'd Death."

Over the tree-tops I float thee a song!
Over the rising and sinking waves—over the myriad fields, and the
    prairies wide;
Over the dense-pack'd cities all, and the teeming wharves and ways,
I float this carol with joy, with joy to thee, O Death!

That is the solution, the end, the emancipation. Once more the poet sings joyously of Death as he had in "Song of Myself" before he was familiar with it. And whereas he sang then of happiness and friendship and of how he walked the city streets with arms about the waists of two friends and "I in the middle" ("Song of Myself," Section 33), the theme has now undergone a noteworthy change.

Then with the knowledge of death as walking one side of me,
And the thought of death close-walking the other side of me,
And I in the middle, as with companions, and as holding the hands
    of companions.

This astounding passage reveals more than any other the development of the Calamus theme in the later editions of *Leaves of Grass*. In the great Lincoln elegy the theme of death reached its lyrical climax in Whitman's poetry, and to some extent its conclusion. There could be nothing new. What came later were only new vibrations within the now firmly established framework of the emotional scale of the collection.

In 1876 the hymn to death, Section 16 of the Lincoln elegy, had a special title, "Death Carol," but in the 1867 edition and in the other later editions the whole poem had a single title. The poem ends with one of Whitman's usual résumés, not with the death song as a climax, but, like almost all Whitman's great poems, with a *dimuendo* in the form of a final reiteration of the motifs of the poem. It became one of Whitman's present-participle passages and really one of his finest.

19 [now 16]

Passing the visions, passing the night;
Passing, unloosing the hold of my comrades' hands;
Passing the song of the hermit bird, and the tallying song of my
  soul,
Victorious song, death's outlet song, (yet varying, ever-altering
  song,
As low and wailing, yet clear the notes, rising and falling, flooding
  the night,
Sadly sinking and fainting, as warning and warning, and yet
  again bursting with joy,)
Covering the earth, and filling the spread of the heaven,
As that powerful psalm in the night I heard from recesses.

20

Must I leave thee, lilac with heart-shaped leaves?
Must I leave thee there in the door-yard, blooming, returning with
  spring?

Must I pass from my song for thee;
From my gaze on thee in the west, fronting the west, communing
  with thee,
O comrade lustrous, with silver face in the night?

In the closing lines he says precisely, so there can be no doubt as to who his comrade is and for whom the memorial is intended, that the poem is written "for the sweetest, wisest soul of all my days and lands." And the poem ends with a peculiarly Whitmanesque enumeration of the three lyric motifs.

Lilac and star and bird, twined with the chant of my soul,
With the holders holding my hand, nearing [*sic*] the call of the bird,
There in the fragrant pines, and the cedars dusk and dim.

It is like a great piece of music concluded with the finest contrapuntal art.

There are two other poems inspired by Lincoln's death, "Hush'd Be the Camps Today" and in the *Sequel* "O Captain, My Captain," which holds a peculiar place in Whitman's work (and has become especially well known through inclusion in many anthologies of American poetry) because it is his only successful attempt to write a "correct" poem in rhyme and meter. It is strictly regular in stanza form, with internal rhyme in the third lines, and conventional meter, but the content and the poetic figure of the ship which returns victorious though with the captain dead, does not rise above a certain bright martial romanticism. There is not a single expression in it which is really Whitmanesque. It could have been written by someone else and reminds us very much of another, not very important, poem of the period, "Abraham Lincoln" ("Not as when some great Captain falls") by Richard Henry Stoddard. Whitman could write conventional verse, but his individualistic form of expression developed and first found its proper medium in his own special prose-verse, which had grown organically out of his peculiar inspiration and diction,[125] as organically as any personal style in world literature.

"Pioneers! O Pioneers!" is an exception to the conventionality and stiffness to which Whitman easily succumbed when he got away from his personal style. Here the form shows no more constraint than when there is no rhyme, though the rhythm is merely a short, choppy marching tune indicative of the progress of the pioneers. The poem is one of the most famous in the collection, and in a new versification sums up the ideas from the earlier poems. America's task in the development of the world is to proceed while the older races rest; the young tan-faced races of the West have great work to do, while the others sit still. It is the theme of America's rejuvenation in the West which he reintroduces. Whitman calls the movement of the pioneers "the Western movement," and thus prepares for his later comments in *Democratic Vistas*, 1871. The poem launches still another symbol for America in *Leaves of Grass*. It is no longer "Mother," now once and for all limited to the concept of death —but "Mistress," in deepest pathos, "Mother-Mistress." Whitman used the expression for the first time to designate himself in the paradoxical 1860 "Inscription" poem, *Chants Democratic* No. 18 (later called "Me Imperturbe"), in which he called himself "Master of all, or Mistress of all"; in 1865 this expression, characteristic of the entire collection, applies to the American nation as a whole.

Raise the mighty mother mistress,
Waving high the delicate mistress, over all the starry mistress,
　　(bend your heads all,)
Raise the fang'd and warlike mistress, stern, impassive, weapon'd
　　mistress,
　　　　　　Pioneers! O pioneers!

The great oral effect of the expression, and the stately reiteration of the word "mistress," once more recalls Poe's studied verse technique, although the language is Whitman's. On the whole, the poem is remarkably rich. From the purely heroic celebration of the westward march of the pioneers, "O resistless, restless race! . . . O to die advancing on!" Whitman expands the sentiment to all humanity in its present stage on the march forward on "the unknown ways" toward the future. All are here, mothers and daughters and new poets ("shrouded bards of other lands! you may sleep—you have done your work!"), all the seamen, all the landsmen, all the masters, all the slaves, but there are many others; the great procession from "Song of Myself" or "Song of the Open Road" continues. Race shall follow the path of race, and behind each press new races "in ghostly millions."

All the hapless silent lovers,
All the prisoners in the prisons, all the righteous and the wicked,
All the joyous, all the sorrowing, all the living, all the dying,
   Pioneers! O pioneers!

 Whitman himself is there.

  I too with my soul and body,
  We, a curious trio, picking, wandering on our way.

The mystical expression produces the effect of a great vision of contemporary humanity, faithful and confident of victory, taking up the task.

We take up the task eternal, and the burden, and the lesson,
   Pioneers! O pioneers!

    . . .

We today's procession heading, we the route for travel clearing.

 The idea of the "pioneers" is used again, with some variation, in one of the poems from the end of the war, "Camps of Green," included in *Drum-Taps*. In this remarkable pantheistic poem, later added to *Leaves of Grass* among *Songs of Parting*, the whole human race passes before the poet like an army which has pitched camp before the great engagement.

Behold the mighty bivouac-field, and waiting-camp of us and ours
 and all.

 The natural conclusion for *Drum-Taps* is the poems from the period of the cessation of hostilities, "Hymn of Dead Soldiers" (later called "Ashes of Soldiers"), "Pensive on Her Dead Gazing," and the four poems from the *Sequel:* "To the Leaven'd Soil They Trod," "Race of Veterans," "Spirit Whose Work Is Done," and "How Solemn as One by One," in which the conquerors hail the flag and the nation and the poet takes leave of all that has meant so much to him. He stands and watches the soldiers file by for the last time and lingers over each face in parting.

(As I glance upward out of this page, studying you, dear friend,
 whoever you are;).

Or in "Hymn of Dead Soldiers," which with "Camps of Green" and "Pensive on Her Dead Gazing" was afterwards transferred

to *Songs of Parting,* he thinks of the enormous number of dead.
At first it is only a new variation of the death motif.

Sweet are the blooming cheeks of the living! sweet are the musical
  voices sounding!
But sweet, ah sweet, are the dead with their silent eyes.

But in the stately "Pensive on Her Dead Gazing" it mounts
to a powerful pantheistic hymn. The great mother of all sits
thoughtfully deliberating and enjoins the earth that nothing
must be lost.

Absorb them well, O my earth, she cried—I charge you, lose not
  my sons! lose not an atom;

                    .   .   .

My dead absorb—my young men's beautiful bodies absorb—and
  their precious, precious, precious blood;
Which holding in trust for me, faithfully back again give me, many
  a year hence,
In unseen essence and odor of surface and grass, centuries hence;
In blowing airs from the fields, back again give me my darlings—
  give my immortal heroes;
Exhale me them centuries hence—etc., etc.

The whole spirit of the end of the war and of the book is in
the poem, "Spirit Whose Work Is Done," in which the poet sees
time bear away all the marching soldiers with their "forests of
bayonets," and once more and for the last time he fills himself
with all the inspiration which these years and these soldiers have
meant to him.

—Spirit of hours I knew, all hectic red one day, but pale as death
  next day;
Touch my mouth, ere you depart—press my lips close!
Leave me your pulses of rage! bequeath them to me! fill me with
  currents convulsive!
Let them scorch and blister out of my chants, when you are gone;
Let them identify you to the future in these songs.

Among the concluding poems in the *Sequel* is "As I Lay,"
a Calamus situation and a Calamus mood which leads directly
into the better and more interesting poem "Chanting the Square
Deific." This has a tone different from that of most of the col-

lection; it points forward and backward in Whitman's work, and it has always given biographers much food for thought. It points backward by being a variant of the old motif, with all its various conflicting potentialities in the poems, that is, the examples of primitive religions that he had already absorbed in himself in "Song of Myself," Section 41.

> Taking myself the exact dimensions of Jehovah and laying them
>   away,
> Lithographing Kronos and Zeus his son, and Hercules his grand-
>   son, etc., etc.

In the present poem he encompasses all the old strong gods, Jehovah, Brahma, and Saturn, the mild forgiving gods, Christ, Hermes, Hercules, likewise the denier and tempter, Satan, and the shining Holy Spirit, Santa Spirita, a home-made but characteristic form of the feminine which has always baffled the philologists among the Whitman disciples. These four elements compose the divine quadrant in human nature, the Satanic element being of equal importance. It is to be noted that the element which otherwise had no voice in *Drum-Taps*—a work heroic or compassionate according to whether it was the Banner and Pennant or the Wound-Dresser who spoke in the poems—assumed significance for Whitman in this collection. The battle of conflicting elements constantly raging in him and defying his efforts to achieve the identity which he celebrated as his goal in the poems as "Essence of forms—life of the real Identities," continued in Whitman's mind. The Washington period did not abolish the contradictions, although it did soften them, and the period after the war was again filled with conflicts.

Whitman stayed on in Washington for eight years after the end of the war, until his illness in 1873 deprived him of his niche in that regular routine where he had found his place. Shortly after the war and soon after he had somewhat recovered from his first attack, the notorious Harlan affair occurred and threatened to take away his means of livelihood. His superior in the Indian Bureau, Mr. Harlan, according to tradition a very upright man, but narrow-minded and conservative, found in Whitman's desk the manuscript of the new edition of *Leaves of Grass* which Whitman was preparing at that time. Mr. Harlan read it with dismay, and a few days later Whitman received a notice that the Bureau would dispense with his services. That was indeed a blow. Whitman's friends, particularly Hubley Ashton, who had some influence in the government, appealed to the higher authorities and made clear what service Whitman had rendered the country during the war. Whitman was continued in government service, but was transferred to another office. To his superior Mr. Harlan used the argument that the dismissal was purely for administrative reasons and that it had been found by investigation that Whitman was the clerk who could be best dispensed with—which may well have been true.

For Whitman the affair was important because it furnished the occasion for the always ebullient O'Connor to dash off in a few days, in the heat of his anger and exasperation, the familiar little essay, *The Good Gray Poet*, which dealt in fiery phrases with the problem of freedom in literature in general, but with particular reference to Whitman's case. Wendell Phillips called it "the most brilliant piece of controversial literature issued during the nineteenth century." [126] And Bazalgette says in his book on Whitman: "In verbal power, in brilliance of imagery, in satirical fervor, it is comparable to the most colorful and most eloquent French prose from Courier to Hugo." [127] The little essay caused a sensation and had no small share in augmenting the growing attention that Whitman's poetry was to receive during these years in America and Europe. O'Connor sent it to a long list of important people, who wrote letters of thanks. Among the many replies and acknowledgments there is a characteristic letter from Matthew Arnold, which Bliss Perry quotes; [128] it is representative of the older generation's opinion of Whitman and young America.

. . . while you think it his highest merit that he is so unlike anyone else, to me this seems to be his demerit . . . a great original literature America will never get in this way, and her intellect must inevitably consent to come, in a considerable measure, into the European movement.

Bliss Perry also prints O'Connor's reply, the essence of which is:

I can't agree that America must come into the European movement, as you say, for, and I am sorry so many Englishmen are blind
to it, America has a movement of her own, the source of her life, the
secret of her power, and I think, if you will pardon me for saying
so, there is far more need and probability of Europe coming into
our movement, than we into hers.[129]

The first sign that Europe would join the current of world
literature called Walt Whitman was already beginning to show
itself. Moncure D. Conway, who had settled in London, wrote
about Whitman in the *Fortnightly Review,* and Lord Strangford, literateur and orientalist, who, like Thoreau, was particularly interested in the oriental traits in Whitman's lyricism, also
wrote about him in the *Pall Mall Gazette* in 1866. At the same
time the circle of young writers and authors such as Symonds,
Swinburne, W. M. Rossetti, Edward Dowden, Buchanan, and
William Bell Scott, who in the future were to spread Whitman's
fame in England, were just beginning to read him with admiration and enthusiasm. In July, 1867, Rossetti wrote an
article about Whitman in the London *Chronicle,* comparing him
with Homer and Shakespeare, and at the same time he began a
correspondence with O'Connor and Whitman himself which led
to Rossetti's important English edition in 1868, the first European edition of Whitman's poems.

Meanwhile, at his office desk Whitman prepared the new
(fourth) edition of *Leaves of Grass,* in which *Drum-Taps* was
to be included. Nothing had happened, but once more Whitman's mood had changed. His sympathy for Negroes was less
pronounced than formerly—a phase of his political convictions
which was to be so decisive in his relations with O'Connor—and
his vision of Democracy had also changed. The American political scene was not encouraging in those years. After the war
and the successful and auspicious peace, there followed a year
of stagnation, caused by Andrew Johnson's incompetency.
Young America remained only a dream. *Democratic Vistas,*
really a violent indictment of America, was first planned during
these years; a small portion of it, under the title "Democracy,"

appeared in *The Galaxy* in 1867. These plans could not fail
to affect the 1867 edition, for they were all part of the same
framework. It is paradoxical in the development of *Leaves of
Grass* that these changing points of view and sentiments should
be carried on year after year in the *same* book. At the time of
the Harlan affair Whitman had admitted to O'Connor that
there were things in his book which he would not now write.[130]
However, he let them stand. *Leaves of Grass* should, according
to the original plan, be a man's whole life in one book. Holloway correctly points out [131] that he could have done it much
better by a series of chronological additions, but Whitman did
not want that.

About his private emotional life during these years we know,
as usual, very little. One result of the diary resolutions at the
outbreak of the war had naturally been a conquest of the
dangerous, the "Satanic" element, in the erotic emotion which
he himself regarded as a threat. Holloway says that in Washington and in the hospitals Whitman learned "to express his
friendship in a more and more paternal manner." [132] And this
paternal sentiment got its fullest release in the famous friendship he formed in 1865 with the nineteen-year-old street-car
conductor Peter Doyle, who was his closest and most intimate
friend until his death. It was these letters, the paternal and
platonic character of which is unmistakable, which Dr. Bucke
published in 1897 under the misleading, but well-considered
title, *Calamus.* There is something very characteristic of Whitman's style and taste in this friendship with an uncultivated
but simple, hearty man of the people whose "education" he
took upon himself, and in whom he found a sort of compensation
for the public among the common people which he never found
elsewhere. Peter himself was scarcely interested in Whitman's
poetry,[133] but such was constantly the poet's fate with those to
whom he felt most strongly attracted. Between Whitman's
"more elegant" friends and the young Irishman there was no
congeniality; Peter was always silent in their company, and
many of them found it difficult to accept him. Only Burroughs
paid any attention to him and could see that in the silent young
fellow there existed a primitive but important emotional life: "A

'mute inglorious' Whitman and a manly and lovable character." [134] Whitman found both refuge and salvation in this peculiar relationship, both release and a certain happiness in that
transformation to the fatherly attitude which has so frequently
been the solution for his psychological type in life and in literature. In the seventies Verlaine tried something similar with less
success.[135] That the relationship was not without temptation for
Whitman we can see in some confused entries in a diary for
1868–70 which Holloway has pointed out.[136] The various passionate exclamations give a tragic insight into his state of mind:

to live a *more Serene Calm philosophic Life—reticent, far more
reticent*—yet cheerful, with pleased spirit . . .

And on the next page:

cheating, childish abandonment of myself, fancying what does not
really exist in another, but is all the time in myself alone—

Later:

. . . —but SAY little—make no explanations—*give no confi-
dences*—

And for June 17, probably 1870:

It is IMPERATIVE, that I obviate & remove myself (& my orbit) *at all
hazards* from this *incessant enormous* & [enormous] PERTURBATION.

The diary concludes with a few sentences, the most important
being three consecutive ones.

Depress the adhesive nature

It is in excess—making life a torment

All this diseased, feverish disproportionate *adhesiveness*

In his book Holloway links these observations closely with the
relationship to Peter Doyle. Especially significant is Whitman's
use of "perturbation" and "adhesiveness," the two words which
in his work are most intimately connected with the Calamus
theme in its dangerous sense. In *Democratic Vistas* he defined
"adhesiveness" as the emotion of comradeship on which this new
democracy is to be founded, the longing for masculine friendship in contrast to "amativeness," which denotes love for woman.

Here suddenly his adhesiveness is "diseased" and "feverish," "making life a torment"! This same word "perturbation" he himself used in a letter to O'Connor as a criticism against the 1860 edition. We have so little "private" material as a guide to Whitman's personality that it is impossible not to ascribe a great deal of importance to that diary fragment.

In Washington, Whitman also knew a number of women, particularly Mrs. O'Connor, Mrs. Burroughs, and Mrs. Ashton. Binns says, "He understood the hearts of women, for there was in him much of the maternal." [137] Like Hans Andersen he had a special talent for talking with women. The question is whether that was all. In the preface to the *Calamus* letters, Dr. Bucke quotes Peter Doyle.

I never knew a case of Walt's being bothered up by a woman. In fact he had nothing special to do with any woman except Mrs. O'Connor and Mrs. Burroughs. His disposition was different. Woman in that sense never came into his head.[138]

Nevertheless, during this period there is a hint of a love affair with a woman. In 1907 Mrs. O'Connor, who after a second marriage was Mrs. Ellen Calder, published some personal recollections of Whitman in the *Atlantic Monthly.* Holloway records that one passage was deleted and he afterwards procured it for his *Uncollected Poetry and Prose of Walt Whitman.* In it Mrs. O'Connor tells how Whitman once confided in her about a friendship he had had with a married woman whose husband discovered their correspondence and because of that attacked and insulted Whitman. In spite of this, the correspondence continued for awhile.

This is the only instance I have known where he was strongly attracted toward any woman in this way. It was this lady for whom he wrote the little poem in "Children of Adam" beginning "Out of the rolling ocean, the crowd." [139]

The poem appeared in *Drum-Taps* and in 1871 was first added as poem No. 7 in *Children of Adam,* where it now stands. Along with "We Two How Long We Were Fool'd," which follows it, it is one of Whitman's most sublime love poems. The poet speaks to a drop which has come to him out of the ocean of the world because of its great longing to do so, but he sends it back to the sea again.

> Return in peace to the ocean, my love;
> I too am part of that ocean, my love . . .

This is not an ordinary erotic sentiment; it is the pantheistic happiness beyond life to which Whitman once more refers and in which he seeks refuge in a way very characteristic of his erotic psychology. Before I understood the stratifications of the book I always associated this poem with Whitman's relationship to Anne Gilchrist, the most serious connection Whitman ever had with a woman. She had actually come over the sea and like the drop had "travel'd a long way merely to look on you, to touch you," and he had sent her away again with a reference to a meeting and a union.

Be not impatient—a little space—know you, I salute the air, the
    ocean and the land,
Every day, at sundown, for your dear sake, my love.

In any case, there is a deeply personal and special meaning, a Calamus meaning, in this poem, which must be explained before it can be understood. It is possible that there were certain points of similarity between his experience with the married woman in Washington and his experience with Anne Gilchrist and that to Mrs. O'Connor he exaggerated his active part in the story. In the same article she says that the reason Whitman never married was that he valued his freedom too highly, and she quoted another exceedingly important observation of his: "He said to me many times *that he did not envy men their wives but he did envy them their children.*" [140]

FOURTH EDITION, 1867

In October, 1867, the fourth edition of *Leaves of Grass* was published, homely in make-up, with 338 pages, and for the first time without a picture of Whitman, but with a carefully revised text and orthography. *Drum-Taps* and the Lincoln poems were not yet placed in all copies; so there are two versions of the 1867 edition. This book contained only a few new poems, among them the first version of the "Inscription" which now introduces the whole book and which in 1867 contributed to the unification of the whole.

SMALL is the theme of the following Chant, yet the greatest— namely, ONE'S-SELF—that wondrous thing, a simple, separate person . . .

. . .

Nor cease at the theme of One's-Self. I speak the word of the modern, the word EN-MASSE.

In "By Blue Ontario's Shore" we have real evidence of Whitman's irresolute and despondent political sentiment while he was working on this edition. This poem had now received its third major revision and for the first time its present title. How accurately Whitman adapted this work to his post-war sentiments is shown by the fact that in the final edition of *Leaves of Grass* it is placed after *Drum-Taps* and the Lincoln poems, not among the earlier poems, although it originated in 1856. In the 1867 edition it is in the appendix following *Drum-Taps* and was included in *Leaves of Grass* proper in 1871. The poem is typical of the period when the first plans for *Democratic Vistas* were buzzing in the poet's head. After the latter work had developed and was published in 1871, many of the hectic, unrestrained foreshadowings in "By Blue Ontario's Shore" were again deleted from the fifth edition of *Leaves of Grass*. Of all Whitman's poems, this one has probably the most varied history. Here in 1867 for the first time its final basic theme runs like a refrain throughout the whole enormously long poem.

As I sat alone, by blue Ontario's shore,
As I mused of these mighty days, and of peace return'd, and the
 dead that return no more,
A Phantom, gigantic, superb, with stern visage, accost'd me;
Chant me a poem, it said, of the range of the high Soul of Poets,
And chant of the welcome bards that breathe but my native air—
 invoke those bards;
And chant me, before you go, the Song of the throes of Democracy.

That is really the important message. For the first time it mentions that Whitman no longer considered himself "The Poet" but wanted other new poets, and refers to the "throes of

Democracy," the pains and aches of democracy. Neither of these things had ever been hinted at before in the book. But in the final version the reference to the poets has characteristically been expunged. Whitman had regained his self-confidence, and the fourth and fifth lines now read:

Chant me the poem, it said, *that comes from the soul of America*
    [that is, his own], *chant me the carol of victory,*
And strike up the marches of Libertad, marches more powerful yet.

But the lines about "the throes of Democracy" were left, and still remain, as a strange and significant revelation in the middle of *Leaves of Grass.* Most of the other additions were about the war, so that the poem would be brought up to date—for example, all of Section 7, which is new, was inclosed in parentheses, a new use of the parenthetical technique in Whitman, and again in Section 11 the long parenthesis about the flag, a line repeated as a refrain in the later version.

Angry cloth I saw there leaping.

Whitman's despondency and distrust are particularly evident when he talks of poets; the idea of the inferiority of American literature had been a constant irritation to him during these years. He expressed himself most emphatically in two places which, like the lines in the introduction, were later removed, the first in 1871 and the second in 1881, because they were discordant with the sentiments of the remainder of the collection. The first passage was in Section 4, immediately preceding the line about "Piety and conformity" which now begins the section.

How dare these insects assume to write poems for America?
For our armies, and the offspring following the armies.

The second and far stronger passage was a part of what is now Section 20 and first appeared in 1867, when it was in Section 22:

Bards for my own land, ere I go, I invoke.

You Bards grand as these days so grand!

.   .   .

Bards towering like hills— . . .

And then the interpolation:

> (no more these dots, these
> pigmies, these little piping straws, these gnats,
> that fill the hour, to pass for poets;).

These parenthetical lines were removed in 1881. "By Blue Ontario's Shore" is thus a typical example of how Whitman revised his book. At the same time it shows no less clearly the dangers of these deposits left from edition to edition. Moreover, the poem is the longest and the weakest in the book. It is inharmonious and lacking in logic. The reasons for these defects are enlightening. It has too many discordant elements in it. The program of 1855 is mixed with the national and democratic sentiments of 1867, and the invocation of *a* poet (all of Section 6) harshly contradicts the appeal for *poets*. The result is inevitably a mighty oratorical mish-mash mingled with a few grains of gold. At the same time it is Whitman's most nationalistic poem, and even prates of a jingoistic nationalism ("Underneath all, nativity," Section 16), which jars violently with the note of universal democracy in the remainder of the collection. But even so, the poem is typical of Whitman's 1867 state of mind.

The new rings added to the old ones of the book clearly indicate what ideas occupied Whitman at that time. Simultaneously with the publication of the fourth edition his reputation began to grow; his future world-wide reputation had its roots in the Washington period between 1867–73. Burroughs published his *Notes on Walt Whitman as Poet and Person* at the time the fourth edition appeared, though it was later superseded by a far more personal and more independent essay in *Birds and Poets*, 1877. Burroughs's *Notes* continued the sentiments of O'Connor's *Good Gray Poet*, and substantially aided the sale of the poetry. In the following year O'Connor's Whitman novel, *The Carpenter*, appeared, the first of the ill-advised attempts to make Whitman into a modern Christ. Most important of all was the English edition of *Leaves of Grass*, called *Poems by Walt Whitman*, selected and edited by W. M. Rossetti, which appeared in February, 1868, and opened to the whole English reading world the poet whose work Rossetti referred to in the preface as no less than "the largest poetical performance of our period." Whitman wanted to write the preface himself and was dissatisfied when Rossetti refused, nor did the choice of poems altogether please him. In reality the English editions of Whitman's poems, even up to the present, have been absurdly cut. Since Whitman refused to have single lines or expressions omitted from his poetry, the result was that "Song of Myself," "The Sleepers," and all of *Children of Adam* were omitted from the English editions.[141] Nevertheless, that English edition naturally had a very definite significance for Whitman's reputation. Notices of approval and admiration poured in. Whitman then began a correspondence with Tennyson, Symonds, Dowden, and Anne Gilchrist. The latter had, through Rossetti, secured a complete American edition, which entirely overwhelmed her. She wrote to Rossetti about the sexual poems.

I will take courage to say frankly that I find them also beautiful, and that I think even you have misapprehended them. Perhaps indeed they were chiefly written for wives!

Her enthusiastic letter about Whitman was afterwards published in 1870 in the *Boston Radical* as the famous article, "A Woman's Estimate of Walt Whitman," which had great influence in America.[142] Edward Dowden, who, with Symonds, was the first English historian of literature to recognize Whitman, wrote an article for the *Westminster Review* in 1871, and the same year Swinburne, who had already discussed Whitman in his book on Blake, 1868, included in *Songs before Sunrise* a poem, "To Walt Whitman in America," with the stately and characteristic Swinburnian verse, which reflected the mood of all young England.

> O strong-winged soul with prophetic
>   Lips hot with the bloodbeats of song,
> With tremor of heartstrings magnetic
>   With thoughts as thunders in throng,
> With consonant ardours of chords
> That pierce men's souls as with swords
>   And hale them hearing along,

> Make us too music, to be with us
>> As a word from a world's heart-warm;
> To sail the dark as a sea with us,
>> Full-sailed, outsinging the storm,
> A song to put fire in our ears
> Whose burning shall burn up tears,
>> Whose sign bid battle reform; . . .

The poem is a typical example of the immediate response Whitman can arouse in youthful readers.

Other countries were also beginning to discover the new American poet. In the *Augsburger Allgemeine Zeitung*, in April, 1868, Freiligrath published the first German article on Whitman. This, along with ten short translations from *Drum-Taps*, is now included in his *Gesammelte Werke*. For Freiligrath, Whitman was "a marvelous phenomenon" who sometimes reminded him of Hamann, sometimes of Carlyle, and about the poetry he exclaimed:

Are we standing before poetic art of the future as a few years ago the music of the future confronted us? And is Walt Whitman greater than Richard Wagner? [143]

Through Rudolf Schmidt, Denmark also had the honor of recognizing Whitman among the first European nations. In February, 1872, Schmidt wrote his great article in the literary review *For Idé og Virkelighed*. And in the same year the first French essay about Whitman appeared, "Un poéte americain," by Th. Bentzon (Mme. Thérèse Blanc) in *Revue de deux Mondes*, June, 1872. Both Freiligrath and Rudolf Schmidt corresponded with Whitman. From one of Schmidt's letters Traubel quotes a remark of Bjørnson's about Whitman: "W.W. makes me a joy as no new man in many years, and in one respect the greatest I have ever had." [144] At that time Burroughs made a trip to England and visited Whitman's friends there and in Ireland—"Whitmaniacs" as O'Connor jokingly called them, a designation Whitman's opponents afterwards appropriated, to O'Connor's delight: "They are indebted to us for even their epithets of abuse." [145]

But his growing reputation, the increasing appreciation

through all these years, was confined exclusively to those interested in literature and did not spread to the greater public.
Whitman continued to write poetry and went on with the little
prose work *Democratic Vistas,* originally intended as a reply
to Carlyle's bitter, spiteful attack on democracy in "Shooting
Niagara," 1867. Gradually it became an American counterpart
of Carlyle's book, and is thus another example of Carlyle's influence on Whitman. *Democratic Vistas* was published in Washington in the fall of 1871, simultaneously with the fifth edition
of *Leaves of Grass,* but received no attention: "it remains entirely unread, uncalled for," Whitman wrote Edward Dowden.[146] Denmark has the honor of being the only country which
in those early days showed any interest in this prose; Rudolf
Schmidt translated it into Danish in 1874 as *Demokratiske
Fremblik af Walt Whitman* (Schønbergs Forlag, Copenhagen).
Naturally this book is extremely interesting now as a supplement to the poems. Whitman's democracy in *Leaves of Grass* is
so comprehensive that it can be appropriated by all democratic
sects, and throughout the years they have, each for itself, proclaimed Whitman as their particular poet. But in this little
book of prose Whitman gave his democracy its accurate definition—and restriction. What Whitman tried to say in the 1855
Preface he now clarified and interpreted out of his new experiences since then. *Democratic Vistas* is invaluable as a statement
of the political and social thinking that actually lay beneath
Leaves of Grass. Rudolf Schmidt noticed that the book was far
from offering any support for the actual social democratic
movements which, in those years, tried to appropriate Whitman.
In the introduction to his translation he said: "Walt Whitman
is not suited to lend a helping hand to our democratic leaders."
Whitman was no more of a social democrat than he was an
abolitionist or an "experimental community man." His democracy transcends the personal limitations, the personal programs.
It is a cosmic, pantheistic democracy.

  Whitman says exactly this in one of the highpoints of the
book:

Disengage yourself from parties. They have been useful, and to
some extent remain so; but the floating, uncommitted electors,

farmers, clerks, mechanics, the masters of parties—watching aloof, inclining victory this side or that side—such are the ones most needed, present and future. *For America, if eligible at all to down-fall and ruin, is eligible within herself, not without;* . . . it behooves you to convey yourself implicitly to no party, nor submit blindly to their dictators, but steadily hold yourself judge and master over all of them.

It is these independent ideas which support democracy. For him democracy means the social condition that offers the best opportunity for the development of self-reliant personalities of real individuality. The aim is for a new and better race. That can only occur in a society in which no one class is privileged, but such is not yet the case in America, where money determines the social standing; and the result is—and this is where Whitman's crushing attack begins—that *morally*, America has hitherto originated nothing. He looks in vain for the typical American personality in oratory or literature. There are some orators and poets, "But touch'd by the national test, or tried by the standards of democratic personality, they wither to ashes." Then follows a typical oratorical passage paralleling the lines quoted from "By Blue Ontario's Shore."

Do you call those genteel little creatures American poets? Do you term that perpetual, pistareen, pastepot work, American art, American drama, taste, verse? I think I hear, echoed as from some mountain-top afar in the west, the scornful laugh of the Genius of these States. . . . The whole present system of the officering and personnel of the army and navy of these States . . . is a monstrous exotic . . .

Earlier he had said:

. . . society, in these States, is canker'd, crude, superstitious, and rotten. . . . Never was there, perhaps, more hollowness at heart than at present, and here in the United States. . . . A lot of churches, sects &c, the most dismal phantasms I know. . . . The depravity of the business classes of our country is not less than has been supposed, but infinitely greater. The official services of America . . . in all their branches and departments . . . are saturated in corruption, bribery, falsehood, mal-administration. . . . In vain do we march with unprecedented strides to empire so colossal, outvying the antique, beyond Alexander's, beyond the proudest sway of Rome. In vain have we annex'd Texas, California, Alaska, and reach north for Canada, and south for Cuba. It is as if we were somehow being endow'd with a vast and more and more thoroughly-appointed body, and then left with little or no soul.

This indictment is remarkable for a poet who is popularly supposed to be an optimistic and almost blind worshiper of his part of the world. Accurately we see Whitman emerge as a forerunner of the modern American writers for whom criticism of their country, for the same reasons as Whitman's, is the chief motif of their work. In *Democratic Vistas* Whitman directed an attack on America as harsh and violent as that of the moderns, and with a foreboding of the dangers which we today glimpse in the works of Upton Sinclair—that democracy as such could become the most appalling failure in history: "The most tremendous failure of all time!" In his last prose article, *A Backward Glance o'er Travel'd Roads,* now included in many editions of *Leaves of Grass,* Whitman repeated, although in milder terms, that "I consider 'Leaves of Grass' and its theory experimental—as, in the deepest sense, I consider our American republic itself to be, with its theory." In *Democratic Vistas* more clearly than elsewhere in Whitman's work we can see the "throes of democracy." It was not a polemic against but rather a confirmation of Carlyle—at whose death Whitman wrote in *Specimen Days:* "I doubt if he ever thought or said half as bad words about us as we deserve." Remarkable words for the poet of democracy.

Therefore it is not right to say that Whitman proclaims his part of the world for what it is; *in his poetry he proclaims what he believes it can become.* Carlyle had questioned ironically whether anyone believed America could gain anything by taking in the scum of all nations. Whitman hoped for a mighty integration, a powerful synthesis—"A teeming nation of nations!" Like De Tocqueville and Fredrika Bremer, Whitman saw the future of the States as lying westward. He took up Carlyle's idea about heroes and great personalities and reshaped them to his program. Such personalities would come from mid-America. The task is to arrange social conditions so that they are favorable for the development of personalities. Equal rights for women is one of the most important items in the program, and complete frankness on the sex question. America must free herself from the women and mothers known in European literature and form her own model woman. The book goes on with demands for great American orators, for a national American opera, and for poets, especially: "I demand races of orbic bards, with unconditional uncompromising sway." Whitman mentions as examples of the "bards" who are his ideals Jesus in Judea and Lucretius in Rome. *Such poets will be able to establish the new cosmic religion which it is the chief function of poetic art to create since science has thrown overboard the old religions.* These poets will break away from all "the grim estimates inherited from the Puritans, hell, natural depravity, and the like." We see to what extent Whitman outlined the program which the more recent American writers have followed. First, the existing material trend in the whole life of the United States must be checked. If it continues "our modern civilization, with all its improvements, is in vain, and we are on the road to a destiny, a status, equivalent, in its real world to that of the fabled damned."

Democratic Vistas was well written, undoubtedly Whitman's finest prose work. Its oratorical character is worth noting, because it gives us an idea of the sort of oratorical presentation which Whitman dreamed of giving. Most interesting are the passages in which the prose, as on previous occasions, slips unconsciously into Whitmanesque verse; this happens particularly at the lyrical climaxes, in descriptions of soldiers during the war or of the ancient poets: "along the great highways of time." Two noteworthy themes are praise of woman in her role as mother—this is where Whitman finds the classics weakest— and finally the invocation of the poet who is fitted to sing "the great poem of death." The danger of the book is the mixture of despair and optimism. In certain ways the duality reminds us of "By Blue Ontario's Shore," but we must remember that it is also the characteristic duality of *Leaves of Grass.*

Democratic Vistas is invaluable as a commentary on *Leaves of Grass:* in the same way as does the 1855 Preface it provides theoretical criteria for Whitman's art. His democracy is far different from what is usually meant by the term. "Produce great individuals, the rest follows" was one of his pronouncements in "By Blue Ontario's Shore." Thus, he approximated Carlyle's hero worship and Nietzsche's theory of supermen. O'Connor must have seen with increasing disapproval that at the end of the 1860's and the beginning of the 1870's Whitman was getting farther and farther away from the tenets of the Democratic party which O'Connor followed. Furthermore, O'Connor was a passionate abolitionist, and after the war Whitman realized that the Negroes were still far from being capable of governing themselves, that their emancipation must proceed slowly and gradually, and he did not agree that they should have membership in Congress. When Bazalgette tried to explain the cause of Whitman's break with O'Connor he said that in Whitman's opinion whatever concerned democracy could be based only "on the consciousness and dignity of the individual." *The paradox is that Whitman, like Hegel, was really a natural conservative.* A break with the petulant, emotional radical O'Connor was unavoidable. One evening in 1871 the two friends had a big quarrel, so violent that for many years they refused to meet, and then would not speak to each other when, four years later, in 1875, they met accidentally at a memorial dinner for Poe.[147]

During the same year that *Democratic Vistas* was published Whitman had two opportunities to appear as a speaker or reader. At the opening of the Exposition held by the American Institute he recited "Song of the Exposition," which he had written for the occasion. The artistic restraint of the poem, with its famous lines about the muse having deserted Europe and now being settled in America, was a glaring contrast to his real opinions during the period. Henry Bryan Binns attempted to free the poem from the thickheaded Americanisms which envelop it by calling it a "half-humorous poem," [148]—an interpretation with which none of the other Whitman scholars agree. The poem is devoid of humor. Later in the year, as a guest at Dartmouth College, he read "As a Strong Bird on Pinions Free." Afterwards he had printed in the Washington *Chronicle* an account of the recital, which Rudolf Schmidt quoted in his

Buster og Masker [149] as a typical American description of Walt
Whitman, though Holloway has pointed out that it was written by Whitman himself, "still under the awkward necessity of
being his own press agent." [150] And it was later revealed that
the invitation to Dartmouth had come about as a joke, a plot
among the students to embarrass their superiors by inviting
a man with such a notoriously bad reputation in academic circles as Whitman.

FIFTH EDITION, 1871

Both "Song of the Exposition" and "Thou Mother with
Equal Brood" (which "As a Strong Bird on Pinions Free" was
finally called in later editions) seem to reveal a decline in Whitman's poetic power, but this can be attributed to the fact that
these poems were commissioned. Actually the fifth edition of
Leaves of Grass, 1871, is one of the finest. It was printed on
thick paper, with a drawing by W. J. Linton, and of the
twenty-eight newly added poems, many are important. "Proud
Music of the Storm" and "Passage to India" are among his best
works. These two poems were not included in the book itself at
first, but were placed in one of the supplements that had now
become almost a regular part of each edition of *Leaves of
Grass.*[151] This fact in itself reveals Whitman's method. The
supplement in this edition took the title of the introductory
poem, "Passage to India."

Among the new poems are a great many "Inscriptions," of
which the most famous are "As I Pondered in Silence," now
second in the book, about the poetic genius of old lands who
looks at the poet of the new world with flaming eyes and asks,
"What singest thou?"; "In Cabin'd Ships at Sea"; and "When
I Read the Book, the Biography Famous," concerning how
little we really know regarding a poet's life. A second group of
poems treats of death: "Darest Thou Now, O Soul," "Of Him I
Love," "Whispers of Heavenly Death," "Pensive and Faltering," "Thought" (afterward called "As They Draw to a
Close"), "The Last Invocation" and "Now Finalé to the Shore."
The latter, now next to last in the section called *Songs of Part-
ing,* tells of the farewell of an old sailor who prepares for his

last interminable cruise—a fine poem, but notorious because of
the home-coined word finalé in the title, all the more astonishing
because it comes next to the end of the collection.[152]

During the course of the years the number of poems between
those forming the introduction and the conclusion in *Leaves of
Grass* constantly increased. In addition to the general ones recently added, this edition contains several fine "occasional
pieces," for example, "The Singer in Prison," about the concert
given in Sing Sing by Parepa Rosas; "Brother of All, with
Generous Hand," a memorial poem to the philanthropist, and
Maecenas, George Peabody; and finally, along with a few new
poems in *Drum-Taps*, such as "Ethiopia Saluting the Colors,"
"Marches Now the War Is Over" (later "Adieu to a Soldier"),
there is the great poem "Carol of Harvest for 1867" (later called
"Return of the Heroes"), with the interesting introductory lines
in Section 5: "When late I sang, sad was my voice," which reflect the sentiments of both 1860 and 1867 and is one of the
clues Whitman has left in the book as evidence of the
widely different moods in which its various sections were written.

All these poems were only additions to the book as it then
stood, variations on the familiar themes. They do not denote
any growth, only a static condition. The enrichment of the collection is in "Proud Music of the Storm" and "Passage to India," two of Whitman's most characteristically great poems.
"Proud Music of the Storm," which is quite unjustifiably often
omitted from collections of his poetry, gives a most interesting
insight into how much Whitman's inspiration was affected by
music. It is a further development of the theme in the shorter
poem, "That Music Always around Me," from 1860, originally
a *Calamus* poem, and a continuation of the motif of the tenor,
"large and fresh as creation" in Section 26 of "Song of Myself,"
conveying the mood of inspiration and ecstasy which music
aroused in him. In *Democratic Vistas* he had invoked, along
with the new school of poets, the great new American opera
which must come. We see in "Proud Music of the Storm" what
opera music really meant to him, how the moods and motifs
from operas he had heard, including *Norma, Lucia, The Hugue-*

nots, Don Juan, Ernani, Robert le Diable, along with memories
of his mother's voice, the voice of the rain, and the scream of
the wild bird, have been reset in inspired lines of verse. Whitman's entire world is pictured for a moment as a musical composition.

Now the great organ sounds,
Tremulous—while underneath, (as the hid footholds of the earth,
On which arising, rest, and leaping forth, depend,
All shapes of beauty, grace and strength—all hues we know,
Green blades of grass, and warbling birds—children that gambol
    and play—the clouds of heaven above,)
The strong base stands, and its pulsations intermit not,
Bathing, supporting, merging all the rest—maternity of all the
    rest.

In this poem Whitman succeeds in giving the impression of
how he conceives all creation as a humming orchestra "of winds
and words and mighty ocean waves," which the great director
controls with his hand.

Tutti! for Earth and Heaven!
The Almighty Leader now for me, for once, has signal'd with his
    wand.
The manly strophe of the husbands of the world,
And all the wives responding.

The tongues of violins!
(I think, O tongues, ye tell this heart, that cannot tell itself;
This brooding, yearning heart, that cannot tell itself.)

The composition reminds us of "The Sleepers." Even the
detailed description of the orchestra and the thousands of voices
occurs in a dream from which the poet, as in "The Sleepers,"
awakes and goes out into the day "refreshed by his celestial
dream." But at the same time the dream was a hint to the poet
and his soul as to the kind of poem it was now his duty to write
since he had heard that great symphony of creation.

But, to a new rhythmus fitted for thee,
Poems, bridging the way from Life to Death, vaguely wafted in
    night air, uncaught, unwritten,
Which, let us go forth in the bold day, and write.

It is noteworthy that that command, that inspiration, does not apply to the poems of *Leaves of Grass* so far written, but only *to some new poems which Whitman, now fifty years old, had planned to write.*

"Passage to India," the second major poem, was originally considered an introduction for a whole new collection of poetry which, in continuation as well as in contrast to *Leaves of Grass,* would celebrate life after death, the invisible world in contrast to the visible and real.[153] Some of the short poems of 1871 show the influence of this new plan, for example, "Joy, Shipmate, Joy," which the poet shouts to his soul in the hour of death. But this one poem was the only novelty, and even "Passage to India" was, before its completion, fitted into the general tone of the old collection, which was strengthened by its high poetic quality.

This poem starts with a celebration of two great triumphs of modern technicians in the years just preceding: the opening of the Suez Canal and the completion of the Pacific Railroad in 1869, "surmounting every barrier." In "Starting from Paumanok" Whitman had celebrated the great trans-Atlantic cable, and now he celebrates these new miracles, "strong light work of engineers." Just as in the older poem the heartbeats of Europe and America met under the sea and answered each other, so now shall peoples and races of the earth meet and be united.

> The races, neighbors, to marry and be given in marriage,
> The oceans to be cross'd, the distant brought near,
> The lands to be welded together.

For the poet this event has not only practical, but, to a far greater degree, ideal significance.

> You, not for trade or transportation only,
> But in God's name, and for thy sake, O soul.

The new route to India shall again revive for humanity the old sagas and legends, the old language and dreams. This is the way to India of which Columbus also once dreamed.

> (Ah Genoese, thy dream! thy dream!
> Centuries after thou art laid in thy grave,
> The shore thou foundest verifies thy dream!)

The reference to Columbus is typical and important. For Whitman, as later for Johannes V. Jensen, he represents the incarnation of all human yearning beyond the daily routine, a yearning which Whitman also knew, and which might find fulfillment in these new events.

After the seas are all cross'd, (as they seem already cross'd,)
After the great captains and engineers have accomplish'd their
    work,
After the noble inventors—after the scientists, the chemist, the
    geologist, ethnologist,
Finally shall come the Poet, worthy of that name;
The true Son of God shall come, singing his songs.

This is the chief content of the first part of this enthusiastic and optimistic poem. This constitutes the *universal* in it, the poet's hope for humanity; he is already far beyond the narrow materialism of 1867. In the latter part of the poem he speaks of his own personal longing, and here the mood is obviously a continuation of the 1860 tone in the poetry of death. For the poet the way to India is a future world in this life, a world where

All affection shall be fully responded to—the secret shall be told;

.   .   .

(O pensive soul of me! O thirst unsatisfied! waitest not there?
Waitest not haply for us, somewhere there, the Comrade perfect?)

We see the poet's personal longing and pain expanding into a religious emotion. "The Untold Want," the title of one of the little "Inscriptions" originally intended as an introduction to the new collection about the future world and the kingdom of the soul, is now significantly found among the *Songs of Parting*. Here the unspoken wish is the wish for death, once more the pantheistic longing for release and fulfillment, union with the divinity.

    Bathe me, O God, in thee—mounting to thee,
    I and my soul to range in range of thee.

There is a basis for comparison of this emerging religious emotion with the old Christian mysticism, or with Swedenborg, who also expected the ideal love in the future world. The optimism of the poem, then, is that of the poet and his soul in their eagerness for the journey to the great "India."

O we can wait no longer!
We too take ship, O soul!

.   .   .

Amid the wafting winds, (thou pressing me to thee, I thee to me,
    O soul,). . .

Long enough have we stood like trees in the ground; now we shall go out onto the deep waters.

Passage to more than India!
O secret of the earth and sky!
Of you, O waters of the sea! O winding creeks and rivers!
Of you, O woods and fields! Of you, strong mountains of my land!
Of you, O prairies! Of you, gray rocks!
O morning red! O clouds! O rain and snows!
O day and night, passage to you!
O sun and moon, and all you stars! Sirius and Jupiter!
Passage to you!

Passage—immediate passage! the blood burns in my veins!
Away, O soul! hoist instantly the anchor!

.   .   .

O my brave soul!
O farther, farther sail!
O daring joy, but safe! Are they not all the seas of God?
O farther, farther, farther sail!

This is a pantheistic religious hymn, the climax of which is the description of consummation, of fulfillment, of the great meeting.

As, fill'd with friendship, love complete, the Elder Brother found,
The Younger melts in fondness in his arms.

We recognize the theme of earlier poems, from "Song of Myself" the visit to the "orchard of the spheres," from "Song of Joys" the "swelling ship of Joy" which launches out from the land with all sails set. The note of personal suffering and despair that, as already pointed out, inspired the last dream-wish of

1860 have in 1871 been refined to a completely religious poetry, in which the "shout of joy" is repeated with deeper meaning. Since 1860 Whitman had been to war and heard "the great poetry of death." [154]

Thus, "Passage to India," instead of becoming the introduction to a new collection of verse with new content, became instead a poetic climax to *Leaves of Grass*, a strengthening and refining of earlier motifs. The farewell that Whitman intended to mean a farewell to the poetry he had written about life became a farewell to life—in any case, a conclusion, not a beginning. "Passage to India" took its place among the many *Songs of Parting* in *Leaves of Grass*. During the twenty years Whitman still had to live as a crippled old man, incapable of any active labor, he continued to get his book ready, but did not begin a new one. And his songs about the strange spheres he took, "uncaught, unwritten," with him on his own Passage to India.

Holloway called the years of Whitman's life after the 1871 *Leaves of Grass* the "Long Afternoon," and it was fundamentally colored by his illness and invalidism, which throughout the whole time made him dependent on strangers, often in an embarrassing way. At best it was a twenty-year battle with death, with periods of comparative good health and periods of frightful weakness and depression.

It was in January, 1873, in his fifty-fourth year, that paralysis, which seven years before had given its first warning, returned and tied him to his bed. For a few months his condition wavered between hope and despair. In May he recovered sufficiently to go to his mother's sick-bed in George's home, in the industrial town of Camden, New Jersey, outside Philadelphia, but his mother's death shocked him so that his own condition grew worse, and he was unable to return to Washington. He had to stay in Camden, dependent on his brother, who did not understand him, cut off from all connection with his most intimate friends, from Burroughs, and above all, from Peter Doyle, who had a permanent position as baggage-master on the Baltimore and Ohio Railroad. Whitman's position in Washington was kept open for him until the middle of the following year, when he was discharged and someone else took his place. By that time he could hobble around with a cane, but only as an invalid. His letters to Peter Doyle reflect his helpless condition and his grief over his mother's death. In 1874 he wrote a few poems, of which "Prayer of Columbus" is the most important because it so completely expressed his Camden mood. Whitman identified himself with the aged Columbus.

A batter'd, wreck'd old man,
Thrown on this savage shore, far, far from home,
Pent by the sea, and dark rebellious brows, twelve dreary months,
Sore, stiff with many toils, sicken'd, and nigh to death,
I take my way along the island's edge,
Venting a heavy heart.

Columbus is cast off, but is still certain that his work has not been in vain.

For that, O God—be it my latest word—here on my knees,
Old, poor, and paralyzed—I thank Thee.

Others will complete what he has begun; Europe's dead cross shall grow flowers and leaves here in America; other ships shall sail in her cool waters.

Shadowy, vast shapes, smile through the air and sky,
And on the distant waves sail countless ships,
And anthems in new tongues I hear saluting me.

The sentiment is clear and strong, a continuation but also a limitation of the theme from "Passage to India"—it is no longer the poet who travels, but others. The poem marks a gain for the book and it takes its place there as a direct addition to "Passage to India." From the same period comes "Song of the Redwood Tree," the content of which is a résumé of earlier themes, but within their frame Whitman now identifies himself with "the mighty dying tree in the redwood forest," which at its fall will make room for those who come after it. It is in the same mood as the Columbus poem.

We welcome what we wrought for through the past,
And leave the field for them.

But in the editorial integration this poem was moved forward in the collection, and now stands among the great oratorical poems, where it is deprived of its association with the Camden poetry.

Whitman now had only his book to live for, and for twenty years the rearrangement and expansion of it was his aim and occupation. His straitened economic condition was his worst handicap. But help came from England in 1876, when Robert Buchanan published an open letter in the London *News* describing Whitman's illness and peculiar situation, without recognition in his native country and reduced to being his own publisher. At the same time there was an appeal for subscriptions to the new edition of his book, the sixth edition of *Leaves of Grass*, the so-called Centennial edition of 1876. This was merely a reprint of the 1871 edition with the added supplement *Two Rivulets* which contained *Democratic Vistas* and a few new poems, among them "Eidólons" and "Song of the Universal." The book sold for ten dollars, but many of the English subscribers, including people outside the regular group of Whitman admirers, for example, Edmund Gosse and George Saintsbury, followed the example of Tennyson and Ruskin in paying double or treble the price. The sale was on the whole very successful, and for a time Whitman could feel economically secure.

George William Curtis replied to Buchanan with an open letter in *Harper's Monthly* for June, 1876, denying the accusation that Americans rejected Whitman.

Mr. Whitman has had the same opportunity that Mr. Bryant and Mr. Longfellow have had. His works have been very widely read and criticised. He has found a place in several of the chief magazines. . . . There is no conspiracy against Mr. Whitman, nor any jealousy of him among the acknowledged chiefs of American literature.[155]

Curtis had a certain amount of truth on his side. Although the New England poets, with Lowell and Holmes in the lead, were always unreasoningly opposed to Whitman, this was not true of the younger circle of American intellectuals. Members of the new school of writers, Bret Harte, Mark Twain, Joaquin Miller, and later Hamlin Garland clearly recognized Whitman's importance. It is characteristic that the large American anthology of a century of American lyrics, published by W. J. Linton, in

London, in 1878, had Linton's own portrait of Whitman as a frontispiece, the only picture in the book, and included eight poems by Whitman, a number equaled only by Bryant, Longfellow, Whittier, and Lowell. Even the stories of the completely "unappreciated Walt" have grown into a myth.

In his room at George's home on Stevens Street, and after 1883 in the unattractive little house in Mickle Street which he bought with funds from the sale of his book, Whitman received visits from curiosity seekers and readers, especially those belonging to the inner circle of special admirers who in later years would do the real work of spreading his fame. In 1877 he received the first visit from young Edward Carpenter, who had read him at a very early age, and whose psychological make-up was similar to that of Symonds. Later his own collection of poems, *Towards Democracy*, became the most obviously direct imitation of *Leaves of Grass* in world literature. That same year came Dr. Maurice Bucke (1837–1902), a gifted Canadian doctor, but also something of a mystic. He found kindred traits in Whitman and proclaimed, after he knew him more intimately, that he was "one of the greatest men, if not the very greatest man, that the world has so far produced." But his blind admiration lessened his value as an objective critic. After him came the well-known orator Colonel Robert Ingersoll, who was Whitman's admirer, and later, among other services, delivered a memorial address at his grave. William Sloan Kennedy (1850–1929), then living in Philadelphia, visited Whitman repeatedly, and throughout the years was one of the most zealous and most eloquent of "the hot little prophets." In a letter to Burroughs in 1881, which Clara Barrus quotes, Kennedy placed Whitman on a par with Jesus: "I think him the equal, and in many respects the superior of the much misunderstood Jesus, and I have said so." [156] We can get some idea of Whitman's astonishing personal magnetism, noticed by Moncure Conway earlier, by observing his effect on all these young men, in spite of his affliction. Three other young Philadelphia journalists, Talcott Williams, Harrison Morris, and Thomas Donaldson, each later wrote books and articles about Whitman. The most intimate of all these young friends was Horace Traubel, a

young poet, who simply consecrated his life to Whitman. He
spent a part of each day with him for the last ten years of Whitman's life, and after Whitman's death was, with Thomas B.
Harned and Dr. Bucke, his literary executor. He published a
paper, *The Conservator* (1890–1908), in which many Whitmanesque themes were thoroughly aired and discussed. Traubel had scarcely any outstanding ability, as is plainly evident
from his three volume book *With Walt Whitman in Camden*,
to which Burroughs objected when the first volume appeared,
in 1906: "There is too much of it. . . . After a while this tires
one. It might have been equal to 'Eckermann's Conversations
with Goethe' if there had been an Eckermann instead of a Traubel to do it." [157] Ernest Boyd, in a Whitman study in the
American Mercury, December, 1925,[158] referred to Traubel as
a "pseudo-Whitman and a pseudo-Boswell." Like Carpenter,
Traubel published a Whitmanesque collection of poems, *Chants
Communal*, 1904, which is entirely worthless. But one can only
agree with Bliss Perry when he says, "of Mr. Traubel's loyal
discipleship it is impossible to speak too highly." [159]

From England, where Whitman found his most zealous readers, there were many visitors. Dowden had written about him
in *Studies in Literature*, in 1878, Stevenson in *Familiar Studies
of Men and Books*, 1882, and in 1883 George Meredith wrote a
poem to him.[160] Visits by notable Englishmen became a regular
occurrence. Henry Irving, Edmund Gosse, Ernest Rhys, Sir
Edwin Arnold, Oscar Wilde, and Frank Harris were among
those who came to Camden, and many of them wrote about their
visits.[161] Most of these accounts show the astonishing and tremendous impression Whitman made on those who met him personally. Frank Harris says he heard him deliver an address on
Tom Paine and considered him a failure as a speaker, but on
closer acquaintance found him "a personality of a new type,
which in the course of time became more and more precious as
one of the best America has produced." [162] This interest in and
admiration for Whitman also put its stamp on the English
novel. George Gissing, in his novel *Thyrza*, 1887, described a
Whitmanian, Walter Egremont, who regards it as his life-work
to further the recognition of Whitman. "Whitman is a tonic be-

yond all to be found in the druggist shop. I imagine that to live with the man himself for a few days would be the best thing that could befall an invalid; surely vital force would come out of him" (*Thyrza*, Chapter XXXV). A similar character is found in Lucas Malet's (pseudonym of Mary Kingsley Harrison) success-novel *The Wages of Sin*.

Among the English friends and admirers, Anne Gilchrist naturally deserves a more detailed discussion because her famous friendship for Whitman, which Binns, not without reason, compared to that between Michael Angelo and Vittoria Colonna,[163] was really a pitiful tragedy. That first became obvious in 1918, when her letters to Whitman were made public and another one of the myths about him was destroyed, to the dismay of the prophets.

Anne Gilchrist was born in 1828, and in 1861 was left a widow by Alexander Gilchrist, whose book on Blake she finished and published with the help of the Rossettis. She was a gifted woman, not beautiful, but because of her broadmindedness she played a certain role in the literary England of the sixties. Tennyson, Carlyle, and the Rossettis thought very highly of her. We know the impression Whitman's book made on her through her article, "A Woman's Estimate of Walt Whitman," which was so important in the growth of Whitman's reputation. In gratitude Whitman sent her his picture through William Rossetti. Formal and purely businesslike as was this link between a poet and one of his admirers, yet it was for her the beginning of a passionate and unhappy love for Whitman, which we can follow throughout all its phases in her correspondence with him between 1871 and her death in 1885—though correspondence is scarcely the word. Beside her many long, eloquent, always well-written but frankly passionate letters we find Whitman's few, very brief, awkward, and reserved replies, in which he is always trying to bring the relationship into focus as a correspondence between a poet and his reader, not between a man and a woman. But her ardor was only heightened by Whitman's reticence, and if a letter did not come—and that occurred frequently—she redoubled the violence and frankness of her expression. For example, when he did not answer her first direct proposal of marriage in a letter of September 3, 1871, she repeated it in even stronger terms on October 23, and almost begged him for an answer.

It is scarcely too much to say that nowhere in all world literature is there another case of a woman offering herself so completely and unreservedly as Anne Gilchrist did in this letter to Whitman. In her first letter she had dismissed her first marriage by denying that she had ever seriously loved her first husband; she accepted Whitman's language and manner of speaking in his poetry and construed it as a personal declaration of love.

Besides, it is not true thou hast not sought or loved me. For when I read the divine poems I feel all folded round in thy love: I feel often as if thou wast pleading so passionately for the love of the woman that can understand thee—that I know not how to bear the yearning answering tenderness that fills my breast. I know that a woman may without hurt to her pride—without stain or blame— tell her love to thee. I feel for a certainty that she may. Try me for this life, my darling—see if I cannot so live, so grow, so learn, so love, that when I die you will say, "This woman has grown to be a very part of me. My soul must have her loving companionship everywhere & in all things. I alone & she alone are not complete identities—it is I and she together in a new, divine, perfect union that form the one complete identity." [164]

We understand in what a dilemma such a letter placed Whitman, who did not want it and had given no occasion for it. His answer, short and noncommittal as it was, ought to have stopped her. Even after that letter, he treated her only as an enthusiastic reader. "Enough that there surely exists so beautiful and a delicate relation, accepted by both of us with joy." [165] But in spite of that "enough," which he repeated several times, she persisted. From 1872 on she wanted to come to him, but he ignored her wish. His illness gave her an excuse: "I believe, my dear love, that what you need to help on your recovery is a woman's tender, cherishing love and care . . ." [166] Her expressions grew warmer and warmer. To the modern reader they sound almost comic in their unequivocal frankness. In a letter in November, 1875, she no longer asks whether she could come to him, but slips in sentence after sentence which gradually reveal the fact that she is coming. The letter probably embarrassed Whitman terribly. In a short note he tried to stop her, but April 21, 1876, she replied:

Do not dissuade me from coming this autumn, my dearest Friend. I have waited patiently—7 years—patiently, yet often, especially since your illness, with such painful yearning your heart would yearn towards me if you realized it—I cannot wait any longer.[167]

And in the autumn of 1876 she went from England to America with two of her children, Herbert, who was to become a painter, and Beatrice, who was to be a nurse, and established herself in Philadelphia near Whitman.

Without knowing any of the details of the two years she lived there, it is still possible to glimpse the disappointment and pain this situation must have caused a woman of her sensibility, although Whitman and she saw each other and he often spent evenings with her and her children. In 1878 she moved to New York, and the correspondence was renewed. In 1879 she returned to England. Whitman seems to have gotten on well with the children, *but he did not write her a line when her daughter died, in 1881.* His letters to her during the last years were mostly composed of newspaper clippings about himself from the local paper. His attitude toward her is both understandable and pardonable. The situation of 1864 with the woman in Washington was repeated, only more cruelly, because Whitman was now done with life and had no strength for new complications. Illness had aged him. She was the drop which came to him from the ocean and which he sent back to the ocean again.

But as for me, for you, the irresistible ocean is to separate us, although both were part of the same ocean.

From a literary point of view their correspondence is one of the most interesting in modern times, because it presents a case in reverse of the usual in world literature—the woman here taking the active role; the man the passive. But humanly speaking, it is tragic and painful to read, and we can understand the indignant protests which arose when it was first published. Clara

Barrus discusses it in her book.[168] Anne Gilchrist's younger daughter, Mrs. Grace Frend, protested in the London *Nation* in 1918 against the publication. In any event, it is obvious that all the biographers and friends, especially Binns and Bazalgette, who had deliberately glossed over the relationship between Whitman and "his noblest woman friend," were irrevocably discredited. As Kate Buss wrote in the Boston *Transcript* for the Whitman centennial in May, 1919, "Anne Gilchrist to Walt Whitman, Some Comments on the Love Letters of a Woman to the Great American Poet": "To have guarded the legend of Whitman Mrs. Gilchrist's letters should not have been published."

Whitman had a rural retreat outside Philadelphia which played an important role for him during these years.[169] This was Timber Creek, ten miles out in the country, where each summer he boarded with the Stafford family, bathed in the creek, took sun baths, and slowly wrote the greater part of the memoranda he published in 1882 under the title *Specimen Days*. Although these diaries from nature are not worthy to be compared with Thoreau's, still there are a number of details that reveal Whitman's unusual ability to observe nature; therefore, they throw some light on his descriptions of nature in his poetry. They contain accounts of nocturnal flights of birds, of beautiful starry nights, lists of names of trees and birds which the poet wanted to impress on his memory, and finally mystical, pantheistic passages, such as the one on man's primitive fear of nature:

. . . for somebody to appear, or start up out of the earth, or from behind some tree or rock? . . . It is not at all nervousness or fear. . . . Nay, it is quite certain there is—some vital unseen presence.[170]

The first part of *Specimen Days* is war memoranda, the second part descriptions of nature from Timber Creek, and the third diary notes describing experiences of these last years. The many obituaries, funerals, commemorations (Bryant, Longfellow, Carlyle) show that it is an old man's diary. There are also descriptions of the few trips he took, in spite of all the difficulties, to Burroughs's home on the Hudson River, to New York, which he scarcely recognized, and from September to December, 1879, a longer trip inland to visit Jeff in St. Louis, which was extended to Denver, Colorado. He wanted to see his country once more. For the first time he was on a sleeping car, and it filled him with a sort of naïve patriotism reminiscent of earlier days. The West, as always, is the land of the future, the Mississipi River, "earth's most important stream." On the way home he visited Dr. Bucke, in Ontario, and even stopped in Boston to visit Emerson. In Boston he saw a collection of Millet's paintings, one of the greatest art experiences of his life.

Never before have I been so penetrated by this kind of expression. . . . Will America ever have such an artist out of her own gestation, body, soul? [171]

He also visited Hawthorne's and Thoreau's graves. But one evening with Sanborn, Emerson, Alcott, and Louisa Alcott seems to have been the high point of his trip, an acknowledgment and corroboration, in spite of everything, of his friendship with Emerson, "a long blessed evening with Emerson" as he called it.[172] *Specimen Days* was published in Philadelphia in 1882 after Whitman had agonized long over a title for such a curious work. We have a characteristic list of titles, of which the most expressive are the following: "Notes after Writing a Book," "Sands on the Shores of 64," "Again and Again." He himself had a feeling that it was not a real book—at most it could be called a commentary on the only book that would bear his name in world literature.

That single book, *Leaves of Grass*, was once more to meet difficulties now gestating. The distinguished publishing firm James R. Osgood, of Boston, had in 1881, on their own initiative, asked Whitman about publishing the definitive edition of *Leaves of Grass*. Of course he delightedly agreed, and went to Boston to help with the final arrangement of the poems. The seventh edition of *Leaves of Grass*, with the exception of the annexes, is the basis for all the present editions. Beside the separate sections, *Children of Adam, Calamus*, and *Drum-Taps*, the rest of the poems were finally divided into the present groupings: *In-*

scriptions, Birds of Passage, Sea Drift (the poems of despair
from 1860), *By the Roadside, Autumn Rivulets, Whispers of
Heavenly Death, From Noon to Starry Night,* and *Songs of
Parting,* in the order Whitman then thought they ought to be
—and which on first acquaintance with the book seems so admirable and impressive.

The new edition appeared in November, 1881, and in the
first few months sold 1,600 copies. Then, in April, on moral
grounds, the sale was forbidden, banned by authority of the
State of Massachusetts, or more correctly by determination of
Anthony Comstock and his "moral police." There was some
negotiation, and the ban could have been lifted if Whitman had
agreed to delete "A Woman Waits for Me," "To a Common
Prostitute," and the new and strong poem "Dalliance of the
Eagles." But Whitman refused, and the publisher had to stop
all further sales, whereupon Whitman, after some delay, made
an arrangement with Rees Welsh, Philadelphia, to bring out
another issue of the book. The American press sided with Whitman against the Boston prudery, and Whitman himself took
the whole affair philosophically. Perhaps it stimulated the sale
of the book. At any rate it was from the proceeds of this edition that he was able to buy the house on Mickle Street, his home
during his last years.

Pictures from this period show Whitman as a very old man.
He liked to be photographed. A private edition of Whitman
photographs (Toronto, 1911) contains eighty-four different
portraits, of which seventy-five were taken in old age, and Dr.
Bucke is said to have had two hundred photographs, all different. The painters Eakins, Herbert Gilchrist, Alexander, and
Kurtz painted and drew him; sculptors Morse, St. Gaudens,
Quinn, and Murray modeled him. He emphasized his resemblance to the prophets so very assiduously that it became a dis-
guise (later both Burroughs and Bucke in their old age tried
to imitate him). There are some really comic pictures of him
with King Lear, Moses, or Wotan-like characteristics in addition to some which remind us of Victor Hugo and Tolstoy. They
are all links in the series of types which Whitman at various
stages of his life wished to associate with himself—the vagabond

type of the early years, the Quaker type later, the social reformer, the "bard," and the "prophet" at last. But it is impossible for any of these masks to obscure the reality of the
weak, dreamy, passionate countenance, "with its sensuous
mouth" which his American admirers [173] preferred to forget
and he himself tried to hide behind the prophet-mask. Even he
had a feeling that he was not playing quite an honest game
with the pretentious prophet pictures. At any rate, he chose
the far more natural, much "softer" picture of himself sitting
with a butterfly on his hand as the one for the frontispiece of
the final edition of the book.

The best picture and the most convincing description of the
real old-age Walt Whitman is in Edward Carpenter's *Days with
Walt Whitman*, 1906. There Carpenter, on the basis of his
association with Whitman between 1877 and 1884, not only in
private also but in the company of the Gilchrists, the Staffords,
and the wealthy Quaker family of Logan Pearsall Smith, in
Germantown, one of Philadelphia's older residential sections,
drew a detailed picture of him in everyday life. Carpenter was
a close observer. He saw plainly that the inner circle of Whitman's friends were "more concerned to present an ideal personality than a real portrait." [174] Even he stressed the acquired
peace that he found most characteristic of Whitman's behavior,
"bearing the mark of life-long passion and emotion." [175] Regarding his personal magnetism, Carpenter, like everyone else,
mentioned "a certain radiant power . . . yet something of
reserve and sadness in it too, and a sense of remoteness and in-
accessibility." [176] We find that in company Whitman did not
talk much—often true of authors who are very eloquent in
their writings. He liked to read aloud, not only from his own
poems but also from favorite authors. Carpenter heard him read
Tennyson's *Ulysses*, one of his favorites. Clifton J. Furness has
made up a list of Whitman's oral readings.[177] The most important are: "The Diver," by Schiller, "Ode on the Passions,"
by Collins, Anacreon's "The Midnight Visit," translated by
Thomas Moore, and Poe's "The Raven." Whitman was very
affable when in public, Carpenter notes, but could also become
moody and strange and leave the group suddenly, or get a

spell of Quaker stubbornness, when he could be neither pushed nor pulled. Logan Pearsall Smith jokingly speaks of Whitman's "magnificent No," so familiar and dreaded by his friends. Whitman's "cussedness" and his "tenacity" are two peculiarities Carpenter particularly emphasized, naturally along with his reticence and "caution," which the phrenologist said was one of his strongest traits,[178] and Carpenter felt that this was really important because it concerned Whitman's complete silence about the inside story of *Leaves of Grass*. We are confronted with a man who had decided for himself exactly what he did and did not want to be known. The most devoted of his friends never doubted that he deliberately and determinedly kept something secret. One day he said to Carpenter: "I think there are truths which it is necessary to envelop or wrap up." [179]

Naturally Carpenter was unwilling to give up trying to get as much information as possible. On the last day with Whitman, June 30, 1884, he asked once more about the secret of *Leaves of Grass*. Whitman, who was sitting at the window looking into the garden, gave him an answer, surprisingly devoid of pose and almost joking in tone, a marked contrast to his usual attitude. It is one of Whitman's most important (and heretofore almost unnoticed) observations about himself, and throws real light on the remarkable genesis of *Leaves of Grass*.

What lies behind "Leaves of Grass" is something that few, very few, only one here and there, perhaps oftenest women, are at all in position to seize. It lies behind almost every line; but concealed, studiedly concealed [N.B.] ; some passages left purposely obscure. There is something in my nature *furtive* like an old hen! You see a hen wandering up and down a hedgerow, looking apparently quite unconcerned, but presently she finds a concealed spot, and furtively lays an egg, and comes away as though nothing had happened! That is how I felt in writing "Leaves of Grass." [180]

In spite of the human frailties and the paradoxical contradictions which Carpenter finds in Whitman's nature, he declared:

I am impressed more than ever with Whitman's contradictory, self-willed, tenacious, obstinate character, strong and even extreme moods, united with infinite tenderness, wistful love, and studied tolerance.[181]

But Carpenter still could not help seeing in Whitman a higher stage in human evolution, just as Dr. Bucke did, and as did practically everyone who came in personal contact with him. The effect is incomprehensible to outsiders, and in any event impossible to discuss.

In everything concerning Whitman personally Dr. Bucke was one of the believers, and Carpenter's "higher stage" as a description of Whitman's personality originated in Carpenter's own highly personal belief that the blending of the male and the female within one person is nature's own experiment with a higher stage in the development of humanity. This idea is felt as an undercurrent in Carpenter's whole sex psychology. He built his life-attitude on it. Carpenter referred to this theory both in *Days with Walt Whitman* and, more emphatically, in *Some Friends of Walt Whitman*, which was issued in 1924 as one of a series of sexual studies published by the British Society of Sex Psychology. There can be no doubt that Whitman's personality was strengthened, probably doubly strengthened, as a result of his struggle to achieve spiritual equilibrium. We know from both literature and history that the struggle to rise above sex, to fight natural impulses, can sometimes endow a personality with something of the superhuman. Both Carpenter and Bucke considered that Whitman's greatest power lay in his "cosmic consciousness." Since this quality has been deeply impressed on his lyricism and is one of the strongest attributes of the book, we feel for the poetry something of what Dr. Bucke and Carpenter felt for the author personally.

Whitman was in straitened financial circumstances during his last years. He gave a few lectures, including a repetition of his 1879 Lincoln memorial address, and twice subscriptions were started for his benefit under the auspices of Andrew Carnegie and Mark Twain. The prose works of his later years, *November Boughs* (1868), and *Good-Bye My Fancy* (1891), must be regarded as products of his need for money. *November Boughs* had essays on Father Taylor, Burns, Tennyson, Lincoln, George Fox, and Elias Hicks. *Good-Bye My Fancy* had, besides the prose, a few poems which he himself called "parrot-like repetitions." A few of these are touching, for example, the little

poem "As I Sit Writing Here," in which he describes his fear
that the weakness of old age, all the physical ailments that ac-
company age, "may filter in my daily songs"; or the poem,
"After Supper and Talk," in which he compares his continuing
to write poems after the book is finished and done to an old
man who has difficulty in breaking away from dear friends: "A
far-stretching journey awaits him, to return no more." He
pauses, first in the entry, then in the door, and on the steps, to
say good-bye once more, "Garrulous to the very last." The poem
that probably gives the most tragic picture in the collection
is "The Dismantled Ship."

In some unused lagoon, some nameless bay,
On sluggish, lonesome waters, anchor'd near the shore,
An old, dismasted, gray and batter'd ship, disabled, done,
After free voyages to all the seas of the earth, haul'd up at last
    and hawser'd tight,
Lies rusting, mouldering.

The imagery of the ship, throughout the growth of *Leaves
of Grass* one of Whitman's favorites to express all his moods,
we now find here used in a poetic conclusion of peculiarly affecting simplicity.

With the addition of "A Backward Glance o'er Travel'd
Roads," from *November Boughs*, which was introduced in 1889
into the eighth edition and in 1892 into the ninth and final edition of *Leaves of Grass*, the book is concluded in an impressive
manner. Proudly and modestly the poet looks back over the
thirty years growth of his book and his nation and once again
(though for the only time in the book as it is now arranged)
outlines his plan and intention. For Whitman poetic art is evolutionary; each step in the development of the literature of his
country and his own book has to him been logical and inevitable,
projected by America herself between 1850 and 1880.

"It were useless to attempt reading the book without first
carefully tallying that preparatory background and quality in
mind." The poet has purposely turned his back on many things
that distinguish foreign literature "in respect to pictorial talent,
dramatic situations, and especially in verbal melody and all
the conventional technique of poetry." But if America is to

develop a literature, it is necessary to turn away from everything that is not native to its own shores. Whitman names the special characteristics of his book in four words: "suggestiveness," "amativeness," "sex," and "animality." His poetry is cosmic and dynamic. By writing so many notices of himself Whitman had gradually acquired a great precision in stating what he considered essential. But the book also requires cooperation from the reader. "The reader will always have his or her part to do, just as much as I have had mine." That is almost like a direct reply to Hamsun's comment about the inspiration which is demanded of the reader to understand *Leaves of Grass.* Above all the book is himself. It is "an attempt, from first to last, to put a person, a human being (myself, in the latter half of the nineteenth century, in America) freely, fully and truly on record."

And now, when the poet sits considering the finished work "in the early candlelight of old age," it shows itself clearly to him, not as a unit, but as an evolution or growth: "Result of seven or eight stages and struggles extending through nearly thirty years." There it is and we may accept it as we please. It is his "carte visite to the coming generations of the New World." For this study of *Leaves of Grass* there is a single passage concealed in a parenthesis right at the beginning which is significant.

(. . . some lengthen'd ship-voyage, wherein more than once the last hour had apparently arrived, and we seem'd certainly going down [N.B.]—yet reaching port in a sufficient way throughout all discomfitures at last.)

This prose article was the period for *Leaves of Grass.* Just before his death, in 1892, he sent Kennedy the final edition, into which it had been fitted, and wrote in the book: "The volume is more a person than a book." He himself saw that the contrasts and self-contradictions had not been eliminated, for he mentioned them in the article. But we cannot deny that "A Backward Glance o'er Travel'd Roads" heightens the impression of the book as an active, living human being. Whitman was not successful in conquering the conflicts in himself or in his book, but he did succeed to a remarkable degree in becoming identified with his book, which affected *all* its characteristics good or bad. The whole man is in it. In this one sense he achieved the desired identity and synthesis which he sang in the poem, "Good-Bye My Fancy."

> Then if we die we die together, (yes, we'll remain one),
> If we go anywhere we'll go together to meet what happens.

The poet Edmund Clarence Stedman, whose criticism Bliss Perry admits had done more for Whitman's case in America than the blind advertising of the prophets, wrote Burroughs after Whitman's death: "Before he died, in fact, he rose to synthesis, and his final arrangement of his life-book is as beauteously logical and interrelated as a cathedral." [182]

Whitman in World Literature

—————✦◆◆►—————

O strain, musical, flowing through ages—now reaching
    hither,
I take to your reckless and composite chords—I add to
    them, and cheerfully pass them forward.
                              "Proto-Leaf," 1860 [1]

TO DISCUSS WHITMAN in world literature is to discuss
those he resembled and those who resemble him. If we
limit the problem to include only his imitators and followers
in modern literature, we rob it of the greater share of its interest. In the relationships of literary history the influence of
one author on another is only half the story, and often the least
interesting; on the other hand, the problem of types, of parallel
intellectual development of authors who may never have heard
of each other, is a genuine and truly interesting one. In the history of literature the apparent influence of one author on another can often be explained by a similarity in the personality
of the writers or by the use of common motifs originating in
parallel or similar temperaments. Whitman's successors are,
therefore, not primarily those who slavishly imitated him (they
are of little interest), but those whose perception of life he had
anticipated in his book and who have thus found in *Leaves of
Grass* a natural model for what they themselves had in mind.
Frequently later poets will appear to have remarkable affinities
with Whitman, although their knowledge of him was demon-
strably inaccurate and superficial. We shall find Whitmanesque
poets even in the literature preceding him, and the whole problem becomes entirely one of the type. An example of the same
idea having found expression through the ages in the work of
various authors ("O strain, musical, flowing through the
ages . . .") makes a discussion of a relationship in world litera-

ture twice as exciting as merely a discussion of a poet and his imitators.

Earlier in this book the oriental aspect of Whitman's poetry was mentioned. This is largely a matter of temperamental similarity. More accurately, it is really the mystic temperament which we recognize in the Chinese *Taoteking,* the Indian *Bhagavadgita,* the Persian Rumi, and in European literature in Angelus Silesius and William Blake. The oldest Chinese poet said in his pantheistic dreams:

> My being is one with the primeval spirit.
> I am a wave in the river of light and darkness.
> All creation is my father and my mother.
> The sky is my bed and the earth my cushion.

Though these phrases are closely parallel to Whitman's, there is no question of any influence. It is the mystic perception that is the same, working spontaneously and using instinctively the same motifs as those in Whitman's poetry. In Laotse we find the theme of defeat as the real victory, and the ninth and tenth chapters of *Bhagavadgita* have the reiterations, the catalogue of everything which the "I" embraces in its various shapes. "I have established and continue to establish all the universe by one portion of myself," as J. C. Thompson puts it in his 1855 English translation, which Whitman saw first after his meeting with Thoreau, and thus after he had written "Song of Myself."

There is a striking personal similarity between Whitman and the Persian Rumi (1207–73), in whose ghazals, or mystic odes (which we know through Rückert and the *Mesnevi,* translated by Friedrich Rosen in 1913), there is not only an obvious Calamus motif and a concept of the divinity exactly parallel to Whitman's "Great Camerado," but in Rumi's poetry there is also a long list of individual Whitmanesque images. We encounter themes such as the path from primeval life to the existing "I," the spotted hawk shaking its wings before it takes leave of the visible world, the thousands of mutations of the "I," the abrogation of all religious sects because the poet encompasses each of them in himself and hence declares all equally

good. There is no question of influence, because Rumi was not
translated into English until 1881. When Rumi exhorts human
beings to become compost gladly so that the nutritious grass can
sprout, or when in the intoxicating idea of universal unity he
and his "dancing dervishes" represent the dance of the spheres
around the sun, we are reminded of passages from Whitman.
These express a primary mystic emotion, peculiarly oriental
and familiar in the East even today. Whitman's contemporary
in India, Bramakrisna (*ca.* 1850), withdrew to the forest to live
with nature, and in the streets he would salute prostitutes with
the respect accorded fine ladies because they were all images
of the divinity. Likewise in modern times Krishnamurti rejected all religions and replaced them with the worship of life
in all its forms. He set up as his inexorable motto: "Follow no
one; follow only thyself," a doctrine the same as Whitman's
and inspired by a similar idea.

It is that similarity of temperament, common to all mystics, that we must clearly understand when we consider points
of resemblance between Whitman and like phenomena in world
literature remote in time or space. The pantheistic note characteristic of all mystic temperaments can be especially misleading and cause us to trace connecting lines where there is no real
connection. The mystic sentiment, the cosmic perception, often
expresses itself in inconsistent ways, as we are well aware in
Leaves of Grass. What Poul Tuxen says in his introduction to
the Danish edition of the *Bhagavadgita* about "contradictions
turned out to graze peacefully side by side" applies with equal
accuracy to the Indian work, to Whitman's *Leaves of Grass*,
and to Angelus Silesius's *Cherubinische Wandersmann*—a book
which, like Whitman's, was composed in strata over a period
of years (1656–74) and contains many contradictions. In
Silesius's famous little apothegms we find whole Whitmanesque
sentences paralleling sections of "Song of Myself." [2] And truly
in his time the American poet was a "cherubic wanderer." Whitman has much in common with the seventeenth-century Silesian
mystic without having known him except as he was extant in
the German romantic philosophy and thus indirectly nurtured
Transcendentalism and Emerson. The similarity is in the exalta-

tion of humanity, of Christ in each individual, of each person who has his church within himself and has no need of a special sect or of divine service. The words of Böhme and Silesius, "Mensch, werde wesentlich" [Mankind, develop essentiality], are surely as Whitmanesque as anyone could wish. In Silesius's personal life his relationship with his mother and an insane brother is also like Whitman's.

We find traces of neo-Platonism, Persian Sufism, and Jewish Chassidism in Whitman, all colored with the common pantheistic characteristics; in them individuality is lost in the All like a drop in the sea. Chassidism, which arose in protest against orthodox Judaism, is strongly stamped by the Cabalistic, but "Asceticism is sinful" is one of its chief tenets, and in Rabbi Baal Schem, its founder (1706–60), we have a Polish Jewish Rumi, or Whitmanesque figure. His remarkable preference for ordinary, elemental people, for artisans and cab-drivers, is one of the points of resemblance, but even more important is the notorious chassidistic cult of friendship for which the Rabbi recruited young men from their homes and their work to follow him on "the great highway" in the same peremptory fashion that Whitman used in "Song of Myself" and "Song of the Open Road." The most interesting thing about Whitman as a mystic type is that in his book we can find the typical characteristics of absolutely all the various mystic doctrines. Without having read them, or heard of them, they arose naturally out of his own temperament, and he has developed characteristic mystic tenets, often even more striking and paradoxical than those of his predecessors.

In the sobriety and abstention that he adopted at the crisis in his life, Whitman held ideas of personal conduct similar to those of Swedenborg, who played an important role in the American thought of that period. In Whitman's fragmentary diaries written after the crisis in his life, he exhorted himself once more to approach his ideal man in a manner parallel to Swedenborg's sudden resolution to live more soberly as a "novus homo in Christo" [a new man in Christ]. Just as Whitman occupied himself with his daily visits to the soldiers, Swedenborg, a great friend of children, took them for daily outings. While the

Swedenborgian visions of a future community of angels and of "the relationship of angels" have no counterpart in Whitman's dream of the future, nevertheless they were highly pathological, and thus the visions of each were similarly motivated. Swedenborg's eccentric idea of "neighborly affection" is like Whitman's "comradeship" and "democracy," which likewise embraced the heathen and the most remote strangers. According to the latest investigations, it now appears that much of Swedenborg's prophetic disposition can be explained only as coming from lack of sexual satisfaction; his instincts were poetized in his heated visions of paradise as were Whitman's in his own way. Swedenborg, like Whitman, regarded the human form as the norm for all creation and believed in corporeal immortality.

The doctrine of achieving the divine through a beautiful physique is an old Platonic idea. Neo-Platonism certainly warns against Narcissism, the losing of the self in worship of its own image and forgetting the higher ideal behind it. It cannot be denied that at times Whitman is like the Greek Narcissus. But at the same time he has a strong sense of reality, a healthy enthusiasm for things themselves, which prevents him from being merely a mystic. In this he reminds us of Goethe, whose ideas of nature he also shared in so many ways. For the Spinozan Goethe the discovery of the human body was of similar major importance as for Whitman; he called it, as is often quoted, "The alpha and omega among all familiar things." Goethe made the discovery through ancient Greek art in the museums of Rome, a fact that definitely separates him from Whitman. But his outcry to naked human nature, "Lord, I will not let you go until you have blessed me," has a paradoxical similarity to Whitman's many outbursts on the divinity of the human body.

Whitman has more in common with the older authors of antiquity than with the younger. He himself always mentions, besides Isaiah, Homer and Lucretius. With Isaiah I can see no similarity except the rolling diction and the call to listen— "Listen, O Isles" (Chapter 49), and the catalogic reiterations in Chapter 2. The gloomy doomsday preacher Isaiah was temperamentally very remote from Whitman. Nor is there any temperamental similarity with Homer, but in the oldest Greek poetry the grass was called "the great Mother's hair," an expression rejected by the Renaissance esthetes as vulgar, but it was revived in modern literature by Whitman and by Swinburne in "Hertha." In classical literature we meet the first Whitmanesque type in Lucretius (96–55 B.C.), with his long didactic poem, *De rerum natura.*[3] The didactic element in *Leaves of Grass* is something which has particularly interested English esthetes. Whitman shares in part the poetic fantasy of Lucretius, who in similar fashion was able to use successfully the outline and catalogic devices. Lucretius, exactly like Whitman, early taught the theory of the atom and the infinity of space and matter—all existence eternally the same. In his Fourth Book the description of love as a natural function cannot fail to suggest Whitman, as does also his homage to nature's permanence, his enthusiastic celebration of *natura creatrix*, and his violent attacks on the official religion. Noteworthy also is Lucretius's treatment of the hexameter, which he used almost like free verse. Moreover, his unusual vocabulary and unconventional word-order are interesting reminders of Whitman. About Lucretius personally we know less than about Whitman, who paid homage to him in *Democratic Vistas.*

Otherwise it is in eighteenth-century world literature that Whitmanesque figures are mainly revealed in Rousseau, Blake, and the young Goethe. Here two intellectual streams have joined to form the Whitmanesque type, especially in Spinozan pantheism, which was so significant in young Goethe's interpretation, and later for the romantics. This is also the century of Toland, Linné, and Buffon. In his youth Goethe was a vagabond, a wanderer: the young Werther calls himself "a pilgrim on the earth." Werther, like Whitman at the opening of "Song of Myself," lies in the woods ("the bank by the wood," "Song of Myself," Section 2), or like Franz Werfel later, wholly submerged in the feeling of peaceful existence.

I lie in the high grass near the tumbling brook and the earth near me is covered with a thousand small grass blades; completely absorbing and engrossing, I feel the myriads of a whole little world among the blades, with the small worms, gnats, countless, and unfathomable forms near to my heart. . . . Alas, then I pine and think: Oh, if thou couldst express that, couldst breathe out on paper what lives so vividly, so warmly in thee! [4]

The same love of nature produces the same kind of lyrical imagery. In his letters to Frau von Stein, Goethe talks about "reading in the landscape's mile-long pages," [5] and in the "Parables" of 1775 he compares himself to "a cedar which grows high above the other trees and has brothers, but on other mountains." [6] That is Whitman's Redwood Tree. Even Goethe's moral sentiments—moral as opposed to natural—grew out of his constant contemplation of nature, which is "beautiful and ugly, good and bad, all existing side by side with equal right." [7] Likewise is there something of the Whitmanesque in his effort to comprehend the *whole* reality through poetry and science combined. Especially in the young Werther's glorification of ordinary human nature, of simple folk, of the common people, is there a democratic feeling less prominent later in Goethe's life which contributes largely to mark in that period a resemblance to the Whitmanesque type.

In the century of Rousseau and the French Revolution this very democratic disposition determined the second tendency, which is fully as essential as the first for the formation of the special type in literature. This is the ideal of world citizenship of Lessing and Schiller, and in Denmark of Jens Baggesen, as one phase of the democratic sentiment, a "love for the world," as when Schiller wanted to clasp millions to his breast ("An die Freude," 1785), or when Baggesen, in 1789, on Arminiusburg wished to unite all the nations of the earth under his world citizenship: "Strive to be at home anywhere; be German in Germany, Swiss in Switzerland, French in France, Lutheran with the Lutherans, Catholic with the Catholics, heathen with the heathens, sorrowful with the sad, joyous with the joyful —human everywhere and all humanity respecting!" Not only the grammatical structure but also the whole high-flown diction makes this passage from Baggesen a sort of Salut-au-Monde in the Whitman manner a century before Whitman.[8] But the comparison is not in this sentiment alone, for it can often be found in poets who are otherwise different from this type: more important is the desire for social reform; the pro-

phetic tendency in combination with this sentiment produces
the type. With MacPherson and Klopstock, Whitman had only
the prophetic style in common. Their psychology is different
from his, although in a few of his odes Klopstock did express
Whitmanesque sentiments, for example, when he celebrated first
his friends and then his "future" friends. But there are often
very striking similarities in two other prophets of that prophetic
century. I refer to Blake and Thorild.

Whitman himself had no interest in Blake, although their
resemblance is very interesting. Blake's active imagination followed an entirely different path from Whitman's; he drew his
metaphors from the Bible, from gnosticism, and, to an astonishing degree, from Swedenborg, but in the vital emotion he is far
closer to Whitman than Swedenborg. The origin of this emotion is simply his rejoicing over the diversity of creation. "Everything that lives is holy," in "A Song of Liberty," and each
entity has its own law. Only by being himself, loving, hating, and
fulfilling the desires of body and soul, can a human being find
immortality. Self-development for Blake, as for Whitman is a
fundamental principle. The difference between them is in their
kind of imagination. But even in such a remarkable poetic
work as Blake's *Marriage of Heaven and Hell*, 1790, there is
no denying the similar psychology. Many apothegms and sentences, especially in "The Voice of the Devil" and "Proverbs
of Hell," are completely Whitmanesque.

Man has no Body distinct from his Soul; for that call'd Body is a
    portion of Soul . . .
To create a little flower is the labour of ages . . .
The head Sublime, the heart Pathos, the genitals Beauty, the hands
    and feet Proportion . . .
The man who never alters his opinion is like standing water . . .
Any man of mechanical talents may, from the writings of Paracelsus
    or Jacob Behmen, produce ten thousand volumes of equal
    value with Swedenborg's, and from those of Dante or Shake-
    speare an infinite number.

And even the cosmic vision:

. . . then I flung myself with him directly into the body of the
sun . . . and passed all the planets till we came to Saturn, here

I stay'd to rest, and then leap'd into the void between Saturn and the fixed stars.

This heightens the impression that we are face to face with a fundamental poetic emotion paralleling the mutable sections of "Song of Myself." The same observation applies to the vision of creation, *The Four Zoa or Vala*, 1797–1804, in which the newly created soul runs out into the garden in the dawn, which opens "with vocal harmony," and is sad on first discovering that it is no more than the grass "and so shall pass away," but is soon comforted by the promise that "thou shalt ever flourish," and yields to the sentiment of universality with all creation, with "the branching trees," "the green pastures," "the sweet smelling ground," and "the tender grass," like St. Francis of Assisi feeling that the animals are "my brethren" and the birds "my sisters." As a rule the poem is written in long rhythmic prose lines, an experiment in Biblical style as people at that time imagined it appeared in the original—a concept that was also important as a model for Whitman.

Besides the great visions there is in the shorter poems of Blake, especially in *Songs of Innocence* from his early period, a lyrical emotion astonishingly like Whitman's. In "London" Blake passes through streets and adopts the themes of the city and its thoroughfares as Whitman did on Broadway. He hears the desperate shriek of the Soul, "the cry of Youth I hear," as Whitman heard "secret convulsive sobs from young men, remorseful after deeds done." In "A Little Girl Lost" Blake addresses himself to youthful readers of the future ("Children of the Future Age!") and describes the earth's golden age before mankind was ashamed of its nakedness. He has a "Laughing Song":

> When the green woods laugh with the voice of joy
> And the dimpling stream runs laughing by!

And a poem "On Another's Sorrow," in which the poet *must* share each sorrow he meets on his way. But foremost is the poem of morning joys, in which the poet in true Whitmanesque fashion talks about "the vigorous joys of youth!" Curiously enough, though Blake was a far more masculine poet, his rhythm can be smooth in a way that never occurs in Whitman. But in spite of differences, it is evident that in the English world Blake prepared the way not only for Wordsworth and Shelley but just as surely for Whitman.

Another eighteenth-century poet, a contemporary of Blake, the Swedish Thomas Thorild (1759–1808), surprisingly anticipates Whitman, not only in his social ideas about equal rights for women, and so forth, but in his lyrical form, which boldly broke all poetic rules and was composed in prose lines, rhetorically divided by proclamation and acclamation. Also in his famous determination to interpret all nature and to reform the whole world he is truly a forerunner of Whitman. Unlike Blake, he wanted to break with all metaphysics. To him certainty and reality were the most important things. Thus, starting with ideas similar to Goethe's and H. C. Ørsted's, he prepared for the "scientific" poetry of the next century. As a social reformer he was a pupil of Rousseau and Franklin. Along with his feeling of kinship with everything he wanted to educate men for universal citizenship. Each according to his capacity should absorb the whole world into himself, scorning nothing and denying nothing. Existence, he said, is holy, and every morning should be greeted with a hymn. (That is Whitman's joy at dawn, which filled him with resounding happiness—"Song of Myself," Section 24). The greatest of all joys is the joy of feeling that for which we have the greatest capacity. Along with his great objectivity, Thorild was subjective in the same way as Whitman, and was likewise devoid of irony and humor. His buoyant delight in life occasionally grew into self-adoration. Vedel says in his great book *Svensk Romantik* [Swedish Romanticism], 1894, that Thorild's style has a lyrical swelling subjectivity. His ego breaks out in noisy, almost insolent violence—Thorild preached a communistic democratization which pointed directly to the next century. Fredrika Bremer found resemblances to Emerson: how much more striking they are to Whitman.

They shared two special themes in common: the theme of encompassing the whole world in one's self, a theme which Goethe so largely made his own and which aroused enthusiastic

response in two such different intellects as Chénier in France
and Steffens in Germany (both of whom wanted to write "An
Epic All-Encompassing"—though it was never written) ; and
the theme of democratic social reform. In three other Scandinavian authors, all from the beginning of the following century, the Danish Sibbern, the Swedish Almquist, and the Norwegian Wergeland, we catch a curious and surprising glimpse
of the basic characteristics of the Whitmanesque personality.

Gabrielis Breve [Letters of Gabrieli] and *Efterlade Breve af
Gabrieli* [Posthumous Letters of Gabrieli] by F. C. Sibbern
(1785–1872) are Danish parallels to Goethe's Werther. Sibbern
was psychologically a "wanderer" like Werther, Hans Andersen, Whitman, and Nietzsche. He was intoxicated by all the
forms of expression in nature, from the antics of the sparrows
to the sunbeams. He wrote in a letter to his sister: "Make of
what surrounds you a heaven filled with joy." That is the
"music of life" that, in 1825, Gabrieli talked of finding in nature, and he preferred to mingle with the common people, in
whom he found great riches. Professor Harald Høffding, in the
introduction to the fifth edition of *Gabrielis Breve*, 1893, mentions Sibbern's peculiar "joy in living" and his "immense belief in the rights of the individual." In his philosophy we find
the typical characteristic of the pantheistic cohesive sentiment,
along with a tolerance which, in spite of being a Christian himself, made him concede that "polytheism might have its good
points." Instead of limiting himself to a single book, the Bible,
he wanted to keep to Nature's book, the great book of life on
earth. His humanized figure of Jesus is completely Whitmanesque. "Jesus is a man in whom the force of life moves
in a special way." With his pupils he was in many ways the
Whitmanesque ideal of a teacher, especially in his "undemand-
ing discipline." He differs most from the Whitmanesque type
in not being in any real sense a poet, though on the whole he did
use an essentially poetic form to express the abundance of poetic
visions that agitated him. But in the astounding and "apocalyp-
tic" book of 1828, *Meddelelser om Indholdet af et Skrift fra
Aar 2135* [Information on the contents of a book in 2135] he
gives a prophecy about "Lavmandsfolket" (that is, the com-

mon people), his term for democracy, and about the future
happiness which is to come in a sort of communal society that
will remedy the defects of the present state—a kind of Danish
Democratic Vistas and astonishingly Whitmanesque in spirit,
often with sentiments that remind us of Whitman's "Crossing
Brooklyn Ferry" when he speaks to future generations, or of
Hans Andersen's *Vort Aarhundredes Musa* [Muse of our Cen-
tury].

The similarities of the Swedish Carl Jonas Love Almquist
(1793–1866) to Whitman are very interesting because his pronounced pathological type helps in many ways to explain Whitman's relation to much subtler intellects than his own—such as
the eccentric German romantics as well as to Wilde and Nietzsche. In his youth Almquist was strongly influenced by both
Rousseau and Thorild, and during his whole life he was ruled
by a pantheistic democratic sentiment that expressed itself particularly in his descriptions of the common people, in his writings on "The Dignity of Labor," and "The Meaning of Swedish
Poverty." With a knapsack on his back he made walking trips
through the Swedish provinces. And on a farm in Värmland he
tried to establish an "experimental community" like those in
contemporary England and America. His "Thorn-rose philosophy" came out of that experiment. In its expression it is
more subtle and more sentimental than Whitman's democratic
dream and was deeply influenced by German romanticism. But
the subject matter is the same as Whitman's. He praised the
conditions before the flood just as Whitman praises his "divine
savage"; mankind is commended for, as he puts it, almost de-
serving the honorable name of child or animal. And even in the
most romantic novels of the "Thornrose series," subtitled "Imagination Unbound," 1832–50, we find astonishingly lyrical pantheistic passages in the Whitmanesque style. Likewise, Almquist's self-portrait, Richard, is always contrasting the situation of the common people with that of the aristocratic milieu
used as the setting of the story. Almquist's writing had a marked
pedagogical character and bore the stamp of social reform; he
wanted to reform marriage and talked of criminals and prostitutes as sympathetically as Whitman did, and probably because

of a like spiritual inclination. The poet felt in himself potentialities that gave him a shuddering sympathy with those in
whom these traits had caused their downfall. Because of a criminal mistake—he was actually suspected of embezzlement—
Almquist had to flee from Sweden in 1851, and for fourteen
years he lived in the United States, chiefly in New Orleans,
where he supported himself by teaching and journalistic work.
But in Almquist the Whitman-psychology is emphasized by
more degenerative traits. He advocates reckless development
of self, as did Whitman in "Song of the Open Road," the soul's
"free course"; one of his most notorious metaphors is about
Ormus, the Ruler God, whom he said hampers and brings death
to all life.[9] He advocated a break with society as a way to find
one's self. This is certainly a characteristic we recognize in
Blake, Goethe, and Whitman, but in Almquist the stronger
emphasis carried the same idea to the lengths of a Wilde or a
Nietzsche. It is interesting in this connection to note the relation which may be observed between Whitman and the fin-de-
siècle European writers, often intellectual artists who would
otherwise seem far from him, but who, nevertheless, had a declared affection for him. The case of Almquist shows us an
exciting example of both types united in one poet.

While in the form and kind of their work Sibbern and Almquist were widely separated from Whitman, it is interesting to
find Henrik Wergeland (1808–45), in such a far corner of
the world as Norway, starting with similar qualifications and
really creating a similar art. Of course, it is the impetuous, all-
encompassing cosmic feeling itself in Wergeland's temperament that primarily determines the resemblances, and it extends
beyond subject matter into the form, which often slips naturally
from conventional verse into prose. Gerhard Gran called Wergeland "our great barbaric poet who sees everything around him
for the first time" and says:

He thinks in images that bubble up in overwhelming numbers out
of his brain; he rarely takes time to choose, one image pressing
on another in long parentheses which often make his poetry into a
wildly growing jungle that requires patience to penetrate.[10]

Could not that have been written of Whitman? Wergeland
shared Whitman's conception of the poet's great task in
modern culture. Whitman referred to American poetry as
"confectionary" or "piano strumming," and Wergeland con-
temptuously called the Dano-Norwegian poetry of his age "sofa-
literature." In his opinion poets worthy of the name should en-
compass the whole knowledge and development of the race and
if possible hasten the development. The poet should be the guide
and reformer of the people. Wergeland, like Whitman, railed
at the ruins of the past and used similar grotesque expressions.

Let the shields lie, let the bones moulder,
Let the antiquarian ants creep about on the mound;
A little dust will arouse them to enthusiasm like snuff an old
        woman.[11]

And his "Mankind" is a tribute to man's victorious progress
toward perfection. In his interpretation of nature Wergeland
is quite as enthusiastic as Whitman; "stretched on the grass"
is a frequently recurring starting point in his poetry for describing nature's "affectionate whispers" around him in the
trees, the waves, flowers. Animals are his friends and relatives;
in his little rabbit he sees a being "a little further down the scale
of creation," but in its eyes he glimpses the "wide heavens"
opening. Only one place is gloomy and sinister to Wergeland,
and that is a church. Outside, in nature, he sees "God's thoughts
stamped on the frail blades of the grass." Like Whitman, too,
Wergeland also gets his lyric erotic imagery from animate
nature, for example, the two intertwined mountain ashes that
die together in "The Intertwined Trees," or the two willow
trees that love one another so tenderly in "The Willow Trees
and the Axe"—or the picture of broken friendship, the two
clouds separated from each other in "One Time Friends,"
Wergeland's parallel to Whitman's "We Two How Long We
Were Fool'd." And even more important, in his astonishingly
frank erotic descriptions Wergeland's inspiration follows the
same path as that of Whitman, not only in *Creation*, in his
vigorous and healthy description of Adam and Eve's love (Eve
speaks of her body as "a lump of tepid mud" and Adam of his

loins which "like heaven may burst with a benediction as with luke-warm rain"—expressions that correspond to Whitman's language in *Children of Adam*) but also in the short "Address to the Humanity in Man." In the latter there is an outright Whitmanesque situation in "the love-intoxicated heath cock" which, "at the moment he bows over his loving mate, drops his wings and closes his eyes so that she will not be frightened by the fire and dark yearning that burns in them." That is Whitman's "Dalliance of the Eagles," or the "clinging bee" in "Spontaneous Me." It is astonishing to learn how two poets with like temperaments have arrived at the same expressions and imagery. In his two poems "Migselv" [Myself] and "To Spring," from 1841 and 1845 respectively, Wergeland's diction is so much like Whitman's that one might be mistaken for the other.

I in a bad mood? I who only need a glimpse of the sun
to burst out laughing with joy which I cannot explain?

When I smell a green leaf, overwhelmed I forget poverty, riches,
    friend and foe.

My cat rubbing against my cheek soothes the heartache,
    the eyes of my dog receive like a well my grief . . .

I who read ecstasies in every leaf of the gift of spring, the centifoil
    rose,
should a poor paper make me kill a second with annoyance? . . .

As if I should heap ashes on my hair not yet turned gray
and throw away the glitter of diamonds time still sprinkles on
    it . . .

I hate? When a bird flies over my head my hate is a mile away.
It melts with the snow, follows the first waves from the shore far
    out to sea.

What riches to a mortal man!
My soul delights in the vernal joy of heaven and will share that of
    the earth.

Its sparkle is brighter than the stars of spring, soon it will bloom with the flowers.[12]

And in "Til Foraaret" [To Spring] he says:

> Your early grass is more to me than emerald,
> your anemones I call the glory of the year . . .
> bear witness despised dandelion and cut-grass
> that more than gold I have valued you—children of spring.[13]

Wergeland even used the metaphor of the ship in his "South Sea Sails" [14] in definitely Whitmanesque forms and in pure prose-verse.

Happy Ship! Your pennants laugh, your full-bosomed sails are like a flock of exultant swans. How your breast swells as if there were a soul there, and you rejoice in the speed toward your destination, toward the warm green shores I seem to have seen in my childish dreams!

That is Wergeland's "Passage to India." In his remarkable book on Wergeland, Vilhelm Troye, commenting on the imagination that led Wergeland to use exotic pictures of places he had never visited, remarks that they appear before his eyes with "clairvoyant vividness, almost like a memory." [15]

The mystic, the colossal, the overflowing style in Wergeland is the product of an overwhelming masculine erotic sensitivity. He was constantly in love, and there are still tales told of his "double love affairs" and his stormy friendships. We find the "Calamus" side of Wergeland in the play *The Venetians*, which is exclusively about friendship, and in the poem "To Joy," in which the friends "drink each other's souls" in the same way that Whitman's friends "take the hearts out of each other's lives."

Literary historians have hitherto ignored the striking similarities of Wergeland and Whitman, except for the German Otto Hauser, who in his *Weltgeschichte der Literatur* [History of World Literature], speaking of Wergeland's "streckverse" observed in passing that "Klopstock, Blake and Whitman arrived at a similar diction." [16] But it is more than diction; it is disposition. In Wergeland's great universal epic, *Creation, Man, and Messiah*, 1830, with its subtle theory regarding the original union and later disunion of the souls here on earth, where they yearningly seek each other, he is influenced by German romanticism in an entirely different way from Whitman. Here the two circles of culture diverge. But in the cosmic fantasy ranging from Thebes to China, from the deserts of the East to the icebergs of the Arctic, there are many characteristics in common with Whitman: their belief in human evolution is identical. Wergeland's faith in democracy is also the same as Whitman's, and was repaid by the unlimited confidence of the common people. He was beloved by the masses, though they understood his poetry as little as most Americans did Whitman's. "In streets he was radiant, an old man told me," Troye quotes in his book,[17] corresponding to what the prophets told and quoted about Whitman. In writing and speaking Wergeland worked for the people, and his "public spirit," a strong conviction of his, exactly corresponds to Whitman's idealistic and pent-up democracy. Like Whitman, Wergeland mingled violent patriotism with an "all-inclusive" world sentiment. During most of his life Wergeland was misunderstood and slandered in Norway, as Whitman was in America. The contempt shown him by older colleagues, especially Welhaven, corresponds closely with the attitude of the Bostonians toward Whitman. Without doubt this great similarity between Wergeland and Whitman, two major figures in world literature, throws a special and suggestive light on the question of literary influence. If they had lived nearer and had read each other, they would hardly have escaped the accusation of having influenced or even imitated each other.

Among European romanticists there are three more personalities with whom we can find interesting points of comparison with Whitman: Bettina (or Elizabeth von Arnim, 1785–1850), Hans Andersen, and—naturally—Victor Hugo. At first glance any similarity between "the child" Bettina and Whitman seems almost absurd, but on closer examination we see that she illuminates the peculiarly feminine quality of Whitman's inspiration, particularly as it is expressed in the *Calamus* poetry. Bettina's inspiration in her letters to Goethe, 1835, which are really not letters, but a collection of pantheistic prose poems, are literary works like Whitman's. Ricarda Huch says, "She let a row of imaginary images, restless as magic lantern slides, flow past her inner eye and thus overwhelmed herself." [18] At the same time, the very emotion by which she is animated corresponds to Whitman's. In one of her letters she wants to "fly aloft and drive before the wind," and she writes one poem of unsatisfied yearning, which in every detail could have been taken from *Calamus* as a parallel to "When I Heard at the Close of the Day." She sits in a valley in the sunshine under the blue sky "and knows that in the evening some one is coming who has thought of me, for whom I wait all day as the sunny hours pass —and the shadowy hours with the silvery crescent moon and the stars bring the friend who finds me at the foot of the mountain, running to meet him with open arms, my heart suddenly full of a burning love!" [19] Goethe was *her* "great Camerado." She experienced the same impassionated feeling of friendship for Karoline von Günderode. Like Whitman and Wergeland she read a meaning in the eyes of animals. To her everything in nature became a symbol of her own emotions, which she interpreted in phrases indicating that where Almquist was the borderline between the Whitmanesque type and the decadents, she is the link between him and the orientals. We find again the imagery of Rumi in Bettina; "The beloved at night is the blanket she creeps under." She hopes some day to dance for him, to surprise him "at the wisdom with which I dance for you." Julius Schmidt says for her the dance is a means of expressing her intuition about the next world.[20] Whitman, strangely enough, has in "The Sleepers" the mystic imagery of the dancers, reminding us of Rumi's dervishes, afterwards consciously introduced by Nietzsche into *Zarathustra*.

Bettina was inspired by music, as Whitman was. She found her own "better nature" in music and strove to hold it fast "under the eternal pain of inspiration," an exact parallel to Whitman's ecstasy in "Song of Myself." Bettina is, above all, a typical example of the androgynous type in literature, and therefore important for comparison with Whitman. Her whole emotion, erotic and lyrical, lies on the sexual borderline. She is an Elisabeth Bergner type from the romantic period, who

liked to wear boy's or men's clothes on her trips. At times, as
she says herself, Bettina felt the call to be a modern Joan of
Arc and reform the world. She liked to associate with poor Jews,
beggars, and artisans. The Tyrolean battle for freedom aroused
her enthusiasm. During the cholera epidemic in Berlin in 1832
she nursed the sick with indefatigable devotion, and afterwards
in *Dies Buch gehört dem König* [This Book belongs to the
King], 1843, she discussed state socialism and democracy. Julius
Schmidt, in his excellent characterization of Bettina, says that
in her expression of feeling she lacked the grace of modesty,[21]
an objection which may occasionally be raised against Whitman
as well. Unlike Whitman, but like so many German romanticists, Bettina lacked the ability to grow old gracefully.

Similarities between Hans Andersen (1805–75) and Whitman have been mentioned before. They become doubly plain
when Wergeland is considered as the connecting link. In Wergeland's tales we find the same talent for animating little things
as in Andersen and obvious similarities of inspiration between
Wergeland and Andersen's angelic tales and two of Whitman's
little stories of the early forties. The expansive power in Andersen's fantasy particularly reminds us of Whitman's. Andersen was a fanciful traveler, a real world-wanderer, and we find
his Salut-au-Monde in his first little book of prose, *Fodrejse fra
Holmens Kanal til Østpynten af Amager* [Walking Trip from
Holmen's Canal to the East Point of Amager], 1829, in which
he first took an imaginary flight out into the planetary system
and then over the whole earth.

Truly this was the place for ideas to buzz. Now it seemed to me I
was walking on the Finnish Bay, or on the Arcadian Nova Scotia;
then I wandered through the Gobi Desert to visit the Dalai Lama
in Tibet, or through the Sahara to find the source of the Niger
River. Now I followed a caravan to Holy Mecca and then stood
among the Eskimoes on Hudson Bay.[22]

While this is nothing but the sportive outcome of a cosmic fantasy, in two later books, *Picture Book without Pictures*, 1840,
and *A Poet's Bazaar*, 1841, which influenced Johannes V. Jensen when he took up themes similar to Whitman's, the motif became serious and wholly Whitmanesque. Instead of reading the

Bible, as did his companions on the mail coach, Andersen observed nature, which he called "my big Holy Bible." Like Goethe he read in the mile-long pages of the landscape.

A poet sings because, like a bird he cannot help it. The burden swells in his breast and in his thoughts, the song will out, *it flies like the light, it lifts itself like the waves* [Whitman's "Salut au Monde"]. But frequently a sheet of music from Nature's great book is opened wider for the poet and this is an invitation to sing. Then he sings from the page.[23]

In *A Picture Book without Pictures* the similarity to Whitman is even clearer. This is a Whitmanesque series of vivid little pictures of real life in all lands as seen by the moon: a Swedish river where a steamboat scares the fish among the rushes, excavated Pompeii's deathly quiet lava streets, China, Greenland, the Louvre, or the convent church at Wreta—all very graphically drawn as in Whitman's "great catalogue," with brief pictorial adjectives, none of them superficial or failing their mark. The climax is the picture of the wedding night when the bridal pair stand looking out the window before going to bed, and the poet exclaims: "Woman! Kiss the poet's harp when he sings of the mysteries of life," just as Whitman did when he proclaimed his reverence for womanhood and celebrated it. In ebullient prose lyrics both Whitman and Andersen expressed delight in photography, in the railroads, and in the telegraph. In *Om Aartusinder* [In a Thousand years] Andersen looked into the future as Whitman did in "Crossing Brooklyn Ferry." The story of "The Last Dream of the Old Oak Tree" is a pantheistic vision paralleling Whitman's "Song of the Redwood Tree." Professor Hans Brix says of Andersen, "His spirit loves the purely human but is a stranger on ground peculiar to the male." [24] In this characteristic there is the essence of his psychological connection with Whitman. Like Whitman, he developed throughout his life the "myth" of his own story. Like Whitman he himself wrote a number of those literary or journalistic biographical sketches which his contemporaries believed were written by others. He was no less sentimental about friendship than Whitman, and in his stories he enjoyed, as did Whitman, assuming the female role in situations that disclose his own most

intimate hope and dreams. The mother- and father-complex
are identical in Whitman and Andersen. In all Andersen's
stories there is not a single father-image.[25]

Whitman has much in common with Victor Hugo (1809–85),
not only externally but also in the kind of inspiration and the
dominantly oratorical manner of the lyricism. Like Whitman,
Hugo is all-encompassing in his poems (so are Blake and
Wergeland). "The Prayer for All" from *Autumn Leaves*, 1831,
is a typical title. Hugo's rhetorical construction is far more
consciously academic than Whitman's, but the content is often
the same. Everything attains its goal: the bird reaches its nest,
the river the ocean, the horse his stall, and so forth—so will *I*
also reach my goal. Frequently, from a purely accidental starting point he can begin, as could Whitman, an endless oratorical
parade through all the associations suggested by the original
subject. The generations and races of the past and of the future pass before him in his long visionary *Contemplations*. But
in all his poetic work throughout the years we can find poems
or titles of poems which reveal similarity in thought and inspiration: from *Les Chants de crépuscule* [Songs of twilight], 1835,
the great "Hymn de la nature et de l'humanitie"; from *Les
Rayons et les ombres* [Lights and Shadows], 1840, the poem
"Oceano Nox" [Night at Sea] ("Oh, how many sailors, how
many captains"); from *Les Contemplations*, 1856, "One day
I saw the crest of the surging waves," "I am the dreamer, I am
the comrade," "Tears in the night," and "At the window in the
night." [26] During his long exile from France from 1852 to
1870 Hugo's somewhat boastfully victorious lyricism first revealed notes of gloom and pain reminiscent of the mood of the
1860 *Leaves of Grass*. *La Légende des siècles*, 1859–83, shows
more definite rhetorical similarities to Whitman, in the preliminary "Hymn to the Earth," which introduces the work, as
well as in "All the Past and All the Future" which constitutes
the forty-fourth section. "The Epic of the Worm" has lines
which are as baroque as any in "Song of Myself." For example:

I am in the dead child, in the lover deserted,
In widowhood quick to laugh, in the atheist, in all the forgotten
    moods of depression.

All profligates are my brothers.
It is from me that the fakir wants to send forth pupils of the
vague spectre Iblis . . .

I am the final being. I am in all . . .

I inhabit Ombos, I inhabit Elis, I inhabit Rome.[27]

And the poem "Open Sky," especially the section "Where goes
this ship?" can in one sense be called Victor Hugo's "Passage to
India." [28] The remarkable affinity with Whitman is recognizable throughout Hugo's lyrical work. Indeed Whitmanesque is
the early poem of the cow that stood to be milked while in her
eyes, undisturbed by mundane affairs, was mirrored a dream of
her god.[29] Hugo's youthful self glorification recalls Whitman.
In *Autumn Leaves*, 1831, he compared himself with the mountain Atlas, which supports a world on its shoulders. And even
in his youth Hugo assumed the Whitmanesque role of the
preacher. But Hugo ended as a real "seer," as the magnificent
poet of the sea and the poet of democracy who promulged a new
civilization. In Hugo's preaching a strong pantheism is ever
present. In his serene life, his vigor, and his living to an ad-
vanced age, he was like a European counterpart of the ideal
poet that Whitman envisioned in America. It is well known that
Whitman once delighted in having his picture taken à la Victor
Hugo.

With Hugo we have reached Whitman's own time and a group
of authors whose contemporaneity probably determines their
resemblance. In this "era of affirmations," as Henry Bryan
Binns calls it, the tendency of the century, the ideas, are expressed in a similar manner by the poets of all lands. It is no
longer merely a question of the Whitmanesque type, but of the
spirit of the time which, along with the other influences, put its
stamp on Whitman's poetry. Binns calls it the era of Mazzini,
Browning, Ruskin, and Emerson. We might mention many
other names. But why? It is sufficient to notice that, like Hugo
in France, Nekrassow (1821–77) in Russia wrote of social
incongruities and of the modern city in a similarly vigorous,
oratorical style often on the borderline between prose and verse,

though in a darker mood, and he outlined his democratic vistas in sentiments corresponding to those of Hugo and Whitman. He celebrated a wandering peddler's romantic pilgrimage through vast Russia in tones that call to mind "Song of the Open Road," and he pictured the Russian mother and the Russian prostitute with the same sympathy as Whitman did, only with more romantic sentiment. And Nekrassow lacked Whitman's gift for original expression. We can best observe this in poems in which the themes are comparable. But the problem is whether the period determines the resemblance, or is it only the type? Frequently important diversities between those social reformers of the same period who have used the same themes are revealed in their dissimilar temperaments, as between Whitman and Nekrassow, but even more between Whitman and Tolstoy (1828–1910), who have occasionally been compared. The similarity is really only in prophetic and ascetic externals, and in their common debt to the ideas of Rousseau. Temperamentally they are vastly different. In the youthful Tolstoy's ecstatic intoxication with life and the lyrical expression he gave it in his early work, there is some emotional similarity to Whitman, for example, Tolstoy's occasional descriptions of soldiers may have something in common with *Drum-Taps*. But the differences in their literary works are very pronounced, and the older Tolstoy is even more divergent. His peculiar "malicious intolerance," discussed by Arseniew in *Russische Literatur der Gegenwart* [Contemporary Russian Literature], 1929, no less than his disavowal of his own poetry and its import, shows the chasm between the types. Tolstoy "was an incarnation of Russia as Whitman was of America," as Binns says,[30] but we dare not carry the comparison any further. They are contemporary and co-ordinate types of the nineteenth-century social literature, but they are not synonymous. Above all, we must bear in mind the lyrical quality of Whitman's whole temperament and inspiration. This naturally confines the comparison to types of real and close affinity.

    With Tolstoy we have reached the extreme limit in the exploration of the problem of the Whitmanesque type in literature. When we again consider the question of influence, we are confronted with Nietzsche, whose influence on modern thought frequently converges with Whitman's despite the paradoxical difference between the two poets. *Les extrêmes se touchent!* Whitman is crude where Nietzsche is refined; Nietzsche's superman theory, with its scorn of the common people, seems at first glance to differ as widely as possible from Whitman's democracy, yet there is a certain accord between Nietzsche's "grosse Individuum" and Whitman's "great individuals," and particularly, as Johannes Schlaf noted, is there an undeniable kinship in their lyrical inspiration. The resemblance is limited to *Thus Spake Zarathustra*, 1883–85, but there it is so striking that it must be commented upon. Nietzsche's original poetic impulse, his enthusiasm for music, and his delight in oratorical effects has produced a prose lyric which follows the same ideas and uses the same imagery familiar to us in *Leaves of Grass*. The very way in which the book came into being in a truly open-air inspiration, such as Whitman often celebrated, contributed to the resemblance. Nietzsche wrote it during a long tramp through the Alps and on the Riviera. Just Bing says, "He went after his thoughts, grasped each impression in the open air, and wrote it down in his notebook." There is nothing to indicate that Nietzsche knew Whitman; the first translation of *Leaves of Grass* into German (Knortz and Rolleston) came out four years after *Zarathustra* was written. The similarity to Indian and Persian lyricism is common to Whitman and Nietzsche. Finally, *Zarathustra* also has the *international* sentiment, for he recognized no national barriers. He always spoke of humanity's progress toward possession of the earth. Like Goethe, Wergeland, Whitman, and Emerson, Nietzsche was an enemy of history ("History weakens the personality"). For him only the present and the future counted. He broke with conventional morality in the same way that Whitman did, and continually carped at scientists and priests. As for the personal resemblance between Whitman and Nietzsche, there are Nietzsche's hectic, enthusiastic, but always disappointing friendships, his longing "for perfect friends," which his sister reports was the personal background for all his work on the book, and can be traced in the Calamus-motivated poem, "The Friend" in Part I of *Zarathustra*. Furthermore, Nietzsche served as nurse in the Franco-Prussian War (his later illness has been attributed to overexertion in that period, exactly as with Whitman), and in his illness and insanity we find the same Christ-complex that Whitman had in a much less pronounced degree. Nietzsche even signed his letters with the name of Christ.

All these comparisons would be only a freak in literary history concerning two vastly different intellects of the nineteenth century if the lyrical inspiration of the two poets had not, simultaneously and in the most remarkable fashion, led to a common form of expression, a common imagery, almost a common language. In the "Prologue" to *Zarathustra* there is the incident of the dead rope-dancer:

And thou, my first companion, rest in peace! Well have I buried thee in thy hollow tree; well have I hid thee from the wolves.[31]

In the First Part, Zarathustra celebrates the body and the soul as one, but with a peculiarly Whitmanesque duality when he has "the Self" carry on a conversation with "the I" exactly like Whitman's dialogue between soul and body. In the Second Part there is the talk with friends in which Zarathustra's "wild wisdom" runs about and seeks "soft sward." ("On the soft sward of your hearts, my friends!") And later the Whitmanesque outburst:

Verily, through a hundred souls went I my way, and through a hundred cradles and birth-throes. Many a farewell have I taken; I know the heart-breaking last hours.[32]

And like Whitman in "Song of Myself," he says of the priests:

. . . but although they are mine enemies pass them quietly and with sleeping swords!
Even among them there are heroes;

.   .   .

But my blood is related to theirs; and I want withal to see my blood honored in theirs.[33]

(Cf. "Crossing Brooklyn Ferry.") Or when he compares his song to a sail at sea:

Have you ne'er seen a sail crossing the sea, rounded and inflated, and trembling with the violence of the wind?[34]

In the Third Part, as a divine vagabond he calls his disciples out of houses as did Whitman in "Song of Myself."

And these rooms and chambers—can *men* go out and in there? They seem to be made for silk dolls; or for dainty eaters, who perhaps let others eat with them.[35]

And like Whitman he talks of his flourish of trumpets and herald cry. Then Zarathustra praises his own body, and says:

—From the powerful soul, to which the high body appertaineth, the handsome, triumphing, refreshing body, around which everything becometh a mirror:

—The pliant, persuasive body, the dancer, whose symbol and epitome is the self-enjoying soul. Of such bodies and souls the self-enjoyment calleth itself "virtue." [36]

Zarathustra teaches his disciples to wait "but only for me." Even through prison walls and to prisoners in prison he blows his buoyant spirit. What is the highest entity? That is the soul:

—The most comprehensive soul, which can run and stray and rove furthest in itself; the most necessary soul, which out of joy flingeth itself into chance:—

—The soul in Being which plungeth into Becoming; the possessing soul, . . .

.   .   .

—The soul most self-loving, in which all things have their current and counter-current, their ebb and their flow: . . .[37]

And so Zarathustra wishes for men and women, "the one fit for war, the other for maternity." But above all he loves the *sea* and everything belonging to the sea, "and am fondest of it when it angrily contradicteth me."

If the exploring delight be in me, which impelleth sails to the undiscovered, if the seafarer's delight be in my delight:

If ever my rejoicing hath called out: "The shore hath vanished,— now hath fallen from me the last chain—

The boundless roareth around me, far away sparkle for me space and time,—well! cheer up! old heart!" [38]

And like Whitman he praises life as it draws to a close.

O afternoon of my life! O happiness before eventide! O haven
upon high seas! . . .[39]

And in the Fourth Part, in which Zarathustra has grown old,
he speaks almost literally like Whitman in his old-age poetry.

—As a ship that putteth into the calmest cove :—it now draweth
up to the land, weary of long voyages and uncertain seas . . .

As such a ship huggeth the shore, tuggeth the shore:—then it
sufficeth for a spider to spin its thread from the ship to the land.
No stronger ropes are required there.

As such a weary ship in the calmest cove . . .[40]

And later:

O happiness! O happiness! Wilt thou perhaps sing, O my soul?
Thou liest in the grass. But this is the secret, solemn hour, when
no shepherd playeth his pipe . . .

.   .   .

Do not sing, thou prairie-bird, my soul! . . .

And at his departure Zarathustra calls himself the dancer,
the fledgling, ready to fly, who waves farewell to all the birds,
but will come again. Despite the differences, such as Nietzsche's
lack of sympathy, his conscious intolerance, his making mouths
at the common people, his anger at corroding antiquity, and his
fastidiousness, still we find an unmistakable leaning toward
Whitman or the Whitmanesque type. It is clear from the above
quotations how astonishingly alike they were in their lyrical
mentality. The wandering and the awakening, the theme of the
ship, the complete intoxication with nature and oratory, the
frequent long lyrical passages similar in construction and content to Whitman's, the oriental imagery of the dancers reap-
pearing again and again in Nietzsche's book, all unite to produce a resemblance that paradoxically makes intelligible what
Isadora Duncan meant by the strange observation in her memoirs that since her youth she had chosen "three masters in the
art of the dance: Rousseau, Walt Whitman, and Nietzsche!"
The gifted danseuse has actually given expression to a sensational relationship in world literature, and it could not be more
effectively phrased by a professional critic.

The comparison with Nietzsche is the natural conclusion for

a discussion of the problem of "the Whitmanesque type." At the same time, the fact that the astonishing similarities are found in one of Whitman's contemporaries who had not read him provides a suggestive opening for beginning a treatment of Whitman's influence on modern literature.

The European country in which Whitman first exercised the most widespread literary influence was unquestionably Germany, but it was also the country in which the most bitter conflict raged over the nature and value of his art, his teaching, his personality, and his type, especially between 1905 and 1912. The poet was no longer a novelty, and the early enthusiasm was followed by discussion.

The pantheistic character of Whitman's lyricism, the mystic and universal quality of his emotion of life, were naturally elements that aroused a direct response in the German temperament. He acted both as a poetic announcer of a new reality and as a secret inculcator of a primeval emotional and esthetic tradition. Frequently when we find "the Whitmanesque" in recent German poetry we discover on further examination that it is not merely Whitmanesque but rather a blending of the Whitmanesque revolt with the traditional emotion and expression of the medieval German mystics, Angelus Silesius, Jacob Böhme, Goethe, the earlier romanticists (especially Novalis), and the later romanticists (especially Leopold Schefer), and then—naturally, Nietzsche. The Germans themselves were aware of some of the connections and relationships. Fritz Lienhard, in *Wege nach Weimar* [Road to Weimar], Vol. I, 1906, proclaimed Whitman as Goethe's pupil nearly equal to the master, and Eduard Bertz, in his various Whitman studies, pointed out his similarity to Novalis.

Whitman had never actually read Novalis, but Carlyle's quotations from Novalis on the sacredness of the human body—"a Revelation in the Flesh," "we touch Heaven when we place our hands on a human Body" (*Sartor Resartus*, Book III, Chapter 6)—had undoubtedly been one of the effective and decisive cues which had aroused Whitman's inspiration before he wrote *Leaves of Grass*. Then Whitman's book—in a new, more forceful, but congenial form—brought this inspiration back to the nation which had a peculiar capacity for accepting and understanding it. The kinship of temperament and perception explain the interest with which Whitman was discovered and accepted by the German prose writers and lyricists of the turn of the century.

He exerted an even stronger influence on the poets of the First World War period when the arguments had subsided after the bitter discussion over his psychology and sexual type, around 1906. That is, after Dr. Magnus Hirschfeld had included Whitman (among other great names of world culture) in his "scientific humanitarian" study, had accredited, and, it seemed irrefutably, classified the great American poet as a peculiarly typical example of a sexual "Zwischenstufe." The debate raged in Germany on this whole dangerous and vital subject, most acrimoniously during the disastrous Eulenberg scandal which swept Germany in 1907, and was both good and bad for Whitman's German reputation. First hailed as a social or religious "prophet," then brought into disrepute as a "Zwischenstufe" (to the dismay and sorrow of his first naïve admirers), Whitman finally won and held a great poetic following as a cosmic lyricist with a universal emotional appeal.

Regardless of kinship of temperament and poetic type, the influence of a poet in a foreign country is naturally always dependent on the number, and particularly on the quality, of the translations in which he is presented—especially on his first appearance in the language of the country. In no other country are there so many and such widely differing translations of Whitman as in Germany. Freiligrath began the movement on his return from his political exile in London, where he had read Rossetti's *Selections from Whitman's Poems.* In April, 1868, he wrote an article in the Augsburg *Allgemeine Zeitung* and soon afterwards published some translations of poems from *Drum-Taps.* In 1870 there followed the *Amerikanische Antologie,* by the critic and translator Adolf Strodtmann, in which Whitman was more copiously represented, still without attracting great public attention. Ernst Otto Hopp's translation of "O Captain, My Captain!" in an anthology called *Unter dem*

Sternenbanner [Under the Starry Banner], 1877, was comparatively unnoticed.

The first really significant translation was the more comprehensive *Grashalme*, by T. W. Rolleston, in collaboration with Karl Knortz, published in Zurich in 1889. Although it was marred by great linguistic faults,[41] it included the complete "Song of Myself" and a number of the most typical and important poems, among others "Starting from Paumanok," "Out of the Cradle Endlessly Rocking," and "The Mystic Trumpeter." And they were basically in Whitmanesque language; thus interest was aroused, the ice was broken, the road opened. The German critics began to write articles about Whitman, the literary public pricked up its ears, and many translations appeared. In 1900 Thea Ettlinger published *Novellen von Walt Whitman*, and in 1904 William Schölermann and Karl Federn, working independently in Leipzig and in Munich, respectively, each presented an utterly different interpretation and selection of *Grashalme*. O. E. Lessing published Whitman's *Prosaschriften*, Leipzig, 1905, and the following year the first German rendering of "When Lilacs Last in the Dooryard Bloom'd" appeared in his *Aus fremden Zungen* [From Foreign Tongues], Berlin, 1906. Finally, in 1907 Johannes Schlaf's translation of *Grashalme*, which was so significant and achieved such widespread recognition not only in Germany but also throughout Europe because it was published in the popular and inexpensive Reclambibliotek—Reclams Universal Bibliothek—and thus for many years was responsible for the opinion the average German reader got of the American poet. When we read it today Schlaf's translation reveals obvious poetic qualities, but suffers from strange linguistic errors. And the choice of poems is narrow, undeniably distorting, or at least disfiguring *Leaves of Grass* by the gaps and omissions. *Children of Adam* is translated in full, *Calamus*, on the other hand, only meagerly. The "standard" German edition of Whitman thus forms a very strange contrast to "the British Whitman," in which a parallel but differently motivated appraisal instituted almost the opposite censorship. This example puts the question of the moral concepts of two different but equally "moral" nations in an amusing light and tempts one to make a sociological analysis of the question.

The first really satisfactory recreation of Whitman in German was Hans Reisiger's two-volume edition in 1922. With its well-informed introduction and its admirable choice of poems, it can justifiably be called a literary event. The writers Gerhart Hauptmann, Thomas Mann, and Hermann Hesse, all three German Nobel prize winners, greeted its appearance as an occasion of far-reaching importance.

It is noteworthy that no long book about Whitman has ever been written in German. Schlaf wrote an essay in the well-known series of elegant little monographs "Die Dichtung," in 1904, and in 1907 translated Henry Bryan Binns's biography, which had some influence but was also severely criticized because of the careless, arbitrary way in which Schlaf had treated the English text. In the early nineties Schlaf had discovered Whitman for himself, had attempted to "take out a patent" on him, and in numerous longer or shorter articles constituted himself the only legitimate agent of Whitman in the German domain. The efforts to formulate the facts and reach an understanding of Whitman which had been made at the turn of the century by such writers as Federn, Bertz, and O. E. Lessing he had patronizingly characterized as "dirt-cheap, weakly esthetic essays." These writers now forcefully turned against him. O. E. Lessing said of Schlaf's study in "Die Dichtung": "This little book is an unparalleled example of high-handed arrogance, cowardly imposition, and utter ignorance." [42] That is a harsh denunciation, but the harshness is a measure of the passionate expression that German discussion of Whitman generally attained.

The most valuable critical contributions to Whitman research in Germany were made by writers with a first-hand knowledge of English and American intellectual life. Schlaf lacked such experience and based his Whitman-creed on the accounts of the "hot little prophets," which he supplemented with his own poetic wishful thinking. But Knortz and Eduard Bertz, like the two real pioneers Strodtmann and Freiligrath, had spent important parts of their lives in England or America

and wrote their first enthusiastic Whitman articles as early as
1882 and 1889. Bertz, the most talented and brilliant of these
men, was a loyal Whitman apostle in his youth (it was he who
was the model for the Whitmanite Walter Egremont in George
Gissing's *Thyrza*), but when he corresponded with the admired
American bard, he received, in the customary manner of Whitman's old age, a bombardment of reviews and newspaper clippings, and these produced exactly the opposite of the effect
desired by Whitman. "Walter Egremont" came to "help people to understand Whitman" (*Thyrza*, Chapter XXXV) in a
way quite different from his intention in his youthful transports. His critical faculty was aroused without his opinion of
Whitman's poetic greatness having been changed in any way.
He made Whitman's personality and mentality the subject of
an increasingly intensive psychological evaluation and analysis,
which culminated in the sensational article "Walt Whitman ein
Characterbild" [Walt Whitman, a Character Study], first
printed in Hirschfeld's *Jahrbuch für sexuelle Zwischenstufen*,[43]
and it was one of that much-discussed yearbook's finest contributions. Later, Bertz formalized and emphasized his ideas about
Whitman in his argument with Schlaf and published *Der
Yankee Heiland* [The Yankee Saint], 1907, but without add-
ing anything material to his first detailed "character study."
The publication of Bertz's forcefully expressed hypotheses
and detailed examples aroused opposition and horror, though
their psychological validity has not apparently been refuted by
later research. Schlaf rejected them with blustering but not
very convincing moral indignation. O. E. Lessing, on the other
hand, accepted them as the clearest and most accurate critical
statement made up to that time about Whitman as a poet and a
psychological type.[44] In 1905, in his introduction to his Whitman translation, Lessing hailed Whitman as the greatest poet
since Goethe ("He is the embodiment, the representative and
the illuminator of American literature in the same sense that
Dante is of the Italian, Shakespeare of the English, and Goethe
of the German"), but unfortunately this new conviction totally
changed his point of view about Whitman's poetic rank, and in
1910 he placed him far below Goethe and Emerson, even turned

directly against him with almost the same fanatical aversion he had formerly felt toward Johannes Schlaf—though for diametrically opposed reasons. He was cured of his Whitmania, "that dangerous malady," as he put it quite unreasonably, but with a convert's passion.

In the same vein as Bertz (and Havelock Ellis and Carpenter), but much less successfully, Knortz, in 1911, as the result of his enthusiastic life-long study of Whitman, wrote *Walt Whitman, Beitrag zur Literatur der Edelurninge* [Walt Whitman, a Contribution to the Literature of the Noble Uranians]. It was the work of an old man, and it did not make a favorable, much less a profound impression.[45] Enough of that. This survey of both important and obscure Whitman literature in Germany serves as an imperfect background for Whitman's real influence, direct and indirect, on German poetry since Freiligrath first discovered him in 1868—and he can now be discussed as an influence and a force in the literary sense of the word.

In the German lyricism of the late nineteenth century we can already hear Whitmanesque notes. In Liliencron (1844–1909) the resemblance is probably accidental, although in the early seventies he had visited America and had become acquainted with Whitman's poetry. His soldier lyrics for the Austrian and Franco-Prussian Wars are somewhat reminiscent of *Drum-Taps*, and his autobiographical novel, *Leben und Lüge* [Life and Lies], has a Calamus incident in which the veteran officer thinks of his youth and imagines that he finds under the lilacs the body of a dear friend lost in battle years ago.

Dost thou bloom again, gentle lilacs, to bring me greetings from my dead friend? He on whose head hung the springlike curls was indeed my friend in joy and sorrow; many hours we wasted in youthful folly until the dawn heard the clink of our glasses. That ended when the eagle of battle spread his broad wings in rage and the destructive cloud of shells filled the air like butterflies. Our flag, red in the evening light, fluttered in sign of victory. On all the hills and in the valleys the dead slept all too fraternally. Far from the song of victory, in the cool evening freshness of the garden, under the quiet shade of the lilacs, I found my friend.[46]

And Liliencron has an instinctive sense of life similar to Whitman's, an innate "awareness of life and a memory of an infinite past," which is a natural link in his whole vivid lyrical personality.

Whitman's direct influence on Rilke and Dehmel was more pronounced. With Rainer Maria Rilke (1875–1926) this influence united with the influence of Baudelaire and that of Silesian mysticism.[47] And Rilke's weak, effeminate temperament fused the two influences in its own decadent, lyrical disposition in the same way that a decadent such as Stanislaw Przybyszewski, this "Jeremiah of the degenerate instincts," as Dehmel liked to call him, "interpreted" Whitman in his work. It was the cosmic, pantheistic emotion in Whitman that made an impression on Rilke and left its mark, especially in his earliest poetry. Like Whitman, he goes out into the surf to show the sun and the sea that "I am young," and the waves sportively stretch their arms toward him as in Whitman's poems. But Rilke lacks Whitman's strong, simple joy in the poetic situation; his emotions are fear and loneliness. And in his imagery the animation of nature, which plainly carries a Whitmanesque stamp, lacks color. Like Whitman, he identifies himself with the storm and the waves, but preferably "with the pale, ashen, spring-frosted birches." He has the same awareness of the struggle of generations before he was born ("Many who lived before us are woven into my soul"), but most of all it is the feminine attitude in both lyricists which is responsible for the similarities. In his poetry Rilke liked to take the feminine roles. He sits like an old woman outside the hut and thinks of his youthful smile, the way you remember an old song. Sorrow over his "disappointed motherhood" runs like a *leit-motif* throughout his lyrics. This expression is also applicable to Whitman. But there is no possible comparison of the artistic form or presentation of these two eminent lyricists.

In Richard Dehmel (1863–1920) there is a noticeably greater likeness of personality. He represents his own time just as Whitman did his, and Johannes V. Jensen does ours. Like Nietzsche he despises dead culture: ruins, archaeology, and monuments seem to him only hindrances to human progress. He praises modern methods of communication at the expense of romanticism. Like Whitman and Nekrassow, Dehmel is a social lyricist and likewise a poet of the city. He protests against the pallid lyricism of the nineties and introduces a new, more vigorous poetry under the motto "Decadence lies behind us." As an erotic lyricist he has characteristics in common with Whitman, for "the holy spirit of the flesh" is one of his regular phrases.[48] The only divinity he recognizes is that which each human being discovers in himself; he is strongly impressed by the Hegelian (N.B.) idea of our consciousness as God's self-consciousness. In *Leben und Lüge* Liliencron characterized him as a man whose sympathy was as great as his self-esteem. He is like Whitman in that very blending of brotherly love and self-love. On the whole, *Mitgefühl* (sympathy) is for Dehmel one of the prime essentials for the society of the future, and it was the lack of that quality in Nietzsche that repelled him—although he, like the rest of his generation, was indebted to that great erratic personality. In his pantheistic sentiment he vigorously approaches the Whitmanesque lyric; in his North Sea poems he speaks of the rhythm of the sea in his blood, and he refers to the sea as "the Mother of Life." In *Aber die Liebe* he has a "Landstreichers Lobgesang" [Vagabond's Hymn], and in *Schöne wilde Welt*, a poem on "Der Schwimmer" [The Swimmer], both of them Whitmanesque motifs. Dehmel shared Whitman's conception of the poet as a prophet and preacher—and he further emphasized the oratorical nature of his poetry by innumerable reading trips throughout Germany. To him, as to Whitman, the spoken word meant more than the written word; poetry should be heard, not read. Julius Bab says pertinently of this phase of his work: "The inclination to pathos is in the last analysis only the conscious strength of a religious cosmic emotion." [49] Dehmel confessed his debt to Whitman and Verhaeren, whom, says Bab, "as the great rhetoricians of pure consciousness" he was now and then tempted "to deny the true rank of poets." Once when the conversation turned on Whitman, he jumped to his feet and exclaimed that here at last was a poet who wanted more "to influence and shape people than just to make poems." Dehmel was more genuinely masculine than

Whitman; in spite of his fifty years, he volunteered in the First World War. His idea of that war, the achieving of a Franco-German intellectual unity worth fighting for, paralleled Whitman's "ideal of the Union." The Calamus note appears in his lyrics of the first year of the war in the fanatical sentimental attachment for Liliencron, whom he saw during the war, six years after Liliencron's death, in a vision in the trenches, as his old "war-comrade,"—and his war lyrics, like Liliencron's, have some characteristics in common with Whitman's. Although in his earlier collections he carefully kept away from the Whitmanesque verse form, there are in his later volumes some poems which in style approach the long lines of Whitman and Verhaeren.

Otherwise it was the Whitmanesque form that at first exerted the most direct influence in Germany. In many ways it was important for the young radical lyricists around 1900, who sought a new lyrical form and for a time used rhymeless verse as the only medium worth while. Klopstock and Goethe had written unrhymed verse, it is true, but it was Whitman who carried rhymelessness as far as it would go. Alfred Mombert (b. 1872), whom Kurt Pinthus, in the anthology *Menscheitdämmerung* [Twilight of Humanity], 1919, mentions along with Whitman and Rilke as the three most significant impulses of modern German lyricism, had written unrhymed poetry as early as 1896, in his collection *Der Glühende* [The Glowing], dedicated to Richard Dehmel, and thus had prepared for "the dissolution of form" which two years later Arno Holz carried through. In Mombert's *Der himmliche Zecher* [The Celestial Drunkard], 1909, a collection of earlier poems amalgamated in a manner comparable to *Leaves of Grass*, we can certainly detect similarities to Whitman—in spite of the metaphysical stamp of all Mombert's refined and discerning intellectual lyrics, which Dehmel liked to read aloud. Mombert, like Whitman, declares his love for all creatures as "my fellow-humans, my earth brothers," when he lies "intoxicated among the flowers, in the midst of heaven, in the garden the world," [50] Whitman's "To the Garden the World."

But the theoretician among these lyricists was Arno Holz

(1863–1929), who in his *Revolution der Lyrik*, 1899, propounded the theories of verse which he himself had already used in 1898 in his *Phantasus* poems, a lyricism that renounces rhythm, word music, all techniques and mechanics, "and lives only through that which strives for expression through it," a characterization especially applicable to Whitmanesque verse. Arno Holz teaches: "Express what you feel and you have it (that is, rhythm). You grasp it when you grasp the things. It permeates everything. All the rest (rhythm, strophe, and so forth) you can dispense with." [51] He is acutely aware of the mechanism of all earlier poetic art; even in the poetry of Goethe and Heine he seems to hear "the furtive barrel-organ." Holz had a great reverence for Whitman, and in 1905 he declared to Amalia von Ende that to him Whitman was the dearest name in world literature, but that for a poet he seemed too much an orator, although the greatest orator in world lyricism. In contrast to Whitman, Verhaeren, and Dehmel, Holz wanted his own lyrics to avoid all pathos, all declamation, and to create for themselves a sort of telegraphic style. Like Mombert he desired poetry to be "white hot," to possess "intensity." Whitman's influence on *Phantasus*, however, is unmistakable. The point of departure of "Song of Myself" is directly transferred.

> Beautiful, soft green grass
> In which I lie . . .[52]

And in the many lyrical "anecdotes" we find characteristics of Whitman's lyricism. There is the evolutionary retrospective look into the world of transmigration.

> Seven billion years before my birth I was an iris . . .[53]

Whitman's cosmic vision is repeated in similar enumerative style.

> In new wandering, growing, fluctuating, brewing, bubbling, revolving world circle
> Grows, climbs, pushes, divided, played, glowed, scattered, quenched the flaming meteor ball . . .
>
> .   .   .
>
> In order to swing my dark metallic, halcyonic, phallic, tinkling, crystal, gigantic flower Scepter-crown . . .[54]

Both "halcyonic" and "phallic" clearly indicate a connection with Whitman—in fact almost a parody of the Whitmanesque. We see how deeply one poet can be influenced by another in Holz's later Whitmanesque poems, though in these he got entirely away from his early youthful theories and ideals. In *Der Blechschmeide* [The Tinsmith], although he uses rhyme and meter, he recreates a completely Whitmanesque situation in the dialogue with his book, in which his "real self," the book, speaks to the poet and towers over him,

> Thou art only the medium! Thou art not the goal! [55]

exactly as *Leaves of Grass* rose superior to Whitman and became the real, vital personality that had merely used the poet and his sufferings as a means to achieve existence. Holz worked with his *Phantasus* collection, integrating and revising it through various phases between 1898 and 1925 in a manner similar to the work of Whitman and Mombert on their collections of poems.

Johannes Schlaf (*b.* 1862), Holz's co-fighter in the days of "consistent naturalism," was as a poet one of Whitman's most vigorous espousers in Germany. How decisive the reading of Whitman was for him is best shown in his little book of prose, *Der Frühling* [Spring], 1894, which was, so to speak, written under Whitmanesque inspiration. It is a sun song, a spring song, a nature hymn in which the poet identifies himself with a venerable, garrulous and ironic eighty-year-old sage, then with a very young child, but is constantly stirred by the music of existence, "the song of power," with its "million-voiced harmony," and wants to yield to it in awe, jubilation, and terror, to join the song which tells simultaneously of the beginning of all life and of the far distant future. And the poet sees before him a future with new conditions of life and a new and better humanity who are all like a radiation of the One.

Everywhere art thou and only thou, and nothing is without thee and nothing beside thee. All is thy image and thy likeness. Today thou art white, tomorrow black, the next day brown, thou art man and woman, child and animal, all, all . . .[56]

That little book, which is one of Schlaf's best and had much influence at the time—among others, on Dehmel—shows plainly what in Whitman interested him. It is the lighter, the affirmative and optimistic, the sunny side of Whitman, if one may use such an expression, which was also dominant in his 1907 translation. Otherwise the Whitmanesque poetry has had no direct influence on Schlaf's work, even though Whitman's social doctrine underlies his great "scientific" and religio-philosophical writing: *Das absolute Individuum* [The Absolute Individual] and *Religion und Kosmos* [Religion and Cosmos] of 1910–11 and the prose-poem *Das Gottlied* [God's Song] of 1922. Schlaf argued against Nietzsche in defense of Whitman and Verhaeren, in whom he saw the type of a future superior humanity. But to an amazing degree Schlaf saw only one phase of Whitman's poetry, the affirmative, and not the profound, tragic contrast between the man and his work, which Bertz and O. E. Lessing first observed and unveiled.

Through Rilke, Dehmel, Mombert, Holz, and Schlaf, Whitman's name and poetic significance reached a wider circle, and his influence is evident in much of the new German lyricism between the turn of the century and the First World War, for example, in Hille and Morgenstern. It was primarily with the younger generation of poets at the beginning of the First World War that Whitman's influence reached its first culmination, because the teachings of Mombert and Holz had just begun to influence the generation following them, and Schlaf's translation, in spite of the controversy over it, achieved its real effect after 1910. For the whole group of young German lyricists the Ragnarok of the First World War was an emancipation, just as in a personal sense the Civil War was for Whitman. Brotherly love, love of humanity, democracy, and cosmic consciousness became the common themes of lyricists such as Alfons Paquet, Ludwig Rubiner, Leo Sternberg, Albert Ehrenstein; Heinrich Lersch and Gerrit Engelke are particularly indebted to Whitman; Arnim T. Wegner and Lersch sent out their first collections of poems, *Das Antlitz der Städte* [The Face of the Cities] and *Herz, aufglühe dein Blut* [Heart, Enkindle Thy Blood], with mottoes from him, and no less obvious is Whitman's influence on Franz Werfel, the most famous of them all. Hatzfeld sings of God, who is in beggars, idiots, in pregnant women,

"and in the enemy whom I stab in the war." Karl Otten wrote
a prose poem to the proletariat, and Ludwig Rubiner published
a whole collection, *Der Mensch in der Mitte* [Humanity in the
Center], 1917, on Whitmanesque motifs: for example, "Der
Mensch" on the human body and "Die Stimme" on the human
voice. We have already mentioned in passing the similarity between *Drum-Taps* and Liliencron's and Dehmel's war lyrics.
Heinrich Lersch (1889–1936) appeared as a new poet, starting
with a similar temperament and also with a strong Whitman influence, and wrote poetry about the First World War which
closely corresponded to Whitman's Civil War poems. As it now
exists, Lersch's first two collections of poetry, *Herz, aufglühe
dein Blut*, 1916, and *Deutschland*, 1917, are scarcely conceivable
without Whitman. Reading *Leaves of Grass* somewhat relieved
the impression the horrors of war made on him and determined
his choice in the form of his expression. It is not merely single
lines or isolated impressions that recall Whitman—such as the
remarkable vision of the dead soldiers marching home, or the
two enemies, a Frenchman and a German, united in no-man's
land—but whole poems are drawn from Whitmanesque motifs.
Whitman's two famous poems from *Drum-Taps* "Pensive on
Her Dead Gazing" and "Vigil Strange" are directly incorporated in "Die Erde singt" [Earth Sings], "Wenn es Abend
wird" [When It Is Evening], and "Totenwatch" [Deathwatch],
in which a soldier keeps watch over his dead comrade:

. . . I am alone with you,
and am father, mother, wife and child, all these am I to you.[57]

In Lersch's postwar poems *Mensch im Eisen* [Humanity in
Iron], 1925, we find a greater independence, although Whitman's inspiration is still constantly evident. He celebrates the
world-wide community of working people; his poem "Der
Schmied reist in den Ferien" [The Smith Travels on His Vaca-
tion] is his "Salut au Monde," and even in the poems of his
later years when the former free and easy vagabond and democratic poet started writing naïve glorifications of Hitler's brown-
shirted "Volksgenossenschaft" the Whitmanesque cadences can
still be heard in poems such as "Sommersonntag" [Sunday in

Summer] or "Der Baum" [The Tree].[58] During Europe's
fateful year the Whitman cult was paradoxically shared by
Nazis and Communists; former friends suddenly became bitter
enemies over the interpretation of the concept "democracy"—
but the tone of the lyrics Lersch wrote remained unmistakably
original and gave evidence of his combined poetic emotion and
oratorical disposition.

Gerrit Engelke, an early friend of Lersch, was also a work-
ingman and soldier who was killed in the war just before the
armistice in 1918. The Whitman influence is conspicuous in
his *Rhythmus des neuen Europa* [Rhythm of the New Europe],
which Jakob Kneip published after Engelke's death. Engelke
had a volume of Whitman with him in the trenches. Dehmel
read Engelke's poems in manuscript and praised them warmly,
although he did object to the monotonous "cosmic ring" in all
of them. They unite the democracy of Whitman and Dehmel.
The themes are reminiscent less of Whitman than of Lersch,
but in his call to the "soldiers of all armies" his diction comes
as close to Whitman's as this:

> You Frenchman from Brest, Bordeaux, Garonne,
> You Ukranian, Cossack from the Urals, Dneister and Don,
> Austrian, Bulgarian, Osmanian and Serb,
> All in the raging struggle of action and death—
> You Briton from London, York, Manchester,
> Soldier, Comrade, truly fellow-men and the best—
> Americans from the populous states of freedom . . . etc.[59]

In another poem, "Sonne" [Sun], we meet a Whitmanesque
catalogue.

> Spew, clang, siren-howl, hissing steam, hammer,
> Ocean travel, mammoth ships wallowing in the fog,
> Rhode Island steamer, Hudson pinnace . . .[60]

The short poem "Zu viele Menschen, zu viele Straszen" [Too
Many People, Too Many Streets] shows the temperamental resemblance by expressing a Whitmanesque yearning for all who
pass him on the streets and a regret "that in the quiet of the evening we never meet again in the streets."

But more important than his influence on these poets who

will scarcely outlive their age is Whitman's influence on the most important modern German lyricist, Franz Werfel (1890–1946), with whom there are also striking psychological similarities. Werfel was of Bohemian descent, as were Rilke, Brod, and Kafka, and his temperamental mystic tendencies make a comparison doubly interesting. A basic element of Werfel's imagination is his constant use of the theme of a mother-religion, growing out of the same pantheistic emotion as Whitman's. Enmity to the father and attachment to the mother dominate his numerous poems and is most clearly expressed in his poem "Tag und Nacht Hymnus." [61] Like Whitman's, Werfel's poetic inspiration is to a great degree based on music. In the early poem "Sterben im Walde" [Death in the Wood] he describes a cosmic experience paralleling Whitman's in "Song of Myself," and he mentions "the great Rigoletto quartet of creation"; [62] here also he refers to a four-part division such as Whitman's "divine quadrant." The interest in music which in his novel *Verdi* has made Werfel one of the world's great "musical authors," along with Heine, Hoffmann, Nietzsche, and Rolland—has frequently stamped the form of his lyricism, which now and then becomes a recitative, interesting as a comparison with Whitman's inspiration from the recitative of Italian opera. While in later years Werfel did more and more work as a novelist and playwright, in his younger days he was almost exclusively a lyric poet—and the most typical representative of that generation of world lyricists. He himself took no part in the First World War, but fled to Switzerland and lived there in the international colony of writers and critics. In single poems of the war period he gave expression to typically Whitmanesque sentiments, such as: The real victor is not the heroic and conquering warrior. No, the real victor:

They despise, they prefer the defeated to the victor, they surrender, they let themselves be captured.

.   .   .

For frightful as is humiliation, more frightful is the purity which knows itself and a Tamerlane who gives himself up.[63]

A Whitmanesque idea is clearly expressed here in a manner as baroque as Whitman's own statement that the *real* victor was the general who lost the battle, the one whose ship went down, and all those who were conquered and slain.

The generations of lyricists between 1910 and 1920 were influenced by Rilke, Dehmel, and Whitman. Werfel opposed Rilke's and Dehmel's "Ich bin" with his all-encompassing "Wir sind," which is really Whitmanesque. Werfel's titles are characteristic of the whole generation: *Der Weltfreund* [The World-Friend], 1911, *Wir sind*, 1913, and *Einander* [One Another], 1915, in which the influence of Rilke and Whitman are joined and remarkably blended. But in the early books Whitman is the stronger, completely dominating influence. The young Werfel sings of "beautiful shining humanity" and in "An den Leser" [To the Reader] he opens his arms and heart to all.

Whether thou art Negro, acrobat, or art still resting deep in the
  mother's womb

he knows them all and is in them all.

                          . . . I know
The feeling of the lonely woman harpist in the chapel,
The feeling of the timid governess in the strange family,
The feeling of the debutante who appears before the prompter's
  box.
I have lived in the forest, been a railway official,
Have sat bent over account books and served impatient guests,
As a stoker I have stood before the boilers, my face illuminated in
  the glare,
And as a cooley I ate garbage and kitchen scraps,

So I belong to you and to every one!

                    .   .   .

O that it might be
That we could fall into each other's arms, brother.[64]

In "Nachtfragment" [Night Piece] he wrote his version of "The Sleepers," in which the poet bends over all the sleepers of the world in turn. In "Ein anderes" [A Different One] he tells of his vivid impression of an earlier existence, when he was a forest, a river, or a road, and he still feels these like music within himself. "Jenseits" [Beyond] is of the soul's longing for a reunion with nature.

> We come again, we return home
> To you, our good mother.[65]

Everything returns home, human beings, animals, the sea, the leaves, the clouds, and the "courageous rivers." In his later poetry Werfel outgrew the Whitman influence and became very original and individualistic in his expression, especially in his erotic lyrics, among the finest and most personal in modern literature. But in many of the exalted, ecstatic hymns of the later years, "Unsterblichkeit" [Immortality], "Hohe Gemeinschaft" [Exalted Community], "Hohere Menschen" [Superior Humanity], or in the purely phallic "Weib-Hymn" [Hymn to Womanhood]

> The essence of humanity bows, Giant Phallus,
> To you! [66]

And in his pantheistic visions, for example, the play *Bockgesang* [*Goat-Song*], 1921, we still observe the inspiration Whitman originally gave him. Like Gerrit Engelke, Werfel also expresses a Whitmanesque feeling for strangers in the street, "We are all strangers on the earth," corresponding to Whitman's "To a Stranger"—and as he passes a stranger and looks into his eyes, he feels, as did Whitman, that at some time they were one; the accidental meeting is "a reunion from the era of stars."

How strong Whitman's influence has been on modern German literature, aside from the lyrical writers, is best seen in the debt which Hermann Hesse, Bernhard Kellermann, and Thomas Mann owe him. Hesse used Whitman motifs not only in *Peter Camemczind*, but also in the vagabond novels, *Knulp* and *Demian*, 1919. In *Narciss und Goldmund*, 1939, he came very close to Whitman's thoughts and diction as witnessed by the sentence: "I believe that a petal or a tiny worm on the way has much more to tell me than all the books of a library." [67] Kellermann's prose style in *The Sea*, *The Tunnell*, and *The Ninth of November* is influenced by Whitman in the same way as Johannes V. Jensen's in *Hjulet* [The Wheel]. And Thomas Mann's optimistic view of democracy and world development after the First World War is, as he himself confesses in *Von Deutscher Republik* [On the German Republic], 1923, the result of reading Whitman, or more correctly, of reading Reisiger's German translation of Whitman, 1922.

The history of Whitman in France shows, on the whole, the same course as in Germany, with the difference that his ideas and form of expression seemed much more strange, though it had been foreshadowed in French literature not only by Victor Hugo but also by the historian and philosopher Jules Michelet (1798–1874), "that blend of a Carlyle and a Walt Whitman" as Vald. Vedel called Michelet as early as 1898.[68] Whitman himself began to play a role there in the eighties and nineties. After Mme Blanc's introduction in 1872, articles appeared in various periodicals by Emile Blémont, Léon Quesnel, Gabriel Sarrazin, and Paul Desjardins, and the younger poets began to read and translate him. Quesnel and Sarrazin quoted fragments of *Leaves of Grass* in their articles, and in 1886 for Gustave Kahn's *La Vogue* Jules Laforgue (1860–87) translated "Une femme m'attend" [A Woman Waits for Me] and "O, étoile de France" [O Star of France]. The following year Francis de Vielé-Griffin (*b.* 1864) published "Le chant de la hache" [Song of the Broad-Axe] in *La Revue Indépendante*. Whitman's importance for the French vers-librists was determined by Laforgue, who, having a mentality similar to Holz's, played a similar role in France. His influence supplemented that of German lyricism, especially Goethe's free verse, which earlier French poets had considered barbaric. In his peculiar book *Écrivains étrangers* [Foreign Writers], 1896, Téodor de Wyzewa hailed Whitman as the first great poet from a country which had only two other poets, Stuart Merrill and Francis de Vielé-Griffin. The statement produced almost hysterical merriment among "the prophets" in America; Kennedy declared that he had never heard the names of the two gentlemen before. Naturally, by American poets Wyzewa had meant poets of American birth living in Paris at that time. But the ignorance of Parisian poets about American literature in general could be justly compared only to the almost grotesque ignorance of modern European literature which the American Whitmanians betrayed in their writing. Stuart Merrill (*b.* 1863) was a compatriot of Whitman's in the strictest sense of the word, having been born at Hempstead, Long Island; Vielé-Griffin, who at that time was busy with plans for a translation of Whitman, was born in Virginia. Both of them were among Whitman's most ardent admirers and were leading vers-librists. In his book on French symbolism Lorentz Eckhoff makes much of what appears to him to be the affirmative note in Vielé-Griffin's lyrics, which he takes to indicate that the later symbolists are "singers of joy." He quotes from Vielé-Griffin's "Clarté de vie" [Splendor of Life].

> None of us dies, nothing is futile or vain;
> Life is realized in infinity—[69]

but oddly enough he does not say a word about Whitman's significance for the whole movement, a connection he might reasonably have pointed out. As Holz did in Germany, Stuart Merrill declared that the "innate melody" alone decides a poem's form and rhythm. Through these two Franco-American authors Whitman's name and influence reached these young Belgian poets who took such an active part in the new lyrical school, Verhaeren, Lerberghe, and Maeterlinck.

Through the efforts of Léon Bazalgette (1873–1938) Whitman gained a larger audience in France. His long book on Whitman ("more the work of a disciple than a critic," says his compatriot Valéry Larbaud) appeared in 1908, and a year later his two-volume translation, *Feuilles d'herbe* (Mercure de France). Whitman's influence on the younger French poets, especially on the "Unanimists," to which Bazalgette himself belonged, was increased by these works, as it had been in Germany by Schlaf's translation. Bazalgette's translation was reprinted in a large edition in 1922.[70] Like Schlaf's, to some extent Bazalgette's edition prettified and idealized the material. André Gide protested against its first appearance and set to work to provide a better, more congenial translation, with the result that in 1918 a new French edition of Whitman appeared in Nouvelle Revue Française's admirable series, "Masterpieces of World Literature." A few of Laforgue's and Vielé-Griffin's best translations were used, but the remainder was newly translated by Gide, Larbaud, or Schlumberger; Bazalgette was rejected altogether. But his work had been important in spreading Whitman's influence in France, especially before the First World War. Phileas Lebesque wrote an essay, "Walt Whitman et la poèsie contemporaine," which was included in a book called *Essai d'expansion d'une esthétique* (Bordeaux, 1911), and Guillaume Apollinaire had two articles about him in *Mercure de France* in 1913 and 1915, respectively. About that time a Parisian correspondent for the Chicago literary periodical *Poetry* wrote:

Whitman is today a greater influence with the young writers of the continent than with our own. Not since France discovered Poe has literary Europe been so moved by anything American.[71]

In 1918 Eugène Figuière gave a lecture on Whitman as the first of a series of literary matinees at the Odéon Théâtre in Paris, which was published under the title *Walt Whitman poète américain* (Paris, 1928), with a portrait—not of Whitman, but of Figuière. In 1920 Jean Richepin (1849–1926) published a group of lectures he had given on *L'Âme américaine;* their chief topic was Whitman. From his youth Richepin had been attracted by Whitman, whose lyric mentality, especially the vagabondry and erotic frankness, were in one way or another suggestive of his own *Chansons des gueux* [Songs of the Beggars], 1876, which was his "Song of the Open Road," and *Les Caresses,* 1877, his *Children of Adam.* In Baldensperger's *Revue de littérature comparée* we frequently find Whitman's name, and one of Baldensperger's students, Jean Catel, published in 1929 and 1930 a profound study of Whitman's early years and poetic style.

Among the earlier vers-librists who were influenced by Whitman, we should also mention Hugues Rebell (1868–1905), with his *Chants de la pluie et du soleil* [Songs of Rain and Sun], 1889, and Maeterlinck. The latter, in his early lyrical period, was as different from Whitman as was Rilke in Germany; nevertheless, in *Serres chaudes* [Hothouses], 1889, we can clearly hear Whitmanesque tones, particularly in the two long poems, "Regards" and "Attouchement," in which not only the themes but also the form is Whitmanesque, for example, the use of the parentheses for "asides" in the middle of the poem clearly reveals the relationship. As in Rilke's poems, the influence is curiously blended with that of Verlaine, who was temperamentally much closer to the young poet. But finding his way "through Whitman" determined for Maeterlinck (as it did for Schlaf and Bazalgette) the nature of his cosmic and social dreams in his later books. To the same early period belongs André Gide's (*b.* 1869) first acquaintance with Whitman. Gide, who was at times in and at other times out of the circle of lyricists of the nineties, which included Heredia, Mallarmé, and Regnier, published his first book, *Les Cahiers d'André Walther* [Notebooks of Andre Walther] in 1891. In his famous memoirs *Si le grain ne meurt* [If the Seed Die] he has described the milieu of the period, including, among other things, a valuable characterization of Vielé-Griffin and Stuart Merrill. Not satisfied with a second-hand knowledge of the great American, he early procured an 1855 edition of *Leaves of Grass*. When in 1925 he sold it, along with some other rare books from his library, it was interpreted by the critic Paul Souday as a repudiation of Whitman, but Gide denied this in a rebuttal by insisting that as far as he was concerned bibliographical interest had no connection with literary interest, and that in his library he had a less expensive but far more complete edition of *Leaves of Grass*.

Naturally Whitman's direct influence on Gide is noticeable only in his early work. In *L'Immoraliste* [*The Immoralist*], 1902, the hero, Michel, flees from the bigotry and prudery of the city into the forest, meeting nature naked in a Whitmanesque ceremony, like the poet in "Song of Myself." Still stronger is the influence in the marvelous little book *Les Nourritures terrestres* [*Fruits of the Earth*], 1897, in which frequently the prose-verse is only a variant of Whitmanesque motifs. The book is addressed to an unknown reader and student, a young man whom the author calls Nathanaël in a way reminiscent of Whitman's direct appeal, whom the author wants to leave everything—work, school, home, family—to follow him, just as Whitman demanded in "Song of the Open Road." The very beginning of the book shows to what extent Whitman suggested it.

Nathanaël, do not expect to find God, except everywhere.
Each creature indicates God, none fails to reveal him.
When our attention is arrested, every creature leads us to God.[72]

This could almost be a translation of Whitman. And the book continues throughout to exhort Nathanaël to be as human as possible, to take everything he possesses with him, and always to be prepared to set out—not to read books, but to live.

> To walk wherever a way opens.
> To rest where the shade invites.
> To swim at the edge of the deep water.
> To love or sleep on the edge of every bed.[73]

Even variations of the ship-motif are to be found:

The boats have come into our port carrying ripe fruits from unknown countries.

.   .   .

Let us go, let us go and relieve them of their burden quickly.[74]

.   .   .

Sometimes, hidden by the darkness, I stand bowed against your window for a long time to watch the customs of your house.

He sees the father, mother—and the eldest son.

And my heart swells with yearning to take him with me on the road.[75]

As with Whitman all the wonders of the world could not counterbalance "the lonely view of my hand on the table." And like Whitman he bursts into spontaneous praise of grain and crops in a typically Whitmanesque exclamatory style.

> Piles of grain! I will praise you—my granaries are full.
> Cereals: red wheat rich in hope, priceless store![76]

And, like Whitman, he sings of everything.

Nathanaël, I will teach you that everything is naturally divine. Nathanaël, I will speak to you of all things.[77]

And finally he takes leave of Nathanaël, in the manner of Whitman, who only promised to stop for a few hours: Leave my book, Nathanaël, and find your own way. No one else can find it for you. No one has carried out with more consistency than Gide, Whitman's instructions about "the passionate kisses of parting" in reply to any plea to remain longer in a place.

While earlier scholars, especially in Germany, thought *Les Nourritures terrestres* could have been inspired by Nietzsche, Gide, in the preface to the German translation, *Uns nährt die Erde* (Berlin, 1930), denied that at the time he wrote it, 1895–96, he had read anything of Nietzsche—and strangely enough no one before this has pointed out the indisputable dependence on Whitman.[78] Naturally there are other elements in the book: oriental touches, the influence of Greek lyricism, and an obvious note of Oscar Wilde, so that in his person, Gide, in a very special way united a Whitman and a Wilde. In the person of André Gide, Georg Brandes would have been correct in considering "the two as one" (see page 10). Obviously it is the whole Calamus phase of Whitman that from the beginning especially interested Gide. In *Corydon*, 1911, he effectively argued against Bazalgette's misinterpretation and distortion of the *Calamus* poems,[79] and an important part of the Whitman translation that he sponsored was the complete and correct *Calamus* section translated by Louis Fabulet. Gide himself translated "From Pent-Up Aching Rivers" and "As I Pass'd." In addition to Whitman, Gide also translated Tagore, Blake, and Nietzsche, and thus intentionally emphasized a significant literary kinship.

Now let us turn to Verhaeren and Whitman. As with Dehmel, the first considerations here are similarity of temperament and oratorical power, and we must realize that Victor Hugo was one of Verhaeren's early models among the poets "dedicating their lives to the heart of the universe." [80] But the influence of Jules Laforgue on him, as on all "La Jeune Belgique," was important in helping him to revolt against all traditional form,[81] to find his "free form," "this free verse so satisfying to the contemporary soul," [82] as he puts it in *Impressions III*—no less important than his connection with Whitman, whom he admired. In his first books, especially during his great crisis in the nineties, he reminds us more of Rilke and Maeterlinck, and in his descriptions of modern life we recall Nekrassow's or Dehmel's impressive but macabre fantasies of the great city; they are not hymns to, but lamentations about, the modern cities. It is first in *Les Visages de la vie*, 1899, *Les Forces tumulteuses*, 1902, *La Mutiple Splendeur*, 1906, *Les Rhythmes souverains*, 1910, which was dedicated to Gide, and *Les Poèmes ardents*, 1913, that Verhaeren becomes the enthusiastic singer of modern life, excited by a joy in the world that glows and is as eloquent as Whitman's. The poet wants to feel the whole rhythm of life in his verse, the wind, the forest, the water, and "the thunder's loud roar," the entire world unfolding from North to South, from East to West, from the cities of India and China to the "gleaming cities" along the shores of America and Africa. He wants to share the life of each individual person, whether priest, scientist, soldier, moneychanger, swindler, or sailor.

It is necessary to admire everything to exalt one's self,[83]

and

I no longer distinguish between the world and myself,[84]

he writes in *La Multiple Splendeur*.

In this collection he writes hymns to work and to words, to the wind, which, full of love, roams over the earth, to the grass, into which he throws himself in an excess of happiness, to the enthusiasm which inspires the poets of his day and produces "the new forms for the new time," to the joy in which he, in Whitmanesque phrases, celebrates all parts of his body, and finally to a tree which, like Whitman's live-oak or Goethe's cedar, stands alone and majestic. Although we must continually regard Hugo as the connecting link, each point of Verhaeren's similarity to Whitman seems so overwhelming that their mutual traits are highlighted not only in their themes but also in the forms of expression used by these two great "rhetoricians of pure consciousness," as Dehmel once called Whitman and Verhaeren. The latter even shared some of Whitman's shortcomings. Eckhoff says, "he did not always have the patience to wait for inspiration's precious moment, and is often disposed to treat his themes too vaguely." Verhaeren is also a wanderer, and, as he himself says in *Impressions*, knows, as did Whitman and Gide, the joy of parting.[85] The wander motif is strongly dominant in his poetry. His love of nature is Whitman's pantheism, and for him death is not obliteration, but the way to eternal life. In "Vers la mer," from *Les Visages de la vie*, he gives himself to the sea, as did Whitman, in order to return again after thousands of years. In the more intimate phrases of their language they have much in common. He writes in "L'Effort," from *La Mutiple splendeur*, of his comrades the peasants, the sailors, the porters, the miners.

> I love you, lads of the fair country, beautiful drivers
> Of neighing, gleaming, heavy teams.[86]

In *Les Heures claires* he describes an erotic experience with one he loves on a quiet afternoon, paralleling the mood of Whitman's "I mind how once we lay," and pursuing a theme apparent in all his work, he has a long poem to his eyes—"Mes Yeux" [87]— in which he asks whether in a thousand years anyone will remember the deep love which his eyes helped him to feel for the whole world. Exactly as in Nietzsche we find in Verhaeren the remarkable oriental metaphor of dancing to express lyrical inspiration. He says in *Impressions I:*

There are certain of my verses that I could dance to, . . .
The rhythms run over my muscles and nerves from the summit of
　my head to the soles of my feet. I make a poem with my whole
　being.[88]

Verhaeren's enthusiastic support of the First World War is well known. It is interesting that he shared with Dehmel the expectation of a union of the German and the French intellects to form a superior race, which it was the real purpose of the war to found—two poets striving, each in his own country, and as enemies, for the same goal, like the North and the South fighting over the Union.

Among the Belgians we can also find in Charles van Lerb-

erghe (1861–1907) the Whitmanesque influence, not only in
his free verse but also in the very emotion of his *Chanson d'Eve*,
1904. Eve's discovery of the earth, her delight and joy in
its freshness and newness, her pantheistic feeling toward the
divinity which she finds in the leaves, in the water, and which
possibly at that moment rests in her arms without her being
aware of it, and finally her longing for death as a release, like
a sound, a note in the whistle and roar of the universe. Completely Whitmanesque is the description of Eve's meeting with
the sea. In the waves seeking one another and bursting with love
we recognize the sentiment of "We Two How Long We Were
Fool'd," repeated here in a more artistic, but at the same time
more decadent, poetic variation. Lerbherge reminds us of both
Whitman and Pierre Louÿs. There is a consistent parallel between Whitman and the *fin de siècle* poets that is astonishing.
Eckhoff mentions characteristics of Francis Jammes (*De
l'angelus*, 1898) and Paul Fort (*Vivre en Dieu*, 1910) in a way
that makes it seem probable that these two poets also, both
among the "Singers of Joy" of the later Symbolists, received
impressions from Whitman's poetry.

The next phase of Whitman's history in France was the en-
trance—after the day of the Symbolists and Young Belgians
—of the Unanimists into the literary arena. We might say they
were introduced by Jules Romains's volume of poems, *La Vie
unanime*, 1908, or we could stress Verhaeren's importance in
the whole movement by saying that Unanimism was first introduced by his poem "La Joie," from *La Mutiple Splendeur*,
1906.

> To mingle your being with the *unanimical* forces
> During this one day and this sublime hour
> Makes you like gods.[89]

The Unanimists proclaim a sort of lyrical socialism, paralleling the outburst of the young German poets of the First World
War against individualism. This group tried conscientiously
to achieve Whitman's theory of adhesiveness and "comradeship." In Romains's vagabond novel, *Les Copains*, 1913, we see
the half-humorous glorification of that "manly friendship"
which is simultaneously Calamus sentimentality and riotous

swaggering. In Romains's lyric poetry, with its wholly religious
worship of life in its entirety and its democratic multiplicity,
we have the lyrical side of Unanimism. Hugo, Verhaeren, Whitman, and Claudel were all forerunners and prophets of these
poets, and in general all the unanimistic lyricism can be traced
back to the influence of one of these four. Romains's own lyricism
is the most typical, and at the same time it is most under Whitman's sway. This influence came directly through Bazalgette,
one of the most active members of the group, whose familiarity
with *Leaves of Grass* began about 1908. Romains speaks directly to the reader in the same way that Whitman did. He acts
as a deliverer for his reader.

> To you . . .
> I give you your soul, is that what you want? [90]

And the influence of the poet will invisibly make itself felt
throughout the community.

> And he, later, without having read the book
> Will mysteriously know what I have said.[91]

These poems have single passages comparable to Franz Werfel's, who was a sort of German Unanimist. The section with
the refrain "Dormir sous les feuilles" [To sleep under the
leaves] in *La Vie unanime*, is a notable French parallel to Werfel's "Sterben im Walde."

> To be a body discarded and partly decomposed! [92]

The most important of the other Unanimists is Duhamel, whose
poems *Compagnons*, 1912, are a direct result of Romains's
works, and on the same theme, as also are the writings of Pierre
Jean Jouve and Charles Vildrac. Duhamel's *Vie des martyrs*,
1917, based on his work as a doctor in the First World War, is
a French counterpart of Whitman's Civil War diaries, and in
their early work both Jouve and Vildrac wrote imitative Whitmanesque prose verse. Whitman's form has been the pattern
for the Unanimists. Vildrac shows it clearly in his books *Vers-
librism* and *La Technique poétique*, 1910. Fritz von Unruh,
who visited Paris shortly after the end of the First World War,
described his impressions in *Flügel der nike*, 1925, and recorded
that only to a very limited extent did the "spirit of peace" dom-

inate the new French intellectual life—although he did except
the Unanimists, to whom he gave enthusiastic approval. "The
spirit of Whitman hovers over them"—as over the corresponding authors in his homeland.

The two ultramoderns Panaït Istrati and Valéry Larbaud
were also influenced by Whitman. They were closely linked to
the Unanimists; like them they were internationally-minded and
had a common bond with them in Gide's *Nouvelle Revue Française*, in whose pages the younger French intellectuals found
refuge after the First World War. In the fantastic oriental
Istrati (*b.* 1884), the connecting link with Whitman is primarily a certain sentimental and temperamental accord. In his
novels *Kyra Kyrelina* and *Mikail* he celebrates the poetry of
the vagabond life, of the highway, and of friendship in prose
which almost imperceptibly glides into the Whitmanesque long
line and is definitely influenced by Whitman's phrasing. Istrati
is both primitive and refined, as was Whitman; but his Calamus
motif is sentimental and amoral, as is usual with people who
succumb to crises rather than go through them.

Entirely different as a conscious artist is Valéry Larbaud
(*b.* 1881), whom Gide permitted to write the preface for his
edition of Whitman and to translate "The Sleepers"—a pessimistic, refined intellectual, and a leading critic of modern literature. In addition to his interest in Whitman, he has associated
himself with the most revolutionary of modern European life
by transplanting to France Ramón Gómez de la Serna, D. H.
Lawrence, and James Joyce. In his own work he is a dandy,
a blasé Beau Brummell, and his poetical leading man, the mil-
lionaire A. O. Barnabooth, travels around the world in his
pleasure yacht, or in *de luxe* trains, and cherishes a passive admiration for the incorruptible South Sea Indians and for third-
class passengers.

O the splendors of everyday life and of the day coach![93]

is undeniably a peculiarly modern variant of the Whitmanesque
vagabond. Nevertheless, his famous volume *Les Poésies de
A. O. Barnabooth* (definitive edition 1923), is probably the
strongest proof of the depth of Whitman's imprint on the young
French lyricists of the period.

The book begins like a parody of Whitman, with Barnabooth celebrating the rumbling of his stomach in "The Gurgling."

> The complaints of the flesh unceasingly modified.
> Whisperings of the irrespressible organs.[94]

But soon, through boredom and irony, he adopts the Whitmanesque tone in earnest. He celebrates the trains on all their routes over the continent (cf. "Salut au Monde," Section 5); but he feels alone, as if he were wearing a mask. If only he could approach people more confidentially and more simply. "Oh for a reader, a brother to whom I could speak" to come to him and kiss him. He longs to capture all of life in his poetry, "la vie réelle," without art, without circumlocution.

> Come into my arms, onto my knees,
> Come into my heart, come in my verse, life.[95]

In the poem, "Le Don de Soi-Même" [The Gift of Myself], like Whitman he gives himself to anyone who will have him, and like Whitman, he knows that he must go immediately. Only for "a moment we read and we sing together." Whatever you have to say, say it now! In "Images" he reviews his memories of the whole world, of the women he met at Kharkov, at Rotterdam, at Elsinore, two Lesbian friends at Seville—will he ever meet them again and know them and enjoy them? "Alas, they will not read these poems. They will not know either my name nor the tenderness of my heart; and yet they exist, they are living *now*." And in "L'Innomable" he asks whether these verses will live after him when he is dead.

> Will there remain in these poems any pictures
> Of the many countries, of the many sights, and of all these faces? [96]

Or, like Whitman, he prepares for a meeting with the sea.

> Leave me alone, leave me alone with the sea!
> We have so many things to say to each other, haven't we? [97]

"Europa" is a reworked Whitman poem, in which he salutes and hails all the large cities, seas, and rivers of Europe.

> Europe! you satisfy these boundless appetites! [98]

He praises the libraries.

> Oh to understand everything, oh to know everything! [99]

He wishes to learn quickly all languages: Sanskrit, Greek, Latin, Hebrew.

To read all the books and all the commentaries!

His muse, "daughter of the great capitals," shall help him to capture the rhythm of the cities in his poetry. He himself stops in each city and enters into its life, in workshop, office, theater.

For the hundredth time I play a role in the theater.[100]

He is intoxicated by the life in the streets, runs against the wind "uttering savage cries." Stockholm, London, Berlin, "cities and more cities."

I have memories of cities as one has memories of lovers.[101]

He hopes fervently that he will see them all again. This is "Salut au Monde" in a modern French version. A fastidious artist has fallen so deeply in love with Whitman's poetry that he has copied it not only in content but also in form, with catalogues, participles, shouts, hails, parentheses, everything.

The Symbolists Gide and Verhaeren, the Unanimists Romains, Duhamel, Panaït Istrati, and Valéry Larbaud are the names that most clearly reveal Whitman's really outstanding significance for modern French literature.

Whitman was introduced into Italy in articles by Enrico Nencioni in the Roman periodical *Nuova antologia*, 1885 and 1887, and in 1898 by P. Jannaccone, who published *La Poesia di Walt Whitman e l'evoluzione delle forme ritmiche*, a book championing the same point of view that Laforgue had upheld in France and Arno Holz in Germany, and that was equally important for the younger Italian writers. Like the Symbolists in France, the youthful d'Annunzio was frankly interested in Whitman, and in 1896 he attempted the Whitmanesque style in *Odi navali*, but without the spirit. In 1908 Gamberale published his translation of *Leaves of Grass* (*Foglie di erba*, Palermo), which served in Italy as Schlaf's had in Germany and Bazalgette's in France. Papini reviewed it in *Nuova antologia* and told how much he himself owed to Whitman, who had been his favorite poet from childhood. Papini is an Italian Unanimist, and Whitman's international doctrine has played a great role for him. One of the chapters in *A Man Finished*, 1912, has a motto from Whitman.

> Who has gone fartherest? For I would go farther!

Whitman was translated into Spanish by Cebriá Montolio, (*Fulles d'herba*, Barcelona, 1910), who later wrote a biography of Whitman: *Walt Whitman, l'homme i sa tasca* (Barcelona, 1913). Whitman deeply influenced Federigo García Lorca. When he was in the United States in 1929–30 he was disgusted with the modern American culture, and Walt Whitman was the only redeeming feature, a poet whose attitude to sex inspired García Lorca's own imagery in his beautiful "Ode to Walt Whitman."

In Russia he was discovered in 1883 by P. Popoff, was hailed by Stepniak as one of the poets of the future, and was afterwards translated by the talented Konstantin Balmont (*b.* 1867), a zealous ambassador at the beginning of the century between "Young Russia" and modern world literature, and he clearly reveals a spiritual kinship to Whitman in his own poetry, *In Infinity*, 1896, and *Let Us Be Like the Sun*, 1903. Whitman's influence on the Russian "decadents" was similar to his relationship to the French Symbolists. In Bjely's lyrics, for example, we can trace the influence in the same way as on Maeterlinck and Rilke's early work. Whitman's real pupil in Russia was the strange cosmic pantheistic mystic, Vassili Rosanow (1856–1919), whose *Fallen Leaves* (N.B.), 1913 and 1915, is a collection of aphorisms and reflections in loose prose. He argues for an anticlerical nature religion and is like Whitman in his worship of friendship, vagabondage, the phallus, cultivation of the physical life, and praise of sex in phrases that strain for poetic intuition similar to Whitman's, but in imagery that is frequently much bolder. The whole of human life seems to Rosanow a great sexual act. He compares it now to a swelling blossom, now to a roaring bull. His religious basis is a mother religion. Earth is to him "the great breeding mother." Here are a few sentences.

It is best when I am alone, for then I am with God.
I am like a child in its mother's body, but with no longing to be born.

For me there is no evil because everything is a part of myself.
The little things are my gods.
Everything that is "majestic" is foreign to me—I do not like it
    and I do not respect it.
The physical is above everything, the soul is only a fragrance of the
    body, etc.

They are all familiar Whitmanesque *leit-motifs*. Rosanow is
often lewd, frequently illogical, but at the same time has much
of Whitman's own disarming naïveté and inevitability—and a
share of his creative linguistic power. Hitherto Rosanow has
been almost unknown in Europe. He was first introduced by
Boris de Schloezer in an article in *La Nouvelle Revue Française*, in 1929, which characterized him as an example of "man
before the Fall." In his writing, Rosanow was anti-Nietzschean,
because "Nietzsche always thought in opposition to his body!"
In his violent struggle for a new interpretation of the erotic in
modern society he was a forerunner of D. H. Lawrence, and he
owes a similar debt to Whitman.

It could have been merely a stroke of luck that Denmark was
among the first European countries to "discover" Whitman,
a literary or journalistic accident (every literary critic has
known such fortunate accidents both in the cultural history of
his country and in his own personal experience); but it was
hardly an accident in this instance. There was an obvious intellectual background which explains the discovery and the understanding. Some of the Danish romantic writers had turned their
attention to America just as Goethe did in his old age and as
the younger German romantics did. Carsten Hauch (1790–
1872), in the historic novel *Robert Fulton*, 1853, has a poem
called "Barlow's Poem on America" (an American's salute to
his native land) in which he, in the same spirit and in the same
unrhymed stanzas as Goethe in "To the United States," hails
the great new world as the scene for a reborn humanity, the land
in which mankind

> . . . the races grown old
> yonder in Europe
> can find their youth again
> and again breathe freely

in the mighty forests
close to nature's breast . . .

Furthermore, by temperament and in his interpretation of nature Hauch was profoundly influenced by the pantheism of the German romantic poets, especially by Novalis. Even in his earliest youthful works we find traces of pantheism and mysticism which plainly link him to the Whitmanesque mood, especially in his dramatic poem, *The Hamadryad*, 1830, in which the hero, Richard, mingles with the animals and is seized with a conviction of his kinship to them. For example:

. . . the timid, gentle horse
that suddenly stops and gazes at me sidelong for a moment
  only . . .
and immediately breaks into a gallop.
How splendid it was rightly to understand
the gazelle's course and the eagle's lofty flight,
yes, even the blind mole's burrowing into the earth,
and what language the cranes speak
when they ascend in wedge-shaped formation
and, unseen in the air, their shrieks are heard afar in the foggy
  night.   (Cf. "Song of Myself," Sections 13, 14, 31, 32, 52.)

Among the older Danish writers are several who, as we have seen, had traits in common with the Whitmanesque temperament (Baggesen, Sibbern, Hans Andersen) ; but these points of resemblance were also related to the cultural dependence, the close and traditional kinship between Danish and German ideas in the romantic period. It is quite understandable that Whitman's earliest Danish admirer and translator was a late romantic writer, Rudolf Schmidt (1836–99), a critic who was almost the last representative of the Germanic tradition in our intellectual life. He wrote his first great laudatory article on "Walt Whitman the American Poet of Democracy" in February, 1872, for his and Björnstjerne Björnson's Scandinavian magazine *For Idé og Virkelighed* [For Idea and Reality]. Rudolf Schmidt and Björnson were both friends and followers of that leading Danish critic of the sixties, Clemens Petersen, who would have been editor-in-chief of the magazine had he not, in 1869, been forced to emigrate to the States. In 1874 Rudolf

Schmidt also translated *Democratic Vistas*, as *Demokratiske Fremblik*, the first translation of this book into any European language. Later he carried on a correspondence with Whitman, Burroughs, and Traubel. In 1892 he included the article from *For Idé og Virkelighed* in *Buster og Masker* [Busts and Masks]. In 1888, in *Fra begge Halvkugler* [From Both Hemispheres], he conspicuously reprinted Whitman's lecture on "The Death of Lincoln."

But Rudolf Schmidt's zealous and industrious efforts as a Danish ambassador for Whitman did not produce direct results on the Danish poetry of the period. It happened that his "ideal- istic" tendency promptly came into sharp conflict with Georg Brandes's realistic, French-influenced school, which in the eighties and nineties dominated not only the intellectual life of Copenhagen but also that of all Scandinavia; and this school, in accordance with its policy, swept aside Rudolf Schmidt and all his work as the pale imitation of a mere imitator. It is not unlikely that Georg Brandes's extraordinary life-long disre- gard of Whitman grew out of the fact that the American poet was "discovered," not by him, but by his opponent and arch- enemy, "the insignificant" Rudolf Schmidt. In any event the Whitman cult in Denmark was for at least three decades com- paratively a private phenomenon, restricted to the circle around Rudolf Schmidt and his friends, among whom was the author and translator P. A. Rosenberg, who did not translate Whit- man's poems, but as a direct result of the group's enthusiasm for Whitman named his eldest son after him.[102] The only trans- lation of Whitman's poetry that appeared in Danish before the turn of the century was by the philologist and student of litera- ture Niels Møller (1859–1941), who in his youthful collection of poetry, *Efteraar* [Autumn], 1888, translated seven of Whit- man's old-age poems (*Fancies at Navesink*) into a remarkably archaic, intricate, and obscure rhythmic diction which showed a lack of understanding of Whitman's poetic language and therefore did not tend to further the cause of the great poet in those academic circles to which Niels Møller preferred to at- tach to himself.[103] In the masterpiece of his old age, his com-

prehensive, erudite, but also one-sided *Verdenslitteraturhistorie,*
Copenhagen, 1928–31, Niels Møller disclosed that his admiration was limited and that on decisive points he was just as condescending in his opinion of the American poet as were the
Boston school of academic poets and literati.

But the coming of the new century and Whitman's debut in
Denmark coincided with the appearance of our own important
poet and master of language, Johannes V. Jensen (*b.* 1873).
Throughout a generation he was the strongest stylistic impulse for Danish writers of all kinds exclusive of the dramatists.
Jensen had visited America in 1902–3, and in the same spirit,
but with far more emphasis than the classicist Carsten Hauch
a half-century earlier, he proclaimed the New World as the
new refuge of civilization, the place of regeneration and expansion. Jensen's enthusiastic salute to America was stridently
high-pitched; in tone it was much like Whitman's "Song of the
Exposition," but in word choice startingly original. He saw in
Whitman the poet of this New World, of the new epoch, of modern man. In his early style Johannes V. Jensen was profoundly
inspired by Whitman, and in his novel about America, *Hjulet*
[The Wheel], 1904–5, he translated three poems, "Starting
from Paumanok" (a fragment only) and "A Song of Joys,"
combined with "When I Heard at the Close of the Day." The
three translations, which caused the greatest sensation by their
frankness of language and the complete break with Danish
lyrical traditions, later appeared in Jensen's and Otto Gelsted's
jointly arranged edition of Whitman's poems [*Digte*], Copenhagen, 1919. This was a limited edition, printed in only three
hundred numbered copies, and scarcely aroused popular interest, but it was nevertheless an extremely important edition. It
contained two valuable introductions, one by Jensen and a second by Gelsted (*b.* 1888), who is an intelligent and acute critic
as well as a poet and translator. In Johannes V. Jensen's work
may be traced a direct Whitman influence both in his radical
early lyrics and in many of his so-called *Myter* [myths],
1907–44,—short prose pieces half-fables, half-essays, a mixture of reminiscences, meditations, nature-observations, and

pure fiction—for example, the conclusion of a myth entitled "Hjertet" [The Heart], 1916, seems to be written on a Whitman theme of the pulse beats of Europe and America.[104]

Through the medium of Jensen's translations there was a strong and direct influence on all the younger generation of writers of Whitman's language and expansive interpretation of life, even if frequently the Whitmanesque was mixed with Jensen's characteristic diction, at least in the authors of the period around the First World War. Whitmanesque tones and themes were audible in Thøger Larsen, Otto Gelsted, Ditlev von Zeppelin, Svend Borberg (*Den sejrende Type; Humane Visioner* [The Conquering Type; Human Visions], 1913), Tom Kristensen, Emil Bønnelycke (*Asfaltens Sange* [Songs of Asphalt], 1918), Frederik Hygaard (*Europaskizzer* [European Sketches], 1918), Aage Berntsen (Song of Joy in *Coldevins Bog* [Coldevin's Book], 1927), Johannes Wulff (*Kosmiske Sange* [Cosmic Songs], 1928), Arne Sørensen (*Spark og Kaertegn, Prosadigte* [Kick and Caress, Prose Poems], 1930), and Jens August Schade (*Jordens Ansigt* [Face of the Earth], 1932). For direct imitation of Whitman we can only offer a few minor instances, although similarities of expression are very striking in the above-mentioned books by Borberg, Bønnelycke, Nygaard, Berntsen, and Arne Sørensen.

In Harald Bergstedt (*b.* 1877) modern Danish lyricism has a poet who is in certain ways comparable to Whitman, not only in his long democratic recitatives, in which he often reminds us of Whitman in an awkward way (there may be a certain American block-headedness in Bergstedt's "democratic vistas"); but there are conspicuous lyrical similarities to Whitman in Bergstedt's long prose poems on "Livet" [Life] in *Sange fra Provinsen* [Provincial Songs], 1921, and in "Stjernerne" [Stars] and "Evigheden" [Eternity] from *Bredere Vinger* [Broader Wings], 1919. Not only the Whitmanesque sentiment but also the Whitmanesque expressions are repeated with striking accord. He shares with Wergeland, Whitman, and Dehmel the scorn for ruins and dead cultures. He throws himself into life as the swimmer leaps into the sea. His interpretation of the

Christ-figure is like Whitman's. When he sacrifices to life it is really to himself. He attacks the superman idea. We are all equally great and equally small. In Bergstedt's short poems, as in Whitman's the wild geese fly over the dark earth (cf. "Song of Myself," Section 14, "*Ya-honk* he says and sounds it down to me like an invitation"), or Creation "draws its breath like a wheatfield" in *Bredere Vinger*. In the prose *Under Klokketaarnet* [Under the Clock Tower], 1926, there are Whitmanesque sentence structures.

Incessantly races of man are born . . .

Incessantly children of men play with sticks and sand, shrieking with happiness, quite impossible to make them happier!

Incessantly youth revels, meets and kisses, from generation to generation . . .

Incessantly the young mother sits by the child's cradle, the peace of the starry universe on her forehead, the smile of the eternal primeval power trembling on her lips . . .

The world should go forward to a goal! My dear boy! It is in the center of the goal itself, and has been as long as it has existed.

Bergstedt denies having been influenced by Whitman, though he admits having known him since he began to write. He is, nevertheless, a characteristic example of the literary *type*. He lacks Whitman's dimensions, but in his lyric inspiration similar forces move. Both in his lyrics and in his social agitation he has often used expressions which range between the trite and the completely sublime. In his social theories as well as in his lyrical talent Harald Bergstedt reminds us of Heinrich Lersch in Germany—also in the deplorable fact that after Hitler's rise he placed himself at the service of the National Socialist propagandists, and in contrast to the overwhelming majority of the Danish Whitmanites he held on to the bitter end to the naïve belief that Hitler's demagogic national "Volksgemeinschaft" was a realization of the very democracy Whitman had inaugurated. In recent Danish poetry, that is, since 1940, there can be traced a Whitman influence, but only of a sort of Whitmaniac surrealism corresponding to the Whitmanesque traits of the Spanish poet García Lorca. This is found in poets, among others, such as the talented young prose poet Ole Sarvig (*b.* 1921), *Grønne Digte* [Green Poems], 1943, and *Mangfoldighed* [Manifoldness], 1945.

The dazzling light emitted by Johannes V. Jensen's pioneering translation and interpretation of the diction and expression in Whitman's poetry ended the long years of stagnation of Danish translation (again we see the extent to which the quality and contexts into which Whitman is translated determine the kind and degree of his literary influence and the place he will occupy in the particular country!). Besides Gelsted's contribution to the edition of 1919, the best of which was the translation of "Pioneers! O Pioneers!" that same year—the one hundredth anniversary of Whitman's birth—produced a biographical article by Ingrid de Lorange in *Illustreret Tidende* (August, 1919). The January, 1919, issue of the literary magazine *Tilskueren* [The Spectator] contained a good translation, though in somewhat antiquated academic diction, the first complete version of "Starting from Paumanok," by Ingeborg Raunkier. In July the same author published in *Illustreret Tidende* translations of "Me Imperturbe," "On the Beach at Night," and "A Night on the Prairies." The great Jutish lyricist Thøger Larsen translated "To a Silent Patient Spider" in his collection of poetry *Limfjords Sange* [Songs of the Limfjord], 1925. In 1929 there appeared an attractive illustrated edition of "Song of Myself" and other poems by Børge Houmann (*b.* 1909), the most successful translation being "When Lilacs Last in the Dooryard Bloom'd" (which combined with Jensen's "Song of Joys" and Gelsted's "Pioneers! O Pioneers!" might be used as the basis for a more complete future edition of the best of Whitman's poetry in Danish); and later, in 1933, the present author's translation of, among other pieces, "Song of Myself," [105] "The Sleepers," and "Out of the Cradle Endlessly Rocking," formed a sort of supplement to the present book, the latter being an attempt at the first detailed presentation in a Scandinavian country of Whitman's life and significance in world literature. Whitman has aroused no moral debate here such as that in Germany and France, although naturally some of his admirers have been among those who swore allegiance

to the optimism and sunshine in his message and to the overwhelming expansiveness in his form of expression, while others
have been deeply moved by the conflict, pain, and secret gloom
in the poems of the 1860 edition. Børge Houmann wrote an introduction to his 1929 translation in the edifying tone of Rudolf Schmidt, Schlaf, and Bazalgette, while Johannes V. Jensen, on the other hand, had in 1919 clearsightedly labeled the
brilliant, arrogant favorite poet of his youth as one of "the
great Erratics" in world literature. That did not prevent the
poet Helge Rode (1870–1937), in the midst of a debate in
Denmark over religious ideas during the interim between the
world wars, from hailing Whitman in *Det store Ja* [The Great
Affirmative], 1926, as a prophet and "one of the healthy-
minded great." So long as Whitman is read and imitated, he
will be fanatically discussed. This is a measure of his greatness
and his vitality. When we have unanimously agreed about a
poet he is on the point of dying.

In Sweden and Norway Whitman has not had nearly so much
influence, so many forerunners, or so many followers, as he had
in Denmark; he had no local prophet in the early period and
no great interpreter like Johannes V. Jensen who could make
him an integral link in the development of a modern style.
Therefore Whitman has no real history in either of these countries aside from Andreas Butenschön's enthusiastic essay on
Whitman and her translation into Swedish of "Proud Music of
the Storm" in the Scandinavian magazine *Ord och Bild* [Word
and Picture] in 1905. In the period between the two world wars
some Whitman influence—and Carl Sandburg influence—first
became evident among the Swedish lyricists and prose writers
of the so-called "cult of life" group. Among the adherents were
Harry Martinson, Erik Asklund, Josef Kjelgren, Gustav Sandgren, and especially Arthur Lundkvist, author of the poetic
collections *Glöd* [Glow], 1928, and *Naket Liv* [Naked Life],
1929. *Glöd* is earlier, but *Naket Liv* contains a poem addressed
to Whitman which in poetic conciseness and originality can only
be compared to García Lorca's famous ode to Whitman,
translated into Swedish by Lundkvist immediately after the Second World War. In a long and interesting article called "Whit-

man och den unga svenska Poesin" [Whitman and Recent Swedish Poetry] in the Swedish *Social Demokraten*, September 6,
1931, Leon Fried said: "I am sure that Lundkvist will admit his
indebtedness to Whitman, whose language and imagery are apparent in everything he has written up to now." Lundkvist
(*b.* 1906) *has* acknowledged this debt by writing poetry in the
Whitmanesque vein, and since 1931 he has acted as a well-
informed and stimulating critical essayist who has been of
great importance in orienting the Scandinavian public in the
current of American literature from Whitman to Henry Miller.
Lundkvist's activity as an expert in that sphere deserves to be
recognized and appreciated outside Scandinavia. In Lundkvist's
collection of poetry *Dikter mellan Djur och Gud* [Poems between Beast and God], 1944, the Whitmanesque inspiration is
definitely audible.

The first long Swedish translation of Whitman's poetry,
Strån av Gräs, by K. A. Svensson, was published in 1935. In
his anthology, *Modern amerikansk Lyrik*, 1937, Erik Blomberg
included ten short, newly translated poems with a different and
more heart-felt emphasis than Svensson's, an omen of the awakening and gradually increasing attention to Whitman's lyricism
in Sweden. There the Whitmanesque "temperament" that expressed itself in the great classical Swedish writers Thorild and
Almquist and at the turn of the century could be very super-
ficially traced in isolated passages in the works of Ossian Nilsson and Per Halström, has today such widely differing exponents
as the two contemporary "immortals" (that is, members of the
Swedish Academy), Hjalmar Gullberg and Harry Martinson.

In Norway the picture is quite different and much more complicated. Björnstjerne Björnson knew and admired Whitman,
and early in the seventies propagandized for him whenever he
could. Likewise the less famous but fine and original novelist and
critic Kristian Elster, Sr. (1841–81), one time contributor to
For Idé og Virkelighed, cherished an interest in the new poet of
democracy, and wrote, among other things, a careful and favorable review of *Demokratiske Fremblik*, which not only pleased
the translator Rudolf Schmidt but also delighted Whitman.[106]

While Rudolf Schmidt's efforts aroused the first Norwegian interest in Whitman's life and work and culminated in Kristofer Janson's benevolent discussion of Whitman in his book *Amerikanske Forhold* [American Affairs], 1881, the interest evaporated very quickly, probably because of the influence of the negative attitude of the Brandesians. This opposition increased after the young genius Knut Hamsun's violent—and clever—attack and ridicule of Whitman in *Fra det moderne Amerikas Aandsliv* [On the Intellectual Life of Modern America], 1889, (originally delivered as a paper before a student society in Copenhagen). It was not *comme il faut* to know about the barbaric lyricist from the crude and uncultured New World, a very paradoxical attitude in the fatherland of Henrik Wergeland. To what extent Whitman as a man of letters was outlawed in the literary consciousness of Norway is evident in the offhand way Vilh. Troye mentioned him in his book on Wergeland,[107] which is as characteristic as it is amusing in its confusion of Emerson's and Whitman's given names.

Nevertheless, there was in Norway a natural basis for the understanding of Whitman's new and peculiar lyrical tone, an understanding which found quite different—even contradictory —expressions in Norway and Denmark. Two young Norwegian "decadent" writers became American travelers, two very sensitive and original young poets, Sigbjørn Obstfelder (1866–1900) and Sigurd Mathiesen (*b.* 1871), who in their books turned Whitman's moods into melancholic *fin de siècle* literature in prose, verse, and prose-verse with a gloomy melody similar to Rilke's, Maeterlinck's, and Lerberghe's. In Sigurd Mathiesen's work there is a cosmic-pantheistic feeling united with a half-unconscious reminiscence of the impressions that reading Whitman and Poe had made on him, and it found unmistakable expression in different places in his brilliant, macabre novels *Hide Unas*, 1903, *Augustnatter* [August Nights], 1907, and *Francis Rose*, 1918. On Obstfelder, who in 1890 worked as a mechanical engineer in Milwaukee, the influence is more direct and undoubtedly entirely conscious. A closer examination of this influence, and also of the conflict in style between American and European forms of poetic expression at the beginning of the present era, especially as it reveals itself in the justifiably famous *Digte*, 1893, of Obstfelder, will be a tempting and certainly a rewarding task for literary research.[108]

In the most recent Norwegian literature there is plainly evident a Whitmanesque influence corresponding to that in contemporary Swedish and Danish poetry in Rolf Jacobsen (*Jord og Jærn* [Earth and Iron], 1933); Andre Bjerke (*b.* 1918) (*Syngnde Jord* [Singing Earth], 1940) and the kindred spirit of Ole Sarvig in Denmark, Per Arneberg (*b.* 1901), whose *Vandringer* [Wanderings], 1945, contains a moving and very effective salute to Whitman in a prose poem "Træet" [The Tree]. In 1947 Arneberg published the first original, powerful, and melodious translation of "Song of Myself" into Norwegian, with surrealistic illustrations by Kai Fjell. In his preface to this edition Arneberg calls Whitman: "An American genius whose mighty . . . all-embracing and infinitely tender voice underlies everything which has given America her position in literature today." The way is finally clear for a frank and complete recognition of Whitman in the country where, more than a century earlier, his spiritual kinsman Henrik Wergeland wrote his "Song of Myself." As Per Arneberg says, "A tree has unfolded before thy eyes, a seed has germinated in thy heart." [109]

There remains for discussion Whitman's influence in England, the country in which he was first recognized, first gained a large following, and in which throughout the years have appeared the greatest number of books about him.[110] It is strange that in all this time no school has grown up around him as it did in Germany and France. But this is quite natural, since Whitman wrote in English and was published in one English edition after another, so that he himself is available to the English for reading and comparison; he occupies the place before the literary public which in other countries is open to those who are like him, think as he does, and who imitate him. In England, Whitman is primarily himself. It was not necessary to imitate him in order to introduce his "manner" into the literature.

It is most interesting that when imitators and followers in England do appear, they represent and stress what the English editions of Whitman omit. *Children of Adam* has always been omitted from the English editions, and therefore the Children of Adam motif is the main one taken up and developed by Whitman's two real pupils in English poetry, Edward Carpenter and D. H. Lawrence, who for that reason were both officially outside the English intellectual circle and were regarded as rebels and demagogues.

The cosmic fantasy and pantheistic religion in Whitman's poetry, however, had forerunners in English poetry, not only in Blake but also in Wordsworth and Shelley. The stamp of "romantic poesy" in this cosmic lyricism was transformed by Swinburne into modern philosophical poetry in such compositions as "Hertha" and "Genesis." To compare Swinburne in his early phase with Whitman is natural and taken for granted. In *Songs before Sunrise,* with its salute to Whitman, we find many Whitmanesque passages, not only in "Hertha" with "the soft hair of the grass," but in "The Pilgrims," where the dead become a part of the earth and "the ancient sea, And the heaven-high air August," in the stately "Hymn of Man," in which God "is the substance of men," and finally in "The Litany of Nations," in which the long catalogue bears the Whitmanesque stamp and old Mother Earth, "our mother everlasting," sings, as for Whitman, her own song "hoarse and hollow and shrill with strife." Later Swinburne's enthusiasm for Whitman cooled, and among other things he wrote the article "Whitmania," first published in *The Fortnightly Review,* August, 1887, afterwards included in *Studies in Prose and Poetry,* 1894. He created quite a sensation in England and America by his complete renunciation of a poet to whom he owed so much and whom he had greeted publicly. That was one of the attacks Whitman felt most keenly. It was later revealed in E. F. Benson's valuable Victorian memoirs, *As We Were,* 1930, that Swinburne's diabolically critical friend, Watts-Dunton, inspired the attack, as he also inspired Swinburne's indiscreet and hysterical attacks on Whistler, Matthew Arnold, and Emerson (whom he referred to in a letter as "a debilitated and now toothless ape"). Concerning Whitman's erotic poetry Swinburne wrote in the article:

Mr. Whitman's Eve is a drunken apple-woman, indecently sprawling in the slush and garbage of the gutter amid the rotten refuse

of her overturned fruit stall. . . . Mr. Whitman's Venus is a Hot-
tentot wench under the influence of cantharides and adulterated
rum!

Sherwood Anderson has since taken up this phase of Whitman's
eroticism in *Dark Laughter*, 1926, and has created an unforgettable poetic situation about "the drunken apple-woman"
(Sponge Martin and his wife). Only a minority of Whitman's
contemporary English admirers recognized how great a reputation he would have in the future—not even Stevenson, who
wrote of him in *Men and Books*, 1898, and who on his first reading was as greatly impressed as Symonds and Edward Carpenter. Only Oscar Wilde among "the prominent people" had
any realization of Whitman's future potentialities. He wrote
with extraordinary insight in one of his articles in *The Pall
Mall Gazette*, January, 1889: "He has begun a prelude to
larger themes. He is the herald to a new era."

It was this perception that also inspired Edward Carpenter
and made him imitate Whitman's poetry in his own extensive
work, which is less artistic than propagandistic for social reform and universal education. Carpenter originally intended,
as did Emerson and Carlyle, to be a minister; instead he became an English blend of Freud and Magnus Hirschfeld—if
that is conceivable for an Englishman. He borrowed the ideas
of Whitman's democracy and comradeship, but especially his
sexual innovations. In his valuable autobiography, *My Days
and Dreams*, 1916, he describes his youthful emotion on first
reading Whitman. He was impressed not merely by the poetry
but more especially by the fact that there for the first time he
"met with the treatment of Sex which accorded with my own
sentiments." When he visited America, Niagara Falls was "the
only thing I saw which seemed quite to match Whitman in
spirit." Carpenter kept this loyalty to Whitman's poetry
throughout the years, and in *My Days and Dreams* he put
Leaves of Grass on a par with the *Bhagavad-Gita*, Plato's
Symposium, and Dante's *Divine Comedy*.[111]

Carpenter's many educational and propagandistic books,
*Love's Coming of Age, The Intermediate Sex, Towards Intellec-
tual Freedom*, and others, have no esthetic or literary value

and are worth remembering today only because they all contain Whitmanesque ideas. But his collection of verse, *Towards Democracy*, the poetic qualities of which are undeniable, is probably the most obvious example in world literature of a literary work written directly out of *Leaves of Grass*. It is a real example of a literary teacher and his pupil, such as is not often found.

The first edition of *Towards Democracy* appeared in 1883, the fifth and complete edition in 1905. Afterwards there were innumerable reprintings. The first edition contained only the long poem, "Towards Democracy," which gives the collection its name and which is Carpenter's "Song of Myself"—in 79 sections, while Whitman used only 52. As the book now stands, this is its weakest poem. Carpenter has tried to give it English local color to parallel Whitman's Americanism, but he lacked Whitman's powers of original observation. The poem is only an interesting and monotonous announcement of a new democratic era. The Whitmanesque emphasis is obvious.

I am come to be the interpreter of yourself to yourself.

[Section 44]

.   .   .

I will be the ground underfoot and the common clay;
The ploughman shall turn me up with his ploughshare among the
    roots of the twitch in the sweet-smelling furrow;
The potter shall mould me, running his finger along my whirling
    edge (we will be faithful to one another, he and I);

.   .   .

And to him I will utter the word which with my lips I have not
    spoken.   [Section 47]

.   .   .

All this day we will go together; the sun shall circle overhead; our
    shadows swing round us on the road . . . the evening see us
    in another land;
The night ever insatiate of love we will sleep together, and rise
    early and go forward again in the morning;
Wherever the road shall lead us, in solitary places or among the
    crowd, it shall be well; we shall not desire to come to the

end of the journey, nor consider what the end may be; the end
of all things shall be with Us.   [Section 59]

This is my trade; teach me yours and I will teach you mine.

Are you a carpenter, a mason, a grower of herbs and flowers, a
breaker of horses? a wheel-wright, boat-builder, engine-tenter,
dockyard-laborer?   [Section 60]

Whitman did not write these lines, but we shall have to admit that an imitation could not be more accurate. The poem
ends:

And the fall of a leaf through the air and the greeting of one that
passes on the road shall be more to you than the wisdom of
all the books ever written—and of this book.

In the remainder of the book Carpenter writes better poetry
and is more free, more concise, and more exact, but every poem
continually harks back to a sentence or a mood of Whitman's;
many of the poems have titles corresponding to poems in *Leaves
of Grass:* "To a Stranger," "A Song in Old Age," "The Dead
Christ," "In the Chamber of Birth," "The Dead Comrade,"
"Who but the Lover Should Know," "Who You Are I Know
Not," and so forth, and on every page we find expressions and
ideas from *Leaves of Grass.* Carpenter has also appropriated
Whitman's characteristic dual expressions ("him or her"),
and in one place quotes Whitman directly by mentioning "the
Calamus-sign" which friends exchange as Whitman did in the
Calamus poem "Among the Multitude." There is a *Calamus*
section of twenty poems, "Little Heart within the Cage," and
in Part IV, in the section "O Little Sister Heart," a poem with
the title "O Child of Uranus." But Carpenter's poetry is more
womanly sentimental than Whitman's, and at times seems almost
to coquet with this sentimentality and this peculiar erotic psyche.
It is remarkable that in spite of everything *Towards Democracy*
is indisputably a readable book, almost as if Whitman had written another collection of poems besides *Leaves of Grass.* But
naturally it cannot be considered as an original work of art, and
from the beginning that fact irritated Carpenter. In a foreword
to the later editions of the book he says:

I have said . . . nothing about the influence of Whitman—for the same reason that I have said nothing about the influence of the sun or the winds . . . I find it difficult to imagine what my life would have been without it. "Leaves of Grass" "filtered and fibred" my blood. *But I do not think I ever tried to imitate it or its style.*

If Carpenter really meant what he said, or if what he maintains is true, *Towards Democracy* is a perfect example of the extent to which Whitman, in ideas and language, can influence and permeate his intellectual or sexual kindred—which occasionally comes to the same thing.

But while Carpenter, with only this one book, naturally did not play any considerable role in modern English literature, none other than the most prominent and controversial figure in English intellectual circles of the late 1920's, D. H. Lawrence (1885–1930), is a pupil of Whitman's. *Children of Adam* was a pattern for his work, which was to find and present "the ultimate truth about sex." The problem, as Lawrence himself plainly states it, is: "How to regain *innocence* in sex?" The goal is a new, purer, healthier society, the "new society" that Whitman also announced and prophesied. In *Studies in Classic American Literature*, 1924, Lawrence admitted frankly, "Whitman, the great poet, has meant much to me," and the connection between the two writers is plain and clear. Although, with the exception of Carpenter's verse, Whitman's form has not been important in English lyricism (the "Imagists," the English Symbolists of the First World War, were largely made up of emigré Americans: Ezra Pound, T. S. Eliot, and Hilda Doolittle), yet it was Whitman's direct style that attracted Lawrence, and in the erotic descriptions in *Lady Chatterley's Lover* he used a freedom of speech equal to Whitman's—though Lawrence is rather hysterical where Whitman is naïve. But for his verse, which was originally conventional, he gradually took over the complete Whitmanesque form; it is strongest in *Look We Have Come Through*, 1913, and *Birds, Beasts and Flowers*, 1923. Lawrence wrote a hymn "To Priapus," and Whitman's image of the bee in "Spontaneous Me" is a frequent symbol in Lawrence. The woman's admiration for the man's body is completely Whitmanesque.

Why shouldn't your legs and your good strong thighs
be rough and hairy?—I am glad they are like that.

.   .   .

And I love you so! Straight and clean and all of a piece is the body
    of a man,
such an instrument, a spade, like a spear, or an oar,
such a joy to me—

And the poem continues:

Only God could have brought it to its shape.
It feels as if his handgrasp, wearing you
had polished you and hollowed you,
hollowed this groove in your sides, grasped you under the
    breasts . . .

.   .   .

I admire you so, you are beautiful: this clean sweep of your sides,
    this firmness, this hard mould! [112]

But the man calls attention to all the mysteries and perils which
lurk in him from earlier stages of evolution—a snake, a young
bull.

> Is there nothing in me to make you hesitate?
> I tell you there is all these.
> And why should you overlook them in me?

Finally in *Birds, Beasts and Flowers* Lawrence comes even
closer to Whitman's style. These poems are not erotic, but "natural history." In a poem on fish he goes so far as to follow Whitman's baroque habit of mixing French with English.

Quelle joie de vivre
Dans l'eau [!]
Slowly to gape through the waters,
Alone with the element;
To sink, and rise, and go to sleep with the waters;
To speak endless inaudible wavelets into the wave;
To breathe from the flood at the gills,
Fish-blood slowly running next to the flood, extracting fish-fire;
To have the element under one, like a lover;
And to spring away with a curvetting click in the air,
Provocative.

Dropping back with a slap on the face of the flood.
And merging oneself!

To be a fish.[113]

But Lawrence is a poet of originality, and where Carpenter could only play variations on the Whitman phraseology, Lawrence creates striking, original imagery in the Whitmanesque style. One very eloquent example of the kinship between Whitman and Lawrence is the "Tortoise's Shout," in which there is an unforgettable account of his first childish impression of animal life and of sex-life.

I remember, when I was a boy, [N.B.]
I heard the scream of a frog, which was caught with his foot in
    the mouth of an up-starting snake;
I remember when I first heard bull-frogs break into sound in the
    spring;
I remember hearing a wild goose out of the throat of night [N.B.]
Cry loudly, beyond the lake of waters;
I remember the first time, out of a bush in the darkness, [N.B.] a
    nightingale's piercing cries and gurgles startled the depths
    of my soul;
I remember the scream of a rabbit as I went through a wood at
    midnight;
I remember the heifer in her heat, blorting and blorting through
    the hours, persistent and irrepressible;
I remember my first terror hearing the howl of weird, amorous cats;
I remember the scream of a terrified, injured horse, the sheet-
    lightning

.   .   .

And listening inwardly to the first bleat of a lamb,
The first wail of an infant,
And my mother singing to herself,
And the first tenor singing of the passionate throat of a young
    collier, who has long since drunk himself to death,

.   .   .

Sex, which breaks us into voice, sets us calling across the deeps,
    calling, calling for the complement,

Singing, and calling, and singing again, being answered, having
   found.

Torn, to become whole again, after long seeking for what is lost,
The same cry from the tortoise as from Christ, the Osiris-cry of
   abandonment,
That which is whole, torn asunder,
That which is in part, finding its whole again throughout the uni-
   verse.[114]

It is a splendid poem, but a modernized version of Whitman.
For Lawrence the elemental, the animal, was always the ideal
to which we should turn back. That is Whitman's "flowing savage" and "divine average" in modern dress. One of Lawrence's
frequent erotic figures is "the blazing tiger" that throws himself greedily on his victim.

But what primarily makes Lawrence interesting in this comparison is the tragic circumstances out of which his optimistic
teachings grew in a way which helps to illuminate Whitman's
mentality. Carpenter, in *My Days and Dreams*, had argued that
love poems (his own and Whitman's) did not come from fortunate love, but, on the contrary, were to be regarded as the release of unrequitted, unsatisfied, instinctive yearnings in the
mind of the poet—and as we saw the truth of this fact in Whitman we see it again in Lawrence. He preached his gospel in spite
of his own experience. All his life he fought a desperate battle
to be at one with his own soul, as he himself expressed it in
"Fantasia of the Unconscious," to overcome the contradictions
in himself. He used the title *Rainbow* to signify the bridge that
should span the gap between the conflicting forces in the human mind. This is Whitman's struggle, repeated in similar circumstances by the younger poet. In *Twilight in Italy* Lawrence
refers to the "rainbow" as the Holy Ghost which should con-
quer the duality of soul and body. "To say that the two are
one, this is the inadmissible lie. The two are related, by the in-
tervention of the *third*, into a oneness." That is the Whitmanesque triad, repeated by a kindred spirit. Middleton Murry
pointed out that throughout his life Lawrence was a sexually
frustrated man. Beginning with the unhealthy mother-complex

of childhood and early youth, which led him into a mother-religion similar to Whitman's, only more perverse, through the erotic disappointments of later life, he dreamed of a higher human relationship than the erotic. "We want something broader. I believe in the additional perfect relationship between man and man—additional to marriage," he says in *Women in Love*, 1921. That is Whitman's Calamus-ideal, his democracy, which we see here arising organically in the younger poet, but from the same spiritual experience of failure and disappointment. Out of disappointed love arose a democratic proclamation, a wish-dream, and a gospel. In general, Middleton Murry does not go into Lawrence's literary dependence on Whitman, but referring to Lawrence's understanding and penetrating criticism of Whitman in *Studies in Classical American Literature*, he explains the connection thus: "Lawrence knew only too well, why Whitman ached with amorous love towards the universe!"

Lawrence, who during his lifetime did not win recognition in England, won his first victory and found his first understanding in America, where *Sons and Lovers* and *Women in Love* were very successful and had significant influence on contemporary and younger American writers like Sherwood Anderson, in whom the influence of Lawrence supplemented that of Whitman. Lawrence made a penetrating study of American culture and wrote illuminating essays on Cooper, Melville, Thoreau, Hawthorne, and Whitman. In the friendship between Deerslayer and Chingachgook he sees a Whitmanesque democracy, "a human relationship of two men . . . deeper than property, deeper than fatherhood, deeper than marriage, deeper than love . . . Natty and the Great Serpent are neither equals nor unequals. Each obeys the other when the moment arrives." But at the same time he regards American and existing "democracy" as a fiasco, an illusion. He wrote on Whitman not only in his *Studies in Classic American Literature* but also in a lead article in *The Nation and Athenaeum*, July 23, 1921, in which he emphasized Whitman's importance, but at the same time very significantly pointed out the theme of death in his work. Most people have missed or refused to hear it, but to Lawrence it is the most important in *Leaves of Grass,* because, as he says, Whitman's struggle for democracy was in vain, although he did see the promised land: "*But there is no way down* . . . *Whitman like a strange, modern, American Moses. Fearfully mistaken. And yet the great leader.*" The characterization is very exact and to the point.

In his own work Lawrence was never able to overcome the contradictions in himself and achieve intellectual poise. That certainly made him peculiarly sensitive to the similar duality and division in Whitman. At the same time, characteristically enough, he is the *only one* of Whitman's pupils in modern literature who has noticed that division. Furthermore, he does not think Whitman would have become the poet he is if he had not been disappointed in love, "if he had not taken the last steps and looked over into death."

It is astonishing and remarkable that the school forming around Whitman in modern literature has been attracted by the light and optimism in *Leaves of Grass,* although Whitman was really not the optimist he dreamed of being. It is Whitman's worship of the "I" and of nature, his preaching of the dream of democracy, and of an ideal America of the future that has had the greatest influence. *In the modern consciousness* Whitman has become what he wished to be, and nothing else so clearly reveals the individuality and strength of his book. To some extent therefore, he was right in authorizing the myths about himself, which, in this study, we have tried to penetrate in order to find out in detail how a contribution to world literature came into being. The myths are correct in as far as, in the popular mind, Whitman is identical with the book which it was his function in world literature to write and make known.

I myself but write one or two indicative words for the future,
I but advance a moment only to wheel and hurry back in the
    darkness.

With good reason he kept himself in the shadow and let the book have the future to itself.

Whitman's importance for modern literature lies both in his form and in his content. In the overflowing lyrical abundance of his longer and shorter poems he has suggested a series of

themes which younger poets can take up and develop. We have
observed this in Europe; and it has naturally happened to an
even greater extent in America. Sherwood Anderson, Edgar Lee
Masters, Willa Cather, Carl Sandburg, and William Carlos
Williams, to mention only five of the more important writers,
have found a Whitmanesque cue and played a literary role in
the spirit of Whitman. Their books or poems can often be traced
back to a quotation or sentence from *Leaves of Grass*. In 1915
Van Wyck Brooks in a manifesto for younger American authorship, *America's Coming of Age*, wrote:

Every strong personal impulse, every cooperating and unifying
impulse, everything that enriches the social background, everything that impels and clarifies in the modern world owes something
to Walt Whitman.[115]

And Bliss Perry, whose study of 1906 has been so often quoted
in this work, wrote in 1920 in *The American Spirit in Literature*:

Whitman, like Poe, had defects of character and defects of art.
His life and work raise many problems which will long continue
to fascinate and to baffle the critics. But after all of them have
had their say, it will remain true that he was a seer and a prophet,
far in advance of his own time, like Lincoln, and like Lincoln, an
inspired interpreter of the soul of this republic.[116]

Whitman's influence in world literature shows that in his
poetry he interpreted not merely "this republic" but also the
whole of "the garden the world," which in the first poem of
Children of Adam he triumphantly entered. He did not live to
see the fulfillment of his dream of victorious entry into the world.
That was left for his other soul, his poems. But it is surprising
and encouraging to see how these poems have met with more and
more sympathy from four successive generations: the generation of the seventies, which "discovered" him; the generation of the turn of the century, which discovered him anew; and
finally the lost generations of the First World War and the
Second World War, which made him their poet in earnest and
took him to their hearts because of his great dream of union and
democracy—a dream which we also share and defiantly proclaim.

Notes

INTRODUCTION

1. "Nur eine Zeit, welche . . . von verlechzender Sehnsucht nach dem Neuem erfüllt ist, konnte in diesen siegesgewissen Rhapsodien mehr sehen, als eine von jene Erscheinungen, welche in der gänzlichen Zertrümmerung aller Form . . . den wahren Dichterberuf erblicken." Adolf Stern, *Geschichte der Weltliteratur in übersichtlicher Darstellung*, Stuttgart, 1888, p. 777.

2. Brandes's neglect had the peculiar effect of keeping any knowledge of Whitman's existence and importance from the radical Scandinavian writers and press until the end of the century. In spite of Rudolf Schmidt and Niels Møller, Henrik Cavling, as late as 1887, visited the United States and devoted a whole chapter in his book, *Fra Amerika* (2 volumes) to American literature without even mentioning Whitman.

3. We have destroyed the myths. We know what he did *not* undertake. We know he was not an abolitionist, a Fourierist, an "Experimental Community" man, like Alcott or Hawthorne—or a socialist.

AMERICA IN 1850

1. Fredrika Bremer, *The Homes of the New World; Impressions of America*, translated by Mary Howitt (London, 1853, 3 vols.), II, 380–81. The present translator has edited this quotation somewhat.

2. *Ibid.*, I, xi.

3.
> Amerika, du hast es besser
> Als unser Kontinent, das alte,
> Hast keine verfallene Schlösser
> Und keine Basalte.
> Dich stört nicht im Innern

Zu lebendiger Zeit
Unnützes Erinnern
Und verbeblicher Streit.

From the poem "Den Vereinigten Staaten" in *Zahme Xenien*, IX. (A prose version from 1819 reads: "North America is fortunate to have no basalte, no ancestors and no classical ground.") The finished poem was sent to Zeeter July 17, 1827. Goethe, *Sämtliche Werke*, IV, 127, 309. Even Chateaubriand's René had fled to America to escape his past and the historical past—the ruins.

4. Tocqueville, *De la démocratie en Amérique*, ch. iii: "Etat social des Anglo-Americains: consequences politiques de l'état social des Anglo-Americains."

5. Martineau, *Society in America*, III, 214.

6. "They have no time to read; they are all at work; and if they get through their daily newspaper, it is quite as much as most of them can effect." Marryat, *Diary in America*, I, Part Second, 230–31.

7. *The Cambridge History of American Literature*, I, 335.

8. To Dickens the Transcendentalists appeared as oases of light in the intellectual darkness of the States. "Transcendentalism has its occasional vagaries (what school has not?), but it has good healthful qualities in spite of them; not least among the number a hearty disgust of Cant . . . if I were a Bostonian, I think I would be a Transcendentalist." Charles Dickens, *American Notes*, I, 134; Chapter III, "Boston."

9. Bremer, *The Homes of the New World*, I, 29.

10. *Ibid.*, I, 31.

11. *Ibid.*, I, 151.

12. *Ibid.*, I, 143.

13. *Ibid.*, I, 134.

14. *Ibid.*, I, 175.

15. *Ibid.*, I, 311, 258; II, 43.

16. *Ibid.*, II, 43–95.

17. *Ibid.*, I, 199.

18. *Ibid.*, II, 368.

19. "A determined clique, who attempted to surround the traveller with an atmosphere of their own." Marryat, *Diary in America*, I, 204–5.

20. Bremer, *The Homes of the New World*, I, 305–6.

21. *Ibid.*, III, 386.

22. *Ibid.*, I, 213.

23. *Ibid.*, 1, 36.

24. To Joseph Klemm, on March 6, 1833, Lenau wrote something similar about American women whom he observed at musical performances in society. "Ich vernahm in jeder Note die Resonanz

einer fürchterlichen inneren Hohlheit." [I felt in every note the echo of a frightful inner vacuity.] Nicolaus Lenau, *Sämtliche Werke und Briefe*, III, 200–201.

25. To Anton Schurz from Baltimore on October 16, 1832, he wrote: "Bruder, diese Amerikaner sind himmelan stinkende Krämerseelen. Todt für geistige Leben, maustodt!" [Brother, these Americans have shopkeeper's souls which stink to high heaven. Dead to all spiritual values; stonedead.] *Ibid.*, III, 193.

26. Tocqueville, *De la démocratie en Amérique*, Book I, ch. xiii: "Physionomie litteraire des siècles démocratie"; ch. xvii: "De quelques sources de poésie chez les nations démocratiques."

27. ("apercevant le genre humain comme un seul tout"), *Ibid.*, Vol. II, Book I, Chapter xvii.

28. ". . . l'homme sort du néant, traverse le temps, et va disparaître pour toujours dans le sein de Dieu." *Ibid.*

29. Toutes ces ressources lui manquent; mais *l'homme* lui reste, et c'est assez pour elle. Les destinées humaines, *l'homme, pris à part de son temps et de son pays, et placé en face de la nature et de Dieu, avec ses passions, ses doutes, ses prospérités inouïes et ses misères incompréhensibles, deviendront pour ces peuples l'objet principal et presque unique de la poésie* . . ." *Ibid.* The italics are mine.

30. Emerson's "Merlin"; Lowell's "Ode" ("In the old days of awe and keen-eyed wonder").

31. Bremer, *The Homes of the New World*, I, 171.

32. Lenau, "Eine Niagarastimme gehört dazu un diessen Schuften zu predigte . . ." *Sämtliche Werke und Briefe*, III, 193.

WALT WHITMAN AT THIRTY-SIX

1. Samuel MacPherson Janney, *History of the Religious Society of Friends* (Philadelphia, 1859–67, 4 vols.) Vol. I.

2. Bremer, *The Homes of the New World;* tr. by Mary Howitt, II, 16–30.

3. *Ibid.*, II, 28.

4. In *November Boughs*, which is now a part of the *Prose Works.*

5. The last two sentences of this quotation are in a Whitman footnote.

6. Traubel, *With Walt Whitman in Camden*, II, 19.

7. From "Two Family Interiors," in *Specimen Days.*

8. From "Paumanok, and My Life on It as Child and Young Man," in *Specimen Days.*

9. ". . . the sea-shore should be an invisible *influence* . . . in my composition." From "Sea-Shore Fancies," in *Specimen Days*. The italics are Whitman's.

10. Cf. "Brooklyniana," 1862, in *The Uncollected Poetry and Prose of Walt Whitman*, ed. by Emory Holloway, II, 235. (Hereafter this work will be abbreviated as *U.P. & P.*) See also "My First Reading—Lafayette," in *Specimen Days*, and "Old Brooklyn Days," in *Good-Bye My Fancy*.

11. Bertz, "Walt Whitman, ein Charakterbild," in *Jahrbuch für sexuelle Zwischenstufen*, VII (Part 1, 1905), 155–287.

12. *Ibid.*, p. 205. Bertz quotes from an article in *The Conservator* (Philadelphia), Vol. X (November 9, 1899), and C. P. O'Connor, *Mainly about People* (London, 1899).

13. J. J. Bachofen, *Das Mutterrecht*, auswahl von Rudolph Marx (Leipzig, 1927), pp. 106, 160.

14. *Cf. Democratic Vistas.*

15. *U.P. & P.*, II, 246–49.

16. "Growth—Health—Work," in *Specimen Days*.

17. Bremer, *The Homes of the New World*, I, 16.

18. "Plays and Operas Too," in *Specimen Days*.

19. "The Old Bowery," in *November Boughs*.

20. Henry Bryan Binns, *A Life of Walt Whitman*, p. 22.

21. Catel, *Walt Whitman, la naissance du poète* (The Birth of the Poet). Unfortunately this work has not yet been translated into English.

22. *U.P. & P.*, I, xxix.

23. Johnston and Wallace, *Visits to Walt Whitman in 1890–1891*, p. 71.

24. "Starting Newspapers," in *Specimen Days*.

25. *U.P. & P.*, I, xxxiii. The italics are mine.

26. *Ibid.*, p. 4.

27. *Ibid.*, p. 37. The italics are Whitman's.

28. Leon Bazalgette, *Walt Whitman; l'homme et son œuvre*, pp. 68–69. ". . . superbe animal humain, ivre d'éprouver sa magnifique santé . . . . Il semble prende possession d'un Paradis, inventorier un héritage qui lui est echu."

29. "Poe was very cordial, in a quiet way. . . . I have a distinct and pleasing remembrance of his looks, voice, manner and matter; very kindly and human, but subdued, perhaps a little jaded." "Broadway Sights," in *Specimen Days*.

30. *U.P. & P.*, I, 52.

31. Lombroso, *Genie und Irrsinn* [Genius and Insanity], 1890; Max Nordau, *Entartung* [Degeneracy], 1892.

32. Perry, *Walt Whitman*, p. 19.

33. Binns, *A Life of Walt Whitman*, p. 36.

34. New York *Tribune*, April 4, 1892, and Perry, *Walt Whitman*, p. 28.

35. *U.P. & P.*, I, 60.   36. *Ibid.*, p. 83.

37. *Ibid.*, p. 86.

38. *Ibid.*, p. 152. The italics are Whitman's.

39. *Ibid.*, footnote on p. 126.

40. *Ibid.*, p. 128.

41. *Ibid.*, p. 129. The italics are Whitman's.

42. *Ibid.*, p. 132.

43. Catel examined the significance of the book to Whitman and called it "a Bible of Individualism." Catel, *Walt Whitman*, p. 347.

44. *U.P. & P.*, I, 132.

45. Binns, *A Life of Walt Whitman*, pp. 67–68.

46. *U.P. & P.*, I, 37.

47. But Binns has already commented: "Whitman was nearly twenty-nine, and had not, so far as I can discover . . . experienced . . . any serious affair of the heart." Binns, *A Life of Walt Whitman*, p. 46. Cf. Holloway, *Walt Whitman*, p. 46.

48. From "Starting Newspapers."

49. From "Through Eight Years."

50. Carpenter, *Days with Walt Whitman*, pp. 142–43.

51. Symonds, *Walt Whitman*, p. 93.

52. Barrus, *Whitman and Burroughs*, pp. 336–37.

53. Binns, *A Life of Walt Whitman*, pp. 349–50.

54. Traubel, *With Walt Whitman in Camden*, II, 316, under date of Sept. 13, 1888.

55. Barrus, *Whitman and Burroughs*, p. 339.

56. Binns, *A Life of Walt Whitman*, p. 51.

57. *U.P. & P.*, II, 102.

58. "Quant à placer à la Nouvelle-Orléans un roman d'amour, dont la fin malheureuse aurait été la cause du départ soudain des Whitman, rien n'autorise à le faire." Catel, *Walt Whitman*, p. 258.

59. Bremer described them, *The Homes of the New World*, III, 42.

60. Holloway, *Walt Whitman*, p. 76.

61. Bremer, *The Homes of the New World*, I, 275–76.

62. In "Song of Myself," "These I Singing in Spring," and "I Saw in Louisiana a Live-Oak Growing."

63. "Through Eight Years," in *Specimen Days*.

64. *U.P. & P.*, I, 191; Holloway, *Walt Whitman*, p. 62.

65. Bremer, *The Homes of the New World*, I, 229.

66. Dickens, *American Notes*, I, 287–96.

67. Sibbern, *Gabrielis Breve*, pp. 173–74.

68. Bucke, *Cosmic Consciousness*, pp. 3, 9–10.

69. Sibbern, *Gabrielis Breve*, p. 174.

70. Franz Werfel, *Der Weltfreund* (Leipzig, 1918), "Sterben im Walde."

71. Holloway, *Walt Whitman*, p. 97.

72. "Omnibus Jaunts and Drivers," in *Specimen Days*.

73. Bremer, *The Homes of the New World*, I, 249.

74. *U.P. & P.*, I, 234.

75. "The Swedish Swan, with all her blandishments, never touched my heart in the least," *U.P. & P.*, I, 257. Cf. also "Old Actors, Singers, Shows &c., in New York," in *Good-Bye My Fancy*.

76. Whitman mentions Alboni in Section 3 of "Proud Music of the Storm" and referred to her in several places in his prose writing.

77. *Evening Post*, August 14, 1851; *U.P. & P.*, I, 256–57.

78. *U.P. & P.*, II, 85.

79. Traubel, *With Walt Whitman in Camden*, II, 72.

80. "Paumanok, and My Life on It as Child and Young Man," in *Specimen Days*.

81. "Dearest Friends—An Ossianic Night," in *Specimen Days*.

82. Perry, *Walt Whitman*, p. 72.

83. In one of Whitman's footnotes.

84. In "Old Poets," from *Good-Bye My Fancy*.

85. "Her stories are like good air, good associations in real life," *U.P. & P.*, II, 53.

86. Kennedy, *The Fight of a Book for the World*, p. 199.

87. In "Old Poets," from *Good-Bye My Fancy*.

88. Binns, *A Life of Walt Whitman*, 62–63. The italics are mine. [Recent scholarship has proved that Whitman's reading and knowledge was more accurate and scientific than Binns thought. See Joseph Beaver, "Walt Whitman, Stargazer," in *The Journal of English and Germanic Philology*, July, 1949, XLVIII (July, 1949), 307–19. Translator]

89. H. C. Ørsted, *Aanden i Naturen* [The Soul in Nature]. Especially the section "Naturvidenskabens Forhold til Digtekunsten" [Relationship of Science and the Poetic Art].

90. Binns, *A Life of Walt Whitman*, p. 62.

91. *Ibid.*

92. Bliss Perry has a very interesting account of what two contemporary authors, Tupper and Warren with their *Proverbial Philosophy* and *The Lily and the Bee,* respectively, might have meant to Whitman. Perry, *Walt Whitman*, pp. 91 ff.

93. Thomas Carlyle, *Sartor Resartus*, Book I, ch. iii, "Reminiscences."

94. *Ibid.*, Book I, ch. iv, "Characteristics."

95. *Ibid.*

96. *Ibid.*, Book I, ch. viii, "The World of Clothes," and Book III, ch. ix, "Circumspectives."

97. *Ibid.*, Book III, ch. iii, "Symbols."

98. In "Friendship."

99. Carlyle, *Sartor Resartus*, Book I, ch. xi, "Prospective."

100. Perry, *Walt Whitman*, p. 84.

101. Carlyle, *Sartor Resartus*, Book III, ch. viii, "Natural Supernaturalism." The italics are mine.

102. So was Carlyle's *Heroes and Hero-Worship.*

103. John Burroughs, *Notes on Walt Whitman as Poet and Person*, 2d ed. (New York, 1871), p. 16. Kennedy, *Reminiscences of Walt Whitman*, p. 79.

104. Trowbridge, *My Own Story with Recollections of Noted Persons*, pp. 366–67.

105. Knut Hamsun, in his *Fra det moderne Amerikas Aandsliv* [On American Intellectual Life], (1889), designates that as Emerson's unique and only ability, p. 91.

106. In France, Valéry Larbaud made the same point in his preface to the Nouvelle Revue Française edition of Whitman, in 1918. He said of this essay of Emerson's: "C'est le portrait du poète à peu près tel que Whitman devait le concevoir; c'est même un peu le portrait du Whitman." [It is the portrait of a poet somewhat as Whitman conceived him; it is even something of a portrait of Whitman.]

107. *U.P. & P.*, II, 71, 72, 80.

108. In his prose writing Whitman frequently expressed the same scorn for "piano strings" and "tinkling rhymes."

109. Barrus, *Whitman and Burroughs*, p. 339.

110. Binns, *A Life of Walt Whitman*, p. 78.

111. Carpenter, *Days with Walt Whitman*, p. 6.

LEAVES OF GRASS, 1855–89

1. James Russell Lowell, "Ode" ("In the old days of keen-eyed wonder"), 1841.

2. "Song of Myself," 1855. Quotations have been checked with the editions in each case, but where section numbers are used they follow those of the authorized edition for the convenience of the reader.

3. Carpenter, *Days with Walt Whitman*, p. 30.

4. Ralph Waldo Emerson, "The Poet."

5. On p. 191 of the second edition of *Leaves of Grass*. This passage would follow line 23 in Section 10 of the present reading of "By Blue Ontario's Shore," but was deleted in 1860.

6. See *supra*, p. 58.

7. Whitman himself later marked "A Boston Ballad" for omission, but Trowbridge persuaded him to leave it. It is one of the poems in the collection which needs commentary, and since this is never found in editions of *Leaves of Grass*, the general reader will always feel that it is space wasted.

8. The theme appears in Sections 1, 5, 6, 9, 17, 31, 33, 39, 49, 52.

9. Clifton Furness has preserved a quotation from one of Whitman's notebooks in which he characterized his type of inspiration as a trance. Clifton Joseph Furness, ed., *Walt Whitman's Workshop*, p. 21.

10. Holloway, *Walt Whitman*, p. 123.

11. Barrus, *Whitman and Burroughs*, p. 64.

12. Knut Hamsun, *Fra det moderne Amerikas Aandsliv* (Copenhagen, 1889), p. 79.

13. Regis Michaud, *Littérature américaine* (Paris, 1928), p. 70.

14. Adolf Hansen in *Illustreret Verdens-Litteraturhistorie*, ed. by Julius Clausen (Copenhagen, 1901), III, 23.

15. Johannes V. Jensen, *Hjulet* (Copenhagen, 1905), ch. ii.

16. Perry, *Walt Whitman*, p. 83.

17. *Ibid.*, p. 88. This study has since been published: Fred Newton Scott, "A Note on Whitman's Prosody," *Journal of English and Germanic Philology*, VII (1908), 134–53.

18. Perry, *Walt Whitman*, p. 97. The italics are Perry's.

19. "Notes on Lecturing and Oratory," *Walt Whitman's Workshop*, pp. 33–84. Catel thinks that Whitman's abstention from

tobacco, coffee, and alcohol was originally for the sake of his voice. Jean Catel, *Rythme et langage*, p. 41.

20. *Walt Whitman's Workshop*, p. 67.

21. "Whitman and Oratory," by Thomas B. Harned, in *The Complete Writings*, VIII, 253–54. [In this essay the phrase about the direct address reads ". . . without a pause afterwards, . . ." which does not seem logical; ". . . with . . ." must have been intended.]

22. *Walt Whitman's Workshop*, p. 36.

23. *Ibid.*, p. 35.

24. Perry, *Walt Whitman*, p. 96.

25. *Leaves of Grass*, 3d ed., 1860, p. 240.

26. *Walt Whitmans Werk*, tr. by Hans Reisiger, II, 70.

"Allenthalben gehn sie mit Groschen vor ihren Augen,
Verfüttern rückhaltlos ihr Gehirn an die Gier ihres Bauches,
Verkaufen und kaufen die Eintrittskarten zum Fest, ohne jemals
selber hineinzugehen,
Schwitzen und pflügen und dreschen und bekommen die Spreu zum
Lohn,
Wenige Träge besitzen und fordern den Weizen immer für sich."

27. Perry, *Walt Whitman*, p. 71.

28. A typical example of Whitman's arbitrary use of foreign words is the Italian *finale*. The first time he used it was in "Faces," in 1855:
"Do you suppose I could be content with all if I thought them their own finale?"
But later he changed the word to *finalé* and used it in the well-known "Now Finalé to the Shore," meaning now farewell to the shore. That is one example of what made Henry James complain of Whitman's "too extensive acquaintance with the foreign languages." See Edith Wharton, *A Backward Glance* (New York, 1934), p. 186, in which she, for both herself and James, hails Whitman as "the greatest of American poets."

29. Otherwise there is found in Whitman's work only the Spanish *libertad*, as a designation of the Goddess of Freedom. At a certain period he introduced it into many of his poems in places where he had previously used "liberty."

30. The difficulties of a clear analysis of Whitman's concept of "The Soul" are not lessened when in "Song of Prudence" he uses the terms "my spirit" and "my soul" interchangeably, and in *Specimen Days*, 1892, he speaks of "my other soul, my poems."

31. Kennedy, *The Fight of a Book for the World*, p. 178.

32. In *Specimen Days* Whitman wrote a short essay called "Carlyle from American Points of View," in which he has much to say about Hegel's philosophy and admitted his indebtedness to Gost[w]ick's popularization of Hegel.

33. The whole passage appears as a sketch in *The Uncollected Poetry and Prose of Walt Whitman*, II, 72–73, where the phrases are not so bold, but the association with the cue-word touch are even clearer.

34. In "Faces" he is the flower that calls to the man passing by: "Come here, she blushingly cries. . . . Come nigh to me limber-
hip'd man and give me your finger and thumb,
Stand at my side till I lean as high as I can upon you,
Fill me with albescent honey . . . . bend down to me,
Rub to me with your chafing beard . . rub to my breast and
shoulders."
In modern world literature Verlaine and Rilke have used similar imagery in their lyrics.

35. Perry, *Walt Whitman*, pp. 72–73. Also printed in *The Complete Writings of Walt Whitman*, IX, 39.

36. In 1860, in "Me Imperturbe," he even used this double phrase, "Master of all or Mistress of all" about himself. Involuntarily we think of Shakespeare's "Master-Mistress" in the *Sonnets*.

37. Angelus Silesius, *Cherubinische Wandersmann*, V, 61.
"Der Frosch ist ja so schön als Engel Seraphim."

38. William Blake, *Proverbs of Hell*.

39. Goethe, *Sämtliche Werke*, XXXIX, 324:
"—Aber einfach bleibt die Gestalt der ersten Erscheinung,
Und so bezeichnet sich auch unter den Pflanzen das Kind."

40. Edmund Clarence Stedman, from "Mr. Stedman's Lectures on Poetry" (at Johns Hopkins) as reported by Harrison S. Morris in *The Conservator*, April, 1891. Quoted by Kennedy, *The Fight of a Book for the World*, p. 274.

41. "Leatherdressing, coachmaking, boilermaking, ropetwisting,
distilling, signpainting, limeburning, coopering, etc."
From "Song of Occupations," Section 5.

42. Jean Catel finds the word "fit" very characteristic of Whitman as an expression of the paroxysms under which his poems were brought into existence.

43. Kennedy, in *The Fight of a Book for the World*, p. 55, says that in a way Emerson himself admitted it in a letter to Carlyle,

in which he speaks of Whitman (*Emerson-Carlyle Correspondence*, II, 25) : "the book throve so badly with the few to whom I showed it . . . . !" etc. Also quoted in Perry, *Walt Whitman*, pp. 122–23.

44. "A rude child of the people!—No imitation—No foreigner—but a growth and idiom of America." The style is so obvious that we must marvel that a generation passed before it was recognized that it was written by Whitman himself.

45. Perry, *Walt Whitman*, p. 122.

46. Thoreau, *Familiar Letters*, pp. 340, 345. Perry, *Walt Whitman*, pp. 119–22.

47. In his diary for February, 1862, Emerson wrote of Thoreau's admiration for Whitman: "Perhaps his fancy for W.W. grew out of his taste for wild nature, for an otter, a woodchuck, or a loon." *The Heart of Emerson's Journals*, ed. by Bliss Perry (Boston, 1909), p. 291.

48. According to tradition this was done at the suggestion of Charles A. Dana, editor of Horace Greeley's *Tribune*. According to Holloway's account, however, it was Richard Henry Dana, Jr., author of *Two Years before the Mast*, who was responsible for the *faux pas*. Holloway, pp. 142–43.

49. "Gedenke stets, o Mensch, du bist ein Vieler,
       Ein Tausendfacher bist du durch Entfaltung,
       Ein ganzer Mensch erst bist und wirst du endlich
       Nur durch das ganze Leben. Und nun wisse:
       Der Mensch ist unsichtbar; sein ganzes Wesen
       Erscheinet nie! Nie Kind, und Jüngling, Mann
       Und Greis vereint. Nie sieht der Mensch sich selbst.
       Und Niemand ihn. Vom Schwimmenden im Meer [!]
       Erscheint nur jetzt die Schulter, jetzt der Arm,
       Ein Fuss, die Hand—bis er an's Ufer steigt
       Und herrlich dasteht als der ganze Mensch!"
                              Laienbrevier (Juni XVII)

"Always consider, O Man, that thou art manifold,
A thousand people art thou by development,
A complete man art thou only and first wilt thou be
Through a complete life. And know that
Man is invisible; his complete existence
Never appeared! Nor child, youth, manhood,
Nor age assembled it. No man sees himself,
Nor does anyone else. Like a swimmer in the sea
Who revealed only a shoulder, then an arm,

A foot, a hand, until he climbed on the shore
And emerged magnificently as a complete man."

50. Walt Whitman: *Digte;* i Udvalg og med Indledning af Johs.
V. Jensen og Otto Gelsted [Walt Whitman; poems, selected and
edited by Johannes V. Jensen and Otto Gelsted]. Copenhagen,
1919.

51. Thoreau, *Familiar Letters,* p. 345.

52. Perry, *Walt Whitman,* p. 115.

53. "He masters whose spirit masters, he tastes sweetest who
results sweetest in the long run."
                    Section 13 of "By Blue Ontario's Shore."

54. Perry, *Walt Whitman,* p. 98; *In Re Walt Whitman,* p. 35.

55. Perry, *Walt Whitman,* p. 124.

56. Holloway, *Walt Whitman,* p. 161.

57. Albert Parry, "The Queen of Bohemia," *American Mercury,*
XXI (September, 1930), 97–105.

58. Kennedy, *The Fight of a Book for the World,* p. 58.

59. Binns, *A Life of Walt Whitman,* pp. 140–41.

60. *Uncollected Poetry and Prose of Walt Whitman,* I, 194.

61. Perry, *Walt Whitman,* p. 133; Binns, *A Life of Walt Whitman,* p. 181; Holloway, *Walt Whitman,* p. 185. The italics are
mine.

62. Holloway, *Walt Whitman,* p. 156.

63. *U.P. & P.,* II, 91–92.

64. Two earlier American lyrics had contained a similar theme:
Bryant's "To a Waterfowl" and Dana's "The Little Beachbird."

65. In a parenthesis later deleted from the last section of "Out
of the Cradle" it read:
        "O a word! O what is my destination?
        O I fear it is henceforth chaos!"

66. Holloway, *Walt Whitman,* p. 162.

67. A reproduction of the text from the *Saturday Press* is found
in *A Child's Reminiscence* (University of Washington Bookstore,
1930), p. 13. The italics are mine.

68. In the 1860 edition of *Leaves of Grass,* in a group called
Leaves of Grass, No. 1.

69. The theme of examining the meaning of existence on the
beach of Paumanok is used throughout Whitman's poetry because
he himself had his most moving spiritual experiences while rambling
there. The first time it was used as notes for the two poems just
discussed was in 1856 in the poem "On the Beach at Night Alone,"

in which the poet begged for a clue to the secret of existence, and in the pervading tone of optimism in the second edition he saw that Space unites everything in its great identity. Then followed the two poems just discussed here, which have the same starting point, the poet's wish for a word, an explanation, but with such a tragic climax. Finally in 1871 Whitman again used the title "On the Beach at Night" in a little poem which may be regarded as an answer and a later solution of the despairing "As I Ebb'd with the Ocean of Life." By that time Whitman's spiritual crisis was over. Here he introduced the father answering the child's complaint:

> "Weep not, child,
>   Weep not, my darling,
>   With these kisses let me remove your tears,
>   The ravening clouds shall not long be victorious."

But the poem is weak, and the optimism has far less vitality than the pessimism in "As I Ebb'd." All these night poems about Long Island, with the masterpiece "Out of the Cradle Endlessly Rocking" as the climax, the spirit of which contrasts so remarkably with all the rest of the collection, were in 1871 grouped under the heading *Sea-Shore Memories*, and in 1881 under the present general heading *Sea-Drift*.

70. The picture was reproduced in Johannes Schlaf's *Walt Whitman*.

71. And a larger audience than can be determined learned to know Whitman in the 1860 version. When, on account of the War, Thayer and Eldridge went bankrupt in 1861, the plates for *Leaves of Grass* were sold to a printer named Worthington, who in the following years printed an undetermined number of copies as Whitman's fame mounted, without Whitman's receiving any royalties. In the economically difficult years around 1880, this was a constant source of trouble to Whitman—and is, in fact, a particularly glaring example of how necessary it was to enforce copyright laws against American printers. Previously Marryat and Dickens had fought for an international copyright law during their American tours.

72. The whole prostitute motif played a much larger role in the 1860 edition than in the completed book. Besides "Once I Pass'd" there was also "To a Common Prostitute" in the 1860 edition.

73. Calamus is the name of a particular kind of North American grass with a sharp, penetrating odor.

74. This idea is repeated in a later "Inscription" in *Calamus*,

originally next to the last, but shifted and almost hidden among the others:

"Here my last words, and the most baffling,

Here the frailest leaves of me, and yet my strongest-lasting,

Here I shade down and hide my thoughts—I do not expose them,

And yet they expose me more than all my other poems."

The italics are mine. The final line was deleted in 1867.

75. D. H. Lawrence remarked on this in an article on Whitman in the London *Nation*, July 23, 1921, pp. 616–18. "But what is Woman to Walt Whitman? Not much. She is a great function—no more. Whitman's athletic mothers of These States are depressing. Muscles and wombs."

76. Sappho's "Ode to Anactoria" ("That man whoever he may be," etc.) in *Sappho*, a new rendering by H. de Vere Stacpoole (London, 1920), p. 23.

77. The main theme of the poems of 1860 Whitman had seen correctly as the transformation of his disappointed love into poetry. In "Proto-Leaf" he introduced it into the great résumé of themes, but in this extremely interesting form:

"I will make the songs of passions, to give them their way"

Here Whitman is concerned with the most interesting question in literary psychology: whether to celebrate the passions in order to provide an outlet for them. The result was just as significant for Whitman as it was later for D. H. Lawrence. In both cases the erotic bent was sublimated in their work.

78. Holloway, *Walt Whitman*, p. 173.

79. "Grad und Art der Geschlechtlichkeit eines Menschen reicht bis in den letzten Gipfel seines Geistes hinauf." Nietzsche, *Jenseits von Gut und Böse* (1886), Paragraph 75.

80. In Hafiz Persian love poems there is one with a similar beginning. *Hafis*, CXXXV, translated from the Persian into German by Daumer.

81. It is interesting to note something of the same trait in Emerson. In "Friendship" he proclaims a similar instability, and in "Circles" expresses an erotomania which recalls Whitman. For further illumination of Whitman's restless inconstancy see "To a Stranger" (No. 22 in the 1860 *Calamus*) and two sections of "Poem of Joys," later deleted, but found in the Variorum Readings. The latter is a valuable supplement to the *Calamus* poetry. "Give Me the Splendid Silent Sun" is another example, though it was not published until 1865.

82. Eduard Bertz, in his study of Whitman's sexuality in *Jahrbuch für sexuelle Zwischenstufen*, VII, 155–287, came to a similar conclusion. The strong auto-erotic trait which Catel found so predominant in all Whitman's work can be explained in this way.

83. Holloway, *Walt Whitman*, p. 173.

84. "Niemals ist das Recht der wissenschaftlichen Kritik das Geschlechtleben eines bedeutenden Mannes unter die Lupe zu nehmen, so offenbar wie dann wenn er sein abnormes Empfinden als das normale verkündet und ein Evangelium, ja eine Religion daraus macht." Bertz, "Walt Whitman," in *Jahrbuch für sexuelle Zwischenstufen*, VII, 169.

85. Holloway, *Walt Whitman*, p. 173.

86. William James, *Varieties of Religious Experience*, Lectures IV and V, "The Religion of Healthy-Mindedness."

87. Johannes V. Jensen, *Hjulet*, ch. viii.

88. In much the same way the criminal Protos "uses" Whitman in his relationship with the young Lafcadio in André Gide's *Les Caves du Vatican*.

89. In one poem, "To One shortly to Die," in the section called *Messenger Leaves*, he congratulates the person who is about to die.

90. Kennedy, *The Fight of a Book for the World*, p. 202.

91. The motif is repeated in *Calamus* No. 40 (later "That Shadow My Likeness").

92. Binns, *A Life of Walt Whitman*, pp. 148–49.

93. Kennedy, *The Fight of a Book for the World*, p. 110.

94. Henry Bascom Rankin, *Personal Recollections of Abraham Lincoln* (New York, 1916), p. 126.

95. Holloway, *Walt Whitman*, pp. 198, 218.

96. Perry, *Walt Whitman*, p. 151.

97. Holloway, *Walt Whitman*, p. 200.

98. *Ibid.*, pp. 200–205.

99. *Ibid.*, pp. 202–4.

100. Binns, *A Life of Walt Whitman*, p. 180; Holloway, *Walt Whitman*, p. 188.

101. Barrus, *Whitman and Burroughs*, p. 339.

102. Dickens, *American Notes*, I, 281–82.

103. "Abraham Lincoln" and also "No Good Portrait of Lincoln," both in *Specimen Days*.

104. "Calhoun's Real Monument," in *Specimen Days*.

105. "The Weather—Does It Sympathize with These Times," in *Specimen Days*.

106. "Attitude of Foreign Governments during the War," in *Specimen Days*.

107. *Ibid.*

108. "A New Army Organization Fit for America," in *Specimen Days*.

109. "Death of a Hero," in *Specimen Days*.

110. Clara Barrus quotes a hospital doctor, Dr. D. W. Bliss: "From my personal knowledge of Mr. Whitman's labors in Armory Square, and other hospitals, I am of the opinion that no one person who assisted in the hospitals during the War accomplished so much good to the soldiers and for the Government as Mr. Whitman." Barrus, *Whitman and Burroughs*, xxix.

111. Holloway, *Walt Whitman*, pp. 206–7.

112. *Ibid.*, p. 199.

113. Perry, *Walt Whitman*, p. 143. Part of the same letter is quoted also in Barrus, *Whitman and Burroughs*, p. 13.

114. Clara Barrus has a characteristic example of such a woman who previously was a Whitman opponent, but changed her mind after meeting him: "I admit that I should be more than ordinarily pleased with him. His photographs are base slanders. He looks a thousand times better than any of those pictures." Barrus, *Whitman and Burroughs*, p. 22.

115. *Ibid.*, xviii and xxii.

116. Burroughs never included this book in his collected works.

117. There is the same sort of myth that Nietzsche's illness was caused by his hospital work.

118. Perry, *Walt Whitman*, p. 150.

119. "Whitman never fully recovered." Binns, *A Life of Walt Whitman*, p. 204.

120. Algernon Charles Swinburne, *William Blake; a Critical Essay* (London, 1868), p. 303.

121. Perry, *Walt Whitman*, p. 157.

122. The erotomania theme is likewise strikingly apparent in "Give Me the Splendid Silent Sun":

"Give me faces and streets! give me these phantoms incessant and
　　endless along the trottoirs!
Give me interminable eyes! give me women! give me comrades and
　　lovers by the thousand!
Let me see new ones every day! let me hold new ones by the hand
　　every day!"

123. *U.P. & P.*, I, 72, reprinted from *The Democratic Review*, X (March, 1842), 259–64.

124. To make the connection with this poem unmistakable Whitman deliberately repeated the phrase, "the echo arous'd in my breast" from the bird's song.

125. The fourth short poem which is now in the section *Memories of President Lincoln*, "This dust was once a man," first appeared in 1871.

126. Kennedy, *The Fight of a Book for the World*, p. 18.

127. "Comme puissance verbale, . . . comme éclat des images, comme verve satirique, elle s'apparente aux morceaux les plus colorés et les plus éloquents de la prose française, de Courier à Hugo." Bazalgette, *Walt Whitman, l'homme et son œuvre*, p. 257.

128. Perry, *Walt Whitman*, p. 178.

129. *Ibid.*, p. 179. Later Matthew Arnold, while in America in the 1870's, wanted to visit Whitman, but Lowell dissuaded him by insisting that it was not worth the trouble. Barrus, *Whitman and Burroughs*, p. 142.

130. Holloway, *Walt Whitman*, p. 224.

131. *Ibid.*, p. 225.   132. *Ibid.*, p. 232.

133. Carpenter says Peter Doyle never read *Leaves of Grass* or took much account of it. Carpenter, *Days with Walt Whitman*, p. 151.

134. Barrus, *Whitman and Burroughs*, p. 351.

135. Eckhoff, *Paul Verlaine og Symbolismen*, p. 87.

136. *U.P. & P.*, II, 94–96. The italics are Whitman's.

137. Binns, *A Life of Walt Whitman*, p. 234.

138. *Calamus*, ed. by R. M. Bucke. Also in *Complete Writings*, VIII, 7.

139. *U.P. & P.*, I, note on pp. lviii–lix.

140. *Ibid.*, I, lix. The italics are mine.

141. That is true not only of Rossetti's edition but also of Ernest Rhys's in 1886, which later became the Everyman edition.

142. The article was later included in *The Letters of Anne Gilchrist and Walt Whitman*, ed. by Thomas B. Harned, pp. 3–22. Also in *In re Walt Whitman*, pp. 41–55.

143. Ferdinand Freiligrath, *Gesammelte Dichtungen* (Stuttgart, 1877), IV, 86–89. "Stehen wir vor einer Zukunftspoesi, wie uns schon seit Jahren eine Zukunftsmusik verkündigt wird? Und ist Walt Whitman mehr als Richard Wagner?"

144. Traubel, *With Walt Whitman in Camden*, I, 274.

145. Barrus, *Whitman and Burroughs*, p. 241.

146. Perry, *Walt Whitman*, p. 201.

147. Binns, *A Life of Walt Whitman*, p. 258.

148. *Ibid.*, p. 245.

149. Rudolf Schmidt, *Buster og Masker* (Copenhagen, 1882), p. 188.

150. Holloway, *Walt Whitman*, p. 246.

151. The final edition was no exception. The poems he had written during the last three years of his life, but had not fitted into the book, now form the three "Annexes": *Sands at Seventy, Good-Bye My Fancy*, and *Old Age Echoes*.

152. Besides using *finalé* in *"Faces,"* in 1855, Whitman had used it once in *Democratic Vistas*.

153. The shifting of many of the old poems having death as their theme to the supplement of the fifth edition stands as a reminder of that intention.

154. The extent to which Whitman had in 1871 united his personal emotion with a religious feeling can be seen in the little poem "To a Noiseless Patient Spider," which was originally to have been a *Calamus* poem about the poet's longing for friends and lovers. (Holloway found the first draft in a notebook dated 1862.) Now it is a purely religious poem about the efforts to make the connection with strange spheres. That in a nutshell gives us an idea of the development Whitman had experienced in ten years.

155. George W. Curtis, "Editor's Easy Chair," *Harper's Magazine*, LIII (June, 1876), 141–42.

156. Barrus, *Whitman and Burroughs*, p. 201.

157. *Ibid.*, p. 342.

158. Ernest Boyd, "The Father of Them All," *American Mercury*, VI (December, 1925), 451–58.

159. Perry, *Walt Whitman*, p. 250.

160. "An Orson of the Muse," in George Meredith, *Poetical Works* (London, 1912), p. 187.

161. Henry Irving, *Impressions of America* (Boston, 1884), 211; Matthew Arnold, *Seas and Lands* (London, 1891), 74–78; Oscar Wilde, *Impressions of America* (1906), 10; Frank Harris, *My Life and Loves* (Paris, 1926), ch. xii; Edmund Gosse, "A Note on Walt Whitman" in *New Review*, August, 1894, afterwards reprinted in *Critical Kit-Kats* (London, 1896).

162. Harris, *My Life and Loves*, ch. xii.

163. Binns, *A Life of Walt Whitman*, p. 265.

164. *The Letters of Anne Gilchrist and Walt Whitman*, p. 66.

165. *Ibid.*, p. 67.   166. *Ibid.*, p. 121.

167. *Ibid.*, p. 149.

168. Barrus, *Whitman and Burroughs*, pp. 153–58.

169. "Dear, soothing, healthy, restoration-hours—after three confining years of paralysis," from "New Themes Entered Upon, 1876, '77," in *Specimen Days*.

170. "One of the Human Kinks," in *Specimen Days*.

171. "Millet's Pictures—Last Items," in *Specimen Days*.

172. "A Visit, at the Last, to R. W. Emerson," in *Specimen Days*.

173. Kennedy wanted the "shirt-sleeve portrait" of the 1855 edition ("this repulsive, loaferish portrait") omitted from future editions of *Leaves of Grass*. Kennedy, *The Fight of a Book for the World*, pp. 240, 248.

174. Carpenter, *Days with Walt Whitman*, p. 52.

175. *Ibid.*, p. 50   176. *Ibid.*, p. 6.

177. *Walt Whitman's Workshop*, p. 205.

178. Carpenter, *Days with Walt Whitman*, p. 38.

179. *Ibid.*, p. 43.   180. *Ibid.*

181. *Ibid.*, p. 38.

182. Barrus, *Whitman and Burroughs*, p. 318.

WHITMAN IN WORLD LITERATURE

1. "Proto-Leaf" first appeared in the 1860 edition of *Leaves of Grass*. In 1867 the title was changed to "Starting from Paumanok."

2. From Angelus Silesius, *Cherubinischer Wandersmann:*
"Ich bin so grosz als Gott: Er ist als ich so klein;
Er kan nicht über mich, ich unter Ihm nicht sein." Book I, 10.
(I am as great as God, He as small as I;
He can not be over me, nor I under him.)

"Wie mag dich doch O Mensch nach etwas thun Verlangen,
Weil du in dir hältst Gott, und alle Ding' umbfangen?" Book I, 88.
(O Man how canst thou long for anything
When within thyself thou containest God and everything?)

"Je mehr du dich ausz dir kannst auszthun und entgiessen
Je mehr musz Gott in dich mit seiner Gottheit fliessen." Book I, 138.
(The more thou pourest forth and disseminatest thyself
The more must God flow into thee with his divinity.)

"Die Welt ist mir zu äng, der Himmel ist zu klein:
Wo wird doch noch ein Raum für meine Seele sein?" Book I, 187.
(The world is too cramped for me, Heaven is too small:
Where then will I find room for my soul?)

3. Among the Whitman holograph manuscripts now in the Library of Congress is a summary of Lucretius's *De rerum natura.* [Translator]

4. ". . . ich dann im hohen Grase am fallenden Bache liege, und näher an der Erde tausend mannigfaltige Gräschen mir merkwürdig werden; wenn ich das Wimmeln der kleinen Welt zwischen Halmen, die unzähligen unergründlichen Gestalten der Würmchen, der Mückchen näher an meinem Herzen fühle . . . ach könntest du das wieder ausdrücken, könntest du dem Papiere das einhauchen was so voll, so varm in dir lebt . . ." Johann Wolfgang Goethe, *Die Leiden des jungen Werthers*, entry for 10th of May 1771.

5. Simonsen, *Goethes Naturførlelse*, p. 44.

6. "Parablen," in Goethe's *Sämtliche Werke*, Jubiläums Ausgabe, XXXVI, 106–7.

7. ". . . schön und hässlich, gut und bös Alles mit gleichem Rechte neben einander existierend." "Aus den Frankfurter gelehrten Anzeigen (1772) Die schönen Kunste in ihren Ursprung, ihrer wahren Natur und besten Anwendung, betrachtet von J. G. Sulzer." *Ibid.*, XXXIII, 16.

8. Jens Baggesen *Danske Værker*, VIII, 387. The whole burden of the world-citizenship exhortation in its rhythmic form and its ideas has even more surprising similarities to "Pioneers, O Pioneers!" *Ibid.*, 356–78.

9. Vedel *Svensk Romantik*, p. 383. "Ormus, the Ruler God hampering and killing life whereas Ariman represents the revolt against rules, the deep freedom-loving religious need," Vedel says in his analysis of the fable "Ormus and Ariman," from *Tornrosens,* Book IV.

10. Gran, *Norsk Aandsliv i 100 Aar*, I, 7–8.

11. From "To a Young Poet," Wergeland, *Samlede Skrifter*, I, 229.

12. "Migselv," Wergeland, *ibid.*, II, 208–10. tr. by Jørgen Andersen.

13. "Til Foraaret," Wergeland, *ibid.*, II, 346. tr. by Jørgen Andersen.

14. From "Sujetter for Versemagere" [Subjects for Poetasters], Wergeland, *ibid.*, II, 202.

15. Troye, *Wergeland og hans Digtning*, p. 184. Troye (1851–1905) with a similar personal disposition has played the same role as a disciple of Wergeland that Whitman's admirer and friend Edward Carpenter played in England. That is a parallel of temperament admiring parallel types of expression. As a curious fact, Troye and Carpenter got to know each other and were friends for a long time (Troye lived with Carpenter in England), but Troye was a litterateur of the old school and completely lacked understanding of Whitman. He mentions him only once in reference to the haphazard, negligent aspect of Wergeland's poetry, "a contempt for the academic elaborate expression as in hardly any other poet." A footnote is added saying that there may be one exception: "the American Ralph [*sic*] Whitman, if those inarticulate cries and exclamations count as poetry." *Ibid.*, p. 38.

16. Otto Hauser, *Weltgeschichte der Literatur* (Leipzig, 1910, 2 vols.), II, 286.

17. Troye, *Wergeland og hans Digtning*, p. 152.

18. ". . . sie liessen eine Reihe von Vorstellungsbildern, die rastlos wie einer Lanterne Magica einander folgten, an ihrem inneren Auge vorüberziehen und sich davon überwältigen." Ricarda Huch, *Ausbreitung und Verfall der Romantik*, p. 180.

19. ". . . und wüsste, dass am Abend einer käm', der meiner eingedenk ist, und ich wartete den ganzen Tag, und die sonneglänzenden Stunden gingen vorüber und die Schattenstunden mit der silbernen Mondsichel und dem Stern brächten den Freund, der fänd mich an Bergesrand ihm entgegenstürzend in die offne Arme, dass er mich plötzlich am Herzen fühlte mit der heissen Liebe . . ." *Goethes Briefwechsel mit einem Kinde*. From a letter to Frau Rat Goethe written by Bettina from Winkel on 25 June [1808].

20. Schmidt, *Geschichte der deutschen Literatur seit Lessings Tod*, 4th ed., II, 176.

21. *Ibid.*   22. In ch. viii.

23. Hans Andersen, *A Poet's Bazaar;* XXII, "The Steamer's Passage."

24. Hans Brix, *Danmarks Digtere*, p. 181.

25. Vilhelm Andersen, *Illustreret dansk Litteraturhistorie* (København, 1924), p. 547.

26. Hugo, *Le Œuvres complètes de Victor*. Ed. definitive, III, 158, 562; V, 109; VI, 197, 243.

27. "Je suis dans l'enfant mort, dans l'amante quittée,
    Dans le veuvage prompt à rire, dans l'athée,

Dans tous le noirs oublis,
Toutes le voluptés sont pour moi fraternelles.
C'est moi que le fakir voit sortir des prunelles
Du vague Iblis . . .

Je suis l'être final. Je suis dans tout . . .

J'habite Ombos, j'habite Élis, j'habite Rome."
Ibid., VIII, 10, 18–19.

28. *Ibid.*, IX, 291, 307.

29. "La vache" was published in 1837 in *Les Voix interieures*, now included in *Œuvres*, III, 289.

30. Binns, *A Life of Walt Whitman*, p. 295.

31. [The translations from *Also Sprach Zarathustra* in the text are based on that of Thomas Common.]
"Und du, mein erste Gefährte, gehab dich wohl! Gut begrub ich dich in deinem hohlen Baume, gut barg ich dich vor den Wölfen."
Prolog, Section 9.

32. "Wahrlich, durch hundert Seelen ging ich meinen Weg und durch hundert Wiegen und Geburtswehen. Manchen Abschied nahm ich schon, ich kenne die herzbrechenden letzten Stunden." Part II, ch. xxiv, "Auf den glückseligen Inseln."

33. "Hier sind Priester: und wenn es auch meine Feinde sind, geht mir still an ihnen vorüber und mit schlafendem Schwerte!
Auch unter ihnen sind Helden; . . .
Aber mein Blut ist mit dem ihren verwandt; und ich will mein Blut auch noch in dem ihren geehrt wissen—" Part II, ch. 26, "Von den Priestern."

34. "Seht ihr nie ein Segel über das Meer gehn, geründet und gebläht und zitternd vor dem Ungestüm des Windes?" Part II, ch. xxx, "Von den berühmten Weisen."

35. "Und diese Stuben und Kammern: können Männer da aus- und eingehen? Gemacht dünken sie mich für Seiden-Puppen; oder für Naschkatzen, die auch wohl an sich naschen lassen." Part III, ch. xlix, Section I, "Von der verkleinernden Tugend."

36. "—aus mächtiger Seele, zu welcher der hohe Leib gehört, der schöne, sieghafte, erquickliche, um den herum jedwedes Ding Spiegel wird:—der geschmeidige überredende Leib, der Tänzer, dessen Gleichniss und Auszug die selbst-lustige Seele ist. Solcher Leiber und Seelen Selbst-Lust heisst sich selber: 'Tugend.' Part III, ch. liv, Section 2, "Von den drei Bösen."

37. "—die umfänglichste Seele, welche am weitesten in sich

laufen und irren und schweifen kann; die nothwendigste, welche sich aus Lust in den Zufall stürzt:

Die seiende Seele, welche in's Werden taucht; die habende . . .

Die sich selber liebendste, in der alle Dinge ihr Strömen und Widerströmen und Ebbe und Fluth haben . . . Part III, ch. lvi, Section 19, "Von alten und neuen Tafeln."

38. "Wenn jene suchende Lust in mir ist, die nach Unentdecktem die Segel treibt, wenn eine Seefahrer-Lust in meiner Lust ist:

Wenn je mein Frohlocken rief: 'Die küste schwand—nun fiel mir die letzte Kette ab—

—das Grenzenlose braust um mich, weit hinaus glänzt mir Raum und Zeit, wohlan! wohlauf! altes Herz!' " Part II, ch. lx, Section 5, "Die Sieben Siegel."

39. "Oh Nachmittag meines Lebens! Oh Glück vor Abend! Oh Hafen auf hoher See! . . ." Part III, ch. xlvii, "Von der Seligkeit wider Willen."

40. "Wie ein Schiff, das in seine stillste Bucht einlief:—nun lehnt es sich an die Erde, der langen Reisen müde und der ungewissen Meere. [That is Whitman's "The Dismantled Ship."]

"Wie solch ein Schiff sich dem Lande anlegt, anschmiegt:—da genügt's, dass eine Spinne vom Lande her zu ihm ihren Faden spinnt. Keiner stärkeren Taue bedarf es da. [Whitman's "A Noiseless Patient Spider."]

"Wie solch ein müdes Schiff in der stillsten Bucht . . ."

.   .   .

"Oh Glück! Oh Glück! Willst du wohl singen, oh meine Seele? Du liegst im Grase. Aber das ist die heimliche feierliche Stunde, wo kein Hirt seine Flöte bläst . . ."

•   •   •

"Singe nicht, du Gras-Geflügel, oh meine Seele!"

Part IV, ch. lxx, "Mittags."

41. "The version is rather crude, at times even faulty, neither German nor English," wrote O. E. Lessing in "Whitman and the German Critics," *Journal of English and Germanic Philology*, IX (1910), 88.

42. *Ibid.*, p. 91.

43. Bertz, *Jahrbuch für sexuelle Zwischenstufen*, VII (1905), 153–287.

44. "Dr. Bertz," he wrote, "had the courage to face the truth and he had the scholarly equipment to prove the truth . . . he proved himself definitely the superior of any Whitman student on the

Continent." Lessing, "Whitman and the German Critics," *Journal of English and Germanic Philology,* IX (1910), 92–94.

45. Urning or Uranian, so called from Uranus (see Plato's *Symposium* and Friedrich W. von Ramdohrs *Venus Urania,* Leipzig, 1798) is the scholarly designation for the homosexual type used by the German Judge H. H. Ulrichs in 1864. The term was later deliberately favored by Hirschfeld and Carpenter and also occasionally by André Gide—though still not accepted in everyday speech.

46. "Was blüht ihr wieder, heitere Syringen, wollt ihr mir Grüsze eines Toten bringen? Er war mein Freund, er wars in Lust und Leiden, um dessen Stirn die Frühlingslocken hingen. Uns schwanden manche Stunden, jugendtolle: Das morgenrot noch hörte Becherklingen. Das nahm ein Ende, als die Schlachtenadler die Flügel breiteten auf Sturmesschwingen, und der Granaten unheilvolle Wolken in Lüften spielten gleich den Schmetterlingen, als unsere Fahnen, rot in Abendgluten Sieg kündend flatterten nach heiszem Ringen. Auf allen Höhen, in den Tälern, schliefen, die gar zu brüderlich den Tod empfingen, und unter ihnen fand in einem Garten, von fern herüber tönte Siegessingen, den Freund ich, abendkühl, wie schlafbezwungen, beschattet still von blühenden Syringen." Detlev von Liliencron, *Leben und Lüge,* in *Sämtliche Werke,* XV, 180. In the same volume are some hospital and battlefield sketches which are written in a terminology much like Whitman's in *Drum-Taps;* cf. pp. 138–39.

47. Cf. footnote 2 of this chapter, p. 347.

48. At the same time, we find in his erotic lyricism some strong erotomaniac traits paralleling those we found in Whitman. Whereas Whitman continually longed for new faces, new people, Dehmel longed for the unknown. *It is in itself a kind of erotic desire to meet new people*—quite like that of the American. And just as Whitman wished to "save," to "free," young men who crossed his path, Dehmel, in a seductive way, wanted to do the same for the young girls he met. "I am thy savior!" Young people will first become conscious, first recognize their own individuality when the poet has aroused them. This sentiment is identical in Whitman and Dehmel.

49. "Der Mut zum Pathos ist ja am Ende nichts als die bewusste Kraft eines religiösen Weltgefühls." Bab, *Dehmel,* p. 123.

50. ". . . mein Menschen-Bruder—oh, mein Erde-Bruder!

·   ·   ·

. . . trunken zwischen Blumen,
Mitten im Himmel;
in dem *Garten der Welt*."

Alfred Mombert in *Der himmelische Zecher*, quoted from
Alfred Soergel, *Dichtung und Dichter der Zeit*, 4th ed.
(Leipzig, 1927), p. 238. There is a discussion of Whitman,
pp. 665–69.

51. "Drücke aus, was du empfind'est, und du hast ihn (den
Rhythmus). Du greifst ihn, wenn you die Dinge greifst. Er ist allen
immanent. Auf alles übrige (Reim, Strofe, u.s.w.) verzichte."
Arno Holz, in *Revolution der Lyrik*, quoted from Soergel, *Dichtung
und Dichter*, 20th ed. (Leipzig, 1928), p. 683.

52.   "Schönes, grünes weiches Gras.
                 drin liege ich."
Arno Holz, *Phantasus*, Section II, Paragraph 6. Also quoted by
Soergel, *Dichtung und Dichter*, 20th ed., p. 686.

53.   "Sieben Billionen Jahre vor meiner Geburt
                 war ich eine Schwertlilie,"
Holz, *Phantasus*, Section I, Paragraph I. Also quoted by Soergel,
Dichtung und Dichter, 20th ed., p. 695.

54. "In neue wallende, werdende, wogende, brauende, brodelende,
          kreisende, Weltringe,
       wuchs, stieg, stiess, steilte, teilte, speilte, verglühte, zer-
       strömte, versprühte sich Flammenkugelmeteore,

                    .   .   .

       um sich schwingschluedernd meine dunkel mettalische, hal-
          kyonisch phallische, klingend kristallische Riesenblü-
          ten-Szepterkrone."
Holz, *Phantasus*, quoted from Soergel, *Dichtung und Dichter*,
20th ed., p. 697.

55. "Du bist nur Mittel! Du bist nicht Zweck!"
Arno Holz, *Der Blechschmiede*, letzte Ausgabe, 1924. Also quoted
in Soergel, *Dichtung und Dichter*, 20th ed., p. 701.

56. "Überall, überall bist du und nur du, und nichts ist ohne
dich und nichts auszer dir. Alles ist dein Bild und dein Gleichnis.
Du bist das liebe Mädel, das mich neulich erfreute. Du bist heute
blond, morgen schwarz, übermorgen braun, bist Mann und Weib,
Kind und Tier, alles, alles . . ." Johannes Schlaf, *Frühling*. Also
in Soergel, *Dichtung und Dichter*, 20th ed., p. 392.

57.   "Ich bin allein mit dir,
          und Vater, Mutter, Weib und Kind

> das alles bin ich dir."
>
> Heinrich Lersch, "Totenwacht," in *Deutschland*, 1917.

58. Heinrich Lersch, *Briefe und Gedichte aus dem Nachlass* (Hamburg, 1939), pp. 18, 20.

59. "Franzose du, von Brest, Bordeaux, Garonne,
> Ukrainer du, Kosak vom Ural Dnjestr und Don,
> Österreicher, Bulgare, Osmanen und Serben,
> Ihr alle im rasenden Strudel von Tat und von Sterben—
> Du Brite aus London, York, Manchester,
> Soldat, Kamerad, in Wahrheit Mitmensch und Bester—
> Amerikaner, aus den volkreichen Staaten der Freiheit . . ."
>
> Gerrit Engelke, "An die Soldaten des groszen Krieges," in *Rhythmus des neuen Europa.*

60. "Gefauch, Geklirr, Sirenen-Heulen, zischender Dampf, Gehämmer,
> Ozean-Riesen, Mammut-Schiffe wühlen aus dem Dunstdämmer,
> Rhode-Island-Dampfer, Hudson-Pinassen . . ."
>
> Engelke, *Rhythmus des neuen Europa*, "Sonne."

61. Franz Werfel, "Tag und Nacht Hymnus," in *Gedichte, Gesammelte Werke* (Berlin, 1929), I, 329–31.

62. From "Sterben im Walde," in *Der Weltfreund.*

63. "Sie verachten das Wort, sie ziehn die Niederlage dem Sieg vor, sie ergeben sich, sie lassen sich gefangennehmen

> .　　.　　.
>
> Denn furchtbar ist der Demütige, furchtbarer der Reine, der sich erkennt, und ein Tamerlan, wer sich aufgibt."
>
> Werfel, "Aus einem Denker" quoted in Soergel, *Dichtung und Dichter*, 20th ed., 333–34.

64. "Bist Du Neger, Akrobat, order ruhst Du noch in tiefer Mutterhut,

> .　　.　　.
>
> Das Gefühl von einsamen Harfenistinnen in Kurkapelen,
> Das Gefühl von schüchternen Gouvernanten im fremden Familienkreis,

Das Gefühl von Debutanten, die sich zitternd vor den
    Souffleurkasten stellen.
Ich lebte im Walde, hatte ein Bahnhofsamt,
Sasz gebeugt über Kassabücher und bediente ungeduldige
    Gäste.
Als Heizer stand ich vor Kesseln, das Antlitz grell über-
    flammt,
Und als Kuli asz ich Abfall und Küchenreste.

So gehöre ich Dir und allen!

             .   .   .

O, könnte es einmal geschehn,
Dasz wir uns, Bruder, in die Arme fallen!"
                Franz Werfel, "An der Leser," in *Weltfreund.*

65.   "Wir kommen wieder, wir kehren heim
       In dich, du gute Mutter unser."
                Franz Werfel, "Das Jenseits," in *Einander.*

66.   "Des Menschen Wesen bäumt sich
       Riesiger Phallus dir zu!"
                Franz Werfel, "Das Weib Hymnus."

67. Herman Hesse, *Narciss und Goldmund* (Berlin, 1930), ch.
V, p. 85.

68. Vald. Vedel, in the article on French literature in Julius
Clausen's *Illustreret Verdenslitteraturhistorie* (Copenhagen, 1898–
1901), 3 vols.

69. "Rien ne mourra de nous, rien n'est futile et vain:
     La vie se réalise a l'infini—"

70. Bazalgette also edited a translation of *Specimen Days* (Walt
Whitman, *Pages du Journal* (3d ed., Paris, Mercure de France,
1926). Like Schlaf, Bazalgette wrote about Verhaeren and published several moralistic philosophical works: *L'Esprit nouveau,*
1898; *Le Problème de l'avenir Latin,* 1903; etc. His last writing
about Whitman was *Le Poème-Evangile de Walt Whitman* (The
gospel poem of Walt Whitman, 1921), in which his idealization of
the Whitman figure was too much even for the prophets in America.
"It idealizes Whitman rather too much." Kennedy, *The Fight of a
Book for the World,* p. 50.

71. Paul Scott Mowrer, quoted in "Editorial Comment," *Poetry,*
I (December, 1912), 88.

72. "Ne souhaite pas, Nathanaël, trouver Dieu ailleurs que partout.

Chaque créature indique Dieu, aucune ne le révèle.

Dès que notre regard s'arrete à elle, chaque créature nous détourne de Dieu."

    André Gide, *Les Nourritures terrestres*, Livre I, Section 1.

73. "de marcher où s'ouvrait une route;

de repos, où l'ombre intitait;

de nage, au bord des eaux profondes,

d'amour ou de somneil ou bord de chaque lit . . ."

    Ibid., Livre I, Section 3.

74. "Des bateaux sont venus dans nos ports apporter les fruits mûrs de plages ignorées,

.   .   .

Allons! Allons!

Déchargez-les de leur faix un peu vite . . ."

    Ibid., Livre II, Section 1.

75. "Parfois, invisible de nuit, je suis resté penché vers un vitre, à longtemps regarde le coutume d'une maison.

.   .   .

Et mon coeur se gonfla du désir de l'emmener avec moi sur les routes!"   *Ibid.*, Livre IV, Section 1.

76. Monceaux de grains, je vous louerai—mes fermes sont closes! Céréales: blés roux; richesse dans l'attente; inestimable provision!   *Ibid.*, Livre V, Section 3.

77. Nathanaël, je t'enseignerai que toutes choses divinement naturelles.

Nathanaël, je te parlerai de tout.

    Ibid., Livre VI.

78. Since the Danish edition of this book appeared, S. A. Rhodes has discussed the Whitman-Gide relationship in "The Influence of Walt Whitman on André Gide," *Romanic Review*, XXXI (April, 1940), 156–71.

79. Like many of the older translators of Roman love poetry, Persian lyrics, or Michelangelo's sonnets—and for the same reasons—Bazalgette changed the sex in the poems at will; for example, he translated "the friend whose embracing arm awakes me," into "l'ami*e* qui . . ." etc.

80. ". . . dediant leur vie au coeur de l'univers," quoted by Edmond Estève, *Verhaeren* (Paris, 1928), p. 222; *Impressions* III.

81. ". . . m'insurger donc contre touts forme réglementée," quoted by Estève, *op. cit.*, p. 40; *Impressions* I, 15.

82. ". . . ce vers libre," si adéquat à l'âme contemporaine," quoted by Estève, *op. cit.*, p. 221; *Impressions* III.

83. "Il faut admirer tout pour s'exalter soi-même," in "La Vie."

84. "Je ne distingue plus le monde de moi-même," in "Autour de ma maison."

85. ". . . la joie des departs," from "Au retour," *Impressions* I, quoted by Estève, *op. cit.*, p. 96.

86. Je vous aime, gars des pays blonds, beaux conducteurs
    De hennissants et clairs et pesants attelages.

87. "Mes Yeux," in *Les Flammes hautes*, 1917. According to Estève, *op. cit.*, "Mes Yeux" was first published in the posthumous *Les Flammes hautes* in 1917, but it had already appeared in Stefan Zweig's famous translation: *Verhaeren Ausgewählte Gedichte*, zweite vermehrte Ausgabe (Leipzig, 1913), p. 169, with the title "An meine Augen."

88. "Il est certains de mes vers que je danserais.

.   .   .

    Les rythmes parcourent mes muscles et mes nerfs, du sommet de ma tête à la plante de mes pieds. C'est avec tout mon être que je fais un poème."

Impressions I, 29–30.

89. Jusqu'a mêler ton être au forces *unanimes*
    Pendant ce jour unique et cette heure sublime
    T'a fait semblable aux dieux!

90. "Toi . . .
    Je te donne ton âme, est-ce que tu en veux?"

Preface of *La Vie Unanime*

91. "Et des hommes, plus tard, n'ayant pas le livre,
    Sauront mystérieusement ce que j'ai dit."

Ibid.

92. "Etre un corps defait et presque dissous!"

93. "O splendeurs de la vie commune et du train-train ordinaire." The Countess of Noailles, in *Les Eblouissements* [The Glamorous] (1907), expressed a similar Whitmanesque world-yearning, in the character of a first-class passenger!

94. "Plaintes de la chair sans cesse modifiée,
    Voix, chuchotements irrépressibles des organes!"
    "Prologue."

95. "Viens dans mes bras, sur mes genoux,
    Viens dans mon coeur, viens dans mes vers, ma vie!"
    "Musique après une lecture."

96. "Restera-t-il dans ces poèmes quelques images
    De tant de pays, de tant de regards, et de tous ces visages?"
    "L'Innomable."

97. "Laissez-moi seul, laissez-moi seul avec la mer!
    Nous avons tant de choses à nous dire, n'est ce pas?"
    "A. M. Tournier de Zamble en lui envoyant d' 'Europe'," Section XI.

98. "Europe! Tu satisfais ces appétits sans bornes!"
    Ibid., Section III.

99. "Oh! tout apprendre, oh, tout savoir . . ."
    Ibid., Section II.

100. "Ou jouer pour la centième fois un rôle dans un théâtre!"
    Ibid., Section III.

101. J'ai des souvenirs de villes comme on a des souvenirs d'amour!
    Ibid., Section IX.

102. P. A. Rosenberg, *Erindringer* (Reminiscences) (Copenhagen, 1934), p. 150, a passage concerning Rudolf Schmidt and *For Ide og Virkelighed.*

103. Three fragments of Niels Møller's translation were later reprinted in the anthology *Fransk og engelsk Poesi fra 1450 til 1900*, edited by Christian Rimestad, Gyldendals Bibliotek Bd. 22 (Copenhagen, 1930), 227–30.

104. Johs. V. Jensen, *Myter*, Vol. III, 1914–1924. (Copenhagen, 1924).

105. An abstract of the translation of "Song of Myself" had already been printed by Vilh. Grønbech and Aage Marcus, eds. of Gyldendals Bibliotek Bd. 9, *Mystik og Mystikere* (Mysticism and Mystics), Copenhagen, 1930.

106. See memorial article on Elster in *Buster og Masker*, especially pp. 37–38.

107. See *supra*, p. 349, note 15.

108. Kristian Elster's son, the author and critic Kristian Elster the younger (*b.* 1881), in his *Illustreret norsk Litteraturhistorie*, Anden Udg. (Oslo, 1935), V, 141, discussing Obstfelder's *Pampas-*

Sange (Songs of the Pampas), has given a clue for such an examination which ought not to be ignored, much less unfulfilled. It will reveal still another suggestive line of association in the currents and a further link between the temperaments of world literature.

109. *Vandringer,* p. 107.

110. Besides Symonds's, Binns's, Carpenter's, and Selincourt's there was published a little book by John Bailey in 1926. He supports Bazalgette and Selincourt and tries to make Whitman into a "dressed-up lion."

111. Carpenter's admiration for Whitman reached such a point that he even had himself photographed in a Whitman pose, see especially the picture on p. 109 of *My Days and Dreams,* in which he appears as a composite of the 1854 and 1855 pictures of Whitman.

112. "She said as Well to Me," in *Look We Have Come Through* (New York, 1918).

113. From "Fish" in *Birds, Beasts and Flowers.* The italics are mine.

114. "Tortoise Shout," from *Tortoises* (New York, 1921).

115. Van Wyck Brooks, *America's Coming of Age* (New York, 1915), pp. 118–19.

116. Perry, *The American Spirit in Literature,* p. 205.

Bibliography

EDITIONS OF WHITMAN'S WORKS

Leaves of Grass. Brooklyn, 1855.

Leaves of Grass. Brooklyn, 1856.

Leaves of Grass. Boston, 1860–61.

Leaves of Grass. New York, 1867.

Democratic Vistas. Washington, 1871.

Two Rivulets. Camden, 1876.

Leaves of Grass. Boston, 1881.

Specimen Days and Collect. Philadelphia, 1882–83.

November Boughs. Philadelphia, 1888.

Complete Poems and Prose of Walt Whitman, 1855–1888. Philadelphia, 1888.

Leaves of Grass, with Sands at Seventy, and A Backward Glance o'er Travel'd Roads. Philadelphia, 1889.

Leaves of Grass. Philadelphia, 1891–92.

Complete Prose Works. Philadelphia, 1892.

The Complete Writings of Walt Whitman; ed. by Richard Maurice Bucke, Thomas B. Harned, and Horace L. Traubel. 10 vols. New York, 1902.

Calamus [Letters to Peter Doyle]; ed. by Richard Maurice Bucke. Boston, 1897.

The Letters of Anne Gilchrist and Walt Whitman; ed. by Thomas B. Harned. New York, 1918.

The Gathering of the Forces; ed. by Cleveland Rodgers and John Black. 2 vols. New York, 1920.

The Uncollected Poetry and Prose of Walt Whitman; ed. by Emory Holloway. 2 vols. New York, 1921.

Walt Whitmans Werk, ausgewählt; übertragen und eingeleitet von Hans Reisiger. 2 vols. Berlin, 1922.

Walt Whitman's Workshop, a Collection of Unpublished Manuscripts, ed. by Clifton Joseph Furness. Cambridge, Mass., 1928.

BIOGRAPHIES

Barrus, Clara, *Whitman and Burroughs;* Comrades. Boston, 1931.

Bazalgette, Léon, *Walt Whitman; l'homme et son œuvre.* Paris, 1908.

Bertz, Eduard, *Walt Whitman: ein Charakterbild.* Berlin, 1905. [The earlier essay published in *Jahrbuch für sexuelle Zwischenstufen* was re-printed separately.]

Binns, Henry Bryan, *A Life of Walt Whitman.* London, 1905.

Burroughs, John, *Notes on Walt Whitman as Poet and Person.* New York, 1867.

Carpenter, Edward, *Days with Walt Whitman; with some Notes on His Life and Work.* London, 1906.

Catel, Jean, *Rythme et langage dans les "Leaves of Grass."* Paris, 1930.

—— *Walt Whitman; la naissance du poète.* Paris, 1929.

Holloway, Emory, *Walt Whitman; an Interpretation in Narrative.* New York, 1926.

In Re Walt Whitman, edited by Horace Traubel, Richard Maurice Bucke, and Thomas B. Harned. Philadelphia, 1893.

Johnston, John, and J. W. Wallace, *Visits to Walt Whitman in 1890–91 by Two Lancashire Friends.* London, 1917; New York, 1918.

Kennedy, William Sloane, *The Fight of a Book for the World; a Companion Volume to Leaves of Grass.* New York, 1926.

—— *Reminiscences of Walt Whitman.* London, 1896.

Perry, Bliss, *Walt Whitman; His Life and Works.* London, 1906.

Symonds, John Addington, *Walt Whitman; a Study.* London, 1893.

Traubel, Horace, *With Walt Whitman in Camden.* 3 vols. Boston, 1906; New York, 1908; New York, 1914.

Trowbridge, John Townsend, *My Own Story; with Recollections of Noted Persons.* Boston, 1903.

HISTORY OF AMERICAN LITERATURE

Cambridge History of American Literature, The. 4 vols. New York, 1917–21.

WHITMAN'S AMERICA AND HIS CONTEMPORARIES

Blake, William, *Poetical Works.* Oxford, 1925.

Bremer, Fredrika, *Hemmen i den nya Verlden.* 3 vols. Stockholm, 1853–54.

—— *The Homes of the New World; Impressions of America*, tr. by Mary Howitt. 3 vols. London, 1853.

Bryant, William Cullen, *Poetical Works*. Boston, 1883.

Carlyle, Thomas, *Works*. 13 vols. London, 1889.

Cooper, James Fenimore, *Excursion to Switzerland*. Paris, 1838.

Dickens, Charles, *American Notes*. 2 vols. London, 1892.

Emerson, Ralph Waldo. *Writings*. 8 vols. Boston, 1855–65.

Emerson-Carlyle Correspondence, The. 2 vols. London, 1883.

Holmes, Oliver Wendell, *Writings*. 13 vols. Boston, 1892.

Lenau, Nicolas, *Sämtliche Werke und Briefe*, herausgabe von Eduard Castle. 6 vols. Leipzig, 1910–23.

Lowell, James Russell, *Writings*. 9 vols. Boston, 1891.

Marryat, Frederick, *Diary in America*. 3 vols. London, 1839.

Martineau, Harriet, *Society in America*. 3 vols. London, 1837.

Raumer, Frederic von, *Die Vereinigten Staaten von Nordamerika*. 2 vols. Leipzig, 1845.

Sealsfield, Charles, *Lebensbilder aus der westlichen Hemisphäre*. 4 vols. Stuttgart, 1835.

Thoreau, Henry David, *Familiar Letters*, Boston, 1894.

Tocqueville, Alexis de, *De la démocratie en Amérique*. 2 vols. 13th ed. Paris, 1850.

Trollope, Frances, *Domestic Manners of the Americans*. 2 vols. London, 1832.

RELIGION, MYSTICISM, PSYCHOLOGY

Arseniew, Nikolai Sergeyevich von, *Die russiche Literatur der Neuzeit und Gegenwart*. Mainz, 1929.

Bab, Julius, *Dehmel*. Leipzig, 1926.

Baggesen, Jens, *Danske Vaerker*. 12 vols. Copenhagen, 1827–32.

Bhavadgita, oversat af Poul Tuxen. Copenhagen, 1920.

Bucke, Richard Maurice, *The Cosmic Consciousness; a Study in the Evolution of the Human Mind*. New York, c. 1923.

Bing, Just, *Verdens-Litteraturhistorie; Grunnlinjer og Hovedvaerker*. [History of World Literature; Foundations and Masterpieces.] 3 vols. Oslo, 1928–34.

Brix, Hans, Danmarks Digtere [Denmark's Poetry]. Copenhagen, 1925.

Brooks, Van Wyck, *America's Coming of Age*. New York, 1915.

Duncan, Isidora, *My Life*. London, 1928.

Eckhoff, Lorentz, *Paul Verlaine og Symbolismen*. Christiania, 1923.

Ellinger, Georg, *Angelus Silesius*. Breslau, 1927.

Ellis, Havelock, *The New Spirit*. 4th ed. London, 1926.

Forst-Battaglia, Otto, *Die franzöische Literatur der Gegenwart*. Wiesbaden, 1928.

Gran, Gerhard, *Norsk Aandsliv i 100 Aar* [Norwegian Spiritual Life for 100 Years].

Grønbech, Wilhelm, and Aage Marcus, *Mystik og Mystikere* [Mysticism and Mystics]. Copenhagen, 1930.

Huch, Ricarda, *Ausbreitung und Verfall der Romantik*. Leipzig, 1902. [Republished as Vol. II of *Die Romantik* in 1920.]

Hugo, Victor, *Œuvres completes*. Ed. definitive. 48 vols. Paris, 1880–83.

James, William, *Religiøse Erfaringer;* pas Dansk ved Edv. Lehmann. 3d ed. Copenhagen.

Jesaja, oversat af Eduard Brandes. Copenhagen, 1902.

Lamm, Martin, *Swedenborg*. Stockholm.

Laotse, *Taoteking*, oversat af Victor Dantzer. Copenhagen, 1924.

Lawrence, D. H., *Studies in Classic American Literature*. London, 1924.

Liliencron, Detlev von, *Sämtliche Werke*. 15 vols. Leipzig, 1904–8.

Murry, J. Middleton, *Son of Woman* [D. H. Lawrence]. London, 1931.

Ørsted, H. C. *Aanden in Naturen* [The Soul in Nature]. 3d ed. Copenhagen, 1856.

Perry, Bliss, *The American Spirit in Literature*. New York, 1920.

Rimestad, Chr., *Belgiens store Digtere* [Great Belgian Poets]. Copenhagen, 1915.

Rose, William and Isaacs, Jacob, *Contemporary Movements in European Literature*. New York, 1929.

Rumi, *Mesnevi;* übersetzt von Fr. Rosen. Munich, 1913.

Schloezer, Boris de, *Rosanow*. Paris, 1929.

Schmidt, Julian, *Geschichte der deutschen Literatur seit Lessings Tod*. 4th ed. 3 vols. Leipzig, 1858.

Sibbern, F. C., *Gabrielis Breve*. 5th ed. Copenhagen, 1893.

Simonsen, Konrad, *Goethes Naturfølelse* [Goethe's Feeling for Nature]. Copenhagen, 1909.

Soergel, Albert, *Dichtung und Dichter der Zeit*. 2 vols. Leipzig, 1928.

Stolpe, Sven, *Livsdyrkare* [Worship of Life]. Stockholm, 1931.

Swinburne, Charles Algernon. *William Blake*. London, 1868.

Troye, Vilhelm, *Wergeland og hans Digtning* [Wergeland and His Work]. Christiania, 1908.

Vedel, Valdemar, *Svensk Romantik* [Swedish Romanticism]. Copenhagen, 1894.

Wergeland, *Samlede Skrifter* [Collected Works]. 9 vols. Christiania, 1852–57.

Wild, Frederich, *Die englische Literatur der Gegenwart*. Wiesbaden, 1928.

Index

Aber die Liebe (R. Dehmel), 282
Abolitionists, 20, 21, 22, 24, 56, 61, 224
"Abraham Lincoln" (R. H. Stoddard), 204
"Address to the Humanity in Man" (Wergeland), 262
Adhesiveness: a favorite Whitman expression, 112; first used in "Poem of the Road," 132, 168; defined in *Democratic Vistas,* 212, 300
"Adieu to a Soldier" (Whitman), 226
"After Supper and Talk" (Whitman), 245
Ahnung und Gegenwart (J. Eichendorff), 16
Alboni, Marietta, 62, 334, n. 76
Alcott, Bronson, 21, 22, 129, 184, 240
Allen, E. M., 188
"All Is Truth" (Whitman), 177
Almquist, Carl Jonas Love, 85, 258, 259-60, 265
Amativeness: as defined in *Democratic Vistas,* 212
America: at time of Fredrika Bremer's visit, 15 ff.; varying European concepts of, 17 ff.; political issues, 24 f.; religious sects, 26; "Mistress" as symbol for, 205; *Democratic Vistas* an indictment of, 210, 220 f.
"American Feuillage" (Whitman), 171
American Institute Exposition, 224
American literature: Whitman as first representative of, 6 f.; literary milieu of the 1850s, 16 ff.; criticism of native land, 17; anti-puritan authors influenced by Whitman, 156
American Notes (Dickens), 18, 20
American personality: as depicted by Whitman, 7
American Scholar (Emerson), 20, cited, 72

American Spirit in Literature, The (B. Perry), 327
America's Coming of Age (Brooks), 327
Amerikanische Antologie (A. Strodtmann), 276
Amerikanske Forhold (K. Janson), 315
"An den Leser" (Werfel), cited, 290
Andersen, Hans, 168, 213; similarities between Whitman and, 46, 47, 67, 258, 259, 264, 266-68, 307
Anderson, Sherwood, 87, 318, 325, 327
"Angel of Tears, The" (Whitman), 47, 48
Angelus Silesius, 122; mystic temperament, 249ff., 275; quoted, 347-48, n. 2
Antlitz der Städte, Das (A. T. Wegner), 286
Apollinaire, Guillaume, 294
"Army on the March, An" (Whitman), 196
Arneberg, Per, 316
Arnim, Elizabeth, von, *see* Bettina
Arnold, Sir Edwin, 235
Arnold, Matthew, quoted, 209, 317, 345, n. 129
"As a Strong Bird on Pinions Free" (Whitman), 224, 225
"Ashes of Soldiers" (Whitman), 206
Ashton, Hubley, 187, 209
"As I Ebb'd with the Ocean of Life" (Whitman), 46, 145; mother motif, 149; reference to his father, 150, 341, n. 69
"As I Lay with My Head in Your Lap, Camerado" (Whitman), 192, 207
"As I Pondered in Silence" (Whitman), 225
"As I Sit Writing Here" (Whitman), 245

Asklund, Erik, 313
"Assurances" (Whitman), 136
"As the Time Draws Nigh" (Whitman), 177
"As They Draw to a Close" (Whitman), 225
"As Toilsome I Wander'd" (Whitman), 186, 197
As We Were (E. F. Benson), 317
Atlantic Monthly (periodical), 145
Augustnatter (S. Mathiesen), 315
Aus fremden Zungen (anthology), 277
Autumn Leaves (Hugo), 268, 269

Baal Schem (Rabbi), 251
Bab, Julius, quoted, 282
"Backward Glance o'er Travel'd Roads, A" (Whitman), 75, 222, 245, 246
Baggesen, Jens, 254, 307, 348, n. 8
Balmont, Konstantin, 305
Bancroft, George, 22
"Bardic Symbols" (Whitman), 145, 149
"Barlow's Poem on America" (C. Hauch), 306
Barrus, Clara, 11; quoted, 53-54, 104, quoted, 188, 234, 239, quoted, 344, n. 114
Bazalgette, Léon, 5, 45, 53; interpretation of *Calamus,* 159; attempt to present Whitman as prophet and reformer, 169; quoted, 209; quoted, 224, 239, 295, 301, 304; his contributions to Whitman's French reputation, 293, 294, 313, 355, n. 70
"Beat, Beat Drums" (Whitman), 191
Beaver, Joseph, 334, n. 88
Beecher, Henry Ward, 61, 62; visits Whitman, 128
Benson, E. F., 317
Bentzon, T., 219
Bergstedt, Harald, 310, 311
Berntsen, Aage, 310
Bertz, Eduard, 37; quoted, 169; Whitman studies, 275, 278-79
"Bervance, or Father and Son" (Whitman), 46
Bettina (Elizabeth von Arnim), similarity between Whitman and, 264 f.
Bettini (opera singer), 62, 64
Bhagavadgita, 129, 249, 250, 318
Bing, Just, quoted, 10, 271
Binns, Henry Bryan, 4; quoted, 47, 49-50, 52, 54, quoted, 67-68, 75, 143, 179,

213; interpretation of *Calamus,* 159; attempt to present Whitman as prophet and reformer, 169, quoted, 224, 236, 239, 269, 270, 278; quoted, 333, n. 47
Birds and Poets (Burroughs), 217
Birds, Beasts and Flowers (D. H. Lawrence), 321, 322
"Bivouac on a Mountainside" (Whitman), 196
Bjely, André, 305
Bjerke, Andre, 316
Bjørnson, Bjørnstjerne, 170; quoted, 219; interest in Whitman, 307, 314
Black, John, 5
Blake, William, 10, 122, 218, 236; mystic temperament, 249, 253; similarities with Whitman, 255 f., 257, 263, 268, 297, 317
Blanc, Thérèse, *see* Bentzon, T.
Blechschmeide, Der (A. Holz), 285
Blémont, Emile, 292
Blomberg, Erik, 314
Bockgesang (Werfel), 291
Böhme, Jacob, 8, 59, 73, 251, 275
Böcklin, I. P., 15
Bønnelycke, Emil, 310
Booth, Junius Brutus: admired by Whitman, 40; as an orator, 107
Borberg, Svend, 310
"Boston Ballad, A" (Whitman), 82, 83, 336, n. 7
Boston Radical, 218
Boston Slave Delivery, 25
Boyd, Ernest, quoted, 235
"Boy Lover, The" (Whitman), 46
Bramakrisna (Indian mystic), 250
Brandes, Georg, quoted, 3, 10, 13, 297; indifference to Whitman, 308, 329, n. 2
Bredere Vinger (H. Bergstedt), 310
Bremer, Fredrika: visits America, 14 f.; introduction to American literature, 22; interest in slave question and in religious sects, 25, 26; describes Quakers, 32, 39; her novels reviewed by Whitman, 49; zoological and botanical observations made in South, 56, 58; hears Henry Ward Beecher, 61-62, 172, 222, 257
Brenton, James S., 42
Brenton, Orvetta Hall, quoted, 42-43
Brinton, D. G., 38
British Society of Sex Psychology, 244
Brix, Hans, quoted, 267

"Broad-Axe Poem" (Whitman), 135, 136, 139
Broadway Journal (newspaper), 45
"Broadway Pageant" (Whitman), 190
Brook Farm, 21
Brooklyn: Whitman's early impressions of, 35 f.
"Brooklyniana" (Whitman), 36, 38, 40, 184
Brooks, Van Wyck, quoted, 327
"Brother of All, with Generous Hand" (Whitman), 226
Bryant, William Cullen, 19, 22, 40, 42, 45, 58, 66, 132, 233, 234, 239
Buchanan, James, 179
Buchanan, R. W., 210, 233
Bucke, Richard Maurice, 4, 9, 60, 61, 176, 182, 211, 213, 234; belief in Whitman, 235, 240, 241, 244
Bull Run, Battle of, 184
"Bunch Poem" (Whitman), 137 f.
Burns, Robert, 65, 66
Burrit, Elihu, 22
Burroughs, John, 4, 11; quoted, 53, 54, 56, 71; quoted, 75; reads "Out of the Cradle," 151; quoted, 183, 187, 235; Whitman's influence on, 188 f.; interest in Peter Doyle, 211, 217, 219, 231; quoted, 235, 240, 247, 308
Buss, Kate, quoted, 239
Buster og Masker (R. Schmidt), 224-25, 308
Butenschön, Andreas, 313
"By Blue Ontario's Shore" (Whitman), 80, 137, 140, 154; poem's history, 215 f.; discordant elements, 217; similarity to *Democratic Vistas,* 221 ff.

Cahiers d'André Walther, Les (Gide), 295
Calamus (Whitman), 4; erotic interpretation, 52-53, 55, 79; germs in 1855 "Song of Myself," 10, 138; appearance in third edition of *Leaves of Grass,* 153; misunderstood, 157; a collection of love poems, 158, 159; offers clues for understanding Whitman, 161; deleted poems quoted, 162-64; central nervous system of *Leaves of Grass;* 167, 168, 170, 182; similar idea in *Drum-Taps,* 191; scantily represented in Schlaf's German edition, but complete in Gide's

French edition, 277; ideas re-appear in Edward Carpenter's work, 320
Calamus (Whitman's letters to Peter Doyle), 211
Calder, Ellen, quoted, 213
Calhoun, John Caldwell, 24, 185
"Calhoun's Monument," 185
Camden, New Jersey, 231
Camerado: a favorite Whitman expression, 112
"Camps of Green" (Whitman), 206
Caresses, Les (J. Richepin), 294
Carlyle, Thomas, 8, 49; influence on Whitman, 68 f., 73; criticisms of American democracy, 220 f., 222, 224, 236, 239, 275, 318
Carnegie, Andrew, 244
"Carol of Harvest for 1867" (Whitman), 226
Carpenter, The (W. D. O'Connor), 187, 217
Carpenter, Edward, 5; quoted, 9, 75, 50, 53, 79, 165, 235, 242-44; visits Whitman, 234, 280; pupil of Whitman, 317-21, 323, 324; friend of Vilhelm Troye, 349, n. 15
Catalogues: in "Song of Myself," 97, 101 ff.; in second edition of *Leaves of Grass,* 135-36; in third edition, 155; in *Chants Democratic,* 171; in "The Lady of Ships," 192
Catel, Jean, 11, 40, 51; quoted, 55, 119, 161; profound Whitman student, 294, 336, n. 19, 338, n. 42
Cather, Willa, 327
"Cavalry Crossing a Ford" (Whitman), 196
"Centenarian's Story, The" (Whitman), 195
Channing, H. W., 21
Channing, W. E., 20, 49, 68, 140
Chanson d'Eve (Lerberghe), 300
Chansons des queux (J. Richepin), 294
"Chanting the Square Deific" (Whitman), 207-8
Chants Communal (H. Traubel), 235
Chants de crépuscule, Les (Hugo), 268
Chants de la pluie et du soleil (H. Rebell), 294
Chants Democratic (Whitman), 171-73, 175; use of term "mistress," 205
Chassidism, 251
Chateaubriand, F. R., 16
Cherubinische Wandersmann (Angelus Silesius), 250

Children of Adam (Whitman), 54, 55, 79, 112; foreshadowed, 120, 123, 137, 153; appearance in third edition of *Leaves of Grass;* impersonal quality of, 156, 157, 158; theme and motif, 160 f., 213; omitted in English editions, 218, 262, 294, 316-17; a pattern for D. H. Lawrence, 321; translated in full in Schlaf's German edition, 277

"Child and the Profligate, The" (Whitman), 46

"Child's Reminiscence, A" (Whitman), 145

"Circles" (Emerson), 73

Civil War: its significance to Whitman, 181, 191

Clare, Ada, 142

Clarke, Edward, 38

"Clarté de vie" (Vielé-Griffin), 293

Classical literature, 253 f.

Claudel, Paul, 106

Clay, Henry, 25

Clements, S. E., 38

Coleridge, Samuel Taylor, 16, 85

Columbus, Christopher, 228, 229, 232

"Come Lovely and Soothing Death" (Whitman), 202

"Come up from the Fields Father" (Whitman), 38, 197; cited, 199-200

Communism, 15

"Community of Fruitlands," 21

Compagnons (Duhamel), 301

Compromise of 1850: 15, 25

Consuelo (G. Sand), 66

Conservator, The (periodical), 235

Contemplations, Les (Hugo), 268

Contemporary literature: an "era of affirmations," 269; Whitman's influence on, 275-327; in Germany, 275-92; in France, 292-304; in Italy, 304; in Spain and Russia, 305; in Denmark, 306-13; in Sweden and Norway, 313-16; in England, 316 ff.; *see also under names of countries, e.g.,* Danish literature

Conway, Moncure D., quoted, 53; visits Whitman, 128-30; 176; writes about poet, 210, 234

Cooper, James Fenimore, 6, 17, 18, 19, 28, 38, 40, 66, 98, 325

Copains, Les (Romains), 300

Corydon (Gide), 297

Cosmic consciousness: of Whitman, 9, 59-60; in Bucke's and Werfel's writings, 60-61; in "Song of Myself," 85; a unity of body and soul, 113, 114; in Wergeland's writing, 264

Creation, Man, and Messiah (Wergeland), 263

Crescent, The (New Orleans newspaper), 51 f., 55, 57

Criterion (periodical), 127

Critic (periodical), 128

"Crossing Brooklyn Ferry" (Whitman), 79, 132, 133, 259

Crystal Palace Fair (1853), 61

Curtis, George William, quoted, 233

Cushman, Charlotte, 23

Daily Eagle (Brooklyn newspaper), 5, 45, 48, 65

"Dalliance of the Eagles, The" (Whitman), 73, 241, 262

Danish literature: recognition of Whitman, 219; translation of Democratic Vistas, 220; background of discovery of Whitman, 306; kinship between Danish and German ideas, 307

D'Annunzio, Gabriele, 304

"Darest Thou Now, O Soul" (Whitman), 225

Dark Laughter (S. Anderson), 318

Das absolute Individuum (J. Schlaf), 286

Days with Walt Whitman (E. Carpenter), 5; cited, 53, 79; descriptions of Whitman's old age, 242-44

Death: as the culmination, 92; as theme of "Out of the Cradle," 145 f., 159; in *Calamus* poems, 159; underlying theme in *Drum-Taps,* 201; "Come Lovely and Soothing Death," 202; D. H. Lawrence's recognition of theme in *Leaves of Grass,* 325

"Death Carol" (Whitman), 203

"Death in the Schoolroom" (Whitman), 45

"Death of Lincoln, The" (Whitman), 308

"Death of the Nature Lover, The" (Whitman), 46

Debris (Whitman), 172

Dehmel, Richard, 167, 281 f., 286, 290, 297, 298, 310, 352, n. 48

De la démocratique en Amérique (De Tocqueville), 18

Demian (Hesse), 291

Democracy, 7; De Tocqueville's study,

18, 19; Whitman's interest in transcendental, pantheistic democracy, 84; erotic freedom, 156; as conceived by Whitman, 191, 220 ff.; in eighteenth century, 254

"Democracy" (Whitman), 210

Democratic Review (periodical), 45

Democratic Vistas (Whitman), 7, 168, 205; as an indictment of America, 210, 215; "adhesiveness" defined, 212; a reply to Carlyle, 220; Danish translation, 220, 308; oratorical character, 223; added as supplement to sixth edition of *Leaves of Grass*, 233, 259

Demokratiske Fremblik (Whitman: Schmidt), 220, 308, 314

De rerum natura (Lucretius), 253

Desjardins, Paul, 292

De Tocqueville, Alexis, 18, 19; belief in the future of American intellectual life, 27, 28; quoted, 28, 68, 83, 172, 222

Deutschland (H. Lersch), 287

Dial, The (periodical), 21

Diary in America (F. Marryat), 18, 58; quoted, 330, n. 6 and n. 19

Dickens, Charles, 18; quoted, 184-85, 20, 23, 26, 58, 142; quoted, 330, n. 8

Die Vereinigten Staates von Nordamerika (F. von Raumer), 19

"Dignity of Labor, The" (Almquist), 259

Digte (S. Obstfelder), 316

Digte (Whitman: Jensen and Gelsted), 309

Dikter mellan Djur och Gud (A. Lundkvist), 314

"Dismantled Ship, The" (Whitman), 245

Divine average, the, 7, 172

Divinity: Whitman's identification with, 89 f.

Domestic Manners of the Americans (F. Trollope), 18

Donaldson, Thomas, 234

Doolittle, Hilda, 321

"Dough-Face Song" (Whitman), 58

Dowden, Edward, 210, 218, 220, 235

Doyle, Peter, 4, 211 f.; quoted, 213; Whitman's separation from, 231, 232, 345, n. 133

Dreams: succession of images in "The Sleepers," 100

"Dresser, The" (Whitman), 195, 196

Duhamel, Georges, 189, 301, 304

Duncan, Isadora, quoted, 274

Eckhoff, Lorentz, 293; quoted, 299

Ecrivains étrangers (T. de Wyzewa), 292

Eddy, Mary Baker, 6

Efteraar (N. Møller), 308

Efterlade Breve af Gabrieli (F. C. Sibbern), 258

Ehrenstein, Albert, 286

Eichendorff, Josef, 16

"Eidólons" (Whitman), 233

"Eighteen-Sixty-One" (Whitman), 191

Einander (Werfel), 290

"Ein anderes" (Werfel), 290

Eldridge, Charles, 184, 187, 189

"Elemental Drift" (Whitman), 149

Eliot, T. S., 321

"Elizabeth" (ship), 35

Ellis, Havelock, 198, 280

Elster, Kristian, 314

Emerson, Ralph Waldo, 8, 16; as a Transcendentalist, 20, 21; Fredrika Bremer's opinion of, 22, 23, 28; quoted, 29, 34, 48; lectures, 49, 58; influence on Whitman, 71 ff.; pantheistic creed, 73; wavering attitude, 77 f., 79, 80, 120, 128, 130; letter to Whitman, 126-27; quote, 129; letter and copy of *Leaves of Grass* from Whitman, 139-40, 141; comment on Whitman's Bohemianism, 142; conversation with Whitman, 151, 184, 188; Whitman's last visit to, 240, 250, 257, 269, 271, 279, 315, 317, 318; quoted, 338, n. 43 and 339, n. 47

Ende, Amalia von, 284

Enfans d'Adam see *Children of Adam*

Engelke, Gerrit, 286, 288

English language: Whitman's eulogy of, 82

English literature: early interest in Whitman, 210; first English edition of *Leaves of Grass*, 217, 218; Whitman's influence in England, 316 ff.

"Epic of the Worm, The" (Hugo), cited, 268, 269

Epictetus, 65

"Eris, a Spirit Record" (Whitman), 47, 48

Eroticism: in Whitman's personality and poetry, 51; New Orleans period, 52 ff.; idea of identity, 117; fusion of erotic and pantheistic emotions in

Eroticism (*Continued*)
"Bunch Poem," 137; the sea as a tragic motif in "Out of the Cradle," 145; erotic themes enumerated in "From Pent-up Aching Rivers," 155; erotic freedom necessary in Whitman's plan for democracy, 156; eroticism merges with religious emotion, 162; its influence on his interpretation of the world, 165; conflicting emotions in the third edition of *Leaves of Grass,* 166; instability of his emotional attachments, 167

Essays (Emerson), 16, 73

"Ethiopia Saluting the Colors" (Whitman), 226

Ettlinger, Thea, 277

"Europe . . ." (Whitman), 58, 83

European literature: its influence on early American writers, 7; early critical reactions to Whitman, 10; interest in America reflected in writings of romantics, 16 f.; attitude of English writers toward America, 17; travel books, 17 f.; early recognition of *Leaves of Grass,* 78; fourth edition marks beginning of world interest, 217 f.; *see also* Contemporary literature *and under names of individual countries, e.g.,* Danish literature

Evangeline (Longfellow), 22, 29

Evening Post (New York newspaper), 45, 58

Evolution, theory of: accepted by Whitman, 67, 68

"Excelsior" (Whitman), 136

Excursions in Switzerland (J. F. Cooper), 19

"Experimental communities," 15, 259

Fable for Critics, A (Lowell), 16, 24, 28, 29

Fabulet, Louis, 297

"Faith Poem" (Whitman), 136

Fallen Leaves (V. Rosanow), 305

"Fame's Vanity" (Whitman), 44, 46

Fancies at Navesink (Whitman), 308

"Fantasia of the Unconscious" (D. H. Lawrence), 324

Father, the: as a negative principle in Whitman's poetry, 38; in a short story by Whitman, 46; kinship with, expressed in "As I Ebb'd with the Ocean of Life," 150; a negative principle in "Song of the Banner at Day-Break," 193; father-image absent in Andersen's stories, 268; *see also* Mother, the

Faust (Goethe), 17, 69, 92

Federn, Karl, 277, 278

Feminine point of view, in first edition of *Leaves of Grass,* 119; key to feminine emotion provided by Whitman, 138, 160; effeminate traits in Whitman's erotic psychology, 162; feminine traits apparent in his nursing talents, 187

Feuilles d'herbe (Whitman), 293

Fight of a Book for the World, The (W. S. Kennedy), 115; quoted, 176

Figuière, Eugène, 294

Fjell, Kai, 316

"Flood of Years" (W. C. Bryant), 132

Flügel der nike (Unruh), 301

Fodrejse fra Holmens Kanal til Østpynten af Amager (Andersen), 266

Foglie di erba (Whitman: Gamberale), 304

Forces tumulteuses, Les (Verhaeren), 298

For Idé og Virkelighed (Danish periodical), 219, 307, 314

Fortnightly Review (English periodical), 129, 210, 317

Fort, Paul, 300

"For You, O Democracy" (Whitman), 158, 170, 191

Fourierism, in America, 17

Four Zoa or Vala, The (Blake), 256

Fowler and Wells's Bookshop and Phrenological Institute, 49, 75, 130, 140

Fox, George, 8, 31, 70, 244

Fra begge Halvkugler (R. Schmidt), 308

Fra det moderne Amerikas Aandsliv (K. Hamsun), 104, 315

Francis Rose (S. Mathiesen), 315

Franklin Evans (Whitman), 40, 44; its literary failure, 47

Freeman, The (newspaper), 58

Free Soil party, 24

Free verse: its effective introduction by Whitman, 9; Emerson's experiments in, 74; Whitman's construction of his poetry, 106; his own organically developed style, 204; Lucretius's treatment of hexameter, 253; in German lyric poetry, 283; *see also* Vers-librists

Freiligrath, Ferdinand: 78; inaugurates Whitman movement in Germany, 219, 276, 278

French literature: influence of Whitman on, 9; sympathetic interpretations of America, 18; first essay on Whitman, 219; Whitman's influence on, 292-304; Bazalgette's translation, *Feuilles d'herbe,* 293; Unanimists, 300 f.

Frend, Grace, 239

Fried, Leon, quoted, 314

"Friendship" (Emerson), 73

"From Pent-up Aching Rivers" (Whitman), introductory poem for *Children of Adam,* 153; translated into French by Gide, 297

"From the Desk of a Schoolmaster" (Whitman), 42

Frühling, Der (J. Schlaf), 285

"Full of Life Now!" (Whitman), 178

Fuller, Margaret, 16; advocate of Women's Rights movement, 21; rumors about, 23, 24, 35; Whitman's approval of, 49, 66, 142

Fulles d'herba (Whitman: Montolio), 305

Furness, Clifton J., 11, 242, 243

Gabrielis Breve (F. C. Sibbern), 59, 258

Galaxy, The (periodical), 211

Gamberale, Luigi, 304

García Lorca, Federigo, 305, 311, 313

Garland, Hamlin, 233

Garrison, William Lloyd, 20, 22, 61

Gathering of the Forces (C. Rodgers and J. Black), 5, 48, 51

Gelsted, Otto, 170, 309, 310

"Genesis" (Swinburne), 317

German literature: Whitman's influence on, 9, 275-92; sympathetic interpretations of America, 18; beginning of Whitman appreciation, 219; early period of his influence, 275-76; First World War period, 276-91; translations of Whitman, 276 ff.; Reisiger's edition, 278; books on Whitman, 278 f.; Whitman's literary influence on German poetry, 280 ff.; on other German literature, 291-92

Geschichte der nordamericanischen Literatur (L. Kellner), 10

Gide, André: as a disciple of Whitman, 96; translator of Whitman, 293-94, 297; influenced by Whitman, 295 ff.; 298; 299; 302, 304

Gilchrist, Alexander, 236

Gilchrist, Anne, 75, 214; quoted, 218; friendship for Whitman, 236-39

Gissing, George, 235, 279

Gleanings in Europe (J. F. Cooper), 17

Glöd (A. Lundkvist), 313

Glühende, Der (A. Mombert), 283

Goethe, Johan Wolfgang von: 9, 11; quoted, 16, 17, 27, 34, 67, 68, 69; belief in the future, 70, 74; on metamorphosis of plants, 122, 235; Whitman's ideas of nature similar to, 252; pantheism of, 253f., 257, 258, 260, 264, 265, 271, 284, 292, 298, 306

Gold: discovery of, 16

Gómez de la Serna, Ramón, 302

Good-Bye My Fancy (Whitman), 34, 49; author's musical interest revealed in, 62; cited, 67; reference to Emerson, 71; its literary value, 244

Good Gray Poet, The (W. D. O'Connor), 4, 185, 209, 217

Gosse, Edmund, quoted, 10, 233, 235

Gottlied, Das (J. Schlaf), 286

Gran, Gerhard, quoted, 260

Grashalme (Whitman: Rolleston), 277

Grass: used as a metaphor, 122

Greek poetry, 252-53

Grønne Digte (O. Sarvig), 312

Gullberg, Hjalmar, 314

Günderode, Karoline von, 265

Hafiz (Persian poet), 159

Halstrom, Per, 314

Hamadryad, The (C. Hauch), 307

Hamsun, Knut, quoted, 104, 105, 129; criticism of Whitman, 155, 315

Hansen, Adolf, quoted, 106

Harlan affair, 208-9

Harned, Thomas, 3, 5, 235

Harrington (W. D. O'Connor), 188

Harris, Frank, quoted, 10, 120; visits Whitman, 235

Harrison, Mary Kingsley, *see* Malet, Lucas

Harte, Bret, 233

Hatzfeld, Adolf, 286-87

Hauch, Carsten, 16, 306
Hauptmann, Gerhart, 278
Hauser, Otto, quoted, 10, 263
Hawthorne, Nathaniel, 7, 24, 29, 45, 240
Hegel, G. W. F., 8, 66, 67, 115
Hero worship, 224
"Hertha" (Swinburne), 253, 317
Herz, aufglühe dein Blut (H. Lersch), 286, 287
Hesse, Herman: as a disciple of Whitman, 96; a modern mystic, 133, 278; Whitman's influence on, 291
Heures claires, Les (Verhaeren), 299
Hiawatha (Longfellow), 29, 141
Hicks, Elias, 31; described by Whitman, 32 f., 65, 89; as an orator, 107, 123, 244
Hide Unas (S. Mathiesen), 315
Higginson, T. W., 183
Hille, Peter, 286
Himmliche Zecher, Der (A. Mombert), 283
Hine, Charles (painter), 152
Hirschfeld, Magnus, 276, 279, 318
Hjulet (J. V. Jensen), 170-71, 292, 309
Høffding, Harald, 258
"Hohe Gemeinschaft" (Werfel), 291
"Hohere Menschen" (Werfel), 291
Holloway, Emory, 5, 6, 11, 40, 42; quoted, 48, 51, 54-55; quoted, 56, 62; quoted, 100, 124, 142, 143, 144, 161, 168; quoted, 169, 181, 182; quoted, 187, 211, 212; quoted, 225, 231
Holz, Arno, 9, 283; quoted, 284-85, 292, 293, 304
Homes of the New World (F. Bremer), 14, 15
Homosexuality, problem of: in artists and writers, 167, 168; *see also* Eroticism
Hopp, Ernst Otto, 276
Horse: as a symbol of "life-force," 87
Houghton, R. M. M., Lord, 128
Houmann, Børge, 312, 313
"Hours Continuing Long" (Whitman), 164, 200
Howells, William Dean, 11, 142
"How Solemn as One by One" (Whitman), 206
Huch, Ricarda, quoted, 265
Hugo, Victor, 11, 47, 85, 264, 268-70, 297, 298, 301
Human body: its importance for

Goethe and Whitman, 252; Carlyle's quotation from Novalis, 275; in Dehmel's lyrics, 282
"Hush'd Be the Camps Today" (Whitman), 204
Hygaard, Frederik, 310
"Hymn de la nature et de l'humanitie" (Hugo), 268
"Hymn of Dead Soldiers" (Whitman), 206
"Hymn of Man" (Swinburne), 317
"Hymn to the Earth and Ocean" (Whitman), 100, 101

Identification of poet with universe, 87; with divinity, 89 f.; duality of the "I," 112 f.; eroticism in poet's idea of identity, 117; identity with animals, 133-34; mystic "I" of second edition, 134; identity with felons and prostitutes, 175-76
Identity, 123, 152, 153, 194
Illustreret Tidende (Danish periodical), 312
"Imagists," 321
Immoraliste, L' (Gide), 295
Impressions III (Verhaeren), 298
"In cabin'd Ships at Sea" (Whitman), 225
Ingersoll, Robert, 234
In Infinity (K. Balmont), 305
Inner light, the, 8
"In Paths Untrodden" (Whitman), 157
Insanity, in great artists, 40; Whitman's interest in, and fear of, 46, 47
Intermediate Sex, The (E. Carpenter), 318
Interpretations of Poetry and Religion (Santayana), 169
"Intertwined Trees, The" (Wergeland), 261
Irving, Henry, 235
"I Sing the Body Electric" (Whitman), 123, 124; social program, 156
"I Sit and Look Out" (Whitman), 172
Istrati, Panaït, 302, 304
Italian literature: Whitman's influence on, 304

Jacobsen, Rolf, 316
Jahrbuch für sexuelle Zwischenstufen, 279
James, Henry (the elder), 22
James, William, 59; quoted, 169, 198

Index

Index

Jammes, Francis, 300
Jannaccone, P., 304
Janson, Kristofer, 315
"Jenseits" (Werfel), 291
Jensen, Johannes V., quoted, 8, 85, 106, 129, quoted, 138, 160, 170; influenced by Whitman, 170-71, 229, 266; as representative of our time, 281, 292; his importance to Danish literature, 309 f.; translator and interpreter of Whitman, 312 f.
Johnston, John, 41
Journalism: Whitman's early interest in, 41 f.
Jouve, Pierre Jean, 301
Joyce, James, 100, 302

Kahn, Gustave, 292
Kellermann, Bernhard, 291
Kellner, Leon, quoted, 10
Kemble, Fanny, 23; admired by Whitman, 39
Kennedy, W. S., quoted, 66, 115, 176, 234, 246, 292
Kjelgren, Josef, 313
Klopstock, F. G., 255, 283
Kneip, Jakob, 288
Knortz, Karl, 277, 278, 280
Knulp (Hesse), 291
Krishnamurti, Jiddu, 250
Kristensen, Tom, 310
Kyra Kyrelina (P. Istrati), 302

Lady Chatterley's Lover (D. H. Lawrence), 321
"Lady of Ships, The" (Whitman), 192
Lafayette, Marquess de, 35
Laforgue, Jules, 292, 297, 304
Laienbrevier (L. Schefer), 134; quoted, 339, n. 49
Laotse (Chinese philosopher), 249
Larbaud, Valéry, 293, 302-4; quoted, 335, n. 106
Larsen, Thøger, 310, 312
"Last Invocation, The" (Whitman), 225
Last of the Mohicans, The (J. F. Cooper), 17
"Last of the Sacred Army, The" (Whitman), 195
"Laughing Song" (Blake), 256
La Vogue (periodical), 292
Lawrence, D. H., 10, 87, 120, 302, 306; a pupil of Whitman, 317, 321-26; quoted, 342, n. 75 and n. 76

Leader (periodical), 128
Leaves of Grass (Whitman): its influence in Europe, 3; author's religious belief in, 6; intended for the people, 7; traces of Quakerism and Unitarianism in, 8, 9; lack of chronological sequence, 12; significance of its publication date, 29; nature descriptions based on Long Island, 34; attempts to mystify reader, 55; trip to New Orleans as first impulse toward, 57; "musical passages," 62; early tentative sketches, 63 f.; parallels to Emerson's writings, 73; development of Calamus theme in later editions, 203; a man's life, 211; changing points of view and sentiments, 211; continual revising, 217; English edition, 217; comprehensiveness of democratic concept, 220; Whitman's description of, 246; a natural model for Whitman's successors, 248; didactic element, 253; kinship with Zarathustra, 271; first German translation, 271; Rolleston and Knortz Grashalme, 277; Schlaf's German translation, 277; Reisiger's edition, 278
Drum-Taps (Whitman), 38, 79; a part of Leaves of Grass, 181-82; source, 186; author's own opinion of, 189; Lincoln elegy, 190; analysis of, 190ff.; Calamus motif, 191; death an underlying theme, 201; concluding poems; 206, 213, 226, 270; Freiligrath's translation, 276, 287
—— First edition: its failure in United States, 77 ff.; preface and twelve untitled poems, 79 ff.; America as source of inspiration, 80; analysis of "Song of Myself," 81 ff.; wander motif, 90; defects in "Song of Myself," 97 f.; Hamsun's criticism, 104, 105; intended to be spoken rather than read, 107; use of suggestion and parenthesis, 109; adolescent attitude, 118; erotic emotion, 118 f.; feminine point of view, 119; poems other than "Song of Myself," 123 ff.; Emerson's letter, 126-27; antagonistic reviews, 127 f.
—— Second edition: published one year after first edition, 130; a significant expansion, 131; mystical phrases, 133; the mystic "I," 134;

Leaves of Grass (*Continued*)
new poems, 134; pantheistic religion
presented, 135; erotic lyricism of
"Bunch Poem," 137 f.; poetic gist of
second edition in "Broad-Axe
Poem," 139; its failure, 141
—— *Third edition: Calamus* section,
157 ff., 167; *Chants Democratic,* 171-
73, 175; "Poem of Joys," 173-75;
conflict between personal and general pronouncements, 176; "So
Long!" as conclusion, 179
—— *Fourth edition:* nationalism dis-
played in, 186, 217; two versions,
214; varied history of "By Blue Ontario's Shore," 215 f.; despondency
apparent, 216
—— *Fifth edition:* new poems, 225 f.;
"Passage to India," 231
—— *Sixth edition:* known as Centen-
nial edition, 233
—— *Seventh edition:* the basis of all
present editions, 240; sale forbidden,
241
Leben und Lüge (D. von Liliencron),
280, 282
Lebesque, Phileas, 294
Legende des siècles, La (Hugo), 268
"Legend of Life and Love, A" (Whit-
man), 47
Lenau, Nikolaus, 27, 29, quoted, 330-31,
n. 24, n. 25, and n. 32
Lersch, Heinrich, 286, 287, 311
Lerberghe, Charles van, 293, 299-300,
315
Lessing, Gotthold Ephraim, 254
Lessing, O. E., 277, 278; estimate of
Whitman, 279-80; quoted, 351, n. 41
and n. 44
*Letters of Anne Gilchrist and Walt
Whitman* (Harned), 5
Let Us Be Like the Sun (K. Balmont),
305
Liberator, The (newspaper), 20
Lienhard, Fritz, 275
Life in the New World (C. Sealsfield),
18
Life of Walt Whitman, The (H. B.
Binns), 4
Liliencron, Detlev, Baron von, 196, 280,
282
Limfjords Sange (T. Larsen), 312
Lincoln, Abraham: admired by Whit-
man, 7; as "the man from the West,"
172; his importance to Whitman,

180; Whitman's Great Camerado,
184; his comment on Whitman, 185;
elegy by Whitman, 190; Whitman's
description of his appearance, 185;
Whitman's lectures, 244
Lind, Jenny, 24, 62; Whitman's comment, 334, n. 75
Linton, W. J., 225, 233-34
"Litany of Nations, The" (Swinburne), 317
Literary history: Whitman's place in
literature, 3, 9; study of types and
parallel intellectual development as
a function of, 248; Whitman's importance for modern literature, 326;
see also Contemporary history *and
under individual countries, e.g.,*
Danish literature
"Little Girl Lost, A" (Blake), 256
"Little Jane" (Whitman), 46
"Liturgic prose" in Whitman's work,
106
London, Jack, 87
"London" (Blake), 256
Longfellow, Henry Wadsworth, 4, 22,
29, 45, 239
Long Island: the Quaker element, 31;
in Whitman's youth, 34-35; beach of
Paumanok in Whitman's poetry,
340-41, n. 69
Long Island Democrat, The (news-
paper), 42, 50
Long Islander (Whitman's news-
paper), 42
Long Island Patriot, The (news-
paper), 38, 42
Long Island Star (newspaper), 38-39
Look We Have Come Through (D. H.
Lawrence), 321-22
Lorange, Ingrid de, 312
Loüys, Pierre, 300
Love's Coming of Age (E. Carpenter),
318
Lowell, James Russell, 4, 16, 22; meet-
ing with Fredrika Bremer, 23;
quoted, 28-29, 40, 68; failure to rec-
ognize Whitman as new poet, 78 f.,
183, 190, 224, 233, 234, 345, n. 129
Lucretius, 253
Lundkvist, Arthur, 313, 314

MacPherson, James, 255
Maeterlinck, Maurice, 293, 294-95, 298,
315
Malet, Lucas, 236

Man Finished, A (Papini), 305
Mangfoldighed (O. Sarvig), 312
"Mankind" (Wergeland), 261
Mann, Horace, 22
Mann, Thomas, 278, 291, 292
"Marches Now the War Is Over" (Whitman), 226
"March in the Ranks Hard-prest, A" (Whitman), 186, 197
Marriage of Heaven and Hell (Blake), 255
Marryat, Frederick, 18; quoted, 20, 25, 41
Martin Chuzzlewit (Dickens), 18
Martineau, Harriet, 18, 19, 20, 25
Martinson, Harry, 313, 314
Masters, Edgar Lee, 327
Mathiesen, Sigurd, 315
Mauprat (G. Sand), 16
Mausoleum: Whitman's preoccupation with his, 6
"Meaning of Swedish Poverty, The" (Almquist), 259
Meddelelser om Indholdet af et Skrift fra Aar 2135 (F. C. Sibbern), 258
"Me Imperturbe" (Whitman), 205, 312
Men and Books (R. L. Stevenson), 235, 318
Melville, Herman, 7, 29, 30; Whitman's review of book by, 49, 87, 141, 174, 325
Menscheitdämmerung (K. Pinthus), 283
Mensch im Eisen (H. Lersch), 287
Mensch in der Mitte, Der (L. Rubiner), 287
Mercure de France (French periodical), 294
Meredith, George, 235
"Merlin" (Emerson), cited, 74
Merrill, Stuart, 292, 293, 295
Mesnevi (Rumi), 249
Messenger Leaves (Whitman), 175
Mexican War, 16
Michaud, Régis, quoted, 10, 11
Michelet, Jules, 292
Mickle Street (Camden, New Jersey), 241
Migrations to the West, 16
"Migselv" (Wergeland), 262
Mikail (P. Istrati), 302
Miller, Joaquin, 233
Millet, Jean François, 240

"Miracle" (Whitman), 72
Mistress, The: as a symbol for America, 205
Moby Dick (Melville), 29, 39, 174
Modern amerikansk Lyrik (E. Blomberg), 314
Modern literature, *see* Contemporary literature
Møller, Niels, 308
Mombert, Alfred, 283, 286
Montolio, Cebriá, 305
Morgenstern, Christian, 286
Morris, Harrison, 234
Mother, The: its dominant role in Whitman's poetry, 38; poet's identification with, in first edition of *Leaves of Grass,* 119; assumes mythical proportions in "The Sleepers," 126; the earth as the old mother in "Song of the Rolling Earth," 133; the sea as mother in "Out of the Cradle," 146; despair in "As I Ebb'd," 149; Whitman's mother-instinct released in his hospital work, 181; the grieving mother in "Come Up from the Fields," 199-201; takes final form as death, 202, 205; *see also* Father, The
Mother-Mistress, The: as a symbol for America, 205
Mother-religion, 38; Werfel's use of theme, 289
Multiple Splendeur, La (Verhaeren), 298, 299, 300
Murry, Middleton, 324
Music: its critical influence on Whitman's poetry, 62 ff., 226-27; Werfel's interest in, 289
My Days and Dreams (E. Carpenter), 318, 324
My Life and Loves (F. Harris), 10
Mysticism: in Whitman's work, 8, 9; similarity to famous mystical poets, 93, 122; use of mystical phrases in second edition of *Leaves of Grass,* 133; the "mystic third" in third edition, 152; as expressed in "Passage to India" and "The Untold Want," 229; Whitman's resemblance to mystic temperament of Oriental and other writers, 249 f.; *see also* Pantheism
"Mystic Trumpeter" (Whitman), German translation, 277
Myter (Jensen), 309

"Nachtfragment" (Werfel), 290
Naket Liv (A. Lundkvist), 313
Narcissism: in Whitman's personality, 252
Narciss und Goldmund (Hesse), 291
Nationalism: in fourth edition of *Leaves of Grass*, 186
"Native Moments" (Whitman), 155, 175
Nature: Whitman's interpretation of, 122
Nature (Emerson), 20; cited, 72
Negro: Whitman's opinion of, 56; poet's identification with fugitive slave in "Song of Myself," 98; Whitman's lessening sympathy, 210; his belief in slow emancipation, 224
Neighbors (F. Bremer), 14
Nekrassow, N. A., 269, 270, 282, 298
Nencioni, Enrico, 304
New England: center of intellectual life, 22
New Harmony Colony, 17
New Orleans: Whitman's stay in, 51 ff.
New World, The (newspaper), 44
New York: in Whitman's early manhood, 39
Nietzsche, F. W., 3, 8, 96; quoted, 165, 224, 258, 265; his influence on modern thought, 270 f.; kinship with Whitman, 271, 272, 282, 287, 297; quoted, 342, n. 79
"Night on the Prairies, A" (Whitman), 312
Nilsson, Ossian, 314
Nina (F. Bremer), 14
Ninth of November, The (Kellermann), 291
Norwegian literature: Whitman's influence on, 313-16
Notes on Walt Whitman as Poet and Person (Burroughs), 4, 188, 189, 217
Notions of the Americans Picked Up by a Travelling Bachellor (J. F. Cooper), 17
Nourritures terrestres, Les (Gide), 295-97
Nouvelle Revue Française (French periodical), 302
Novalis (German poet): Whitman's similarity to, 133, 275, 307
Novellen von Walt Whitman, 277
November Boughs (Whitman), 31, 34, 40, 65, 66; literary value, 244

"Now Finalé to the Shore" (Whitman), 225, 337, n. 28
Nuova antologia (Italian periodical), 304

Obstfelder, Sigbjørn, 315
"O Captain, My Captain" (Whitman), 204; translated into German, 276
"Oceano Nox" (Hugo), 268
O'Connor, C. P., 38
O'Connor, William D., 4; meets Whitman, 151, 182, 184, 187; defends Whitman in Harlan affair, 209; quoted, 210; quoted, 219; break with Whitman, 224
O'Connor, Mrs. W. D., *see* Calder, Ellen
"Ode to Walt Whitman" (García Lorca), 305, 313
Odi navali (D'Annunzio), 304
"Of Him I Love" (Whitman), 225
"Of the Terrible Doubt of Appearances" (Whitman), 177
Old Bowery Theater (New York), 40
Om Aartusinder (Andersen), 267
"O Magnet South" (Whitman), 57
Omar Khayyám, 34, 122
Omoo (Melville), Whitman's comment, 49, 174
"On Another's Sorrow" (Blake), 256
"Once I Passed through a Populous City" (Whitman), 53; cited, 54, 55; translated into French by Andre Gide, 297
"One Time Friends" (Wergeland), 261
"On the Beach at Night" (Whitman), 312, 341, n. 69
"One Wicked Impulse" (Whitman), 46
"Open Sky" (Hugo), 269
Oratory: Whitman's interest in, 61, 62; *Leaves of Grass* intended to be spoken, 107
Ord och Bild (Swedish periodical), 313
Oriental literature: mystic temperament of Whitman similar to Oriental writers, 8, 9, 249 ff.
Ørsted, H. C., 15, 67, 257
Osgood, James R., 240
Ossian, 65
Ossoli, Margaret Fuller, *see* Fuller, Margaret
"O Star of France" (Whitman), 292
"O Tan-Faced Prairie Boy" (Whitman), 196

Index

Otten, Karl, 287
"Out of the Cradle Endlessly Rocking" (Whitman), 124, 145; cited, 145-47; revelation of tragedy in author's life, 147 f., 154, 159, 164; reappearance of theme in "When Lilacs Last," 201; German translation, 277; Danish translation, 312
"Our Future Lot" (Whitman), 46
"Out of the Rolling Ocean" (Whitman), 213
Over-Soul, The, 21
"Over the Carnage Rose Prophetic a Voice" (Whitman), 191
Owen, Robert, 17
"O you whom I often and silently come" (Whitman), 160-61

Panaroma de la littératur américaine contemporaine (R. Michaud), 10
Pantheism: in "Song of Myself," 84 ff.; in "As I Ebb'd," 150; in "Song of Joys," 174; pantheistic nature of Whitman's democracy, 220 f.; "Passage to India," 230; common to all mystic temperaments, 250, 251; Andersen's and Hugo's work, 267, 269; its expression in Dehmel's work, 282; mother-religion theme used by Werfel, 289; *see also* Mysticism
Papers on Literature and Art (M. Fuller), 16
Papini, Giovanni, 304
Paquet, Alfons, 286
Paralysis: hereditary trait in Whitman family, 38
Parenthesis, use of: in *Leaves of Grass*, 109
Parker, Theodore, 21, 22, 141
Park Theater (New York), 39
Parnassus (Emerson), 79
Participles: translation difficulties, 110
"Passage to India" (Whitman), 67, 124, 225, 226; its importance, 228; cited, 230; a poetic climax, 231, 232, 263
Pathological study of Whitman, 37
Paumanok, *see* Long Island
Peabody, George, 226
Peace movement: emergence of, 15
"Pensive and Faltering" (Whitman), 225
"Pensive on Her Dead Gazing" (Whitman), 196, 206-7, 287
Perceptiveness of Whitman's poetry, 9

Perry, Bliss, quoted, 4, 5, 6, 13; quoted, 47, 54, 106, 111, 129, 140, 182, 187; quoted, 190, 209, 210; quoted, 235, 247, 327, 335, n. 92
Personal Recollections of Abraham Lincoln (H. B. Rankin), 180
Peter Camemczind (Hesse), 291
Petersen, Clemens, 307
Pfaff's German Restaurant, 142, 143, 182
Phantasus (A. Holz), 284, 285
Phillips, Wendell, 22, 61, 184; quoted, 209
Philosophy: its influence on Whitman, 8, 66
Phrenological Journal (periodical), 128
Phrenology: Whitman's interest in, 49; its contribution to Whitman's vocabulary, 54, 112, 128
Picture Book without Pictures (Andersen), 266, 267
Pieces in Early Youth (Whitman), 58
"Pilgrims, The" (Swinburne), 317
Pinthus, Kurt, 283
"Pioneers! O Pioneers!" (Whitman): 190; wander motif in, 91; identity of body and soul in, 115; included in *Drum-Taps*, 190; exceptional style, 204, 205; Danish translation, 312; compared to Baggesen's style, 348, n. 8
Plato: *Leaves of Grass* ranked with *Symposium*, 318
Poe, Edgar Allen, 6, 7, 46, 47; Whitman's verse technique reminiscent of, 195, 205, 242; Whitman's meeting with Poe, 332, n. 29
Poèmes ardents, Les (Verhaeren), 298
"Poem of Joys" (Whitman), 173, 179
"Poem of Many in One" (Whitman), 80; eulogy of English language, 82; sex program, 136, 137; title changed, 154
"Poem of Procreation" (Whitman), 136, 137
"Poem of Salutation" (Whitman), 131, 136
"Poem of the Proposition of Nakedness" (Whitman), 136
"Poem of the Road" (Whitman), 132; use of the mystic "I," 134
"Poem of the Sayers of the Words" (Whitman), 133

"Poem of Wonder at the Resurrection of Wheat" (Whitman), 135
"Poem of You, Whoever You Are" (Whitman), 132, 136
Poems by Walt Whitman: English edition of *Leaves of Grass,* 217, 218
Poesia di Walt Whitman, La (P. Jannaccone), 304
Poésies de A. O. Barnabooth, Les (V. Larbaud), 302
"Poet, The" (Emerson), 72; cited, 77
Poetry, the emotional quality of: in *Leaves of Grass,* 9; suggestive nature of emotion in "The Sleepers," 124; love as an emotion celebrated in *Calamus,* 158; Whitman's emotional instability, 167; *see also* Free verse; Vers-librists
Poetry (periodical), 294
Poet's Bazaar, A (Andersen), 266
Popoff, P., 305
Postl, K. A., *see* Sealsfield, Charles
Pound, Ezra, 321
Powers, Hiram, 23
"Prayer for All, The" (Hugo), 268
"Prayer of Columbus" (Whitman), 232
Preface, 1855, analysis, 79-82, 140; turned into poetry, 152; interpreted in *Democratic Vistas,* 220, 222
President's Daughters, The (F. Bremer), 14
Prohibition movement: emergence of, 15
Prophetic style, 255
Prosaschriften (Whitman: Lessing), 277
Prose verse, *see* Free verse; Verslibrists
"Proto-Leaf" (Whitman), 29, 115; poetic form of 1855 Preface, 152, 154, 162, 248
"Proud Music of the Storm" (Whitman), 62, 225; its importance, 226, 227; Swedish translation, 313
"Proverbs of Hell" (Blake), 255
Przybyszewski, Stanislaw, 281

Quakerism: in *Leaves of Grass,* 8, 34; in Whitman's ancestry, 31; Fredrika Bremer's description, 32; Whitman's "inner light," 122, 123; in "To Him That Was Crucified," 175
Quesnel, Léon, 292
Quincy, Josiah, quoted, 140

"Race of Veterans" (Whitman), 206
Rainbow (D. H. Lawrence), 324
Rankin, Henry Bascom, quoted, 180
Raumer, Friedrich von, 19; praised by Whitman, 49
Raunkier, Ingeborg, 312
Rayons et les ombres, Les (Hugo), 268
"Real War Will Never Get in the Books, The" (Whitman), 186
Rebell, Hugues, 294
"Reconciliation" (Whitman), 196
Reisiger, Hans, 43; Whitman translator, 110, 278, 292
Religion und Kosmos (J. Schlaf), 286
Religious aspects of *Leaves of Grass,* 6; Whitman as a prophet, 8, 122; as a lyrical-mystical author, 59, 60; presentation of pantheistic religion in second edition, 135; *Democratic Vistas* calls for new cosmic religion, 223; pantheistic religion in "Passage to India," 230
Religious sects in America, 26
Renaissance in Italy (Symonds), 52
"Respondez" (Whitman), 136
"Resurgemus" (Whitman), 58
"Return of the Heroes" (Whitman), 226
"Reversals" (Whitman), 136
Revolution der Lyrik (A. Holz), 9, 284
Revue de deux Mondes (periodical), 219
Rhetorical style of *Leaves of Grass,* 109, 110
Rhys, Ernest, 235
Rhythmus des neuen Europa (G. Engelke), 288
Richepin, Jean, 294
Rilke, Rainer Maria: influenced by Whitman, 281, 283, 286, 290, 294, 295, 298, 315
Ripley, George, 20, 21
"Rise O Days from Your Fathomless Deeps" (Whitman), 192
Robert Fulton (C. Hauch), 16, 306
Rode, Helge, 313
Rodgers, Cleveland, 5
Rolleston, T. W., 277
Romains, Jules, 300, 304
"Roots and Leaves" (Whitman), 167
Rosanow, Vassili, 305-6
Rosas, Parepa, 226
Rosen, Friedrich, 249
Rosenberg, P. A., 308

Rossetti, William Michael, 210; edits English edition of *Leaves of Grass*, 217, 218, 276

Rousseau, Jean Jacques, 3, 4, 7, 10, 66, 253, 257, 259, 274

Rubiner, Ludwig, 286, 287

Rückert, Friedrich, 249

"Rules for Composition" (Whitman), 111

Rumi (Persian poet), Whitman's similarity to, 93; effeminate traits, 162; mystic temperament, 249, 250; use of similar imagery by Bettina, 265

Russian literature: Whitman's influence on, 305-6

Russische Literatur der Gegenwart (Arseniew), 270

Rythmes souverains, Les (Verhaeren), 298

Sadi (Persian poet), 159

Saintsbury, George, 233

"Salut au Monde" (Whitman), 79, 112, 124, 131, 153, 267, 287, 303, 304

Sanborn, Frank, 127, 140, 240

Sand, George, 16, 66

Sandburg, Carl, 313, 327

Sandgren, Gustav, 313

Sange fra Provinsen (H. Bergstedt), 310

Sartor Resartus (Carlyle), 68-71, 275

Santayana, George, 169

Sappho (Greek poet), 159

Sarrazin, Gabriel, 292

Sarvig, Ole, 312, 316

Saturday Press (periodical), 145, 148

Scarlet Letter (Hawthorne), 24, 29

"Scented Herbage of My Breast" (Whitman), 157, 159

Schefer, Leopold, 134, 275, quoted, 339, n. 49

Schade, Jens August, 310

Schiller, J. C. F. von, 254

Schlaf, Johannes, 4, 52; translator of Whitman, 110; attempt to present Whitman as prophet and reformer, 169, 171; compares Nietzsche and Whitman, 271; his important translation of *Grashalme,* 277; essay on Whitman, 278, 280; an espouser of Whitman, 285-86, 293, 295, 304, 313

Schloezer, Boris de, 306

Schmidt, Julius, 265

Schmidt, Rudolf, 128, 129, 219; trans-

lates *Democratic Vistas,* 220, 224; a romantic writer, 307, 313, 314, 315

Schölermann, William, 277

Schöne wilde Welt (R. Dehmel), 282

Scott, F. N., quoted, 106

Scott, William Bell, 210

Sea, The (Kellermann), 291

Sea, The: its impression on Whitman, 35; erotic connotation, 118, 121, 124, 138; somber motif, 145; its importance in *Zarathustra,* 273

Sealsfield, Charles, 18

Sedgwick, Catharine, 19

"Self-Reliance" (Emerson), 73

Selincourt, Basil de, 5

Sequel to Drum-Taps (Whitman), 190, 192, 196, 206, 207

Serres chaudes (Maeterlinck), 295

Sex: in Whitman's poetry, 9 f.; sexual imagery in "Song of Myself," 95; auto-erotic experience, 117, 118

Shelley, Percy Bysshe, 317

"Shooting Niagara" (Carlyle), 68, 220

Sibbern, F. C., quoted, 60; pantheism of, and Whitman's similarities with, 258 f., 307

"Sight in Camp in the Day-Break, A" (Whitman), 182, 197, 198

Si le grain ne meurt (Gide), 295

Sinclair, Upton, 222

"Singer in Prison, The" (Whitman), 226

Sketches of Daily Life (F. Bremer), 14

"Slang in America" (Whitman), 111

Slavery (W. E. Channing), 20, 68

Slavery: in the United States, 15, 17; a leading political issue, 24

"Sleepers, The" (Whitman), 35, 36, 79; stream-of-consciousness association, 100, 124; its skill-execution and its beauty, 124-26; omitted from English edition, 218; dream technique later repeated in "Proud Music," 227; mystic imagery of dancers, 265; French translation, 302; Danish translation, 312

Smith, Logan Pearsall, 242, 243

Socialism: emergence of, 15

Social reform: combined with ideal of world citizenship, 254

Society in America (H. Martineau), 18

"So Long" (Whitman), 12; significance of, 177-79

Some Friends of Walt Whitman (E. Carpenter), 9, 244

"Song of Joys" (Whitman), 41, 114, 230; Danish translation, 309, 312

"Song of Myself" (Whitman), 7, 35; cited, 44; mystical experience described in section 5, 60; music, Italian influence, 62 ff.; Carlyle's influence apparent in, 70; death theme, 202; omitted from English editions, 218; parallels in Silesius's writing, 250; in Rabbi Baal Schem, 251; wander motif in *Werther* similar to, 253; similarities in Blake's poetry, 256; Thorild's joy in life similar to, 257; parallels in Bettina's writing, 265; similarities in *Zarathustra*, 272-73; Danish edition, 312; Norwegian translation, 316; section 25 quoted, 76; section 1 quoted, 78-79; themes and episodes, 81; chief poem of first edition, 83; pantheistic democracy reflected in, 84; combination of wander motif and religious motif, 87-88; identification with divinity, 89 f.; wander motif, 90; alternation of personal and universal Ego, 91 f., 112; similarity to other mystical poems, 93; sexual imagery, 95; sense of personal communication between poet and reader, 97; defects of poem, 97 f.; American history anecdotes, 98; use of stream-of-consciousness association, 99, 101; the poet as literary pioneer, 100, 106; Section 33, cited, 101-3; oratorical quality, 107 f.; dangers in use of catologues, 104-5; vocabulary, 111; unity of body and soul, 113, 114; auto-eroticism, 117-18; wound-dresser motif, 123; erotic lyricism, 137; its dominant position in all editions of *Leaves of Grass*, 152; its prophecy of author's hospital work, 181, 196

"Song of Occupations" (Whitman), 123

"Song of the Banner at Daybreak" (Whitman), 191, 193-95

"Song of the Broad-Axe" (Whitman), 135, 136; social theme of, 158; French translation, 292

"Song of the Exposition" (Whitman), 7, 67, 70, 224, 225, 309

"Song of the Open Road" (Whitman), 66, 79; wander motif in, 90 f., 132,

205; parallels in writing of Rabbi Baal Schem, 251; Almquist's development of self, 260, 294; similarities in Gide's *Les Nourritures terrestres*, 295-97

"Song of the Redwood Tree" (Whitman), 232

"Song of the Rolling Earth" (Whitman), 133

"Song of the Universal" (Whitman), 233

Songs before Sunrise (Swinburne), 218, 317

Songs of Innocence (Blake), 256

Songs of Labor (Whittier), 29

Sons and Lovers (D. H. Lawrence), 325

Sørensen, Arne, 310

Souday, Paul, 295

"South Sea Sails" (Wergeland), 263

Spanish literature: Whitman's influence on, 305

Specimen Days (Whitman), 34, 35, 41; cited, 51-52, 65; descriptions of hospital work, 182; life in wartime Washington, 185; attempts to publish hospital diaries, 189; observations of nature, 239

"Spirit Whose Work Is Done" (Whitman), 206, 207

"Spontaneous Me" (Whitman), 137; social program, 156; erotic imagery of Wergeland similar to, 262; bee symbol also used by D. H. Lawrence, 321

Spoon River Anthology (E. L. Masters), 176

Stafford family, 239

Standard (Brooklyn newspaper)

"Starting from Paumanok" (Whitman), 29, 76; a poetic preface to *Leaves of Grass*, 152, 153; contains reference to trans-Atlantic cable, 228; German translation, 277; Danish translation, 309, 312

Stedman, Edmund Clarence, quoted, 122, 247

Stendhal, 27

"Sterben im Walde" (Werfel), 289, 301

Stern, Adolf, quoted, 10

Sternberg, Leo, 286

Stevenson, Robert Louis, 9, 235, 318

St. Mawr (D. H. Lawrence), 87

Stoddard, Richard Henry, 204

Store Ja, Det (H. Rode), 313
Stowe, Harriet Beecher, 25, 61
Strån av Gräs (Whitman: Svensson), 314
Strangford, Lord, 210
Stream-of-consciousness association, use of: in "Song of Myself," 99; in "The Sleepers," 100; Whitman's ignorance of modern dream interpretation, 100
Strodtmann, Alfred, 276, 278
Studies in Classic American Literature (D. H. Lawrence), 321, 325
Studies in Prose and Poetry (Swinburne), 317
Studies of Greek Poets (Symonds), 52
Sublimated emotion: its presence in artists, 168
Sue, Eugene, 66
Suggestion: as poetic device in *Leaves of Grass*, 109
Supermen, theory of: approximated in *Democratic Vistas*, 224
Surrealism: foreshadowed by Whitman, 100
Suso, Heinrich, 162
Svensk Romantik (Vedel), 257; quoted, 348, n. 9
Svensson, K. A., 314
Swedenborg, Emanuel, 8, 59; influence on Emerson and Whitman, 74; mysticism of "Passage to India" comparable to, 229; Whitman's ideas of personal conduct similar to, 251, 252, 255
Swedish literature: Whitman's influence on, 313-14
Swinburne, Algernon C., quoted, 190, 210, 218, 253; compared with Whitman, 317
Swinton, John, 187
Symonds, John Addington, 4; quoted, 9; Whitman's letter to, 52-53, 168, 198, 210, 234, 318

Tagore, Sir Rabindranath, 8; quoted, 9, 297
"Tag und Nacht Hymnus" (Werfel), 289
Taoteking, 249
Taylor, Edward Thompson (Father Taylor), 23, 141, 244
Taylor, Zachary, 24
Teaching: Whitman's attempts at, 41

Technique poétique, La (C. Vildrac), 301
Tennyson, Alfred, 66, 218, 233, 242
"That Music Always around Me" (Whitman), 62, 65, 226
Theater, the: its early influence on Whitman, 39 f.
"There Was a Child Went Forth" (Whitman), cited, 30, 36-37, 98; 126
"This Compost" (Whitman), 135
Thompson, J. C., 249
Thoreau, Henry David, 7, 21, 22; visits Whitman, 128, 129; comments on *Children of Adam* section in 1856 ed. of *Leaves of Grass*, 158, 239, 240, 325
Thoreau's Familiar Letters (H. Blake), 129
Thorild, Thomas, 257
"Thorn-rose philosophy" (Almquist), 259
"Thought" (Whitman), 62, 172, 225
"Thoughts of These Years" (Whitman), 172
"Thou Mother with Equal Brood" (Whitman), 225
Thyrza (G. Gissing), quoted, 235-36; 279
"Til Foraaret" (Wergeland), 262, 263
Tilskueren (Danish periodical), 162, 312
Timber Creek, 239
Times (New York newspaper), 184
Times (Brooklyn newspaper), 128, 142
"To a Common Prostitute" (Whitman), 175
"To a President" (Whitman), 172, 179
"To a Noiseless Patient Spider" (Whitman), 312
"To a Stranger" (Whitman), 291
"To Him That Was Crucified" (Whitman), 175
"To Joy" (Wergeland), 263
Tolstoy, L. N., 270
"Tomb Blossoms, The" (Whitman), 47
"To My Soul" (Whitman), 177
"To Oratorists" (Whitman), 175
"To Priapus" (D. H. Lawrence), 321
"Tortoise's Shout" (D. H. Lawrence), 323-24
"To Spring" (Wergeland), 262, 263
"To the Leaven'd Soil They Trod" (Whitman), 206
"To the States" (Whitman), 172
"To Think of Time" (Whitman), 123

"To Walt Whitman in America" (Swinburne), 218
Towards Democracy (E. Carpenter), 234; its direct derivation from Leaves of Grass, 319 ff.
Towards Intellectual Freedom (E. Carpenter), 318
"Træet" (P. Arneberg), 316
Transcendentalism, 8; its demand for original American literature, 16; derivation from Unitarianism, 20, 21, 23, 83
"Transpositions" (Whitman), 136
Traubel, Horace, 4, 234-35, 308
Travel books on America: by Europeans, 17, 18
"Trickle Drops" (Whitman), 159
Trollope, Frances, 18
Troye, Vilhelm, quoted, 263, 315; quoted, 349, n. 15
Tunnell, The (Kellermann), 291
Tuxen, Poul, quoted, 250
Twain, Mark, 233, 244
Twilight in Italy (D. H. Lawrence), 324
Two Rivulets (Whitman), 233

"Ulysses" (Tennyson), 66
Unanimists, 293, 300 f.
Uncle Sam in the Eyes of His Family (J. Erskine), 41
Uncle Tom's Cabin (Stowe), 25
Uncollected Poetry and Prose of Walt Whitman, The (E. Holloway), 5, 42, 142
Under Klokketaarnet (H. Bergstedt), 311
Unitarianism, 8; advocacy of freedom of thought, 20
United States and Democratic Review, The (periodical), 128
Unruh, Fritz von, 301
Uns nährt die Erde (Gide), 297
"Unsterblichkeit" (Werfel), 291
Unter dem Sternenbanner (E. O. Hopp), 276-77
"Untold Want, The" (Whitman), 229

Vandringer (P. Arneberg), 316
Van Velsor, Cornelius, 31
Van Velsor, Naomi Williams, 31
Varieties of Religious Experience (W. James), 59, 169
Venetians, The (Wergeland), 263

Verdenslitteratur-historie (N. Møller), 309
Verdi (Werfel), 289
Verhaeren, Emile, 293, 297-99, 304
Verlaine, Paul, 212, 295
Vers-librists, 9; Whitman's influence on, 292, 294; see also Free verse
Vers-librism (C. Vildrac), 301
Vie des martyres (Duhamel), 189, 301
Vielé-Griffin, Francis de, 292, 293, 295
Vie unanime, La (Romains), 300, 301
"Vigil Strange I Kept" (Whitman), 186, 197-98, 287
Vildrac, Charles, 301
Visages de la vie, Les (Verhaeren), 298, 299
Vocabulary: Whitman's enthusiasm for words, 105, 107; his rules for composition, 111; symbolic wording, 133
"Vocalism" (Whitman), 175
"Voice of the Devil, The" (Blake), 255
"Voices" (Whitman), 108, 175
Von Deutscher Republik (Mann)
Vort Aarhundredes Musa (Andersen), 259

Wages of Sin, The (L. Malet), 236
Walden (Thoreau), 29
Walt Whitman (R. M. Bucke), 4
Walt Whitman (J. Schlaf), 4
Walt Whitman, a Critical Study (de Selincourt), 5
Walt Whitman, a Study (Symonds), 4
Walt Whitman, Beitrag zur Literatur der Edelurninge (K. Knortz), 280
"Walt Whitman, ein Characterbild" (E. Bertz), 279
"Walt Whitman et la poèsie contemporaine" (P. Lebesque), 294
Walt Whitman, la naissance du poète (J. Catel), 11, 40
Walt Whitman, l'homme et son œuvre (Bazalgette), 5
Walt Whitman, l'homme i sa tasca (C. Montolio), 305
Walt Whitman poète américain (E. Figuière), 294
Walt Whitman's Workshop (C. J. Furness), 11, 107
Wander motif: in Leaves of Grass, 90 ff.; expanded concept in "Song of the Open Road," 132; present in Verhaeren's poetry, 299

Washington, D.C.: described by Dickens, 184-85

Watts-Dunton, W. T., 317

"Weather, The,—Does It Sympathize with These Times?" (Whitman), 186

Webster, Daniel, 25

Wege nach Weimar (F. Lienhard), 275

Wegner, Arnim T., 286

"Weib-Hymn" (Werfel), 291

Welsh, Rees, 241

Weltfreund, Der (Werfel), 290

Weltgeschichte der Literatur (O. Hauser), 10, 263

Werfel, Franz, 61, 253, 286; Whitman's influence on, 289 ff., 301

Wergeland, Henrik, 47, 260-64, 271, 310, 315, 316

West, the: migrations to, 16; Whitman's interest in, 172

Westminster Review, 218

"We Two How Long We Were Fool'd" (Whitman), 155, 160, 174, 179, 213, 261, 300

Wharton, Edith, quoted, 337, n. 28

"When I Heard at the Close of the Day" (Whitman), 265; Danish translation, 309

"When I Read the Book, the Biography Famous" (Whitman), 225

"When Lilacs Last in the Dooryard Bloom'd" (Whitman), 190; an example of pure lyricism, 201-4; German translation, 277; Danish translation, 312

"Whispers of Heavenly Death" (Whitman), 225

Whitman, Andrew Jackson, 37

Whitman, Edward, 37

Whitman, George Washington, 37; quoted, 141; drafted in Civil War, 184; Walt forced by illness to live with George, 231, 234

Whitman, Hannah, 37, 76

Whitman, Jesse (Grandfather of Walt Whitman), 31

Whitman, Jesse (brother of Walt Whitman), 37, 38, 76

Whitman, Louisa Van Velsor, 4, 37; her importance in Whitman's life, 38; death, 231

Whitman, Mary, 37

Whitman, Thomas Jefferson, 37, 52, 240

Whitman, Walt, quoted, 3; publication of collected letters, 4; an American poet, 6, 7; philosophy, 8; creator of literary epoch, 9 f.; birth, 30; ancestry, 30, 31; removal to Brooklyn, 32; his recognition of Quaker influence, 34; childhood in Long Island, 35 f.; life in Brooklyn, 35 f.; leaves home, 38, 39; becomes a schoolmaster, 41; founds newspaper, 42; biographical meagerness of New York period, 45, 50; reviews Fredrika Bremer's novels, 49; New Orleans period, 51 ff.; reply to Symonds's letter, 53, 168; return North, 58; friendships with bus drivers, 61; interest in oratory and music, 61 ff.; his review of Bettini concert, 62, 63; his reading, 65 ff.; publishes first edition of *Leaves of Grass,* 76; his "inner light" and role of prophet, 122, 134; writes reviews of *Leaves of Grass,* 128; letter to Emerson, 139 f.; failure of second edition, 141; clues to personal life found in *Calamus* poems, 157 ff., 161; homosexuality, 162-70, 244; instability of his emotional attachments, 167; unfulfilled erotic longings, 168; his place in world literature based on his lyrical gift, 169; contrast in his voice and appearance, 141; crisis in his life between second and third editions of *Leaves of Grass,* 142 ff.; conversation with Emerson, 151; his fate linked to that of his country, 179; his hospital work, 181 ff.; failure to enlist, 183; describes Lincoln, 185; nationalistic sentiments during Civil War, 186; life in Washington, 186 ff.; failing health, 189; publishes *Drum-Taps,* 190; Harlan affair, 208 f.; English recognition, 210; friendship with Peter Doyle, 211 f.; Washington friendships with women, 213; beginning of world-wide reputation, 217 ff.; pantheistic nature of his democracy, 220 f.; break with O'Connor, 224; invalidism and the "long afternoon" of his life, 231 f.; receives financial aid from England, 233; read "Song of Exposition" at Exposition of American Institute, 224; Guest at Dartmouth College, 224-25; personal mag-

386 Index

Whitman, Walt, (*Continued*)
netism, 234; English visitors, 235; relations with Anne Gilchrist, 236-39; journeys, 239, 240; reading aloud from favorite authors, 242; affinities of later writers with Whitman, 248; similarity to other mystics, 250

—— *In literature:* Whitmanesque types, 248-75; in literature of Germany, 275-92; of France, 292-304; of Italy, 304; of Spain and Russia, 305-6; of Denmark, 306-13; of Sweden and Norway, 313-16; of England, 316 ff.; his importance for modern literature, 326

—— *Myths:* growth of, 5 f.; Lafayette meeting, 35; teaching ability, 41; swaggering youth, 47; New Orleans period, 52 ff.; fatherhood, 53; wanderer, 57; Emerson influence, 71; "strong man" stories, 75; Bohemian period, 142 ff.; illness caused by hospital work, 189; justification for, 326

—— *Poetry:* religious aspects, 6, 8, 34; emotional quality, 9; vividness in reproduction of childhood impressions, 36; mother motif, 38; eroticism, 51; poetic inspiration from stay in South, 56; political poems, 58; mystical experience, 59, 60 f.; interest in oratory and music revealed in style, 62 f.; diversity of reading, 65 ff.; philosophy, 66 f.; influence of Carlyle and Emerson, 68 ff.; transition from prose to poetry, 82; first edition of *Leaves of Grass,* 77; Hamsun's criticism, 104, 105; "liturgic prose," 106; identification and suggestion, 109; use of parenthesis, 109; vocabulary, 111 ff.; interpretation of nature, 122; begins work on third edition, 144; *Calamus* poems, 157 ff.; personal meaning of war revealed in his poetry, 186; friendship poems, 198; death theme reaches lyrical climax in Lincoln elegy, 203; Whitman's own description of his work, 246; similarity to writers of antiquity, 252 f.

—— *Portraits:* "Christ" portrait, 75, 187; photographs and drawings during Bohemian period, 143; Hine's portrait, 151-52; similarity to Lin-

coln, 180; Linton portrait, 225, 234; paintings and sculptures in old age, 241; picture à la Victor Hugo, 269

Whitman, Walter, 37, 46, 76
Whitman, an Interpretation in Narrative (E. Holloway), 11, 100
Whitman and Burroughs Comrades (C. Barrus), 11, 53; invaluable sourcebook, 188
Whitmanesque types, 248-75; in German lyric poetry, 280 f.; *see also* Contemporary literature
"Whitman och den unga svenska Poesin" (L. Fried), 314
Whittier, John Greenleaf, 22, 23, 29, 45, 128
"Wild Frank's Return" (Whitman), 46
Wilde, Oscar, 10, 171, 235, 259, 297; quoted, 318
Wilhelm Meister's Travels (Goethe), 16
Williams, Talcott, 234
Williams, William Carlos, 327
"Willow Trees and the Axe, The" (Wergeland), 261
Wir sind (Werfel), 290
With Walt Whitman in Camden (H. Traubel), 4, 235
Woman in the Nineteenth Century (M. Fuller), 21
"Woman's Estimate of Walt Whitman, A" (A. Gilchrist), 218, 236
"Woman Waits for Me, A" (Whitman), 136; social program, 156; French translation, 292
Women in Love (D. H. Lawrence), 325
Women's Rights movement: emergence of, 15; influence of Transcendentalists on, 21, 129
Words, *see* Vocabulary
Wordsworth, William, 85, 317
World citizenship: ideal of, 254
Wound-Dresser, The (Whitman), 4, 182, 196
Wulff, Johannes, 310
Wyzewa, Téodor de, 292

Yankee Heiland, Der (E. Bertz), 279
"Years of the Modern" (Whitman), 190
"Years of the Unperform'd" (Whitman), 190
"Yet, Yet, Ye Downcast Hours" (Whitman), 172

"You Felons on Trial in Courts" (Whitman), 175

Zahme Xenien (Goethe), 16

Zarathustra (Nietzsche), 96, 265, 271; "Prologue," 272; quoted, 272-74
Zeppelin, Ditlev von, 310
Zwischenstufe, 276